GENTLEMEN
IN KHAKI
AND CAMOUFLAGE

By the same author

Hussars, Horses & History
(published by Pen & Sword, 2007)
If by Chance
On Drag Hunting
Churchill and Hitler: In Victory and Defeat
The Duke and The Emperor:
Wellington and Napoleon
Beggars in Red: The British Army 1789-1889
Gentlemen in Khaki: The British Army 1890 – 1990
The Italian Campaign
A History of the SAS Regiment
El Alamein: Desert Victory
The Battle for Berlin
The Battle for the Ardennes
Hitler as Military Commander
The Battle for North Africa

GENTLEMEN IN KHAKI AND CAMOUFLAGE

The British Army 1890-2008

JOHN STRAWSON

Pen & Sword
MILITARY

by

Republishe ... 9 by

Copyright © John Strawson, 1989, 2009

ISBN 978 1 84415 978 9

The right of John Strawson to be identified as
author of this work has been asserted by him in accordance
with the Copyright, Designs and Patents Act 1988

A CIP catalogue record for this book is
available from the British Library

Printed and bound in England
by CPI

Pen & Sword Books Ltd incorporates the imprints of
Pen & Sword Aviation, Pen & Sword Maritime, Pen & Sword Military,
Wharncliffe Local History, Pen & Sword Select,
Pen & Sword Military Classics and Leo Cooper,
Remember When, Seaforth Publishing and Frontline Publishing

For a complete list of Pen & Sword titles please contact
PEN & SWORD BOOKS LIMITED
47 Church Street, Barnsley, South Yorkshire, S70 2AS, England
E-mail: enquiries@pen-and-sword.co.uk
Website: www.pen-and-sword.co.uk

CONTENTS

LIST OF MAPS

ACKNOWLEDGEMENTS

Acknowledgements for the original *Gentlemen in Khaki* are as shown in that volume and are not repeated here. What now follows is an acknowledgement of the assistance which I have received during the preparation of additional text and illustrations for this updated *Gentlemen in Khaki and Camouflage*, including permission to reproduce a number of photographs. I am most grateful to the following:

Tim and Carolin Barker for their help with pictures; Kate Brett, Curator, Naval Historical Branch for her advice; Major-General Patrick Cordingley DSO for reading part of the text and giving me the most valuable advice; Colonel Andrew Cuthbert for directing me to the right source for certain information; General Sir Peter de la Billière KCB KBE DSO MC for permission to reproduce some photographs which appear in his book, *Looking for Trouble*; Major-General Arthur Denaro CBE for allowing me to see and quote from his diary of the First Gulf War, for reading part of the text of this book and giving advice on it; Dr Stuart Griffin for his permission to reproduce pictures from his book, *Joint Operations: A Short History*; Mr Christopher Hobson, Head of Library Services, Joint Services Command and Staff College for his agreement for me to reproduce Lady Butler's painting of *Rescue of the Wounded, Maiwand*; Brigadier Tom Longland CVO OBE for his repeated, instant responses to my requests for information; The History Press for their permission to reproduce pictures from *Battlefield Afghanistan*, ISBN 978-1-86227-390-0 by Mike Ryan; The Random House Group for their advice about pictures; David Robertshaw, Warminster Bookshop for his assistance in obtaining books of reference; Lucie Stones, Press Association Photos for her advice about a picture which appeared in *The Times* of June 10 2008.

As always I would like to thank my wife for her untiring help with the preparation and production of this book.

I am not afraid that this war [Iraq] will fail.
I am afraid it will succeed. I am afraid it
will prove the first in an indefinite series
of American interventions. I am afraid it is the
beginning of a new empire that I am afraid
Britain may have little choice but to join.

Matthew Parris, February 2003

America, Britain and other NATO allies face
their toughest challenge since the end of the
Cold War. They are committing thousands
more troops to Afghanistan in the knowledge
that it will take decades to stabilise the
country. Meanwhile casualty tolls are rising,
public support for the war is dropping and
locals are beginning to wonder if life might
not be better under the Taleban.

Richard Beeston, June 2008

FOREWORD

This book is an extension of a previous work of mine – *Gentlemen in Khaki*, published 1989, which portrayed the British Army between 1890 and 1990 and in particular pointed to both resemblances and contrasts between the size, role and activity of the Army at those two dates separated by a century. This previous work made it clear that to have been a soldier during the latter part of Queen Victoria's reign was to have been more or less continuously on active service. The Queen had herself declared that if we were to maintain our position as a first-rate power, we would have to be prepared for 'attacks and wars somewhere or other' all the time. For these were the days of the Pax Britannica and this peace could only be kept by constantly engaging in campaigns against those subject peoples of the Empire who were disposed to dispute the British belief in their Imperial mission. And although the Army was small – so small indeed when compared with huge conscripted forces of the European powers that Bismarck remarked once that under certain circumstances he would send a German policeman to arrest it – it was highly professional and experienced, composed entirely of volunteers and enjoying a special sort of strength in the tight-knit pride and loyalty of its regimental system.

Although Victoria's 'little wars' might not have prepared the British Army for Continental *grande guerre*, it had been battle-hardened by hundreds of engagements all over the world, was expert at joint operations with the Royal Navy – the *real* preserver of peace and guarantor of the Empire's security – and was unrivalled at improvising to meet changing circumstances and requirements. This adaptability, however, was limited by the Army's experience in colonial wars against 'native' enemies, and its commanders were to receive the rudest of shocks when pitted against the fast-riding, straight-shooting, elusive and determined Boers.

We may already discern some similarities between the Army of

Queen Victoria and that of Queen Elizabeth II towards the end of the last century. In 1990 the Army was still relatively small, had seen a great deal of active service, sometimes to protect national interests – Belize, the Falkland Islands, Northern Ireland; sometimes in support of United Nations – Cyprus; sometimes at the request of a friendly country in trouble – Brunei, the Dhofar. But despite these and other likenesses, for the Army was still composed entirely of volunteers, organized in regiments with the same precious *esprit de corps*, highly professional, spread about the world, skilful at combined operations, instinctively adaptable – there were two striking differences. The first was that the British Army's principal commitment was to NATO with the so-called British Army of the Rhine. In short we were at this time committed to and trained for *la grande guerre*. And there was another colossal change in the military establishment at Queen Victoria's disposal and that which owed fealty to Queen Elizabeth. In the 1890's the Indian Army was some 200,000 strong and altogether at the service of The Queen's Government. How else indeed, how but by the power of the sword, could the Raj have survived?

Moreover the Indian Army did not confine its activities to India. As James/Jan Morris put it: 'You could do things with Indian troops that you could not do with British . . . The Indian Army was like a Praetorian Guard of Empire, set apart from the public control, and available always for the protection of the Inner State'. Now there is no Empire and no Indian Army at our command – a difference indeed. And this great difference was manifest from the middle of the last century, at the very time when our commitment to NATO was becoming paramount.

And now we come to the period post-1990. With imperialism out of fashion and *la grande guerre* rendered improbable by the collapse of the Soviet Union and Warsaw Pact, we may well ask, as Haldane did in 1906, what, apart from defence of the realm, is the Army for? The idea that armed conflict has left the international stage is for illusionists only. Something else has stepped on to it. It is called interventionism, and the British Army has adopted it, if not eagerly then under constraint. We have intervened in Iraq – twice; we have intervened in Sierra Leone, Bosnia and Kosovo; we have intervened in Afghanistan, without the hesitation which a backward glance at previous campaigns there might have induced. What of the future? Is Matthew Parris right in saying that Britain will be dragged into a series of American interventions? Is Beeston right in saying that stabilising Afghanistan will take decades? If so, the British Army will have plenty to do and may be too small to do it. We will examine this point later. But before discussing how the Army's interventionist role might evolve, we would do well to take a look at its origins.

PROLOGUE

AFGHANISTAN*

In Kipling's day long muzzled jezails
Were enough to do for our Beggars in Red;
But now it's a road bomb packed with nails
Which adds to the number of British dead.

And all for what? To deter al-Qaeda?
To try and destroy the Taleban?
Or: is it a case of follow my leader
As Blair trailed Bush to Afghanistan?

The lesson of history's ignored, but returns
When we tell ourselves we mustn't forget
The practical view of Bokhara Burnes -
'You can't settle Afghans with the bayonet.'

No matter how often you make a plan
To dominate the Helmand plain,
You may suceed, but the Taleban
Will wait till you go, then come out again.

So now we play the Great Game once more
With different weapons and a different foe,
And when the time comes to withdraw
Those who have taken part will know

That whether you call them Beggars in Red
Or gentlemen in drab fatigues,
It's all the same when a soldier's dead
Because of No 10's intrigues.

Yet through it all one thing is clear -
The British Army will persevere.

Written by the author early in 2007 for a local Poetry Festival

"A gentleman in kharki."

1

ORIGINS

Was it reasonable ... that an honest gentleman should pay a heavy land tax, in order to support in idleness and luxury a set of fellows [the military] who requited him by seducing his dairy maids and shooting his partridges?

Macaulay

No issue in our political and constitutional history has been more momentous than that of whether or not to have – and if to have, how to control – a Standing Army. This issue was really that of controlling not the nation's sword, but the nation's purse. For the one could not be had without the other. That the governed should seek to ensure that neither was exclusively and permanently manipulated by the governors will excite no special wonder. Even as late as George III's reign one of the main pillars of English justice, as Arthur Bryant has pointed out, was 'a traditional distrust of the standing army which was always kept by Parliament – alone capable of voting funds for its maintenance – at the lowest level compatible with national safety, and often a good deal lower'. If we may date the history of the nation from the century following the Norman Conquest, an Englishman's earliest memories would be of the tyranny exercised by professional soldiers of the day, armoured horsemen issuing from royal or private fortresses to suppress and dictate to all around them, whether in the interests of good rule or misrule. The great popularity enjoyed by the Tudors was in part derived from their having put an end to private armies of the lords and barons and keeping no standing army of their own. So we find the sentiments of the Husbandmen and Merchant, echoed above by Macaulay, in *The Discourse of the Common Weal* in Edward VI's reign. When the Husbandman calls on God to forbid that such tyrants as soldiers should come among them, for they did nothing but steal poultry and pigs without paying, except by ravishing wives and daughters, the Merchant's rejoinder is that, far from quenching 'commotions', the appearance of soldiers among them would stir up commotions, 'for the stomachs of Englishmen would never bear it'.

The Tudors, who loved money almost as much as they loved themselves, preferred to put their faith in Yeomen. They may have raised special bodies, like the Honourable Artillery Company, one of the earliest Volunteer forces and one that has survived with honour until today. But Henry VIII formed it in order to provide officers to command the trained bands of London. The trained bands, the Yeomen, the militia – it was these men, together, of course, with the Navy, who were the real defenders of the country in Tudor times. Indeed the Yeomen had shown what they were capable of at Agincourt. 'And you good yeomen,' exhorted Harry the King, 'whose limbs were made in England, show us here the mettle of your pasture'. Almost a hundred years later their skill and resolution were again demonstrated at Flodden. During the great crisis of 1588 their readiness and spirit were once more not in doubt, although what their performance against the finest infantry in the world would have been, had the Armada enabled Parma to invade England's shores, is another thing. We may recall the answer made by De Vere when Elizabeth asked what he thought of her 'brave army'. 'Your Grace's army is brave indeed. I have not in the world the name of coward; and yet I am the greatest coward here. All these fine fellows are praying that the enemy may land, and there there may be a battle; and I, who know that enemy well, cannot think of such a battle without dismay.' Not for the last time the English Army had cause to be thankful for the English Navy.

There was no better recorder of the times than William Shakespeare who repeatedly held the mirror up to nature and showed the very age and body of *his* time its form and pressure. His portrait of Elizabeth's clownish militia would do little to inspire confidence in such experienced warriors as De Vere. Falstaff explained it all:

> If I be not ashamed of my soldiers, I am a sous'd gurnet ... my whole charge consists of ancients, corporals, lieutenants, gentlemen of companies ... such as indeed were never soldiers, but discarded unjust serving-men, younger sons to younger brothers, revolted tapsters, and ostlers, trade-fallen, the cankers of a calm world and a long peace ... you would think that I had a hundred and fifty tattered prodigals ... I'll not march through Coventry with them, that's flat.

It was a far cry from Falstaff's militia to Cromwell's 'Ironsides', although Cromwell used almost Falstaffian language in pointing out to Hampden what sort of men he should be recruiting. 'Your troopers,' he said 'are most of them old decayed serving men and tapsters and such kind of fellows ... their [the royalists'] troopers are gentlemen's sons, younger sons, persons of quality. Do you think that the spirits of such base and mean fellows will ever be able to encounter gentlemen that have honour, courage and resolution in them?' How capricious therefore are origins! All the great fear of standing armies harboured by freedom-loving citizens of this country has come somehow to be associated with the way in which a Prince, whether Plantagenet, Tudor, Stuart or Orange, would exercise and abuse the power therein accorded to the Crown. How contrary are the facts. It was the very guardian of these liberties, the champion of every free Englishman, the incorruptible source of protecting the constitution, the Houses of Parliament themselves, which in the end enacted that legislation which gave birth to a regular, a standing, army. It was the Ordinance of 15 February, 1645, which established the New Model Army. Its effect on the outcome of the Civil War was decisive. Its later exploits in territorial and continental wars made it the terror of its enemies. Irony did not finish with the origins of a Standing Army. Its very place of creation, that Army whose task would above all be to keep King Charles I in check, was Windsor Park, principal seat of this same royal King. Later, when Charles's second son began to enjoy the taste of power and increased the size of the Army, because his brother's bastard son, Monmouth, raised his doomed standard on England's shores, irony came full circle. Although in 1685 James II raised six regiments of cavalry and thirty companies of foot to keep himself on the throne, before long most of them were fighting to keep him off it.

But if we are to talk of origins we must go further back in history, back even to a time before the Norman Conquest. Just as the Yeomanry of later days were composed largely of landowners who voluntarily gave up their time and joined together under the local nobleman to form mounted squadrons and regiments, so right at the beginning the English national army at its most primitive was founded on military service in payment for the grant of land – in essentials the feudal system itself. Any man between the ages of sixteen and sixty was liable to serve. The source of the word, still in use – *Landwehr* – is thus clear at once. In England the army was known as the fyrd. Each man liable for service could be called upon for two months of each year. It was left to King Alfred to organise the fyrd properly. Dividing the country as he did into military districts,* he assessed that every five hides† of land or more

* The United Kingdom is still divided into military districts for purposes of Army Command.
† A hide of land was between 60 and 100 acres.

would provide an armed man summonable by the King and to be provided with pay and victuals. The owner of five or more hides had to take the field himself in times of national danger, not just for two months, but for the whole of the campaign. This was known as thane's service and the thanes in their turn were organized by shires.

Times of national danger were not infrequent during Alfred's reign. The year 878 saw perhaps the greatest reversal of his fortune. At the beginning of the year his Army had been surprised, confused and dispersed at Chippenham. He himself was in hiding, doing little more than living a guerrilla-like existence and burning bread to the consternation and fury of a cowherd's wife. So confident were the Danes that the game was at last in their hands that they attempted to take Alfred's Exmoor stronghold. But the King's thanes chose victory or death. The victory was theirs; death was reserved for the Danes who lost nearly a thousand men. Ever ready to exploit success, Alfred decided to take the field once more, sent out his messengers to summon the fyrd, who were to assemble at the end of May. Alfred had an army again and in the most decisive battle of his reign he utterly routed the Danes at Edington. Part of his greatness lay in what one of his successors as leader of the nation, and indeed one of his chroniclers, laid down as a rule for the conduct of human affairs: In Victory, Magnanimity.* Alfred, although he had the Viking King, Guthrum, in his power, did not exact revenge. Rather, he divided the land with his rival. Fourteen years of peace ensued. Yet Alfred did not neglect military preparations. He reorganized the fyrd and made it into two. One half would be available for duty, the other half stayed at home looking after the land and the interests of those on service. In this way there would always be sufficient numbers on active service and there would be less temptation to desert. Moreover it was not just on land that Alfred carried out his reforms. Recognizing that an island without some means of commanding the sea would be vulnerable to every buccaneer with a taste for adventure and gain, he founded the English Navy too.

It was not, however, a Saxon king who was the first to balance the inherent weakness of the fyrd system, based as it was on temporary service. We owe the next move in military development to a Dane – the great Canute. After becoming undisputed ruler of the English in 1016, he introduced something new – a royal bodyguard. They were known as house-carles, picked Danish troops, some three to six thousand strong. The idea was that after the conclusion of a campaign and the return of most of Canute's soldiers to Denmark, the house-carles would be kept

---

* *The Second World War*, Winston S. Churchill.

in service here in this country. This combination – which in a sense has survived until today – of the inexpensive levies, the fyrd, and the well-trained, instantly available professional force, remained in being under Harold. Yet all were still dismounted soldiers. The thanes might possess horses and move about on them. For fighting an action, they dismounted. Even the King himself fought on foot, and it was fighting thus surrounded by his thanes at Hastings that Harold received his mortal wound. Then, with the Conqueror, came knight service.

In medieval Europe, at least until the coming of the long bow, battles were dominated by the mounted, armoured knight. Knight service in England during Edward I's reign enabled him to raise a large and balanced Army for the subjugation of Wales. In 1277 he mustered the largest, best-equipped force that England had seen for more than two hundred years. From France he acquired *destriers*, battle chargers and remounts for his household guard, able to carry the most heavily armed nobles. Apart from the feudal levy which raised a thousand armoured horsemen, he put together no fewer that 15,000 foot soldiers, some conscripted from the fyrd, some volunteers recruited by veterans who had fought with him in the Crusade. The King also had bodies of archers and some professional crossbowmen. Within two months of starting his advance from Chester in July Edward had not only subdued the Welsh, but won from Llywelyn of Gwynedd his fealty, the recognition which Edward sought of his own lordship and law.

But the Welsh rose again and this time Edward was determined to have done with it once and for all. In raising another force in 1282, he changed his recruiting methods in order to have under his command not a feudal, but a professional, army. These methods were much resented by two of Edward's principal officers of state – his Marshal, Earl of Norfolk and his Constable, Earl of Hereford – who saw in it the loss of their own independent status. What Edward did was to persuade the barons and knights to contract with the Crown to have their fighting men paid for agreed periods, instead of the former system of having at his disposal the tenants-in-chivalry serving at their own expense for a mere forty days and then free to please themselves. The advantage of this new arrangement, as Arthur Bryant pointed out, was that it enabled the King to muster the type of force he needed for this particular campaign and thus not have to rely largely on heavily armoured knights. 'For war in Snowdonia he required light horse or *hobelars* [for reconnaissance], cross-bowmen and archers, infantry in disciplined companies to contend with the Welsh spearmen; artificers, woodcutters, wagoners and labourers to make and maintain forts and communications'. This sort of balanced army was never obtainable by feudal levy. In Edward's day the armed knight was an expensive, but not a numerous, article. In William the Conqueror's day his tenants had equipped a 'simple mail-coated *miles* or trooper', and William had been able to call on up to six thousand of them. Edward had only a few hundred but they were much finer to look at. Thus the King was not changing the system for the sake of undermining the feudal dignity of his principal barons. He had to do it if he were to raise an effective army at all. Effective it certainly proved to be and, despite set-backs and delays, Edward's armies in conjunction with the sea power he still enjoyed decisively defeated Llywelyn, whose head crowned with ivy was set on a pike to decorate the Tower of London.

Edward's fighting was never done. When he turned his attention to France he sought once more to widen the base of his military power, and in particular to increase the number of armoured knights he could call on. This time he instructed the sheriffs to summon to London not only his military tenants, but all freeholders with lands worth £20 a year. They were not simply to be ready to defend the realm, but to be ready 'to cross with us to foreign parts'. This order was disliked both by those to whom it applied and by the barons who saw in it a usurping of their own military monopoly and a further blow at their independent power. So stubborn was their opposition that when the £20 freeholders actually assembled in July 1297, the Earls of Hereford and Norfolk refused to enrol them. Appointing a new Constable and a new Marshal was an easy matter for the King; appealing to the people was another; yet even abandoning his idea to make £20 freeholders serve overseas gained him only a subsidy from the knights of the shires. Magna Carta was not to be lightly forgotten by the descendants of those who had wrung concessions from King John. Instead of two thousand or so armoured horsemen Edward had hoped to take to Flanders with him, he had to be content with some five hundred.

His campaigns in France availed him little, but the activities of Wallace and Robert the Bruce were means of mending quarrels with his own people. Edward was obliged to acknowledge that even he could not in the end rule without the consent of his subjects. To enable him to concentrate against the Scots, Edward was reconciled to Norfolk and Hereford and by June 1298 he was ready to take his army to Scotland. He crossed the border the following month with an army of some 2,000 horse and over 12,000 foot, supported by the customary collection of supply wagons and artificers. In the one battle he fought with, and defeated, Wallace, it was the Welsh longbowmen which were decisive. They were to remain so for many a campaign to come. But winning a battle did not win the war against Scotland and it was not until 1305 that Wallace was finally taken. By this time twelve years of war had bankrupted the English Crown.

We may perhaps pass over Edward II and Bannockburn, and move straight on to his son, the second great Plantagenet warrior, Edward III. Never was Bishop Stubbs's contention that the history of a people was most truly reflected by the history of its wars than during the time of Edward's campaigns in France, for the need to seek financial aid on a huge scale obliged him to make use of Parliament in a way which had great legal and social consequences. Although the devices for raising soldiers did not themselves change, that is to say, both the domestic army and foreign mercenaries were still based on the contracts of indentures, the money-fief, the Crown's revenue was simply inadequate for making payments. This led King Edward III to augment the sums already available to him – from levies on movable wealth and clerical incomes by virtue of Parliamentary grant – with more regular sources of revenue from customs. In addition, increased taxes on wool were substantial, and lent some justification to the saying that wool paid for the Hundred Years War.

Yet, as many medieval historians have made clear, herein lay the beginning of the endless struggle between Crown and Parliament as to the supply of money for raising and maintaining armies. Supply would be forthcoming from Parliament, but only if the Crown removed grievances. In other words the King would get his money, but Parliament would begin to get the power to control the King's use of this money. 'By observing the forms of parliamentary consultation and ruling with the advice of the great officers of the Church and state in whom the taxpayers' representatives imposed their trust,' wrote Arthur Bryant, 'he [Edward III] could obtain the wherewithal to raise a professional army far superior in quality to anything feudal France could put into the field.' With such financial resources behind him, Edward succeeded in putting together exactly the sort of army he wanted. Indentures made with the lords and other leaders specified what sort of and how many soldiers would be provided, what they would be paid and how long they would serve. These contingents or 'retinues' varied in size according to the stature of the commanders with whom the indenture or contract was made. For these lords and barons the arrangement had many advantages. They were not simply doing the state some service. Personal gain was assured by the Exchequer with the prospect of plunder thrown in.

Most of such retinues they provided would include bannerets – that is knights of proved valour who commanded contingents of the army and thus had vassals under their banners – knights, men at arms and archers. The archers, because of their success in previous battles, formed a major part of the army. They were armed not only with the famous long bow and arrows with the Grey Goose Feather, but had swords, knives and stakes with steel tips to protect their phalanxes against enemy horsemen. The basic disciplinary unit of the army was called a 'lance' [hence lance-corporal] and consisted of the knight who paid the lance, a man at arms, two archers, a swordsman and two pages armed with daggers. Apart from these soldiers the army contained light horsemen [hobelars], artificers, woodmen – for making bridges – miners and those in charge of the baggage wagons. When we remember that the pay of an ordinary soldier in the British Army was right up until the nineteenth century but one shilling a day, we may be surprised that in the army which sailed to Brittany with Edward and his son, the Black Prince, the mounted archers received sixpence a day and even the Welsh spearmen, least regarded of professional soldiers, twopence, With such an army, about 13,000 strong, against the French King Philip's force of four times as many, Edward III immortalized the forest of Crécy in 1346. A later French King, Charles VI, remembered it *without* advantages:

> Witness our too much memorable shame
> When Cressy battle fatally was struck.

Crécy's fame was surpassed only by Poitiers ten years later. By it Edward won sovereignty in Acquitaine, Poitou, Ponthieu and Calais. The English Army that had done it all was not a feudal army made up of vassals bound by fief to the lord from whom they held their land. Nor was it a militia raised by England to defend English soil. 'It was a collection of private war-bands raised by indenture by adventurous nobles and knights for the pursuit of profit' and led by one of the greatest soldier princes to spring from a family renowned for soldier princes. Richard Coeur de Lion's name might shine most brightly in the catalogue of chivalry; Edward III's endures rather for sheer achievement. Yet Edward's triumphs were echoed by his great grandson, Harry of Monmouth, at Agincourt and his later campaigns in France.

The indenture made between King Henry V and a certain Thomas Tunstall Esq. on 29 April, 1415, reads almost like a modern contract between employer and employee. It is filled with conditions of service on the one hand and payment on the other. Thomas is bound to serve the King for a whole year in a 'voyage' which the King will make in his Kingdom of France and Duchy of Guienne. He is to be ready in a month's time, and will bring with him for the whole year six men at arms and eighteen mounted archers. Thomas will have wages of two shillings a day. If the company go to Guienne, he will receive forty marks for the men at arms and twenty for the archers; if they go to

France the wages will be respectively twelve pence and six pence a day.
And so on, dealing with payment for the first quarter, delivery of jewels
to Thomas for surety of payment for the second quarter, moiety for the
third quarter, wages for the last one. Thomas is to be ready to muster
his said people at such and such a time. Shipping for him and his retinue
will be provided, and for his horses, harness and provisions. If Thomas
or his retinue should take prisoner any of the Adversary of France's
Lieutenants or chieftains or cousins, the King shall have them 'and shall
make reasonable agreement with the said Thomas or to those by whom
he may be taken'. Any other likely 'Gaignes de Guerre' – prisoners,
booty, money, gold, silver, jewels – are suitably contracted for. The
whole thing is a bond between plunderers. Henry's Ordinances of War
also make good reading. 'Every souldeour shal obey his captaine in all
lefulle thinges; no man make assault withoute his capiten will it be; no
man shal selle his prisoner, nor make fynaunce, without license of his
capiten'. No wonder Parolles wanted to 'eat and drink and sleep as soft
as captain shall'.

Successful overseas plunder of the sort practised by Henry V made
for a degree of domestic stability in an age renowned for disorder, and
after Henry's death military failure in France simply aggravated internal
disorder. The Wars of the Roses were the result of weakness at the
centre of affairs. Everything hung upon the King. 'If he was wise, of
strong character, and with a firm policy,' observed Professor Dover
Wilson, 'the balance of the commonwealth was preserved; if he was
weak, capricious or evil, the balance was disturbed.' Bastard feudalism,
as history has called it, led the country's great magnates to acquire
supporters, who were neither indentured retainers nor motivated by
anything save personal ambition. So there came about those circumstances in which England, wont to conquer others, once more made
a shameful conquest of itself. With Henry VI out of the way, Edward
of York was strong enough to survive challenges from Warwick and his
faction, but later his brother, Richard III, no matter how able a soldier
and administrator, did not command sufficient loyalty or resources to
withstand the rival claim of the Lancastrian Henry Tudor, despite some
ringing exhortations to his army:

> Fight, gentlemen of England! fight, bold yeomen!
> Draw, archers, draw your arrows to the head!
> Spur your proud horses hard, and ride in blood;
> Amaze the welkin with your broken staves ...

Henry Tudor prevailed at Bosworth and under his wise, cautious, thrifty
dictatorship, the whole of the Plantaganets' military system, which had

brought such triumph to England, was changed. This change was certainly to the good of the realm, for the power exercised by the great lords under Plantaganet rule was open to the very worst of abuse, as was illustrated by the occasion in 1378 when the Commons attempted to restore order in the country – we must remember that the opening years of Richard II's reign [he was after all only ten years old when he succeeded to the throne in 1377] were marred by numerous riots. The trouble was that the order-restorers were themselves retainers of the great lords, and as their method of putting things right was, as we read in *Piers Plowman*, to break into farms, ravish the women, make away with the horses, steal the corn and leave by way of payment a tally on the King, we may readily understand that the people on the whole were not enthusiastic about being robbed and murdered by those who were supposed to be upholding the law.

But as the King's only source of soldiers was that of the great lords, he was unable to impose his own will on that of his own chief magnates. To the extent therefore that the Wars of the Roses and the outcome of those wars so greatly reduced the military power and landed wealth of the nobles, they may be said to have produced some benefits. Tudor policy of actually suppressing the power of their great subjects spelled an end to the system of indenture. At the same time it left the Tudor monarchs without the means of raising well trained armies for foreign adventures. Troops rapidly levied for service on the Continent without training or discipline could not do the great things that had been done under the Plantaganets. So it was that there were no great Continental adventures indulged in by English monarchs between the reigns of Henry VIII and William III, and even the Field of the Cloth of Gold was little more than a pageant. Yet opportunity for learning the profession of arms, whether as a volunteer or as a full-time professional, was not lacking. There was always a war going on somewhere, notably in the Low Countries where Spain endlessly endeavoured to subdue the Protestant cause. Without such events there would have been no Zutphen with its immortal memories of Sir Philip Sidney. The siege of Ostend in 1601 was an occasion for sight-seeing fops and genuine gentleman volunteers to get a taste for coveting or acquiring honour.

At home the conscript militia system – the so-called trained bands – was sufficient to keep the Tudors on the throne in their own realm. The success of Henry VIII's yeoman archers at Flodden was a striking example of it. What is more, while Henry might possess no royal army, he did have control of all artillery and had built strongly on his father's beginnings in founding more firmly the Royal Navy as a standing force in royal pay. The Royal Navy might be expected to keep the King free from outside interference, but no such force existed to enable him to exercise unlimited power at home without interference from his own people. 'It was impossible,' wrote Macaulay, 'for the Tudors to carry oppression beyond a certain point; for they had no armed force, and they were surrounded by an armed people.' The people of England might look on with indifference at Henry's personal tyrannies in executing those who stood in the way of his indulgence in or outside the marriage bed, but no sooner had he issued a demand for money which touched their own pockets than he found that he was dealing with those who regarded themselves as freemen, not slaves. The shires raised their own armies. The King's lieutenants were unable to do so. Henry cancelled his illegal demands and actually apologised in public for having infringed the law.

Thus the great English constitutional issue of purse and sword, which was to reach such heights of controversy and violence during the Stuarts' reign, found expression. The good fortune of being an island made it possible to ignore the existence of great standing armies elsewhere in Europe, for while the English Navy remained in being, these armies posed no threat to England. And the good fortune that the power of the purse remained in the hands of the nation made it impossible for the sovereign to raise great standing armies at home which most assuredly would have posed a threat to England. Only taxation would provide the King with a regular army and only parliament could provide taxation. It was not thus from choice that the Tudors allowed this restriction of their power to come about. It was from necessity. The Stuarts' refusal to recognise the realities of this restriction was what led to their undoing, and the supreme irony of this country's military development was that when the time came to acknowledge a division making the practice of war a distinct and separate calling, with all the social and political consequences which this change entailed, it was not for the confusion of a foreign foe, but for the punishment of an English king.

The father of this particular king shunned the errors of his son. James I pursued a policy of pacification. His neighbours in the Low Countries, in France, Italy and Germany might be treated to the daily spectacle of town and countryside filled with regular soldiers. In Britain there was but the militia. The militia, however, was not enough for Charles I, nor for his faithful minister, Thomas Wentworth, Earl of Strafford. To make Charles as absolute a monarch as possible, Strafford devised his scheme – Thorough. It depended on realizing what had eluded so many former monarchs. 'He saw that there was one instrument, and only one, by which his vast and daring projects could be carried into execution. That instrument was a standing army. To the forming of such an army, therefore, he directed all the energy of his strong mind.' He failed and, with his failure, Charles failed too. It was left to Parliament to form and raise the New Model Army, which in Cromwell's hands arranged first of all for the submission of the Cavaliers and then for the submission of Parliament itself. No objective historian could accuse the English of doing things by halves. Having for almost thirteen centuries resisted and prevented government by military dictatorship, they then set up for thirteen years their own version of government by the sword. The Army may have begun its career as the realm's arbiter by being well-liked and on the whole well-behaved (its efficiency was not in doubt), but when it went to the lengths of closing down race meetings and interfering with its countrymen's other sporting activities, it left a legacy of distrust and hatred which survived for some two hundred years.

Yet paradoxically the original elements of this first of Standing Armies were made up of real volunteers. It was perhaps in some ways the finest Army this country has ever known. It was not composed of the scum of the earth. The men had not enlisted for drink, to avoid gaol or escape from the cloying importunities of womenfolk. They were not eager for plunder or bent upon the rape of fortresses and those inside them. They were not even seeking the bubble reputation. Nor were they concerned not to think meanly of themselves. 'The boast of soldiers, as we find it recorded in their solemn resolutions, was that they had not been forced into the service, nor had enlisted chiefly for the sake of lucre, that they were not janissaries, but freeborn Englishmen, who had, of their own accord, put their lives in jeopardy for the liberties and religion of England, and whose right and duty it was to watch over the welfare of the nation which they had saved.'

And what an army it was! All the opposing forces in Europe went down before it. For the strictness of discipline, for the precision of manoeuvre, for moral and religious fervour, for sheer joy at the sight of the enemy, for certainty of victory – a certainty that was confirmed time and time again – nothing quite like it had ever been seen before. It aroused alike the admiration of its opposing commanders and the grudging pride of its Cavalier observers. It was a model indeed. Its main difficulties arose in the suppression of opposition from its own people, for no sooner had the nation felt the hand of military tyranny than it instantly expressed its distaste by a series of insurrections. In Scotland, in Wales, in East Anglia and Kent, movements to throw off the Army's yoke were at once fierce and numerous. All such expressions of national ill-temper were, however, put down by Cromwell and Fairfax.

Before very long the Army was to do the state one more great service. Having been successful in ridding England of one Stuart King, it now allowed the son of that same King to be restored to the throne without the disturbance of another civil war. How was it that those very soldiers to whom the name of King and the name of Stuart were hateful, who saw that the period of their own supremacy could but be ended by such a restoration, who were still in sufficient strength to sweep aside the rapidly mustering trained bands and militia had they been put to the test – how was it that these men stood idly by when Charles Stuart, the Black Boy, landed in Kent and, amid general festivities and joy, was borne triumphantly to the capital to come into his own again? The answer lay in a single word. They were in the same condition as they had rendered Charles's father – headless. General Lambert was imprisoned; Monk was engaged either in disbanding those regiments most likely to turn words into action or in calming and dividing the rest; the country's provisional government, with the aid of county magistrates and lieutenants, had embodied and organized the militia; in London twenty thousand citizens were armed; the Navy, like the nation, supported the new Parliament, and both Houses had determined their course – the King was invited to return. The Army, divided, discordant and dispirited, with no single leader to direct and guide them, stood sullenly and silently by. They were witnessing the prelude to their own disbandment.

One of the first Acts which received the royal assent formalized once and for all the abolition of tenures by knight service, the feudal system designed to ensure some means of national security. All usefulness of the system had long since passed away. Nothing but a few ceremonial obligations [which were allowed to remain] and some vexatious grievances had survived. The burden which accompanied the holding of land from the Crown by virtue of knight service, that is the paying of a large sum by each landed gentleman on inheriting land, had understandably lapsed with the abolition of the monarchy. That such abuses should be revived was neither to be tolerated by those who would suffer nor to be imposed by him who would benefit. The age of chivalry was pronounced to be at an end. The age of frivolity was about to take its place. Disappearance of chivalry in name was accompanied by dispersion of the standing army in fact, although it was shortly to be replaced by a much smaller royal army. Thus the great aversion to standing armies which prevailed in this kingdom for more than another century, until indeed the realm's security was threatened by the armies of Revolutionary and Imperial France, had been brought about not by a military machine in the hands of a royal tyranny, but by the rule of Cromwell, the Major-Generals and the New Model Army. Whatever the cause, however, the effect was the same. To English ears, as Macaulay put it, the words Standing Army would continue to sound as unpleasing as either Ship Money or Star Chamber.

At the beginning of Charles II's reign the militia, the only army recognized by law, was reorganized by Act of Parliament. An obligation to provide soldiers was based, not on the tenure of land, but on the income derived from land or other sources. Thus those with £500 a year from land or a total estate of £6,000 were required to provide one horseman, equipped and paid. If the amounts were £50 and £600 respectively, a pikeman or musketeer would be furnished. Smaller owners of properties would be grouped together in societies, each society making available a horseman or foot soldier. By this means about 130,000 militiamen, foot and horse, could be mustered. The King was Captain General, his Lord Lieutenants or their deputies were the local commanders. Assembly for inspection and drill would be for two weeks in a year, the cost borne locally. If called out to face a foreign enemy, the Crown would bear the cost. Just as the militia or trained bands came in for a good deal of mockery and contempt by Falstaff, and again in 1642, before the raising of the Roundhead armies ('it was a commonly held view,' wrote Antonia Fraser, 'that the bands when they were assembled trained for drinking rather than any more martial occupation'), so some forty years later the rustic militia were ridiculed by Dryden:

> The country rings around with loud alarms,
> And raw in fields the rude militia swarms;
> Mouths without hands, maintained at vast expense,
> In peace a charge, in war a weak defence.
> Stout once a month they march, a blustering band,
> And ever, but in time of need, at hand.
> This was the morn when, issuing on the guard,
> Drawn up, in rank and file, they stood prepared
> Of seeming arms to make a short essay,
> Then hasten to be drunk, the business of the day.

We may reflect that the Territorial Army of this country did not escape similar charges. But with the people of England at the time of the Restoration, no matter what sallies of wit it had to endure, the militia was intensely popular, simply because it was not a standing army. Nevertheless Charles, in accordance with the practice of maintaining a royal bodyguard, did set about the business of establishing a small body of regular troops. Casual to the point of carelessness though he was – except perhaps in regard to money – Charles not unreasonably felt that the beefeaters and trained bands might not be quite up to guaranteeing the security of his household, particularly if some of these disbanded and not improbably discontented members of his predecessor's Army should take it into their heads to threaten this security. He therefore contrived to put aside sufficient funds, no doubt thereby making a serious sacrifice to his own pleasures and dissipations, which would support a body of guards.

Guards they have been ever since and have won fame and honour throughout the world by their discipline, their devotion and their deeds. Their beginnings were modest. To start with there were no more than three regiments of cavalry, all of which survive to this today, although two of them are now formed into one regiment. The Life Guards were exceptional in almost every way. Their horses were well bred, their accoutrements and trappings rich, their cuirasses at once serviceable and splendid, their officers of the King's household. Even the troopers were called gentlemen of the guard, not without reason for many were of good family and had held commissions in the late wars. Not surprisingly their pay was high. The second regiment was equally well known, and because of their blue coats and cloaks, still worn, were called the Blues. The third regiment, which had returned from Tangier, was the first regiment of Dragoons, later the Royal Dragoons or Royals. Almost 300 years later these two regiments were amalgamated, hence the Blues and Royals of today. A Dragoon was, of course, a foot soldier who used horses to get more quickly to the scene of action. Later he became, as Macaulay put it, 'a mere horse soldier'.

So much for the cavalry. Infantry were more numerous and more familiar with military operations. Foremost among them were the two regiments of Household troops – the first regiment of Foot Guards, later the Grenadier Guards, and the Coldstream Guards, formed from the one surviving relic of the New Model Army – Monk's Regiment which had safeguarded the Restoration by scattering the disgruntled and rebellious Fifth Monarchy Men. Next came the forerunner of the Royal Marines, at this time called the Admiral's Regiment. Then there were four regiments of the line, all of which still exist today, albeit in some cases under different names, because of an endless process of reorganizations and amalgamations. The first, second, third and fourth of Foot are now The Royal Scots, The Queen's Regiment, which as a result of amalgamations includes the Buffs (3rd Foot) and The King's Own Border Regiment. At the time of Charles's accession, whereas the 1st and 3rd Foot had fought respectively under Gustavus Adolphus and Maurice of Nassau, the other two had been recalled from Tangier, 'bringing with them cruel and licentious habits contracted in a long course of warfare with the Moors'. Not for the first time in English history, it was the less fashionable part of the military establishment which was most familiar with actual practice of the military art. In total this establishment amounted to some 1,700 horse and 7,000 foot – 'not very likely to enslave five millions of Englishmen ... indeed hardly able to suppress an insurrection in London, if the trainbands of the City had joined the insurgents'.

Such thoughts no doubt – even before the threat to his position posed by Monmouth's ill-fated challenge – were not absent from the mind of Charles's brother, James, when he succeeded, narrow, bigoted and dull though his mind was. It could hardly be said that the militia, which fought on both sides during this brief affair, displayed a degree of martial prowess calculated to afford a sovereign much confidence in his security, if that security rested largely on the militia. If its loyalty were such that many of them could instantly rally to the standard of his brother's bastard son, even though this son's followers were few and by no means formidable, how would they behave when confronted with large and veteran armies of a foreign invader? The only manoeuvre which the militia seemed capable of carrying out with consistent success was that of running away. Soon after Monmouth had landed at Lyme in June, 1685, he had mustered a force of some 1,500 men. Meanwhile at Bridport the Dorsetshire and Somersetshire militia were gathering, and on 14 June the two forces met. At first the action was distinguished neither by clarity of what was going on nor by decision on either side. What was to be expected when the opposing armies were largely composed of country labourers under the direction of country gentlemen neither of whom had any knowledge or proper training in military matters? Now it seemed that Monmouth's men would prevail; then the militia stood firm; at length the latter's perseverance was enough for the rebels to lose heart and begin to withdraw. Indeed Monmouth's so-called cavalry, peasants and apprentices mounted on unschooled farm horses which became unmanageable as soon as drums sounded or pieces were fired off, galloped away as if Prince Rupert himself were after them and did not stop until they had reached the supposed safety of Lyme.

First honours therefore went to the loyal militia. It would not be long before Monmouth turned the tables on them, albeit temporarily. At Exeter Christopher Monk, Duke of Albemarle and son of George Monk, whose influence in restoring Monmouth's father to the throne had been decisive, was gathering together the local militia and had a total of 4,000 men of the train bands under his command. With this force, sufficient as he thought to deal once and for all with Monmouth's rebellion, he marched eastwards. At Axminster the rebels were drawn up to meet him and had made their dispositions in no contemptible fashion. But it was not so much this which deterred Albemarle, whose superiority in numbers was very great. It was rather fear that if his trainbands caught sight of the immensely popular Monmouth, they would instantly desert him in a body. He therefore resolved upon retreat. Such was the effect on his followers that sober retreat deteriorated into headlong flight. The militia became a rabble of fugitives who seemed unable to dispossess themselves quickly enough of weapons and uniforms.

It could not last, of course. Support for Monmouth was local and limited. His assumption of the royal title – a totally unnecessary step at this stage of the proceedings – was taken ill by the republicans of London who used it as an excuse not to honour whatever obligations they might be supposed to be under. The great men of the realm – however much some of them might dislike the rule of James, whom they had after all sought to exclude from the succession – were not disposed to risk another civil war, the outcome of which was bound to be uncertain, for the sake of Charles's bastard son. Besides, the longer Monmouth's attempt lasted, the more it seemed to falter. It was true that Monmouth was organizing his forces at Bridgewater and that volunteers were still reinforcing him. He now had some six regiments of infantry, many of whom were the very militiamen of Dorset and Somerset. But was it probable that their valour or skill would be much enhanced by serving *under* Monmouth's banner rather that *against* it? It was also true that his cavalry – if the collection of carthorses and coach horses, which, far from being trained to the tumult and discipline of war, were not even schooled to answer to the bridle, could be graced with the name of cavalry – now numbered perhaps a thousand. But the far more numerous forces of James were gathering to put an end to the whole miserable affair. Monmouth's idea of taking Bristol was thwarted by his own dilatoriness and the intervention of the Life Guards, who quickly dispersed what forces opposed them at Keynsham. Meanwhile more Government troops were closing in. The trainbands of Wiltshire assembled under, as was proper, Thomas Herbert, Earl of Pembroke. The trainbands of Gloucestershire under the Duke of Beaufort occupied Bristol. Volunteers from Oxford-shire went to Abingdon. Churchill, with The Blues, showed as much military skill on behalf of the King this time as he was to show political skill on behalf of William three years later. All these forces, together with Feversham from London, were concentrating.

From then on Monmouth dithered. Although it was thought he might raise more reinforcements in Wiltshire and so have enough strength to take on the Royal Army, the Earl of Pembroke soon put paid to such Wiltshire volunteers who ventured to assemble. Monmouth returned ignominiously to Bridgwater where he received a less enthusiastic welcome than he had had ten days earlier. Moreover the Royal troops, now numbering some 4,000, were moving to attack him. The chosen

field of battle was Sedgemoor. Dispersal of Monmouth's cavalry was
followed by the wearing down of his infantry. The presence of the
King's Household troops and regular battalions of Foot had brought
about Monmouth's defeat. In captivity he sadly added disgrace to failure,
and all in all would have done better never to have ventured forth from
Holland from the comforting embraces of Lady Henrietta Wentworth.

Thus James triumphed and the odious Jeffreys set about completing
the work. Now at the zenith of his power, the King turned his attention
to realizing two prize objectives, which of all possible objectives were the
two most calculated to inspire fear and opposition in the House of
Commons – repeal of Habeas Corpus and formation of a great Standing
Army. With these achieved, any curb on his exercising absolute power
would be removed. Although he himself was removed before he gained
either, he did succeed in taking some steps towards achieving the second.
Under the guise of the realm's security during Monmouth's rebellion,
he had greatly increased the strength of regular forces at his disposal by
raising six regiments of cavalry and nine of infantry. James had trebled
the size of his Army and had some 20,000 regular troops under arms,
more than any former monarch had ever had in times of peace. It still
did not satisfy him. He did not quickly forget the number of militiamen
who had formed part of Monmouth's rebel army, nor did he ignore the
plight in which he might have found himself had he been unable to call
on the support of his regular forces. Happily for England, the power of
raising an even larger Standing Army rested upon the ability to pay for
more soldiers. And the power of the purse still rested with the House
of Commons.

So little did James understand the character of the people he ruled
that when opposition to his intention to destroy the Established Church
by using his Ecclesiastical authority reached the point of London's
trainbands refusing to disperse hostile crowds, refusing in short 'to fight
for Popery', he formed a great camp of his Standing Army at Hounslow
Heath. Fourteen battalions of infantry and over thirty squadrons of
cavalry were assembled together with artillery pieces and ammunition –
all with a view to overaweing and subduing the citizens of London. But
James, who usually got his priorities wrong, had completely misjudged
both these citizens and his soldiers, for instead of the soldiers deterring
and forcing obedience on the citizens, the ideas of the citizens took a
grip on the imagination of the soldiers. Apart from this, the Londoners,
once their first apprehensions were overcome, took to the spectacle and
active delights of the camp rather as they would to a gigantic fair or
circus. 'Mingled with the musketeers and dragoons,' wrote Macaulay,
'a multitude of fine gentlemen and ladies from Soho Square, sharpers

and painted women from Whitefriars, invalids in sedans, monks in hoods, and gowns, lacqueys in rich liveries, pedlars, orange girls, mischievous apprentices and gaping clowns, was constantly passing and repassing through the long lanes of tents. From some pavilions were heard the noises of drunken revelry, from others the curse of gamblers.' So much for the effect of James's Standing Army. Two years later, when all was put to the test, it availed him nothing.

Yet even the departure of James Stuart did not bring to an end controversy about the desirability or the danger of a Standing Army. This controversy was raging just as furiously almost ten years after the joint assumption of power by William and James's daughter, Mary. The parliamentary conflict of 1697 produced all the old arguments, the old prejudices and the old inconsistencies that had characterized such conflicts in the past and were to do so again in the future. It was the same old discussion about the respective virtues or dangers of relying on professional soldiers or the militia. Although it was in fact clear enough, indeed always had been clear [and still is Government policy] that only a combination of the two could properly provide effective guarantees against aggression from abroad or disturbance at home, such moderation, such compromise, such common sense, were unlikely to enjoy much of a hearing among those who still remembered the extremes of Strafford's Thorough and the excesses of Cromwell's Ironsides.

The pamphleteers of the late seventeenth century were no different from those of today in combining ignorance of history with abstinence from logic. They made it their business to show by recourse to history that any form of regular armed force was incompatible with the freedom of the people. Whether it was the commonwealth of Greece, the empire of Rome, or here at home recent experience of 'our Chief of Men', who had deposed, then murdered, a King, and afterwards had imposed a tyranny on the people which only the disbandment of the Army had relieved them of – these same pamphleteers sought to prove that their countrymen's liberty would and could never be secure while a standing army existed. The possible dangers of invasion from abroad were shrugged off once more by appeal to the nation's history. Was it not a fact that a largely militia army had triumphed under the Plantagenets at Crécy and Agincourt? To whom did the country owe victory at Flodden, or the host which had turned out at Tilbury – that same host whose likely effect on the enemy had so worried De Vere – if not to the militia? 'In the fourteenth, fifteenth and sixteenth centuries Englishmen who did not live by the trade of war had made war with success and glory. Were the Englishmen of the seventeenth century so degenerate that they could not be trusted to play the men for their own homesteads and parish churches?' The absurd inconsistencies of these arguments were not hard to reveal. The pamphleteers could not have it both ways. If militias in the past had been so successful in dismaying or defeating the regular troops of foreign armies, what was to be feared from a mere handful of regular troops made up of their own countrymen? On the one hand, these scribblers maintained that a standing army of Englishmen would quickly reduce the rest of the country into a state of subjection and slavery; on the other hand, should any foreign invader at the head of one hundred thousand veteran troops, triumphant from unbroken victories throughout Europe, be unwise enough to set foot on English soil, he would instantly be sent about his business with grievous loss and a resolution never to return by the English yeomen and burghers who, without any regular form of training, discipline or knowledge of the affairs of war, would none the less prove irresistible in battle. Yet these same yeomen and burghers would be helpless against an infinitely smaller number of their own countrymen. As Macaulay tells us, whoever denied the serious threat to English liberties posed by creating a standing army was denounced as 'a tool of the Court', while those who in the same breath denied the ability of untrained militiamen to overcome with speed and certainty European veterans was accused of 'insulting and slandering the nation'. It was left to Somers to suggest a means of reconciling these ridiculous contradictions.

Somers' argument was essentially that which has prevailed ever since. To be without the means of defending the realm from a foreign invader was to invite that foreigner to invade and conquer. It was absurd to suppose that the militia, to whom battle would be unfamiliar, could be equal in a fight to those whose entire existence had been one long preparation for battle. 'What he recommended was, not a standing army, but a temporary army, an army of which Parliament would annually fix the number, an army for which Parliament would annually frame a military code, an army which would cease to exist as soon as either the Lords or the Commons should think that its services were not needed.' Such an army is more or less what we have today. But although today too we are quick to endorse Somers' contention that 'the occasional soldier is not a match for the professional soldier', so expensive is the professional that we arrange for his reinforcement by the occasional in time of national emergency. It was essentially Somers' idea which took root and flourished in the eighteenth and nineteenth centuries and is the means of safeguarding the realm today.

Thus it was during the reign of the Stuarts that controversy as to the dangers of having and of not having a Standing Army reached the greatest heights of intensity and bitterness. The compromise proposed by Somers and adopted by William III and the Houses of Parliament greatly reduced that fine army which William had raised and trained, and with which he had helped to restrain the power, ambition and duplicity of Louis XIV. Yet the ironic turns of fate had still a surprise in store. For it was under the last of the Stuart monarchs, Queen Anne, that the splendid machine forged by William achieved its greatest triumphs in the hands of Marlborough. We do not need to look far to discover the reason for these fluctuations in the army's strength and capability. The demands of war would first outweigh the imagined fears and real need for thrift in peace; then with war over for the time being retrenchment would be the order of the day. So that when the Treaty of Ryswick was concluded in 1697, William's army of some 30,000 – half as much again as James II had mustered – was drastically scaled down to a mere 8,000 or so, in short an army of roughly the size that James had inherited from Charles II. But of course peace did not endure long. James II died in 1701; Louis XIV, in a gesture as gratuitous as it was ineffectual, as capricious as it was insolent, recognized James's son as King James III of England and VIII of Scotland in direct contradiction of his undertaking under the terms of the Peace of Ryswick. In England the affront was resented by Whig and Tory alike. The nation became determined for war, but it would be one in which the Grand Alliance would be held together not by William, who died in 1702, but by Marlborough, probably the greatest British general ever to take the field.

During the War of the Spanish Succession the British Army's contribution to the Alliance was substantial. By 1708 almost 50,000 British soldiers were campaigning either under Marlborough in the Low Countries and elsewhere or under Galway and Peterborough in Spain. Marlborough's unbroken run of victories – Blenheim, Ramillies, Oudenarde, Malplaquet – are renowned. 'For the first time since 1588,' wrote Arthur Bryant, 'England basked in the intoxicating glory of military supremacy.' Not only was this success demonstrated by the colours of vanquished enemies being displayed in the streets of London and hung in Westminster Hall, but again as Bryant has it 'the soldier, and particularly the disabled veteran and half-pay officer, became a common feature of the social scene, and even passed over into literature, notably in George Farquhar's play *The Recruiting Officer*.' In Spain results might have been less spectacular but were no less interesting. In the biography of his great ancestor, Winston Churchill pointed out that the success of a commander rarely arises from rigid adherence to sets of rules. He argued that there was no surer road to failure than imitating plans of former heroes and trying to fit them to new circumstances. The point

is notably illustrated by Galway's conduct during the war in Spain.
That Galway was an experienced commander no one would deny. That
he was familiar with campaigning conditions in Spain was equally
recognized. And that his failure in 1707 was a result of his insistence
that war was an exact science from which all original ideas should be
excluded was made equally clear when, having embarked on the Battle
of Almanza in a manner with which the text books could have found no
fault, it took him only a few hours to lose the best part of twenty
thousand men, all his guns and baggage, over a hundred colours, the
campaign itself and almost the whole of Spain. How different a man
was one of his fellow commanders – Charles Mordaunt, Earl of Peterborough. He possessed the very qualities most appropriate to the peculiar
demands of the campaign in which he was engaged. He was able to do
much with extremely slender resources. Audacity and novelty were
second nature to him. He knew when to strike a decisive blow, how to
do so and above all how to exploit success. Having embarked upon a
course of action, nothing could deflect him. He was dismayed neither
by unfavourable odds nor by the inconstancy of the elements. His energy
overcame difficulties which would have caused other men to falter. All
of us must find his eccentricity endearing. 'One day he took towns
with horse-soldiers,' observed Macaulay, 'then again he turned some
hundreds of infantry into cavalry at a minute's notice. He obtained his
political intelligence chiefly by means of love affairs, and filled his
despatches with epigrams.' Yet it was this irresistible capriciousness
which robbed him of his employers' confidence.

Not all the warring against France, however, made any difference to
the Spanish Succession. Philip V, grandson of Louis XIV, remained on
the Spanish throne. In 1713 Queen Anne's principal ministers, Harley
and Bolingbroke, concluded the Peace of Utrecht, and because of the
consequent displeasure of George I, Elector of Hanover, these two
ministers began their secret intrigues with the Pretender. But before her
death Anne dismissed them both, and her appointment of Shrewsbury
as chief minister ensured the proclamation and accession of George I.
This rebuff to the Stuart cause, however, had little effect on the retention
of a standing army. The Stuart rising of 1715 and a further, although
short-lived, war with Spain three years later saw to it that the Whig
government maintained substantial regular forces. In 1715 there were
some 36,000 troops deployed at home and abroad. Those at home
demonstrated once more that a standing army – the Stuarts' formerly
favoured toy for preserving their position and their tyranny – could
effectively be employed, not on the Stuarts' behalf, but to encompass
the dissipation of their hopes. Once again that instrument previously so

dreaded by the English people as being curtailer and destroyer of their liberties came to the rescue as preserver and guarantor of these same liberties. There was not much talk now of disbanding regular forces, and relying solely on the questionable martial soundness of the militia. Under Walpole the military establishment was further enlarged, and, as Arthur Bryant explains 'the three great professions of the Victorian Age, the Army, the Church and the Civil Service were taking shape'.

There was no shortage of activity for these military professionals. The War of the Austrian Succession saw the British Army fighting the French again at both Dettingen and Fontenoy. At the first of these battles in 1743 George II was nominally in command of some 30,000 British troops, but Dettingen was won – if indeed it can be called a victory at all – in spite of, rather than because of, George II. At one stage in the battle George's horse, sensing perhaps that the Earl of Stair, one of Marlborough's lieutenants, was the abler commander, took off, not towards, but away from the enemy. But George was nothing if not resolute. He succeeded in stopping the animal, and, dismounting, returned to the fray on foot. He now realized that Stair's previous dispositions to the north of the River Main, dispositions which he himself had changed, had been proper and in attempting to rectify his former error, he brought about a general action. As so often before and since, poor generalship was rescued by the steadiness and courage of the British soldier. Both horse and foot contributed to a satisfactory result. Our infantry's musketry dismayed and halted the advancing French Guards, and four regiments of our cavalry thrust back the French horsemen. So carried away was George II by the gallant behaviour of one of Rich's dragoons, whose name was Daraugh, in repossessing a Regimental standard, that he not only promoted Daraugh to the rank of cornet, but actually pressed a purse of guineas into his hand.

If the British prevailed at Dettingen, the same could not be said of Fontenoy. This time the Duke of Cumberland, George II's son, was in command and although the British infantry behaved with the utmost gallantry, furious French counter-attacks carried the day, and Cumberland was obliged to leave the field. He was, however, able to indulge his inclination for butchery a year later at Culloden where the Young Pretender's hopes were dashed for ever. In 1748 the Peace of Aix-la-Chapelle brought a temporary end to hostilities between France and England. Eight years later the Seven Years War began, illuminated as far as British arms were concerned by the activities of Clive and Wolfe. It is not hard to divide British military endeavours into two categories – the first a series of bold ventures, like Clive's seizure of Arcot and his triumph at Plassey or Wolfe's capture of Quebec, infinite in their vision, astonishing in their almost insolent disregard for the military odds, incalculable in their political consequences, and reflected by page after page of glorious history; the second a weary, stale, flat and unprofitable catalogue of indecisive, ill-judged and ponderous campaigns, lightened only by perseverance and redeemed only by virtue of possessing powerful allies. This sharp distinction makes it easy to separate wars of Empire from European struggles. The former inspired innovation, freedom of action, boldness of execution and *gain*. The latter produced grievous loss, sick enterprise, shackled manoeuvre and stifled initiative. And the main cause of the disagreeable conditions of these European ventures was almost always the same – heavy odds against this country which in turn meant that there was no alternative to a long haul.

One of the longest hauls was against the storm which Pitt the Younger was required to weather. Macaulay is not kind about Pitt's aptitude for the conduct of war. 'His military administration was that of a driveller.' He reminds us that Pitt misunderstood the nature of the war in which he was engaged and therefore mismanaged it. In spite of extremity of danger, in spite of having absolute command of unlimited resources, Pitt did not create large, well-equipped and successful armies. Instead he embarked upon one disastrous expedition after another and was saved only by the existence of the English Navy and his own eloquence in the House of Commons. After many years of war and countless expenditure of life and treasure, so Macaulay has it, 'the English Army, under Pitt, was the laughing stock of all Europe'. It was left to Sir John Moore and Wellington to reverse this judgment, and we may now perhaps see how this came about.

When Revolutionary France declared war on Britain in 1793, this country was unprepared. There were a mere 15,000 troops at home and another 30,000 at various stations overseas. Pitt at once set about raising more by first introducing a Bill to increase the size of the Army by some 25,000 and also to call up nearly 20,000 from the militia. And as the one thing Britain was not short of was money, he also hired auxiliaries – 14,000 from the Electorate of Hanover, a further 8,000 from Hesse-Darmstadt. But compared with what Carnot, the organizer of victory, was doing, these numbers were contemptibly small. Carnot, with his *levée en masse*, was creating a nation in arms. Twice the Duke of York tried to do something in the Low Countries; twice he was obliged to retreat and return to these shores. But at least something was learned from these disasters. Young Lieutenant-Colonel Wellesley quickly saw that there was nothing wrong with the British soldier if he were properly directed – his own 33rd Foot showed what could be done with good discipline and accurate shooting – but that it was the system itself, of organization, administration and command, which was at fault. Happily he was born to put it right. Captain Calver, who was the Duke of York's aide de camp, had some remarkably pertinent things to say about what was needed;

> We want artillerymen, we want a general officer at the head of the artillery, we want drivers and smiths, we want a commanding engineer of rank and experience – we want, at least, two out of the four brigades of mounted artillery with which his Grace of Richmond is amusing himself in England. We want a total stop put to that pernicious mode of bestowing rank on officers without even the form of recommendation, merely for raising (by means of crimps) a certain number of men, to restore to the Army those independent and disinterested feelings and high principles which should actuate a soldier and form the basis of military discipline of a free country.

But without all these necessary changes, without proper command arrangements or proper supplies, without the organized support of artillery and engineers, without discipline or system, the British Army indulged in a series of expeditions to the Continent only to be beaten, obliged to retire and then subjected to the humiliation either of re-embarking to return to England by favour of the Royal Navy or of capitulating to the enemy. There could be no more dramatic illustration of what depths a defeated and disintegrating army could descend to than Sir John Fortescue's descripton of the retreat at the end of the Duke of York's ill-fated 1794–95 campaign:

> Far as the eye could reach over the whitened plain were scattered gun-limbers, wagons full of baggage, stores or sick men, sutler's carts and private carriages. Beside them lay the horses, dead; here a straggler who had staggered on to the bivouac and dropped to sleep in the arms of the frost; there a group of British and Germans round an empty rum cask; here forty English Guardsmen huddled together about a plundered wagon; there a pack-horse with a woman lying alongside it, and a baby swaddled in rags peering out of the pack with its mother's milk turned to ice upon its lips – one and all stark, frozen, dead. Had the retreat lasted but three or four days longer, not a man would have escaped.

None of these expeditions would have been possible, of course, without the Royal Navy. And it was the Royal Navy which proved to be the one rock which Revolutionary France and Napoleon could neither budge nor outmanoeuvre nor destroy. It was the Royal Navy too which enabled Moore and later Wellington to nibble away at Napoleon's empire in such a way that the cancer of Spain at length did so much to bring about the disintegration of this empire. If Moore and Wellington slowly and patiently remodelled and directed the British Army to their eventual victories, it was Nelson who embodied the spirit, dash, masterly professionalism and invincibility of the Royal Navy. Above all Nelson understood the business of command. 'He reminded the Navy.' writes Arthur Bryant, 'that, whatever the bonds of authority, leadership was not a mere matter of transmitting orders but of evoking the will to serve.' Because of his leadership and the instrument under his hand, Nelson was able to indulge his absolute determination to seek out and bring the enemy to bay, his consuming desire for the offensive which by bringing about what he wanted, a pell-mell battle, enabled him also to take the game-winning trick of annihilating the opposition. Moore, too, understood the need to evoke the will to serve, Wellington perhaps less so, but their campaigns and strategies were very different from Nelson's. If anything they were anxious to *avoid* a great battle, and rather to create a distraction to the enemy's major campaigns elsewhere against England's allies. It was not that they did not understand that the principal feature of war was violence. It was because with the material at their disposal – England's only Army and a small one at that – they could not aspire to more than limited objectives. Moore took great risks when he set his Army across Napoleon's lines of communication, but he made sure, despite appalling difficulties and a virtual breakdown in discipline, that the Army got away after Corunna. Moore's death meant that the next attempt at a Peninsula distraction was carried out by Wellington, the Fabian general, who knew when to retreat and dared to do so on several occasions, remarking as he did that since England had but one Army, they had better take care of it. In one respect, we might say, Moore was a greater commander than Wellington – he understood the need for and insisted on sound training. His outstanding creation was the Rifle Corps.

When Moore formed and trained his special Corps of Light Infantry [today's Green Jackets] he was motivated partly by the need to find some answer to the French *tirailleur*, the swift, sharp-shooting skirmishers which would move ahead of the main columns, both discovering the enemy's whereabouts and disrupting their positions. The idea had originated when the Duke of York ordered a dozen or so infantry regiments to send both officers and men to Horsham in 1799 where they underwent training in light infantry tactics, field craft and shooting. From this modest beginning sprang the famous Rifle Brigade, the 95th Regiment, who fought with Nelson at Copenhagen. Later under Moore himself at Shorncliffe, together with the 43rd and 52nd Regiments, they perfected their methods of disciplined initiative which so distinguished their performance in the Peninsula. It was fitting that there was this connection between Nelson and Moore, for both possessed that indispensable quality of a truly great commander – humanity. 'Moore,' wrote Arthur Bryant, 'faced by a triumph of the natural courage and enthusiasm of the Revolutionary armies, went back to nature to defeat them. He did not discard the traditional discipline of the British Service; he humanized it.' His system was founded on justice, good humour and common sense. As a result he inspired confidence, efficiency and daring.

Training is one thing, war another. In the autumn of 1808 Moore was appointed to the command in Spain: 'His Majesty, having determined to employ not less than 30,000 infantry and 5,000 cavalry in the North of Spain, to cooperate with the Spanish armies in the expulsion of the French from that Kingdom, has been graciously pleased to entrust to you the Command-in-Chief of this force.' It was not, however, the French army which was to be expelled. Napoleon himself took a hand in the game, and in a lightning campaign smashed the Spanish Army and took Madrid. His intention to invade Portugal and destroy the British Army was thwarted by Moore, who set his much smaller force astride the French lines of communication. This chance to get at the British leopards so galvanized the Emperor that he dropped everything else, and, as Sir Charles Oman tells us, 'hurled on to Moore's track not only the central reserve at Madrid, but troops gathered in from all directions, till he had set at least 80,000 men on the march, to encompass the British corps which had so hardily thrown itself upon his comminications'. Moore was obliged to retreat to Corunna, a retreat during which the Army both distinguished itself – the performance of the Light Brigade, which Moore himself had trained, and the cavalry under Paget was magnificent – and disgraced itself by drunkenness and ill-discipline. 'The great fault of our soldiers at this time,' wrote a private of the 71st Foot, 'was an inordinate desire for spirits of any kind. They sacrificed their life and safety for drink, in many ways; for they lay down intoxicated upon the snow and slept the sleep of death; or, staggering behind, were overtaken and cut down by the merciless French soldiers.'

Yet Moore's army succeeded in repulsing Soult's pursuit, and got away by sea to return to the Peninsula before long, this time under Wellesley, for Moore died the death he had always wanted to, and at the rampart of Corunna was left alone with his glory. Within three months of Corunna Wellesley landed at Lisbon and this time the British Army had come to stay. It was to be a long campaign. A. G. Macdonnell described Wellington's task in the Peninsula as the easiest one ever facing a general. With a mercenary army, assured intelligence, a population wholly hostile to his enemy, abundant supplies, interior lines and command of the sea, he had 'the game in his hands, and yet it took him nearly six years to advance from Lisbon to the Pyrenees'. This was an unfair criticism, understandable, for Macdonnell was concerned with extolling Napoleon, but unfair because Wellington's army was always greatly outnumbered by the French and his Spanish allies were notoriously inefficient and unreliable. It would, however, be fair to say that Wellington was always prepared to bide his time. He had infinite patience; he could therefore afford to be cautious; his foresight in building the Lines of Torres Vedras was a master stroke of strategy; and although he might not have appreciated what a cancer to the Napoleonic system Spain would become, he had confidence in keeping the campaign going as a steady drain, a permanent distraction, to the French military machine. He never despaired, partially because he prepared for every contingency, but mainly because despair was foreign to his nature. In 1810 he observed that affairs in the Peninsula always seemed to have the same appearance, the appearance of being lost. 'The contest, however, still continues.' During the contest he formed an army with which, he later said, he could have gone anywhere and done anything. It had its ups and downs all right. In 1810 Wellington defeated Massena at Bussaco, but was soon bundled back to the lines of Torres Vedras; in 1812 he cut up Marmont at Salamanca and took Madrid, only to retire again after a repulse at Burgos; in 1813 he advanced a third time and for once was not required to 'know when to retreat and to dare to do so'. This shuffling to and fro did not turn Napoleon off his throne. It was simply one more illustration of British strategy – engaging the enemy in a relatively minor theatre while the main business of knocking the stuffing out of the enemy's armies was left to some European ally. The destruction of the Grand Army by Russia, Napoleon's failure at Leipzig, the arrival of Blücher's troops at the walls of Paris – these events persuaded the Marshals that enough was enough and that the Emperor must abdicate. It was Wellington, though, who ensured that the Hundred Days were brought to an abrupt and satisfactory conclusion.

It was after Waterloo, so the story has it, that Wellington performed one more incalculably great feat for the nation and the British Army. He invented the Tommy. Elizabeth Longford in her incomparable biography writes;

A military paper had been submitted to him suggesting a typical name for a private. The Duke crossed out the entry and substituted the name of a veteran in his old regiment, the 33rd Foot. Private Thomas Atkins had been with him during the wretched retreat towards Antwerp in 1794. At one tense moment he ordered his 33rd, held in reserve, to form open lanes and let the crumbling first line through to the rear, then fill the gap themselves – a grim manoeuvre. Though they succeeded, Thomas Atkins was one who fell, to become immortal after Waterloo.

Wellington had no illusions about his army – the amateurishness of many officers, the drunkenness of the rank and file – yet he could say of them, 'there are no men in Europe who can fight like my infantry ... my army and I know one another exactly. We have a mutual confidence, and are never disappointed'. Sir John Fortescue's judgment that he alienated the affections of all ranks, parted from them with no regret and never took any trouble about them again is hardly supportable. Apart from his generosity to old soldiers, he became Commander-in-Chief of the Army after the Duke of York's death in 1827. His first General Order to the Army was characteristic of him. Short and to the point, it simply demanded and pledged duty and service. He did not remain Commander-in-Chief long this time because he became Prime Minister early in 1828, but during his Premiership he opposed major reform of the Army, standing out against the abolition of flogging, because he believed that the bulk of Britain's battles would be fought in defence of her empire, that is in unpleasant climates in which only the 'scum of the earth' would be willing to serve, and such men required the deterrent of flogging if they were to be properly controlled. At the same time Wellington is awarded the praise of saving the British Army by hiding it away in these same colonies. And how wholly right he was in judging that Britain's wars would be fought outside Europe. For almost forty years after Waterloo the British Army was engaged in Burma, in South Africa, in Afghanistan, China, New Zealand and, of course, in India. There was but one exception during the rest of the century – the Crimean War. But the wars of Empire went on. The Indian Mutiny, Afghanistan again, Zululand, Abyssinia, the Sudan, Egypt and at the very end of the century, the Boer War – all these kept the Army abroad and fighting. Shortly before Wellington became Commander-in-Chief for the second time, in 1842, four out of five infantry battations were overseas, some twenty in India, Burma and China; a similar number at home; about sixty in the colonies.

Thomas Babington Macaulay is principally remembered as one of the two greatest historians this country has produced, yet in 1840 as Secretary at War in Melbourne's administration he was responsible for introducing the Army estimates. In doing so he proposed a modest increase in the Army's strength – from 110,000 to 120,000 – but this did not go nearly far enough for Sir Henry Hardinge who was to succeed Macaulay as Secretary at War a year later when Peel became Prime

Minister. Hardinge pointed out that the demands of overseas service were such that infantry battalions were more or less 'condemned to perpetual banishment'. There were eighty-four battalions either serving abroad or on passage, and nineteen at home of which eight had just returned. Thus there was no possibility of a sensible and just relief system. In commenting on this Fortescue not only gives us a taste of his own literary distinction, but shows us that little has changed in one hundred and fifty years:

> It does not appear that Parliament was in the least moved by this statement; and indeed members took little more interest in the Army estimates then than in the Indian budget now.* It was only the British Soldier who was concerned, and he always did as he was bidden, and accomplished the tasks that were set to him. It was a matter of small moment to politicians whether he were condemned to continuous exile, so long as they remained at home and could share in the delights of faction.

There is, however, one thing that has changed in one hundred and fifty years. Today's soldier would welcome with the greatest imaginable enthusiasm the opportunity to serve somewhere further afield then Germany or Great Britain. When Hardinge himself was in office he tried to correct the imbalance between home and overseas service, and in part succeeded by increasing the number of battalions at home with organizational adjustments.

In the past France had been Britain's great adversary and although she was never to be again (we may discount the brief, yet tragic, disputes we had with Vichy France in the 1940s), concern with what Napoleon III might do after assuming power in 1851 persuaded the British Government to increase the Army establishment by some 5,000. A further bill to form a local militia of 70,000 men was opposed by Palmerston and caused the Whig Ministry to resign. In Lord Derby's administration which followed, a new Militia Bill provided for 80,000 men to be embodied with voluntary enlistment. In supporting this Bill with all the eloquence and influence at his command, the Duke of Wellington made his last great contribution to the military welfare of his country:

> We have never up to the present moment maintained a proper peace establishment; and we are now in the position that we can no longer carry out that system. You have been carrying on war in all parts of the globe by means of your peace establishment, yet in that establishment you have never had more men than are necessary to relieve the sentries and regiments on foreign service, some of which have been twenty-five years abroad.

* Fortescue was writing in 1930.

Yet from the point of view of the ordinary soldier little had changed since Wellington had been in command of his Peninsular or his Waterloo armies. His pay of one shilling a day was nearly all removed from him in charges for food, laundry, maintenance, 'barrack damages' [a phrase familiar enough to anyone who has been a soldier] and so on. What little he had left might be spent in the wet canteen. Clothing, food, a roof were the consolations for donning a red coat. The officers set over him were for the most part adherents to a regimental code of behaviour which shunned professionalism and demanded only loyalty, courage and character. These, together with the muzzle-loading muskets of a century before, were adequate for fighting local colonial wars against ill-equipped natives. They would not do for taking on a European foe as the Crimean War was shortly to show.

The British soldier has frequently suffered from having incompetent commanders, inferior equipment and no very clear political objective, yet in their preparation for and conduct of the Crimean War even British ministers and generals with a taste for disastrous military adventures surpassed themselves. In June, 1854, after the Cabinet had agreed to propose to the French Government that a joint landing of 60,000 men, half French, half British, should be made near Sevastopol and that the town should then be attacked by land and sea, the Duke of Argyll expressed some concern about the plan to Palmerston, then Home Secretary, who replied: 'Oh, you need not be in the least anxious. With our combined fleets and our combined armies we are certain to succeed. ... We shall have one battle to fight outside the walls and then the siege. The end is certain.' By November of that year, two months after the landings, several battles had been fought, including Alma, Balaklava and Inkerman, with the long siege of Sevastopol still to come. So certain had the Government been that the campaign would be a short one [a certainty that was to recur at the beginning of the Boer War and the Great War with equally disappointing error] that the troops were ordered not to be encumbered with winter clothing. After Inkerman – 'the soldiers' battle' in which the gallantry of the Foot Guards and the rest of the British infantry was outstanding – the troops in the Crimea were to face one of the worst winters of campaigning history, for which no provision had been made. Hurricanes of rain and snow swept away thousands of tents in the English and French camps and destroyed much of the shipping in the harbour; no less than thirty transports foundered and immense quantities of food, medical supplies, clothing, hay for the horses and ammunition for the guns were lost, turning hardship into acute want. Men and horses died in the extreme conditions without food or comforts and during those winter months disease claimed nearly nine thousand lives. It was administrative incompetence that had condemned them to death, not action by the enemy.

Apart from the incompetence of generals like Raglan, Lucan and Cardigan – one member of the 4th Light Dragoons wrote of the two latter that 'two bigger fools could not be picked out of the British Army to take command' – the Crimean campaign is principally remembered for the battle of Balaklava. 'You have lost the Light Brigade!' It was thus that Lord Raglan bitterly reproached Lord Lucan on the evening of 25 October, 1854. As a simple statement of fact the words were not unfounded. Before the charge, according to Captain Portal who rode in it, the Light Cavalry Brigade had mustered on parade some 700 men; after it they numbered a mere 180.* But had *Lucan* lost it? The controversy as to who was to blame has been lengthy. The truth is that many were to blame, Lucan amongst them. It was a coalition of personal ill-feeling, general mismanagement and peculiarly bad orders which led to so great, yet glorious, a blunder. Given the circumstances which prevailed, however – a Commander-in-Chief, Raglan, who had no very clear idea of how to conduct operations and unlike his teacher, the Duke, was accustomed to expressing himself with as little precision and as much ambiguity as the putting together of words would allow; a Lieutenant-General of cavalry wholly at odds with his Commander-in-Chief's direction of the campaign and with his brother-in-law, Cardigan's proprietary handling of the Light Brigade; and an aide-de-camp who at the critical moment of delivering the fatal order was almost insane with impatience and injured pride, so much so that he actually seemed to point to the wrong objective – given these circumstances we may perhaps accept General Airey's epitaph that it was 'nothing to Chillianwallah'.† Although the Light Brigade's loss was grievous, their charge will be remembered, not so much for foolhardiness and sacrifice, but for courage, discipline and devotion to duty.

There were many consequences of the mismanagement that had prevailed during the Crimean War. The Commissariat was overhauled, the medical services improved, the Enfield Rifle introduced, *and* – of great significance for the future of the British Army – The Duke of Cambridge, who had commanded a division in the Crimea with courage, if no imagination, was in 1856 appointed to be Commander-in-Chief of the Army. He was to remain so for nearly forty years.

---

* In fact 607 charged (hence Tennyson's 'noble six hundred'); 198 were at roll-call afterwards.
† In 1849 at Chillianwallah in a battle against the Sikhs the British cavalry disgraced itself. Because of some misunderstanding which led to confusion and panic, a division of cavalry stampeded to the rear.

Shortly after his appointment there occurred another great event which had a profound effect on the military affairs of the nation – the Indian Mutiny, provoked, some would say, by the method of greasing the very Enfield rifle just introduced into service, and so savagely fought by those on both sides that things were never quite the same again for the British in India. One of the most controversial points was how large an army was needed for India and what should be the proportion of British to Indian troops. That there had to be an *Indian* Army was not in doubt, for it would be impossibly expensive and politically absurd to try and hold India with British troops alone. The Committee wrestling with this problem recommended a proportion of between one to two and one to three. By 1863 there were 62,000 British and 125,000 Indian. All gunners, however, except with mountain batteries, were to be European. There was, as James Morris has told us, another effect of the Mutiny on the British attitude to Empire. It was, if nothing else, a practical attitude which now prevailed and one that suited a people dedicated to business: 'The Mutiny had demonstrated indeed that not all the coloured peoples were capable of spiritual redemption ... but the British could always concentrate on material regeneration – the enforcement of law and order, the distribution of scientific progress and lubrication of trade.' The Army would help with all three.

It might have been thought that a senior officer like the Duke of Cambridge, who had taken part in the Crimean War and had personally seen how disastrously commanded, organized, equipped and administered the British Army had been during that campaign would have been the most fervent advocate of reform. Not a bit of it; generally speaking Cambridge, as Commander-in-Chief and as cousin of Queen Victoria, opposed all change.* It would have been difficult to find a man of such limitless good intentions and sparse imaginative powers. Yet during his time as Commander-in-Chief, as Fortescue put it 'the Army was utterly transformed from top to bottom, not always in accordance with his [Cambridge's] own opinion'. Happily the opinion of Cardwell prevailed, but before we see what Cardwell's reforms achieved we may take a look at the Army's establishment in 1859, three years after Cambridge's assumption of command and two years after the Indian Mutiny. In that year the Army totalled 237,000 men, and the principle of having half as many infantry battalions of the line at home as were deployed abroad meant that with fifty battalions in India and a further thirty-seven in the Colonies, there would be forty-four at home. Some

---

* One change was insisted on by the Queen herself – the establishment of her new decoration, the Victoria Cross, which was first distributed in June, 1857.

of those at home had found a new camp and exercising ground which has long been looked upon as a very special preserve of the Army – Aldershot. Those of us who have served there will have mixed views, but on the whole the idea of concentrating troops in one area had beneficial effects. Although there were those who maintained that the Army detested Aldershot, as the wooden huts erected were 'verminous' and there were no amusements for the men except to visit such 'vile places' which sprang up alongside and housed the 'wrens', as the women who hung round the camp were known. Not that the soldier had much to spend on amusements. In 1865 a private soldier in a line regiment was paid thirteen pence a day, a shilling for wages [as it had been during the Peninsula War] and a penny for beer-money. From his shilling eightpence halfpenny was deducted for food, and from the balance he was required to pay for laundry, washing material, renewal of some clothing and 'barrack-damages'. In 1867 some minor addition was made to his pay – a mere twopence a day. Yet soldiers who initially enlisted for ten years' service and had the opportunity for re-enlisting for a further similar period were so impressed by this small improvement to their pay that in 1867 the numbers re-enlisting were some 26,000. In the previous six or seven years the yearly average had been but a tenth of this figure.

The opportunity for making real changes in conditions of service and the systems of both enlisting soldiers and selecting officers for promotion was presented to Cardwell, who was Secretary for War from 1868 to 1874, as a result of the Franco-Prussian war in 1870. The fearsome possibility of a German invasion of this country was for the first time seriously contemplated. Cardwell did not merely enlarge the Army; he completely reformed it. Even before the Franco-Prussian War, he had succeeded in abolishing flogging in peacetime (it was not abolished for active service until 1880) – a totally necessary step if the business of being a soldier in the ranks were to be thought of as a respectable, honourable calling as opposed to what Stendhal called *servitude* for the 'very scum of the earth'. He had also succeeded in introducing measures which enabled the Army to discharge men of bad character. Another step of great significance was to bring back from the colonies some 20,000 men, made possible by the policy of raising local forces in these colonies to assist with their own defence. By concentrating more of the Army at home, it was possible both to build up a kind of strategic reserve and to give this reserve proper training at a formation, as against mere battalion, level. Cardwell did not stop here, however. He abolished purchase, he introduced a system of short service [six years with the colours, six with the reserve], and he subordinated the position of the

Army's Commander-in-Chief to the Secretary of State – much to the Queen's displeasure. He re-equipped the infantry with the first proper breech-loading rifle they had had – the Martini-Henry. And, as if all this were not enough, he changed the entire infantry regimental organization to one which has more or less survived until today – by dividing Great Britain and Ireland into a number of regimental districts, where they would recruit and where their depot would be. In short he territorialized the infantry, which henceforth would be associated with a particular county, rather than simply be known by a number. Each county regiment would have two regular battalions and a number of militia battalions. With two regular battalions it would be possible for each regiment to provide one for foreign service and one at the home depot, where recruits could be trained, and so enable battalions to replace each other at home or abroad without loss of efficiency. The fighting record of the infantry in the numerous wars which took place in the Empire and elsewhere between 1871 and the end of the nineteenth century – Ashanti, Zulu, Afghanistan, Sudan, Egypt – speaks for itself. We shall be looking at some of their activities in more detail shortly. Cardwell's achievements can hardly be overstated, and Sir Robert Ensor in his brilliant *History of England 1870–1914* summed it all up like this:

> His reforms during the quarter of a century following left a broad mark on British history. Without them not only would prompt and crucial successes, such as the Egyptian campaign of 1882, have been unobtainable, but the power-prestige, which Lord Salisbury had behind him in his diplomacy, would scarcely have existed in the same way. Not their least exceptional feature was their economy. Cardwell left the estimates lower than he found them, and yet he had increased the strength of the army in the United Kingdom by 25 battalions, 156 field guns, and abundant stores, while the reserves available for foreign service had been raised from 3,545 to 35,905 men.

Ensor went on to remind us that in two respects Cardwell had fallen short. He had not created a general staff and the Duke of Cambridge was still the Army's Commander-in-Chief, and it is perhaps now time to see what he, the Army, the country and the Empire were up to in the 1890s.

2

HIGH NOON OF EMPIRE

'Ave you 'eard o' the widow at Windsor
With a hairy gold crown on 'er 'ead?
She 'as ships on the foam - she 'as millions at 'ome,
An' she pays us poor beggars in red.
There's 'er nick on the cavalry 'orses,
There's 'er mark on the medical stores -
An' 'er troopers you'll find with a fair wind be'ind
That takes us to various wars.
Then 'ere's to the Widow at Windsor,
An' 'ere's to the stores and the guns,
The men an' the 'orses what makes up the forces
O' Missis Victorier's sons.

Kipling

In June, 1890, when he was only fifteen and at Harrow, the Briton who was to have a more profound influence on the military affairs of the nation during the century to come than perhaps any of his fellow-countrymen was writing to his father, Lord Randolph Churchill, about getting into the Army. He was expressing a wish to effect his entry through the Militia. It would be much more amusing and much easier. Instead of being unacquainted with drill, he would have passed the standard required. Besides, being in the Army class was robbing him of interesting work and spoiling his term. Being at Harrow might be all right for the Preliminary Examination [which in the event Winston passed with some ease] but it would be much better to go in through the Militia because you started much earlier. 'It is a well known thing that a fellow who goes through the militia is always much more use than a Sandhurst Cadet.' Three years later Churchill sat for the Sandhurst Entrance Examination for the *third* time and just passed, not sufficiently high for an infantry cadetship, but enough for the cavalry. Despite Lord Randolph's having warned his son that he should put any idea about joining the cavalry out of his head, Winston was appointed to the 4th Hussars in February, 1895, after the intervention of the Duke of Cambridge himself, still just hanging on to being Commander-in-Chief. Lord Randolph had died a month earlier, but not before he had given his son some excellent advice: 'The Army is the finest profession in the world if you work at it and the worst if you loaf at it.' Military affairs were never far from the mind or hand of Winston Churchill and although he did not remain a regular soldier for long, his interest in and concern for both his Regiment and the Army in general remained alive as long as he did.

At roughly the time when he was writing his letter from Harrow, an event of profound consequences to the British Army and the whole world itself had taken place in Germany. In March, 1890, Emperor William II dismissed his Chancellor, Bismarck.

Having first made Prussia a great European power by a policy of ruthless aggression and then gone on to found the German Empire, Bismarck remained for many years the leading actor on the stage of European affairs. But after obtaining for Germany its supreme position by a series of wars, thereafter Bismarck sought to avoid war, not for the sake of Europe, but for the benefit of the German Reich. Hence his endless negotiations for a system of alliances which would protect Germany from what he saw as the aggressive intentions of France and Russia, and would thereby preserve the peace. He even attempted to bring about an Anglo-German alliance. In 1887 he had written to Britain's Prime Minster, the Marquess of Salisbury, saying that whereas Austria-Hungary, Great Britain and Germany wanted only peace and preservation of the *status quo*, France and Russia were bent on adventure and gain. Austria-Hungary's integrity was necessary to Germany, as was some understanding with Russia for Germany could not risk war on two fronts. Salisbury saw little in this for England, and when two years later Bismarck actually offered him an alliance – against France, but not Russia – Salisbury declined. It was shortly after this that William II got rid of Bismarck and so a restraining influence was removed. Bismarck would never have sent the renowned 'Kruger telegram' (congratulating the Transvaal president on bringing the ill-judged Jameson raid to so humiliating a conclusion) or declared that 'Germany's future lies on the water'. In 1896 the Kaiser did both. We shall see later how the Kaiser's policies led inexorably to war. Whether he had hoisted in Bismarck's prediction that it would be 'some damned foolish thing in the Balkans' which started it all may be doubted. What was not in doubt was that

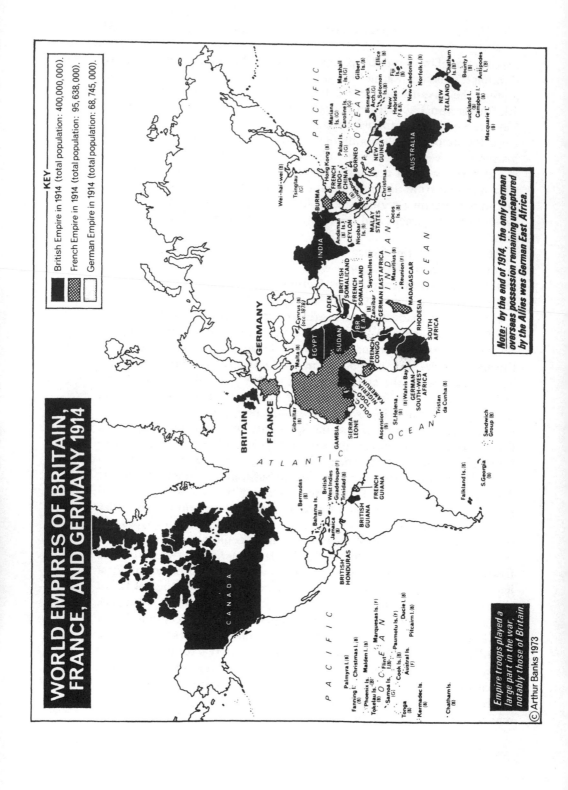

WORLD EMPIRES OF BRITAIN, FRANCE, AND GERMANY 1914

KEY

British Empire in 1914 (total population: 400,000,000).

French Empire in 1914 (total population: 95,638,000).

German Empire in 1914 (total population: 68,745,000).

Note: by the end of 1914, the only German overseas possession remaining uncaptured by the Allies was German East Africa.

Empire troops played a large part in the war, notably those of Britain.

© Arthur Banks 1973

the German Army planned and trained for just such a war. The same could hardly be said of the British Army.

Yet there were those in Great Britain who were trying to set right some of our Army's shortcomings in organization and direction. In 1890 a royal commission charged by Salisbury's government to look into the Army's administration found that its main fault lay in the almost total centralization of control in the hands of the Commander-in-Chief, still at this time the aged Duke of Cambridge. Everything of moment had to pass through his office and he alone was accountable to the Secretary of State. Matters as varied as personnel, fortifications, training, stores, promotions, weapons, the deployment of the Army and even the strategy for which it was deployed – all these were the responsibility of one man, and that man one opposed to any sort of change and almost impossible to get rid of because he was the Queen's cousin. Nevertheless the commission made some important recommendations – many of which mirrored what was done in continental armies. The trouble was that their implementation depended on one crucial step, the first of their proposals, which was not carried out until many years later – abolition of the office of Commander-in-Chief. Following on this indispensable first step it would be possible to do what all European powers had long since done and create a General Staff for forming and executing policy, under the higher direction of a War Office Council, consisting of the Secretary of State, his two junior ministers, the permanent under-secretary and the five senior officers of the General Staff (chief of general staff, adjutant-general, quarter-master general, director of artillery, inspector-general of fortifications). There would also be a general officer commanding the forces in Britain, just as there were in certain overseas stations. The task which was to be given to the General Staff was in essence to collect intelligence, make plans for operations, recommend organization and generally prepare the Army for war. It would be charged with no less a responsibility than the defence of the whole Empire. 'If this programme of 1890 had been carried out even so late as 1895,' observed Sir Robert Ensor, 'when Campbell-Bannerman* at last ejected the obstructive duke, many, if not all, of the army's gross blunders in the South African war might have been avoided. But it was not.' Instead Campbell-Bannerman, who could not conceive what a General Staff would have to do and therefore might think of something disagreeable that should be done, appointed a new Commander-in-Chief in place of the Duke of Cambridge. His choice fell on the hero of innumerable engagements, the victor of so many of Queen Victoria's

* Campbell-Bannerman was Secretary for War 1892–95 and Prime Minister 1905–08.

little wars, Gilbert and Sullivan's 'very model of a modern major-
general', who had given the phrase 'All Sir Garnet' to the nation as a
universal recipe for getting things right, and whom Disraeli called 'an
egotist and a braggart' – Field-Marshal Lord Wolseley.

Like many other soldiers of his time Wolseley enjoyed war for its own
sake. He wrote of the intense, intoxicating joy of leading men in battle,
and regarded it as the duty of young officers to try and get themselves
killed. He certainly tried hard himself in Burma, the Crimea, the Indian
Mutiny and in China. He went on with it even when in command of
expeditions which suppressed a rebellion in Canada's Red River, utterly
destroyed the Ashanti military power in the Gold Coast, and – perhaps
Wolseley's finest hour – inflicted a crushing defeat on Arabi Pasha at
Tel-el-Kebir in 1882, thus ensuring that the British presence in Egypt
would not again be challenged for many a year to come. Yet it was only
two years later in another campaign which began in Egypt with the
purpose of relieving Gordon – Gordon, who was thought of as a unique
Christian hero, a man of infinite truth and integrity, the ever-victorious
general, a legend – that Wolseley met with a check to his hitherto
unbroken run of success, from which he was never quite to recover. Let
us visit him during this last of his campaigns as commander of a British
Army in the field.

Gordon had been sent to Khartoum to evacuate the Egyptian garrisons
in the face of the Mahdi's successful revolt. Sir Evelyn Baring, British
consul-general in Cairo, had opposed the idea, knowing Gordon's
character and courage and fearing that he might take action in the Sudan
that would lead him and the British government into further trouble.
This is precisely what happened. On arrival in Khartoum in February,
1884, Gordon disobeyed his instructions and elected to try and hold
Khartoum and the Nile valley in defiance of the Mahdi. Three months
later Berber and its environments had been taken by Mahdist forces.
Gordon was cut off. Even before this happened there had been urgent
requests by both Baring and Wolseley to prepare for just such an eventu-
ality by getting ready a military expedition to relieve Gordon. Indeed
in April Wolseley had actually produced a plan for what he described
as 'the biggest operation the English Army has ever undertaken'. With
himself in command, his favoured Ring of subordinates there to support
him, a repetition of his former triumphs would establish him once and
for all among the great captains. He might have done it had his plan
been acted on instantly, but the Prime Minister, Gladstone, always
reluctant to indulge in military adventures, was so obsessed with other
matters, notably his Reform Bill, that nothing was done before August,
so that when Wolseley was finally appointed in that month, no proper

preparations for an expedition had been made. Although Wolseley arrived in Cairo in September, he still had to organize the heterogeneous force that had collected in Egypt from England, Gibraltar, Malta, and India. Perhaps the most colourful element of all was the Camel Corps, manned by some of the most fashionable regiments in the British Army – the cavalry, the Foot Guards, Rifle Brigade and even the Royal Marines. In October Wolseley's army set off from Wadi Halfa, travelling up the Nile by courtesy of Thomas Cook's steamers. Time was always going to be against them, four months having been thrown away by Gladstone's dithering, and although Wolseley's force had passed the Nile's first and second cataracts by November, reached Korti the following month, won a battle against the Mahdi's army at Abu Klea on 17 January, and at last on 28 January came within sight of Khartoum from the leading armed steamer, they were just too late. Gordon had been killed two days earlier and the Mahdi's banners were fluttering above Khartoum. Five days before Gordon's death and on receipt of news about the Abu Klea battle, Wolseley recorded in his campaign journal:

> Messengers arrived from Stewart. They left him at Abu Klea wells on morning of 18th instant, so they have come in well, 150 miles in three days on the same camels all the way. Stewart had a real big fight on the 17th inst ... our loss has been heavy arising from the unsteadiness of the Heavy Camel Regt. which allowed the enemy to break into the square. Poor devils they have suffered for it, as out of 64 killed 35 belonged to that Regt. There were 9 officers killed and 9 wounded; amongst the former poor Burnaby who was stabbed by a spear through the jugular. All the correspondents speak most highly of the manner in which our soldiers fought and also of the way in which Stewart handled his troops.

There have been many colourful cavalrymen in the British Army. Burnaby of The Blues might be said to have outshone them all. Six foot four in height, politically active, a balloonist, fluent in eight languages, famous for his adventures like riding across the Russian steppes and commanding a Turkish brigade, correspondent for *The Times* during the 1874 Spanish civil war, best-selling author, his personal courage was outstanding. His biographer, Michael Alexander, described his final moments like this:

> A furious sheikh charged at him on horseback, spear outstretched, but a bullet from the ranks brought him headlong to the ground before they closed. Tribesmen followed close behind and one dashed at him, pointing a long spear at his throat. Checking his pony and slowly reining back, Burnaby leaned forward in the saddle and parried with his sabre. He fenced calmly

and smartly as if he was playing in an assault-at-arms, but the length of his opponent's spear – over eight feet – prevented him from striking back. At that moment another Arab came from the right and with a sudden spring ran his spear-point into Burnaby's shoulder. It was only a prick, but it caused him to turn in the saddle and defend himself from this new quarter ... Burnaby's brief sideways glance gave his opponent the opening he had been waiting for; a heavy spearpoint was driven into his now unguarded throat. He held on for a moment, then fell to the ground. Half a dozen Arabs were immediately upon him, but he somehow got to his feet and with blood spurting from his jugular vein laid about him with desperate sword strokes.

No wonder a young soldier in the Bays wept as he tried to help Burnaby, calling him the bravest man in England; no wonder his own troopers from The Blues who were serving with him then 'sat down and cried'; no wonder *Punch* published a commemorative poem. Nor was this the only poem to be published or the only brave soldier to be mourned. There was Gordon himself:

> Too late! Too late to save him,
> In vain, in vain they tried.
> His life was England's glory,
> His death was England's pride.

Wolseley did not receive the news that Khartoum had fallen until 4 February and then recorded in his journal that, if Gordon had been killed, it were better than captivity and 'the beginning of a glorious new life'. He could not help reflecting that the prize had been so near and yet had been snatched from his grasp. And what a fuss there would be in England! 'If anything can kill old Gladstone this news ought to, for he cannot, self-illusionist though he is, disguise from himself the fact that he is directly responsible for the fall of Khartoum ... that it was owing to his influence, active measures for the relief of Gordon were not undertaken in time ... What an ending to all our labour, and all our bright hopes, is this!!' These bright hopes, however, were to be revived thirteen years later by an officer who fought under Wolseley during this last campaign of his in 1885. The officer's name was Herbert Kitchener. There was, of course, one other great man among the Victorian generals, whose name was closely associated with Kitchener's for their joint efforts in bringing the Boer War to a successful conclusion and who first captured the imagination of Britain and India alike by his classic march from Kabul to Kandahar to relieve the British garrison there in 1880 – Roberts, affectionately known to the British Army and the public alike as 'Bobs'. How different were these three men! Wolseley, as Adrian Preston put it a 'self-advertising hero and reformer' who was convinced 'that he was the greatest commander his country had produced since Wellington'; Roberts, genial, trim and precise, blessed by the ordinary soldier, and as Kipling had it, 'little but wise, a terror for his size, 'An' 'e does not advertise – Do yer, Bobs?'; Kitchener, cold, ambitious, thorough and remote, with occasional flashes of brilliant foresight. All three were in charge of the British Army at one time or another – Wolseley and Roberts both Commanders-in-Chief, Kitchener Secretary of State for War. When it came to the greatest test the Army ever had to face – the Great War of 1914 to 1918, all three had made or were making their contribution. Wolseley and Roberts both had their part in preparing the way for the British Expeditionary Force which first went to France; Roberts went so far as to campaign for compulsory military service; while Kitchener raised the huge armies which fought in France and Flanders, Gallipoli and Mesopotamia.

For this worst of all wars the British Army would resort to conscription for the first time in its history, but in the 1890s the Army was still small and composed entirely of volunteers. In *Pax Britannica*, James Morris explains that at the time of Queen Victoria's Diamond Jubilee of 1897, there were just more than 200,000 men in the Army, field guns numbered 718 and there were 26,000 horses. About half the Army was at home, a third in India and some 30,000 in the colonies. The infantry of the line had about one hundred battalions overseas, of which half were in India, no fewer than twenty-three in Ireland, a further twenty-seven spread out between Malta, Gibraltar, Egypt, Ceylon, Hong Kong, Singapore, South Africa, the West Indies, Bermuda and Canada. The cavalry were deployed in Egypt, India, South Africa and Ireland, apart from those in Britain. 'There were Royal Engineers all over the Empire, building everything from slaughter houses to cathedrals – in British Columbia they had laid out a mining town, New Westminster, complete with Victoria Gardens, Albert Crescent, and little squares named for royal princesses'. When we consider that the greatest Empire the world had ever seen, comprising a quarter of the globe's land, with Dominions, colonies or protectorates in every continent and every ocean, an Empire on which the sun really did never set, containing over 370 million people of different race, religion, customs, laws – when all this depended for its security on so absurdly small an Army, with a few regiments and battalions scattered here and there, we may also consider that the whole thing was a gigantic bluff. So it was to some extent. But of course there was also the Royal Navy. And there was also the Indian Army.

Like the British Army itself, the Indian Army was composed entirely of volunteers and there was never a shortage of them. Recruited from the martial peoples – Mahrattas and Sikhs, Dogras, Rajputs, Muslims and Gurkhas – to whom soldiering was an honourable profession, the Indian soldier fitted easily into the tight loyalties and proud traditions of the British regimental system. In his masterly *The Men Who Ruled India*, Philip Mason has reminded us of the remarkable trust and liking that was established between British officers and their Indian soldiers, bearing in mind the gulf existing between them in race and religion, personal habits and beliefs. This mutual confidence was such that it was enhanced by danger and hardship, but it depended essentially on the soldiers' being under command of the officers they knew. In emphasizing this last point, Philip Mason has a message not only for every officer who has ever commanded or will ever command troops, but for every manager in any business or other organization where leadership and direction are necessary:

> But forget that the army was a living organism, treat it as a dry skeleton, sit at a desk and look at returns of strength, tables of ranks, and rations, send away the officers he knew to other regiments – and the sepoy's confidence would wither. And once his affection was gone, once his confidence had withered, his fidelity to that far extravagance, that shadow of a name, that abstract nothing the Company, was liable to shatter to brittle fragments, at a whisper, at a hint from the bazaar of some imagined peril.

At the time of which we are speaking, of course, it was not to the East India Company, but to the Queen, Empress of India, to whom the Indian Army owed its loyalty. About the same size as the British Army itself, 200,000 or so, this meant that in times of peace, Queen Victoria had at her command some 400,000 soldiers, apart from huge reserves in India which could be called upon if necessary. Often the Indian Army's regiments were of mixed races. Jacob's Horse [later 14th Scinde Horse] had squadrons respectively of Sikhs, Baluchis and Pathans. Originally raised by Major Jacob himself, Philip Mason gives us the flavour of what an Indian cavalry regiment with first-class leadership was like:

> Every man was inspired by his commander's spirit. Instant readiness for action, unshakable tenacity in pursuit of law-breakers – these were the watchwords. Once, when information reached an outpost of the Sind Horse that raiders from the Baluch tribes had carried off some camels, Dunga Singh, the officer in charge of the outpost rode after them at a gallop with fifteen troopers. When at last he came up with them he had covered thirty miles and killed two horses; thirteen of his men had been left by the way with foundered beasts. He and two troopers and a Baluch guide faced an

enemy, perhaps forty strong, who had come to realise how few were their
pursuers. The guide begged him to go back, but Dunga Singh replied that
'he should be ashamed to show his face to Major Jacob if after coming in
sight of the robbers he should retire without killing some of them'.

He thereupon attacked the enemy who, being in overwhelming numbers,
cut him and his two troopers in pieces – but not before they had killed or
disabled fifteen tribesmen. The remnant of the raiding party tied round
Dunga Singh's wrist the scarlet thread, the highest honour the border
tribesmen can bestow on the valiant dead.

You could hardly beat spirit like that. It was the same as that displayed
by Burnaby and his English troopers. And there was plenty of need for
such spirit during Victoria's savage wars of peace. Who could forget the
devotion to duty and heroism of a company of the 24th Regiment at
Rorke's Drift, when a mere hundred British soldiers took on four
thousand Zulu warriors, repelling their repeated attacks and winning
eleven Victoria Crosses between them in a single day and night in
January, 1879? This was subaltern's war at its zenith. Who could forget
the triumphs of organization, leadership and sheer fighting quality that
enabled Wolseley to conquer at Tel-el-Kebir or Roberts at Kandahar?
These savage wars did not always end in success to British arms. Gordon
was not saved; two years before the Mahdi had annihilated an Egyptian
army commanded by Colonel Hicks; Lucknow had been a near-run
thing; the Crimea a sorry tale of mismanagement and muddle; although
Roberts had defeated the Afghans, in a previous war an entire British
army had been wiped out except for one solitary survivor. And worse
was to come in the Boer War at the end of the century, as if to remind
us of Majuba Hill, some twenty years earlier when the Boers attacked
General Colley's force of 400 men, killing 280 of them and causing the
rest to run away in disorder.

Amid all these triumphs and disasters there was no slackening of the
imperial urge. Where to fulfil this urge? – that was the question. India
no doubt had been won by the sword and would have to be kept by the
sword. It was more or less unassailable from the outside, although, as
we shall see, the Great Game went on. There were other parts of the
gorgeous East that Britain held in fee – Burma, Ceylon, Singapore,
Malaya, North Borneo, Fiji; Egypt might be nominally independent,
but in fact it was run by the British; innumerable islands in the Pacific
and the Caribbean flew the Union flag; Gibraltar, Malta and Cyprus
together with the Royal Navy guarded the Mediterranean; Aden coaled
British ships between Suez and Bombay; Australia, New Zealand and
Canada were loyal Dominions. Yet there was one continent where

Britain, despite its hold on parts of that continent's east, west, south and north-east, could indulge in a final effort of expansion, and she would not be without rivals or enemies. This last fling, this new and disillusioning phase of imperialism was known as the Scramble for Africa.

There are two parts of this undeveloped continent where we must follow the activities of the British Army. One is in South Africa where the names of Chamberlain, Rhodes, Jameson and Kruger will set the scene, and soldiers like Buller, Baden-Powell, Roberts, Kitchener, Smuts, Botha and De Wet will rule the military stage; the other which we will look at first, is the Sudan, where Gordon was to be avenged, the Mahdi's successor, Khalifa Abdullahi, to be subdued, and Kitchener to win a peerage by his victory at Omdurman and go on to humiliate the French at Fashoda. In both these theatres of war we shall see playing the sort of part that only 'the most bumptious subaltern in the British Army' could play, the historic figure who introduced this chapter for us – Winston Churchill.

3

THE OMDURMAN CAMPAIGN

The diplomatist said: 'It is to please the Triple Alliance'. The politician said: 'It is to triumph over the Radicals'. The polite person said: 'It is to restore the Khedive's rule in the Soudan'. But the man in the street said: 'It is to avenge General Gordon'.

Churchill

Herbert Kitchener, the most pushing, opinionated and unscrupulous soldier in the British Army until the advent of Henry Wilson in the First World War and Montgomery in the Second, became Sirdar of the Egyptian Army in 1892 and was able to set about preparing for what he had long desired – reconquest of the Sudan. By this time he had been serving in Egypt and the Sudan for some ten years, and had seen various ups and downs in the fortunes both of those countries and of the British Army in its campaigns there. He had first come to Egypt for Wolseley's lightning successes of 1882, in which Kitchener's fluency in Arabic was invaluable. He served again under Wolseley in the Gordon relief expedition and distinguished himself for his energetic courage in collecting intelligence at the front. Then in 1886 as Governor of Suakin he pursued an aggressive policy of harassing the tribes, culminating in a battle with the forces of Osman Digna, a Mahdist Emir, during which Kitchener received a severe wound in the jaw. When the Egyptian consul general, Evelyn Baring, laid down that the future policy in East Sudan would be to stay on the defensive and encourage trade, Kitchener gave up his appointment at Suakin and took up the job of Adjutant General to the Egyptian Army in Cairo, where he reinforced his reputation for intolerance, aloofness and ambition. He preferred expedience to regulations, resented having to explain his actions and avoided whenever he could committing anything to writing. He became known as He-who-must-be-obeyed, and there is an agreeable story that a set of

rules drawn up by some humorist among his subordinates was awarded
a mark of grim approval when it fell into Kitchener's hands. It read: 1.
Never write anything; 2. If you want anything done, catch the AG – he
is sure to be here tomorrow; 3. If you want leave, catch the Sirdar (at

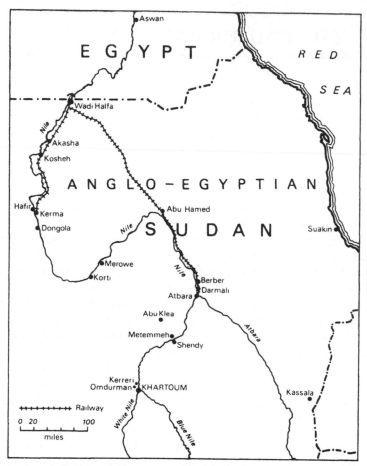

The Nile from Aswan to Khartoum

this time Sir Francis Grenfell); 4. If you get leave, go home at once and
take care never to come back.

In the summer of 1889 Mahdist forces under Wad-el-Nejumi* had
attempted to carry their *jihad* into Egypt, but had been defeated by

---

* The Mahdi himself died in 1885. His successor, the Khalifa, commanded the Dervish
Army at Omdurman. Although he escaped, he was captured and killed a year later.

Grenfell and Kitchener in a battle at Toski, near Wadi Halfa. The new Egyptian Army, trained by Kitchener, had shown its worth in the field. Later that year Baring asked Kitchener to take on the additional task of reorganizing the Egyptian Police with the post of Inspector General. Within a year his policy of reforming the *existing* system, and not trying to alter traditional principles of local government and society, had completely transformed the effectiveness and standing of the Police. It now only remained for Kitchener to step into the position he had so long wanted and expected. In April, 1892, Grenfell resigned and Kitchener took his place as Sirdar. Before long there was to be a government at home which shared his views as to what should be done in the Sudan.

In 1895 Salisbury formed his third administration. He, of course, would continue to be in charge of the Foreign Office, while the Colonial Secretary, an office of his own choosing, would be Joseph Chamberlain. Here was signalled an end to *laissez-faire* in colonial policy and a beginning of what he called investment of British money in estates belonging to the British Crown in order to develop them for the benefit both of the people living there and for those outside – in a word, Imperialism. As we have already noted there were not many areas in the world left for further expansion except Africa, and in pursuing his aggrandisement policies here Chamberlain came up against another European power bent on expansion in Africa – France. In 1890 Britain had signed three agreements, respectively with Germany, France and Portugal, concerning the partition of Africa, but France, particularly in West Africa, consistently ignored the agreement by occupying areas with troops even though those areas had already been conceded to Britain. Chamberlain countered these moves by organizing a West Africa Frontier Force with British officers and Hausa troops with Frederick Lugard in command of it all: Lugard who had fought with Roberts in Afghanistan and Wolseley in the Sudan, who now forestalled the French in lightning marches, and who in the end became what James Morris called 'a dedicated champion of imperial trusteeship' which enabled the indigenous peoples to develop according to their own ways while their territories were developed for wider benefit. It was not only in West Africa, however, that British and French interests clashed. It happened in East Africa too, and one of the most serious incidents arose as a result of Kitchener's reconquering the Sudan. Ironically enough his campaign began because another European power, Italy, appealed to the British government to assist them out of trouble they had fallen into after their army's defeat by the Abyssinians at Adowa, which was followed by a Dervish attack on the Italian position at Kassala.

Accordingly Kitchener's advance began with the initial idea of relieving pressure on the Italians by creating a diversion up the Nile. If ever Montgomery required a demonstration of the soundness of his subsequent cry: No advance without security – it was given to him now. For Kitchener's progress was slow, methodical, relentless, depending essentially on the construction of a railway behind him as he advanced, thus guaranteeing that the sinews of war would always be at his disposal. The whole thing took a long time. It was in March, 1896, that the campaign began. It was September, 1898, when Kitchener entered Khartoum, the Mahdist army shattered and the Khalifa a fugitive in his own land. The bulk of Kitchener's army of over 25,000 men were Egyptian and Sudanese, but there were no less than 8,000 British soldiers too – cavalry, Foot Guards, infantry of the line, artillery and engineers, plus of course a sizeable flotilla of gun-boats commanded by officers of the Royal Navy.

There were three phases to Kitchener's operation. The first was the advance to recapture Dongola province, and by September, 1896, six months after his army had begun its movement south from Wadi Halfa he was in possession of Dongola with only two relatively minor actions at Akasha and Firket to interfere with his progress. Kitchener then sat down for almost a year while his great project of building a railway from Wadi Halfa to the junction of the Nile and the Atbara south of Berber proceeded. The first part of this railway was laid across the desert between Wadi Halfa and Abu Hamed, about 200 miles, dramatically shortening the route via the huge Dongola loop by river. In August, 1897, Kitchener had captured Abu Hamed and the railway reached there by November. There would now be another long pause until the next Nile flood would allow the gunboats and the passage of troops and supplies by river to continue south towards Khartoum. The Khalifa decided to make a stand on the banks of the Atbara and by April, 1898, had established a strongly defended zariba there with some 16,000 men. A reconnaissance of this position carried out by Broadwood and the Egyptian cavalry nearly got into serious trouble because of an enveloping movement by mounted Dervishes, but were extricated by the initiative of a British cavalry officer, Captain Douglas Haig [who was further to distinguish himself in the Boer War and to command the British armies in France in the Great War]. The outcome was fortunate, for not only had Kitchener got the information he required, but the Egyptian cavalry had acquitted itself admirably. Kitchener was able to launch an attack on the zariba three days later. A British infantry brigade led the attack and the whole thing was over in less than an hour.

Private Corbett of the Seaforth Highlanders remembered that during the march southward the only water supplied for them to drink was carried on camels' backs in iron tanks and of course got very hot in the sun. When therefore they found a pool of water in which some local people were bathing, they rushed to refresh themselves with cool water. A warning from the doctor not to drink it as they would die of enteric fever had no effect. They drank it and survived. Corbett also recalled that at one stage in the advance he had been appointed to mount guard over the native women in order to keep intruders away. He was never sure what special qualifications he possessed which caused him to be selected for the job. At the Atbara battle on Good Friday, 8 April, 1898, his regiment together with the Warwicks, Lincolns and Cameron Highlanders were in the brigade commanded by Major-General Gatacre, known by the troops as 'Back-acher' because he loved indulging in forced marches. It was seven o'clock in the morning when they assaulted the zariba and succeeded in surprising the enemy at their breakfast:

> What a surprise it was – bayonets instead of hot cross buns. In less than no time they were rushing about, yelling, the native women screaming – what a pandemonium! There was much hand to hand fighting and bayonet work in this action, and the Dervish women being dressed so much like their men, they could not easily be distinguished, many of them raising their Jebbahs or smocks to prove they were women and so save their lives.

Corbett went on to say that the enemy commander, Nahmud, had dug a number of trenches in preparing the zariba, with its prickly bushes standing as high as a man to protect the defenders, and that he had chained his soldiers by the ankle to prevent their running away. Thus it was that the initial bombardment which had set fire to some of the zariba's bushes accounted for some of the poor defenders who were unable to escape.

By July, 1898, the railway had at last reached the Atbara and the Nile could be navigated to Khartoum. A second British brigade had arrived to reinforce Kitchener, together with a cavalry regiment, which for the last thirty-four years during service in India and Ireland had not seen a shot fired in anger and had thereby earned the motto: *Thou shalt not kill*. Among those who had joined this regiment, the 21st Lancers, largely because of the string-pulling at which he was so expert and much to the annoyance of the Sirdar, was a young lieutenant of the 4th Hussars – Winston Churchill. The third and final phase of Kitchener's campaign began in late August, 1898. At the end of that month Kitchener's advance guards were in sight of Omdurman, and Douglas Haig has a memorable description of what the Khalifa's army looked like as he observed it from the top of Kerreri ridge on the morning of 1 September:

> On reaching the hill a most wonderful sight presented itself to us. A huge force of men with flags, drums and bugles was being assembled to the west of the city; the troops formed on a front some three miles long, and as each body or 'roob'* was complete, it commenced to move northwards. With my glass I saw that they were moving very fast indeed. To my mind we were wasting time where we were.

Haig did not waste any more time but observed what he estimated to be some 30,000 of the enemy deploying across the plain beneath his position. Meanwhile Kitchener's main army had taken up a defensive semi-circular zariba on the west bank of the Nile at El Egeiga. He had some 25,000 men, of which 8,000 were British, no fewer than 7,000 animals, forty-four artillery pieces and twenty Maxim guns, while the gunboats mounted a further sixty guns including twenty-four Maxims. Opposing Kitchener's forces the Khalifa had perhaps 50,000 Dervishes, and their first attack on the zariba was at about 6 o'clock on the morning of 2 September.

Private Corbett tells us what it was like. He and his comrades of the Seaforth Highlanders could see great hordes of the enemy with their flags flying in the breeze. Their numbers seemed to extend as far as they could see. When about a mile distant they began their war chants and the noise seemed to fill the air around them. They kept on advancing and then when about a thousand yards away, Kitchener's artillery opened fire with great effect. On the Dervishes came, however, until they were within some 600 yards, using their rifles [the Mahdist army had many modern rifles captured from the Italians and also Remingtons], although happily for the British their marksmanship was poor. At this point the Maxim guns began their deadly work, firing 200 rounds per minute, and the British infantry were themselves at work, pouring volley after volley into the enemy masses. Corbett remembers what a spectacle it was, shells flying into the Dervishes and exploding with deadly effect on their horsemen and those on foot alike, riderless horses rushing desperately about, but they kept up the fight for some two and a half hours before this first assault had clearly been repulsed. It was then that Kitchener – who at this time was not aware that the Khalifa had huge undisclosed reserves which were shortly to subject his defenders to another furious attack – ordered the 21st Lancers to reconnoitre southwards towards Omdurman itself, as he wished to occupy the town before

* The Arabic for quarter is *rub*.

the Khalifa's forces could and so avoid the dangers and difficulties of street fighting, where his superior fire power would be least effective. So it was that the celebrated charge of the 21st Lancers, in which Winston Churchill participated, took place. The reconnaissance turned out to be a charge through a *khor*, or dry water course, in which several thousand of the Khalifa's men were concealed. In his account of the battle Churchill recalls that suddenly in front of them hundreds of men and some scores of horsemen appeared to rise up out of the ground to confront the galloping Lancers, whose reaction was merely to increase the pace and so, by sheer momentum, get through. As he and his troop closed with the enemy, they seemed to be about four deep:

> But they all fell knocked A.O.T. [arse over tip] and we passed through without any sort of shock. One man in my troop fell. He was cut to pieces. Five or six horses were wounded by back handers etc. But otherwise unscathed. Then we emerged into a region of scattered men and personal combats. The troop broke up and disappeared. I pulled into a trot and rode up to individuals firing my pistol in their faces and killing several – three for certain – two doubtful – one very doubtful. Then I looked round and saw the Dervish mass reforming ... I realized that this mass was about twenty yards away and I looked at them stupidly for what may have been two seconds. Then I saw two men get down on their knees and take aim with rifles – and for the first time the danger and peril came home to me. I turned and galloped. The squadron was reforming nearly 150 yards away. As I turned both shots were fired and at that close range I was grievously anxious. But I heard none of their bullets – which went Heaven knows where. So I pulled into a canter and rejoined my troop – having fired exactly ten shots and emptied my pistol – but without a hair of my horse or a stitch of my clothing being touched. Very few can say the same.

The whole affair had lasted perhaps two minutes and the 21st Lancers had achieved almost nothing except some death and a lot of glory. Some twenty of the enemy were killed. The regiment had lost seventy killed or wounded and more than a hundred horses. Worst of all, the one task they might have carried out of real value – discovering that the bulk of the Khalifa's huge reserve behind Signal Hill was about to emerge and fall on the rear of Kitchener's now advancing army – they totally failed in. But Colonel Macdonald's 1st Brigade of Egyptian and Sudanese Regiments behaved magnificently in repelling the Dervish hordes and when these latter, after suffering appalling losses, saw that Macdonald's brigade was being reinforced, they drew off. Kitchener had won. By a combination of patience, relentless organization, fire power, the steadiness of British and local troops alike, and a goodly portion of luck, he had destroyed the Mahdist army, killing at least 10,000 of them for the loss of only 28 British soldiers.

Private Corbett recorded that they marched into Omdurman at about 6.30 pm, and then had breakfast, dinner and tea all rolled into one. After that they enjoyed a rest. 'We had avenged General Gordon at last.' Two days later Kitchener entered Khartoum itself and at Gordon's residency, over which the British and Egyptian flags were hoisted, a requiem was held. James Morris's portrait of this scene is so brilliantly evocative that we may perhaps recall his reminding us of some of the celebrities who were there; Reginald Wingate, Kitchener's intelligence chief, John Maxwell of the Egyptian Army, Douglas Haig who was to lead the British Army to victory on the Western Front, the Prime Minister's son, Lord Edward Cecil, Lieutenant Staveley R.N., a name long to be famous in naval circles,* and 'at the head of his men, ramrod stiff, one hand on the hilt of his curved scimitar, one booted foot raised upon a convenient boulder, Kitchener himself stood impassive and immaculate ... As the solemn men's voices sang the old words of 'Abide with Me', Gordon's favourite hymn, to the uncertain harmonies of a Sudanese band, a tear was seen to roll down the Sirdar's brown and flinchless cheek ... The parade had to be dismissed by the Chief of Staff, so incapacitated was the victor by his emotions'. His total victory had not only avenged Gordon, however. It had gone far to satisfy Lord Salisbury's concern that in the interests of imperial defence, British control of the whole Nile valley was a necessary measure. Yet there was still a fly in the ointment, or perhaps rather a mosquito, in the form of Captain Jean-Baptiste Marchand of the French Marines who had arrived at Fashoda with a hundred or so Senegalese riflemen 'to establish French claims in the region of the Upper Nile'.

Compared with Omdurman the Fashoda incident was a mere trifle. Yet in dealing with it Kitchener showed an uncharacteristic touch of tact and understanding. He spoke French fluently, of course, and liked French things, so that sailing south with five gunboats [one commanded by Beatty, later to be in charge of the Royal Navy's Grand Fleet], a company of Cameron Highlanders and 2,500 Sudanese askari, he ensured that when they all came within sight of Fashoda he himself was wearing Egyptian uniform as Sirdar and his officers did the same. Kitchener made it plain to Marchand that although he had done a remarkable thing in getting to Fashoda at all, he would not enjoy the backing of the French government. In this Kitchener was right. France was far too concerned with other matters, notably the Dreyfus Affair,

* Admiral Sir William Staveley, his son, is First Sea Lord today (1988).

and the sheer military odds were so wholly in favour of the British. Yet the conditions imposed by Kitchener were generous – the British would establish their own garrison in the area, which was essentially the possession of Egypt's Khedive, but the French flag could continue to fly over Fashoda until the government in Paris decided what was to be done. By December, 1898, they had decided and the French garrison withdrew by way of Djibouti. Marchand got the Legion of Honour. Kitchener did better, was made a peer, given a grant of £30,000 and became Governor-General of the Anglo-Egyptian Sudan. Yet there had been moments when this bizarre affair looked like leading to war between France and England. It would have been a classic example of what Hamlet called finding quarrel in a straw when honour was at the stake. France's honour had already been called into question by the Dreyfus affair and was only to be redeemed by her performance in the Great War, and then at so great a cost that some twenty years later she forfeited this honour once more.

So Salisbury's policies and Kitchener's armies had triumphed in the Sudan and upper reaches of the Nile. It was to be a very different story when they turned their attention to South Africa. Before we look at the Boer War and the initially disastrous performance of the British Army in it, it is necessary to understand two things – first the preparations which had been made by President Kruger, second the absolute lack of preparations by the British. When Sir Alfred Milner arrived in South Africa as High Commissioner in the spring of 1897, he set about studying the whole situation, and what he saw of Kruger's virtual dictatorship of the Transvaal alarmed him. Not only had Kruger initiated a huge re-armament programme, with millions of pounds being spent on fortification, artillery, German advisers and secret service activities in neighbouring British Territories, but Milner was convinced that there was no way out of the political problems in South Africa if there were no reform in the Transvaal, except for war. This was the very last thing that Wolseley, Commander-in-Chief of the British Army since 1895, had in mind. When the royal commission which reviewed the South African war after its conclusion reported on it, one sentence alone was sufficient to condemn the military departments of the War Office for which Wolseley was responsible: 'No plan of campaign ever existed for operations in South Africa'. The mere success of relatively small scale operations against native forces in Africa or Asia had led to two fatal defects – no study of what might be necessary against a better armed, better organized, better led and possibly *European* enemy; and secondly no attempt at organizing the British Army into divsons and corps in *peace* time and then training them under their selected commanders for war, all of which was common practice in foreign armies. On top of all this the intelligence branch at the War Office, together with that of the military in South Africa, was so inadequate that the British, from the Commander-in-Chief in London down to local commanders in Natal and Cape Colony, had no idea of what the Boers' military resources and capabilities were. No wonder that in the early stages of the Boer War the British Army was bewitched, bothered and bewildered.

4

THE ARMY FALTERS

The General saw the mountain-range ahead,
With their 'elios showin' saucy on the 'eight,
So 'e 'eld us to the level ground instead,
An' telegraphed the Boojers wouldn't fight.
For 'e might 'ave gone an' sprayed 'em with a pompom,
Or 'e might 'ave slung a squadron out to see –
But 'e wasn't takin' chances in them 'igh an' 'ostile kranzes –
He was markin' time to earn a K.C.B.

Kipling

You would have thought that the fiasco of the Jameson Raid would have given people like Salisbury, Chamberlain, Rhodes and Wolseley enough food for thought that they would not once again have fallen into the fatal error of underestimating the Boers. The raid which began on 29 December, 1895, and reached its pitiful conclusion in total capitulation on 2 January, 1896, would never have taken place but for the imperial ambitions of Cecil Rhodes, Premier of the Cape, creator and master of Rhodesia, richest and most powerful man in Africa, who genuinely believed that the English should rule the earth. That the Transvaal should be a kind of independent republic outside the absolute dominion of the British Empire was intolerable to him, and because the Uitlanders of Johannesburg (who had done so much to develop the Rand's gold industry) were dissatisfied at having no voice in the conduct of Transvaal's affairs and had formed a Reform Movement, Rhodes and Jameson, Rhodesia's Administrator, had formed the plan of making an armed incursion from Bechuanaland to Johannesburg in order to rouse the Reformers, overthrow the legitimate government of the Transvaal and incorporate the State in British South Africa. There was, of course, no backing of so piratical and dishonourable a scheme from the British

Government, which was not even aware of it. The whole enterprise was an ignominious flop. Jameson had some five hundred British South Africa Company mounted police, some Maxim guns and a 12-pounder. Secrecy would be maintained by cutting all the telegraph wires; stores and fresh horses would be waiting for them en route; they would be met as they neared Johannesburg by horsemen supplied from the Reformers there. All this planning went wrong. The Boers learned about the raid at the outset as the telegraph wires had not all been cut and Jameson wired his intentions to Cape Town. Even information reaching Jameson that the British Government repudiated his action and ordered him to return, plus news that there had not been a successful rising by the Reformers, did not deter him. After advancing about 160 miles, the raiders, tired, dispirited, with worn-out horses and no food, found themselves facing the fresh and skilful Boer horsemen, who led Jameson's men into a trap at Doornkop. Surrounded, running out of ammunition, no hope of succour from any source, they surrendered to Commandant Cronje.* They had had forty men killed or wounded, and had achieved nothing except to debase the whole imperial purpose, awaken profound antagonism in the European powers, especially Germany, as the Kaiser's congratulatory telegram† to Kruger indicated, caused Jameson's arrest and Rhodes's resignation, and aroused in the Boers themselves both a unified purpose and a belief that the British Government had backed the raid, a belief which itself contributed to the eventual outbreak of war. Sir Robert Ensor goes further and points out that the British reaction to the Kruger telegram was so violent – it caused the Government to despatch a 'flying squadron' to sea, strong enough to destroy any other naval force in the world – that this in turn merely fed the fires of anti-British policy in Germany, thus facilitating the creation of a substantial German navy, which was itself one of the conditions leading to another war of far greater consequence to Britain and the whole world. Who would have thought that the crude aggression of the Jameson Raid could have had so powerful an effect on the fortunes of both the Empire and the British Army?

We must now turn our attention to the more immediate causes of the Boer War. Things once more reached a head as a result of the Uitlanders' grievances. Late in 1898 a British worker in Johannesburg was shot and killed by a Boer policeman. To the Uitlanders it seemed like murder.

---

* Whom we shall meet as a Boer general later.

† It read: I sincerely congratulate you that, without appealing for the help of friendly Powers, you with your people, by your own energy against the armed hordes which as disturbers of the peace broke into your country, have succeeded in re-establishing peace and maintaining the independence of your country against attacks from without.

The Boer jury and judge took another view. The policeman was not just acquitted. He was commended. British subjects on the Rand thereupon despatched a petition to Queen Victoria, which reached the Prime Minister, Salisbury, in March 1899. It was signed by nearly 22,000 Britons and was taken seriously by Chamberlain and the government. It led to a series of negotiations between Milner, the British High Commissioner in South Africa, and Kruger. First one side, then the

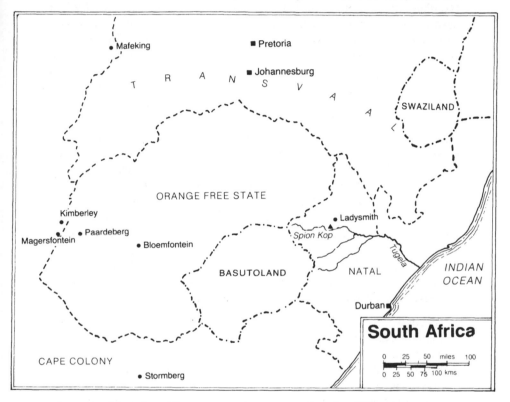

other, would make offers attempting to resolve the differences. At one point, in August, the Transvaal state attorney, Jan Christian Smuts [who was to figure so largely in Boer War itself, the Great War and the Second World War] made proposals which seemed to be acceptable to both sides. But Kruger, who seemed bent on conflict, scuppered them, as he later rejected Chamberlain's conciliatory counter-proposals in September. It seemed that only military measures remained, and in this respect the Boers were not only far better prepared. The whole of their strategy rested on undertaking offensive operations at the very time when the seasonal rainfall was to refresh and renew the grass of the veldt – that is the same time that Kruger was making sure negotiations would fail. He had some reason for confidence. In September, 1899, they had some 50,000 mounted infantry at hand, with ample arms and ammunition. The British had a mere 15,000 regular soldiers in South Africa, although a further 10,000 troops were on their way from India, reaching Durban early in October. Not only therefore had the Boers a two to one superiority in numbers. They were a nation of quick-thinking, fast-shooting horsemen, born to the country, the most formidable and natural guerrilla fighters, with a united sense of justice and brotherhood, that could be imagined. Moreover they were vastly better equipped with artillery. Against this the British had authorized the despatch of a field force from England – as late as 29 September – and had given command of it to General Sir Redvers Buller!* Even before he sailed the Boers had taken the game in their hands. Having issued an ultimatum on 9 October demanding that troops be withdrawn and no reinforcements sent with all the aggressive truculence of which Kruger was such a master, they followed its inevitable rejection with a pre-emptive invasion of British territory, crossing into Natal and Cape Province with the objective of seizing the railway centres of three towns, which were to feature in the British Army's history from that day until now – Ladysmith, Mafeking and Kimberley. Before we follow the fortunes and misfortunes of our soldiers there, however, we may perhaps remind those readers, who will never forget their own experiences aboard a troopship, that not much had changed since the end of the last century, when Private Moffett of the Scots Guards was one of many 'gentlemen in khaki ordered south' and recalled what it was like:

> Breakfast – About three-quarters of a pint of a curious infusion called by courtesy coffee; half a pound of dry bread, with now and again some half-dozen tablespoons of porridge.
> Dinner – Three-quarters of a pint of soup (I suspect this to be water masquerading as soup on the somewhat inadequate grounds that it has been used to boil meat, puddings, or to wash greasy dishes). The meat itself – well, we generally leave it untouched. (I never knew before where all that unwholesomely fat meat one sees at Christmas time goes. I think I know now. It is used to feed the fishes on the Cape route).
> Tea – This meal consists of a pint of 'tea' – a brew which has considerable

---

* Buller, one of Wolseley's 'Ring', had served with him in Canada, in the Ashanti and the Zulu Wars, where he won the Victoria Cross, and was with Wolseley again in the Gordon relief expedition. Renowned for his courage, but not for his tactical sense. A frontal attack against prepared enemy positions seemed to be the height of his military imagination.

claims to be called 'special'. It is certainly like nothing I have ever tasted before. This, with half a pound of dry bread, constitutes the last meal of the day.

Moffett went on to say that there was no 'wet' canteen, only one selling coffee. The day's duties were mess-work, swabbing the deck, guards, pickets, fatigues, together with kit inspections and physical training. There were inevitably the gambling schools – housey-housey and crown and anchor. A concert or sing-song at night, plenty of time to yourself by day for reading or gazing at the dolphins, whales and flying fish. The troop deck with hammocks slung so low was impossible to move about on except by crawling. Many slept on deck.

More serious business awaited them ashore. The Boer War lasted for two years and eight months, and may conveniently be divided into a number of phases. The *first*, from October 1899, to February, 1900, saw the Boer invasion of British territory, the investment of Ladysmith, Mafeking and Kimberley, Buller's blundering efforts to restore the situation (including 'Black Week' in December when Gatacre, whom we last met in the Sudan, was defeated at Stormberg, Methuen was trounced at Magersfontein by General Cronje, and Buller himself trying to relieve Ladysmith was driven back by Botha with severe losses), the arrival of Lord Roberts, with his chief of staff, Kitchener, to take command, further reverses for Buller notably at Spion Kop, and Roberts's victory over Cronje at Paardeberg, followed by the eventual relief of Ladysmith. The *second* phase was Roberts's invasion of the Transvaal and Orange Free State which led to the occupation of Pretoria and Johannesburg, capitulation of the Boer army at Prinsloo and President Kruger's flight from his homeland. By September, 1900, it seemed to Roberts that, with all the main Boer strongholds in British hands and his lines of communication secure, the war was over, and he therefore handed over to Kitchener and went home. But then began a *third phase*, which with various stages of its own lasted a further eighteen months or so – a campaign of guerrilla warfare by the Boers with their commandos. This was perhaps the most terrible part of the war, featuring Kitchener's remorseless policy of concentration camps, scorched earth, block houses linked by wire fences which compartmentalized the country and robbed the Boers of their two principal advantages – mobility and elusiveness. Worse still for the Boers, the concentration camps containing women and children were so ill managed that disease took charge, and between the beginning of 1901 and February, 1902, more than 20,000 – out of a total six times that number – died. In the end the British policy of organizing drives between lines of blockhouses put such military pressure on the Boers that they opted for peace, and on 31 May, 1902, at Vereeniging, terms for ending the war were agreed. These terms were notable for their generosity, and Kitchener who had shown himself so utterly efficient in the prosecution of the anti-guerrilla campaign deserves equal praise for his magnanimity in victory.

Yet this victory had required the British Army to deploy nearly half a million troops, including 250,000 regulars (the rest were made up of troops from the Empire, including India, and a huge number of volunteers, both from Great Britain and the Dominions) against a vastly inferior number of Dutch farmers and it had taken this same British Army, which had throughout Victoria's reign been enjoying an unbroken run of triumphant successes, nearly three years to do it. Something clearly was wrong, but before we see what it might have been, a visit to the actual battlefields of the Boer War will illustrate that whereas the British soldier still possessed those ever to be desired qualities of courage and fortitude, many of those generals in command were both ignorant and incompetent. Moreover, the whole military system – with no general staff, no proper intelligence organization, no sensible division between administration on the one hand and training for war on the other – was such that, had it not been for the reforms instituted by Haldane and others in the years before the Great War, the British Expeditionary Force would never have taken its place beside the French Army in 1914.

Unnecessary battles for unimportant objectives are no doubt a permanent feature in the history of war, and among them must rank high the battle of Spion Kop. After Roberts had taken command at the beginning of January, 1900, he had advised Buller, who had some 30,000 troops in Natal, to remain on the defensive. On Buller's insisting that a further attempt should be made to relieve Ladysmith, however, Roberts contented himself with further advice that the essential thing in taking on an enemy so skilled in the rapid strengthening of defensive positions was – speed of movement. For all the notice that Buller took of this advice, you might have thought that Roberts had instructed Buller to be as dilatory as possible. Having had some success in deceiving the Boers as to his approach route, Buller's army could have advanced to Ladysmith with very little opposition, but instead he concerned himself with his supply columns and handed over the direction of operations to a general even less competent than himself, Charles Warren. At the very time when Dundonald, in command of mounted troops, had succeeded in finding the Boer's right flank at their Tabanyama-Spion Kop position, and asked for reinforcements to exploit this success, Warren sat down to supervise his supply oxen crossing a river. In his report later, Buller conceded that Dundonald's action should have been instantly supported with artillery and infantry, an action which would have turned the whole Boer defences, yet he did nothing to urge Warren forward, nor did he take control himself. Such dithering could only end in failure. Worse was to come at Spion Kop itself, but as usual the ordinary British soldier was able to see what was lacking in delay at Tabanyama and summed it up in the way that only Thomas Atkins could:

'What are we waiting 'ere for? Why don't we go on?'
'Don't yer know?'
'No.'
'To give the Boers time to build up their trenches and fetch up their guns. Fair – ain't it?'

As if this were not enough, Warren then proposed to sit down and do nothing for two or three more days. Buller, impatient though he was, made the unforgivable error of continuing to vacillate. He suggested what Warren ought to do, but did not insist on it. Nor when he saw that Warren was going his own way, did he assume the command himself. When at length an assault on Spion Kop was made – itself a pointless operation, for although Buller and Warren judged it to be the key to relieving Ladysmith, some ten miles further north, it could easily have been outflanked – far too few troops were employed and then they failed to capture the two knolls which overlooked the objective which they had taken. One of Buller's staff, attached to Warren, Lieutenant-Colonel Charles à Court, wrote of it afterwards: 'Some 1,700 men were to assault a hill in the centre of the Boer position, and the rest of Buller's 20,000 men were to look on and do nothing.' Although the assaulting troops under Colonel Thorneycroft reached what they thought was the summit by night attack, in the morning, 24 January, they were subjected to continuous and accurate fire from the Boer artillery and riflemen. It lasted the whole day. 'Pinned to their ground,' wrote James Morris, 'exhausted by desperate attacks and counter-attacks, the British on Spion Kop simply sweated and died through the long day, holding an objective that had no meaning.' So little meaning indeed that when night fell and the Boer shooting ended, Colonel Thorneycroft on his own initiative led his surviving soldiers, including long lines of wounded, back down from that fatal summit and ended the engagement. It had all been for nothing. The battle of Spion Kop had been won by the Boers. If clarity in choosing an objective, precision in giving orders, concentration of force and speed of action in executing those orders can be regarded as sound principles in managing military operations, it was obvious that as far as generals like Buller and Warren went, these principles were more honoured in the breach than the observance.

Roberts, as might have been expected, was doing better. Concentrating his forces, grouping all his cavalry under French (whose success in the Boer War led British politicians to suppose he could command the British Expeditionary Force in France at the beginning of the Great War with equal success – greatly to their disillusion), choosing a clear objective, Bloemfontein, in the centre of the Orange Free State, deceiving the Boers as to his intention, sticking to his course of action even though short of supplies because De Wet captured his supply waggons, he both relieved Kimberley and brought Cronje to battle at Paardeberg. Cronje was forced to surrender with 4,000 men on 27 February, 1900. Next day Ladysmith was finally relieved by Buller – at his *fifth* attempt. One of the soldiers who remembered the march to Bloemfontein and the fighting for it was our old friend, Private Corbett of the Seaforth Highlanders:

> We had won Bloemfontein with men on half rations or quarter rations and whole-day marches, 220 miles in a month. In our long marches we existed on bully beef and hard biscuits, with very little water. We once halted for a rest near an abandoned Boer farm and discovered potatoes and pumpkins etc, while a few comrades captured a goat which was unceremoniously killed, cut into chunks, including skin, which we put into our canteen or mess-tins with our share of vegetables, and cooked over a slow fire ... The bugle just then sounded 'fall in', which was most annoying, for my South African 'Irish' stew was just coming on to boil,* so I had to carry it in one hand with my rifle shouldered with the other, until we came to the next halt about two hours later. It was still warm and I don't think I ever enjoyed a meal better.

Corbett wrote that a combination of forced marches on half or quarter rations and heavy going which slowed down the gun carriages made it seem a wonder that their advance was so successful. They never seemed to get to grips with the Boers for hand-to-hand fighting. Their own artillery would shell the Boer positions on hill-tops, they would advance towards the enemy under cover of this artillery fire, then flatten out on the ground to present minimum targets to the hundreds of Boer riflemen silhouetted on the skyline. Finally when near enough and after a further artillery bombardment they would assault the hill with fixed bayonets. But the Boers had no taste for cold steel and were miles away on their horses which had been tethered on the reverse slopes, leaving only thousands of empty cartridge cases. And so to further marches, drinking water often being in short supply, for the Boers poisoned the wells and

---

* Many were the moments in the Second World War when just as a brew-up was ready, orders to move would come over the radio. Many times too these orders were ignored.

streams with dead animals. A small stone in the mouth would help to keep it moist.

The war in South Africa, like all other wars in which the British Army had taken part, produced its own contribution to the English dictionary. To *maffick* was to exult riotously, because of the extravagant celebrations in London on the relief of Mafeking in May, 1900, after a siege of 217 days. In Mafeking itself joy was more restrained, and for the besieged the principal feature of it all was the jauntiness and style with which Baden-Powell (famed also for establishing and leading the Boy Scout movement) conducted its defence. By exaggerating the dangers and reiterating their defiant confidence in his despatches, he captured the imagination of the world, keeping, as James Morris put it, 'the legend of Empire alive' and with such colourful characters as Lord Edward Cecil, who had been with Kitchener in the Sudan, and Winston Churchill's aunt, Lady Sarah Wilson, who would telegraph home details of her menu – minced mule and curried locusts – with assurances that all was well, the whole affair seemed to confirm that 'British imperialism still had *class*'.

Winston Churchill himself, never one to miss an opportunity for campaigning, was there of course – first as war correspondent for the *Morning Post*, then as a prisoner of war, next, after making his escape, a popular hero, finally as a soldier once more, this time as a lieutenant in the South African Light Horse. As might have been expected he was in the thick of things, and remembered what it had been like to be with Colonel Thorneycroft in the shambles of Spion Kop. Having reconnoitred the position he reported to General Warren's headquarters where he was asked to take a message to Thorneycroft to the effect that fresh troops would be coming and that they would dig in all night to hold the plateau next day. Churchill climbed the mountain, picked his way through dead and wounded, with occasional bullets flying past, found Thorneycroft and handed him his new orders. But Thorneycroft had already decided to retire from Spion Kop, had issued orders to proceed and would not be moved from his decision by anything Churchill said, or indeed when later after reaching the foot of the mountain, they encountered the reinforcing sappers and infantry. He simply ordered the relieving troops to countermarch. Churchill gave it as his opinion that Thorneycroft was wrong to abandon the position that he and his troops had so gallantly held. There was no doubting Thorneycroft's exceptional personal courage. The real mistake lay with Warren and his staff for leaving him so long without orders or assistance. 'A young active divisional general, having made all plans for the relief, would have joined him on the summit at nightfall and settled everything in person.'

Alas, there were to be many further instances in the terrible Great War still to come of generals commanding their troops from the comfort of chateaux far in the rear with no very clear idea of the conditions under which their soldiers were fighting. It is clear, of course, that the retention of Spion Kop would not by itself have ensured the relief of Ladysmith. Nevertheless when the beleaguered town was finally relieved at the end of February, 1900, Winston Churchill with the South African Light Horse was there:

> The next morning, advancing in leisurely fashion, we crossed the river, wended up and across the battle-scarred heights, and debouched upon the open plain which led to Ladysmith six miles away. The Boers were in full retreat; the shears were up over their big gun on Bulwana Hill, and the dust of the wagon-trains trekking northward rose from many quarters of the horizon.

Churchill and his fellow cavalrymen were longing to pursue the enemy and harass them further, but Buller had thought it better to leave them alone now they were going away. No grand Napoleonic idea of pursuing and utterly destroying a defeated enemy appealed to him. Churchill further recalled:

> All day we chafed and fumed, and it was not until evening that two squadrons of the S.A.L.H. were allowed to brush through the crumbling rearguards and ride into Ladysmith. I rode with these two squadrons, and galloped across the scrub-dotted plain, fired at only by a couple of Boer guns. Suddenly from the brushwood up rose gaunt figures waving hands of welcome. On we pressed, and at the head of a battered street of tin-roofed houses met Sir George White on horseback, faultlessly attired. Then we rode together into the long-beleaguered, almost starved-out, Ladysmith. It was a thrilling moment.

After further adventures during Roberts's advance to and capture of Johannesburg and Pretoria, Churchill went home and at the so-called 'Khaki' election – arranged by Chamberlain to exploit the government's popularity in the light of Roberts's victories – was elected to represent Oldham in the House of Commons as a Conservative. His life as a politician was to be even more spectacular than as a soldier, although as we shall see, he had not done with soldiering yet.

The Boer War was not yet over. As we have seen after Roberts's capture of the principal towns of the Orange Free State and the Transvaal, the Boers resorted to guerrilla warfare. They had already demonstrated the supremacy of the mounted rifleman for tactics on the veldt. They were to continue to do so, and when Kitchener assumed the overall command from Roberts* in October, 1900 – at a time when the war had still more than eighteen months to go – he found himself so short of cavalry that a further 30,000 had to be despatched to him. When we consider that more than half-a-million horses were employed by the British throughout the course of the war, it is at once clear how important the mounted arm was. When we further note that the British succeeded in destroying 350,000 of them, we may conclude that horse-management within the British Army had a long way to go. But there were further implications in this emphasis that had to be placed on use of cavalry. Simply because so many of the officers who served under Roberts and Kitchener and who distinguished themselves were cavalrymen – French, Allenby and Haig among them – they came to fill the highest positions at the outset of and during the first European war that the British had fought since the Crimea, at a time moreover when a furious controversy as to the usefulness of horses in war was itself at its height. In short the immense value of the mounted rifleman on the veldt blinded those who put their faith in the 'shock' action of cavalry to the growing predominance of long-range fire power, even though much of this fire power could be in the hands of the mounted soldiers. Roberts saw it all clearly enough in commenting on French's cavalry action at Klip Drift during his operations to relieve Kimberley:

> French's admirable movement at Klip Drift was essentially a rapid advance of fighting men carried out at extended intervals. It was a rapid advance of warriors who possessed the ability, by means of horses and rifles (not swords or lances) to place their enemy *hors de combat*. It was an ideal Cavalry operation but it was not a 'Cavalry Charge', as this term is generally understood, and the arme blanche had nothing to say to it.

Yet in 1903 after the war was over, Haig, who had been in the thick of things at Klip Drift was writing that the cavalry should be armed with both sword and lance, while French, in a paper written a year later, emphasized the overriding importance of the 'cavalry spirit', which he defined as élan and dash, and a determination to take offensive action and seize the initiative. He went on to say that *if* cavalry soldiers were to regard the rifle as their principal weapon and that if shock tactics were only to be employed exceptionally, 'we shall soon find that we have no cavalry in the British army worthy of the name'. He totally failed to see that it was *not* the weapon which created and preserved the cavalry spirit. It was the man. Yet only a few years earlier both he and Haig had seen for themselves what the fire power of rifles in the hands of skilful horsemen could do to dominate a battlefield. And these were the

* Roberts succeeded Wolseley as Commander-in-Chief later that year.

two men who within ten years or so, were to command the British Army
in the most desperate struggle it had yet encountered.

It was not only the regular cavalry that took part in the Boer War.
Innumerable regiments of Imperial Yeomanry were raised – among
them some extraordinarily striking characters. Paget's Horse – nick-
named either the Piccadilly Heroes or Perfectly Harmless according to
taste – led by Major Paget, grandson of Wellington's cavalry commander,
Lord Anglesey – was one of the finest of these regiments. Its commander,
totally indifferent to enemy bullets or appalling weather, indefatigable
on the march, indifferent to wounds, was an inspiration to his troopers.
Rimington's Guides, known also as 'Tigers' from the leopard-skin
scarves wound round their slouch hats, was another remarkable outfit,
recruited largely from Uitlanders who spoke Dutch and the native
languages, invaluable when attached to columns who needed interpreters
and guides. Self-reliance, tactical skill, scorn for the orthodox – these
were their watchwords. And then there was Strathcona's Horse, raised
and paid for by Lord Strathcona (the Regiment is still part of the
Canadian Army), commanded by Colonel Steele of the Mounties and
consisting of 'Canadian-born men and young men from home of the
adventurous type, all mixed up together and held together in a discipline
of iron by Colonel Steele'. The Duke of Wellington had always maintained that the secret of good cavalry was iron discipline. It was a quality
not always recognized or observed by the British cavalry. Another
branch of the Army in South Africa perhaps not noted for this quality
was the Mounted Infantry of the Line, immortalized by Kipling in his
poem *M.I.*:

> That is what we are known as – we are the push you require
> For outposts all night under freezin', and rearguard all day under fire.
> Anything 'ot or unwholesome? Anything dusty or dry?
> Borrow a bunch of Ikonas! Trot out the old M.I.

Kipling, who was there in South Africa working on an army newspaper,
got the feel of it down on paper better than anyone. In his unforgettable
plea for the gentleman in khaki ordered south, the absent-minded
beggar, who was on active service, wiping something off a slate, he began
by inviting you to drop a shilling in the tambourine after you had
shouted 'Rule Britannia' and sung 'God save the Queen'. But Queen
Victoria died on 22 January, 1901. She had always maintained that the
possibilities of defeat did not exist, and by the time she died, this was
clearly true. Yet Kitchener still had a lot of clearing up to do. This was
the least rewarding and most frustrating part of the campaign. The
Boers were expert at guerrilla warfare; the British were slow at finding

answers. It was a pattern to be repeated frequently in the future, especially during the gradual withdrawal from Empire after the Second World War, when with an army still largely composed of national servicemen, Britain conducted its counter-insurgency operations in Malaya, Southern Arabia, Cyprus and Kenya. In 1901 too it was a slow grind, and as Lord Anglesey points out in his masterly history of the British Cavalry, the quality of our troops had fallen after the release of many experienced regiments of the Imperial Yeomanry, while that of the burgher guerrillas was higher than ever. It was at this time also that column commanders tended towards care and caution, in order, as Kipling so sharply put it in the lines which head this chapter, not to jeopardize their K.C.B. No wonder Kitchener resorted to the new tactic of adding to his existing policy of numerous drives between the lines of blockhouses by despatching single columns under vigorous and bold commanders to seek out and bring to book some of De Wet's roving commandos. One such successful encounter was enjoyed by a sixty-three-year-old Canadian, veteran of the Indian Mutiny, when as an acting Brigadier-General and in command of two Imperial Light Horse Regiments and the 11th Imperial Yeomanry, he worsted De Wet himself. Anglesey tells us how the Commanding Officer of the 2nd Imperial Light Horse dealt with the sudden appearance of De Wet's men who had been waiting in ambush:

> He suddenly saw the enemy riding out of the Tiger Kloof Spruit, where they had been concealed (in long grass). They formed up in line like a British regiment and charged over the flat ground. I galloped through a long hollow in front of us, dismounted my men and lined the crest of the ridge, at the same time shouting: 'Now, 2nd I.L.H., you have the chance of your lives!' We opened fire at the approaching enemy and soon checked them. (The closest they got was 150 yards). A few took refuge in a little stone kraal on our left front, and others swerved to our right and worked round our flank. I noticed a high ridge on my left front which commanded my position and quickly sent Captain Jack Duff with his squadron to occupy it. Only just in time, for he sent a message back saying that about 500 Boers (an exaggeration) were riding up to occupy the position, but on seeing him and his men and no doubt concluding that the position was strongly held, returned to the valley.

Here, if ever it were wanted, was further evidence of the superiority of fire power over so-called 'shock action'. De Wet admitted afterwards that everything went wrong.

But such fleeting successes could not win the war. It required Kitchener's grim and inexorable policy of using the blockhouse lines as axes of advance and communication and so stepping up the scale of his 'drives' that the Boer guerrillas could not elude them. This was not always to the Boers' discomforture, however, for as late as March, 1902, General De La Rey overcame a mixed force under command of Lord Methuen with such intrepid tactics – his men charging and firing from the saddle – that Methuen himself was wounded and taken prisoner, losing 200 men killed and wounded and 600 taken. It could not last, of course, and shortly afterwards Kitchener's drives had taken their toll and the Boers sued for peace, but before we see how it ended, let us visit in the company of Private Moffett, Scots Guards, whom we last met on board the troop-ship, one of the blockhouses which were such a cardinal feature of Kitchener's strategy. They proved just the thing, he tells us, to counter the enemy's guerrilla tactics, cutting off their food supply from Basutoland and barring them from escape to the mountains:

> Each blockhouse is enclosed with barbed wire sloping down inwards and outwards from iron standards. This effectually prevents the citadel from being rushed by a superior force of the enemy. In the centre of the wire entanglements is the citadel ... The trench surrounding the citadel may be safely used by troops who stand and fire from this position. Usually about six men and a non-commissioned officer are left in charge of a blockhouse.

Each blockhouse had a water tank with up to 100 gallons, sufficient victuals for two weeks, with reserves of food and ammunition, and the whole line of blockhouses could communicate with one another by telephone or telegraph. If in real trouble, rockets were fired to attract the attention of troops nearby. Along the line appeared larger scale forts, strong enough to withstand artillery fire and more largely garrisoned. Throughout the process of building and manning these blockhouses, horses, cattle and forage from neighbouring farms were removed. It was all a kind of scorched earth policy, unromantic, inexorable and bitter, but it worked. And for Kitchener and the British Government, the overriding necessity was to bring the war to an end.

The Peace of Vereeniging, signed on 31 May, 1902, did precisely this. The burghers were required to surrender with their arms and ammunition; all those prepared to be Edward VII's loyal subjects were repatriated; the official language would be English, although Dutch could still be taught; licensed sporting guns were permitted; self-government to be the aim; no tax towards war costs; and grants for putting farms back in order. All in all it was generous, but the bitterness it left was never to die, and as James Morris pointed out, 'the Boers were to win the Boer War in the end'.

Even though the British had eventually triumphed in 1902, it had

taken the entire resources of their Army to do it. If this was the best
the British Army could do in nearly three years of fighting against a
greatly inferior number of Dutch burghers, it did not augur well for any
future conflict which might arise in Europe. Indeed this weakness did
not go unnoticed in Europe itself, whose powers numbered their armies
in millions. Yet the Army itself took the whole thing in its stride. We are
again indebted to the incomparable pen of James Morris for reminding us
of the comment made by a British officer after one of the many bloody
engagements on the Tugela River before Ladysmith was finally relieved.
There had been a local cease fire while dead and wounded on both sides
were recovered. A Boer soldier had remarked what a rough time they
had all been having. The British officer's reply characterized what has
always been best in our Army's acceptance of hardship – and more –
his absolute commitment to it. While acknowledging that it had been
rough, he added: 'But for us of course it's nothing. This is what we're
paid for. This is the life we always lead – you understand?' Happily for
some of his successors, reforms were on the way. They were going to
be needed.

The war's end saw other changes. Wolseley had already been succeeded by Roberts; Rhodes was dead; Edward VII was on the throne
and before long was to do much to help end Britain's isolation in Europe;
Salisbury had relinquished the Premiership to Balfour, who rapidly
converted the Committee of Imperial Defence from just a name to an
instrument of government, and whose first two Secretaries for War, St
John Brodrick and Arnold-Foster respectively did great things in theory
and in practice. The first produced an idea for six army corps, but it
remained an idea. The second appointed three men – Lord Esher,
Admiral Fisher and Colonel Clarke – to advise how the Army machine
should be reorganized, and the resultant Esher Report whose recommendations were accepted by the government was of profound
importance. At last the General Staff system was to be put into effect;
administration would be handled by districts throughout the country
and would be quite separate from training and preparation for war. The
Field Force would be able to get on with its proper business of training.
It would be for a Liberal Secretary for War in Campbell-Bannerman's
administration – Haldane – to put these essential measures and many
others into effect before the disasters of 1914 overcame Europe like a
summer's cloud, and we shall look at these shortly. First we will turn
away from South Africa, where it had been shown that the Imperial
theme was beginning to go wrong and look eastwards where the Great
Game was still being played and still was enjoying some spectacular
though sometimes fruitless successes.

5

PLAYING THE GREAT GAME

When you're wounded and left on Afghanistan's plains,
And the women come out to cut up what remains,
Jest roll to your rifle and blow out your brains
An' go to your Gawd like a soldier.

Kipling

Disraeli's ideal of an exotic, visionary, benevolent and faintly mystical
Imperialism might have gone. Chamberlain's new Imperialism, brash,
pushing, business-like and rather vulgar, might have faltered. Yet there
were still plenty of influential Britons about who had great faith in the
idea and reality of the British Empire and the Army's [to say nothing
of the Royal Navy's] role in sustaining it. Among them were Cromer,
Milner, Kitchener, Curzon* and, of course, that hero of many imperial
engagements, who was about to make his mark in politics too, who built
his life, as Sir Isaiah Berlin wrote, 'on the supreme value of action', who
is the dominant character in this book and a thousand others – Winston
Churchill. In between his military adventures in the Sudan and South
Africa and even before becoming a Member of Parliament, he had made
a remarkable speech at the Southsea Conservative Association in October
1898:

> To keep the Empire you must have the Imperial spark. Where is the glory
> of an armed sluggard living on the terror he has excited in the past? That is
> the debauched Imperialism of ancient Rome. Where is the glory of the

* Lord Cromer, formerly Evelyn Baring, was British consul-general and virtual ruler
of Egypt 1883–1907; Milner was governor Cape Colony 1897–1901, governor Transvaal
and Orange River Colony 1902–06, war cabinet 1916–19, colonial secretary 1919–21;
Kitchener we have seen in Sudan and South Africa, and will see again as C.-in-C.
India 1902–09, British representative Egypt 1911–14, War Minister 1914–16; Curzon
was Viceroy of India 1898–1905, war cabinet 1916–18, foreign secretary 1919–24.

starving peasant arrayed in purple and in cloth of gold? That is the Imperialism of modern Russia. . . .

To keep our Empire we must have a free people, an educated and well fed people. . . . We would have an Empire and make all share the glory. '*Imperium et Libertas*' is the motto of the Primrose League, and it may also be the motto of Progressive Toryism. You have two duties to perform – the support of the Empire abroad and the support of liberty at home. . . . We want young men who do not mind danger, and we want older and perhaps wiser men who do not fear responsibility. . . . So the great game goes on, and, gentlemen, it is for you to say that it shall go on – that it shall not be interrupted until we are come through all the peril and trial, and rule in majesty and tranquillity by merit as well as by strength over the fairest and happiest regions of the world in which we live.

Churchill in his own person combined the young man who did not mind danger and the older man who did not fear responsibility as perhaps no one before or since has done. It was in his former capacity that he was able to reply to an attack on the British Army for their 'massacring Dervishes at Omdurman' by the editor of a pacifist magazine, *Concord*, making the point that had this editor been there, like himself, he would not have protested at the soldiers' opening fire on 40,000 savages hostilely advancing. It was thus both unfair and unreasonable to disparage the soldiers for simply defending themselves with skill and success. But Churchill did later concede that the killing of wounded [even though at Omdurman many Dervishes feigned wounds in order to attack British soldiers as they advanced past them] had disgraced Kitchener's conduct of the campaign. Little more than two years after making this speech, and with the further excitements of the Boer War behind him, Churchill entered Parliament in the Conservative interest. His speeches in the House of Commons, however, proclaimed him more a Liberal, and he broke with his party on the issue of Protectionism or Free Trade. An ardent Free Trader, like his father, Churchill crossed the floor of the house in May, 1904, and when Campbell-Bannerman formed the new Liberal Government in 1905, Churchill became Parliamentary Under-Secretary for the Colonies. There we will leave him for the moment and look at what another imperialist, and indeed a most superior one at that, was up to – George Nathaniel Curzon, Viceroy of India.

In an article published as recently as 1988 Simon Jenkins recalled the mirth and mockery with which he and his fellow students would regard Curzon's declaration that 'under Providence' the British Empire was the greatest instrument for good the world had ever seen, that there had never been anything so great in the world's history. Yet in this same article Jenkins concludes that all in all the imperial chapter was a creditable one in British history, making great demands on Britain's resources, military, financial and human, and he quotes Marjorie Perham's judgment that Britain was of all modern colonial nations 'the most humane and considerate and did most to prepare her subjects for self-government'. There is an echo of Curzon here, for although he relished the sheer autocratic grandeur of his office, turned his formidable intellect to all aspects of Indian affairs, and seemed to see India as having a kind of suzerainty over its lesser neighbours, yet in the early 1900s he too had observed what he called 'the growing temper of the native' who was 'awaking to a new consciousness of equality and freedom'. No doubt Curzon had been irritated by the ponderousness, pomposity, aloofness and arrogance of Indian Civil Service officials and Army officers alike. Yet he saw that these attitudes must be restrained if rebellious violence were to be prevented. James Morris called him the most Indian of Viceroys, viz. his championing of the Indian – what Lieutenant-Colonel George Younghusband* called an 'attack of poor black man ... protecting the poor Indian from the assaults of the brutal British soldiery'. Unfortunately there were too many instances of just such assaults for it to be brushed aside. Curzon was not willing to condone such behaviour or be party to the idea that 'a white man may kick or batter a black man to death with impunity because he is only a "damned nigger"'. He therefore made sure that both regiments and individuals were properly punished and moreover that such punishments received the sort of publicity which might deter further crime. Thus the West Kent Regiment, some of whose soldiers had been guilty of rape in Burma, was despatched to the less than agreeable station of Aden. A private soldier of the Royal Scots Fusiliers, guilty of murder, was severely dealt with. Curzon's point was that even a few crimes of this sort committed by British soldiers could affect the whole British position in India. The soldier was there to protect the natives, not bully them. If the British could not command themselves, they would lose their control of India itself.

The most celebrated case of all was that concerning the 9th Lancers, two of whose troopers after heavy drinking had so badly beaten a cook called Atu, because he was unwilling to produce a native woman for them, that he later died. The so-called Court of Enquiry was a classic hush-up and refusal to take or consider any real evidence. Shortly

---

* Commanding Guides Cavalry, and not to be confused with Lt.-Col. Francis Younghusband, King's Dragoon Guards, who led the British expedition to Tibet.

afterwards another soldier of the 9th Lancers murdered a punkah-wallah and again local enquiry failed to satisfy Curzon. The egregious folly of General Sir Bindon Blood, who commanded in the Punjab, when he made his comments on the report, comments full of contradictions and absurdities, roused Curzon's ire still more. His 'castigation of Blood', wrote Lord Anglesey, 'running to many pages in his own hand, must surely be unprecedented in the annals of civil/military relations'. The result of it all was that the Commander-in-Chief [at this time Sir Arthur Power Palmer, shortly to be succeeded by Kitchener] recommended that the regiment as a whole should be punished. All those on leave, officers and men, were to be recalled, there would be no further leave for six months, and the 9th Lancers would be excluded from the Coronation Durbar. This last punishment was not exacted, and on the day of the Durbar, some six months later, when the regiment escorted the Duke of Connaught, those in disagreement with Curzon's stand for the rights of the natives made their feelings plain by their demonstrative cheer for the 9th Lancers as they rode by. Curzon subsequently recorded that, conscious as he was of the implications of this demonstration, he was conscious too of pride in having dared to do the right thing. By this time Kitchener had become Commander-in-Chief, India, and although he supported Curzon in this particular matter, he was soon to mount a campaign *against* Curzon in order to secure total control over all military affairs in India, a campaign which ended in Kitchener's triumph and Curzon's resignation.

Before he went, however, Curzon played one more hand in the Great Game, employing men of both the British and Indian armies and achieving at once both a military victory and a further depredation of the Imperial purpose. The Great Game [so memorably portrayed by Kipling in *Kim*] had been principally played in Afghanistan, which divided the British and Russian Empires, and out of which – a cardinal principle of London's foreign policy – Russia must be kept. After all had not Tsar Nicholas II at the time of the Boer War once boasted that he needed only to order his Turkestan army to mobilize and march to India's frontier to transform the course of affairs in South Africa? It was for control of the North-West Frontier that innumerable little wars were fought both by the Indian Army and the British Army in India. No one has written better of them than Philip Mason to whom we must turn for an understanding of why it was described as a game:

Terrible country, harsh, fierce, and jagged; rocky peak, serrated ridge, dry icy upland, stony breathless valley that pens up the heat; a marksman behind every rock; a war of sniping and ambush and long marches at night, occasionally the rush of yelling fanatics sworn to die for the faith of Mohammed ... the extraordinary part about these wars is the spirit in which they are fought; death is real enough, exhaustion, hunger, thirst and above all courage, but across this harsh and bitter landscape will flash suddenly a jagged lightning-streak of humour. It is a game – a contest with rules in which men kill without compunction and will die in order to win, in which kinship and friendship count less than winning – but, in which there is no malice when the whistle blows and the game is over.

It is this that explains why George Roos-Keppel after a successful campaign against the Zakka Khel tribesmen, whose agent he had been, replied, on being asked by them whether they had fought well, that, had they not done so, he would not have shaken hands with them. It explains too why an outlaw called Dilawar Khan, having been persuaded by Colonel Lumsden to join the Guides, stayed on with the regiment, despite a half-admitted intention of learning what he could and then deserting to resume his former life. Something had captured his spirit. It explains why Winston Churchill had used every ounce of 'pull' to get himself attached to Bindon Blood for the Malakand expedition and revelled in his first taste of action, regarding as he did military service as an indispensable qualification for a political careerist. The game amused him, he wrote to his mother, dangerous though it was. It was a strange life, lying in a hole as cover against night firing, with a frightful headache and the sun getting ever hotter. 'But, after all, food and a philosophic temperament are man's only necessities'. Churchill was 22 years old when he wrote this.

Nothing much happened in India between the turn of the century and the Great War, although some 30,000 British troops went from India to fight in the Boer War, and some 1,300 to help suppress the Boxer Rebellion in China.

But at the end of 1903 Curzon extended the playing fields of the Great Game to the north. Russia's own conduct of the game with her seemingly endless expansion to the east and south, the instantly conjured – up threat to India's approaches, had aroused Curzon's profound suspicions, suspicions which were further added to when his agents reported Russian activity in Tibet and rumours of a military mission established at Lhasa. Despite reluctance in London to do anything at all, Curzon was so concerned that no other country should secure undue influence there that he determined to put an end to what he regarded as the aloofness, hostility even, of the Dalai Lama who had had the preposterous insolence to ignore his tentative proposals. In the summer of 1903, therefore, he despatched Lieutenant-Colonel Francis

Younghusband, already renowned as an explorer of Central Asia, as political agent at Chitral and as a leading participant in the Great Game, to cross the Tibetan frontier to position himself at Khamba Jong and open up some sort of negotiations with the Dalai Lama's representatives. Nothing came of it. The lamas who appeared from Lhasa to see what was going on refused to have anything to do with Younghusband and after spending some fruitless months meditating, he returned to report to the Viceroy. This time Curzon decided on harsher measures and instructed Younghusband to put together a military expedition to penetrate deep into Tibet, moreover, as Curzon wished to lose no time, to do so *in winter*. Whatever the rights and wrongs of what amounted to a military invasion of an independent and not unfriendly neighbour, this was the sort of thing the British were best at. Well over a thousand soldiers, Gurkha infantry, Sikh pioneers, a British mountain artillery section, two Maxim gun detachments manned by the Norfolk Regiment, would be supported by ten thousand porters and double that number of every type of beast of burden – yaks, camels, mules, ponies, bullocks and buffaloes. In the middle of December, 1903, this remarkable force crossed Tibet's frontier and made camp.

Thereafter their progress was slow but sure. By the beginning of 1904 they were at Tuha, on a 15,000 feet plain, bitterly cold with snow, and there the lamas made it plain that there could be no negotiating and that the British should withdraw. Younghusband and his force stayed put, however, and then in March advanced again with a view to reaching his initial objective, Gyangtse, some 150 miles inside Tibet. Fifty miles short of this objective, at Guru, they encountered the first attempt by the Tibetans to defend their country – a pathetically inadequate barrier of stones and perhaps a thousand Tibetan soldiers armed with old muskets and swords. The British deployed and manned their guns, tried peacefully to disarm the Tibetans, but a clash between their leader and a Sikh precipitated, not a battle, but a massacre. The maxim guns, the mountain artillery, British and Gurkha musketry were overwhelming. Some 600 Tibetans were killed; half a dozen of Younghusband's men were wounded. The remaining Tibetans simply walked away. The British were sickened by their own victory.

Nevertheless Younghusband and his force persevered. They skirmished their way to Gyangtse, and, reinforced by a battalion of the Royal Fusiliers, entered Lhasa at the beginning of August, 1904. There was no Russian mission, indeed no Russians at all, and the Dalai Lama had gone. The British and Indian soldiers settled down, as they always did in such circumstances, to playing games and watching or harrying wild life, while their camps outside the city took on the normal appearance with flags, crests, bugles sounding and Regimental white-washing and polishing. A month later Younghusband signed a treaty with the lamas, which by its term of imposing a British agent at Gyangtse, an occupying force and an indemnity went so far beyond his instructions simply to make some agreement on trade that it aroused strong protests from the European powers. The British Government then modified it. After Younghusband's expedition left Lhasa a month later or so, everything reverted to what it had been before. Nothing had been achieved – for Curzon, for the British position in India, for the Great Game itself. All that had happened was that the British Army had once more shown how good it was at this sort of operation, involving long marches over hazardous country, with huge lines of communication maintained by a great variety of animals, brushing aside opposition and persisting in the face of delays and difficulties. In short, it was an extraordinary feat, but in their encounter with a so-called enemy, the British soldiers had been almost ashamed of themselves, and in any event a success of this sort could never erase the far greater shame felt by the Army and the nation over its performance in the Boer War.

Kipling, as so often before and after, spoke for the nation when he wrote of our having had 'no end of a lesson' which would 'do us no end of good'. James Morris, with incomparable prose and perception, points out that Kipling was not simply criticizing the Army's structure, which, made up as it was with brave but incompetent leaders and equally brave but unquestioning rank and file, had fallen down on the job. An apparently unending run of success in all Queen Victoria's little wars had made it seem that the British Army was invincible, yet in their attempt to subdue some 35,000 untrained Dutch farmers, it had met with a series of humiliating failures. Kipling, therefore, was calling into doubt the whole hierarchical system, the assumption that 'gentlemen' automatically made good leaders in war, and that all the ordinary soldier needed to do was loyally to follow them. 'The great regiments of the British Army', James Morris wrote, 'the Guards, the Highlanders, the cavalry of the line, were of all British institutions the most devoted to the old order: yet these proud brotherhoods had been seen running for their lives through the South African night, or pinned humiliatingly among the thorn-bushes with the sun blistering the backs of their kilted knees.' If the Marquess of Halifax had been right when he observed that the third part of an army must be destroyed before a good one could be made out of it, the British Army in South Africa had gone some way towards qualifying for this very amelioration. What then was to be done? The Esher Report, as we have noted already, was produced in the spring of 1904. We must now see how Richard Burdon Haldane, perhaps the greatest of all Army reformers, set about implementing its recommendations.

6

AT HOME

'Luckily we live in an island and haven't much fighting to do. If we hadn't live in an island I should never have gone into the army.'

Captain De Baron in Trollope's *Is He Popenjoy?*

Some of the Victorian novelists' idea of a British officer was singular. That unmitigated cad, Lieutenant George Osborne, was thought by his brother officers in *Vanity Fair* to be a regular Don Giovanni, which they regarded as one of the finest qualities to be possessed. He excelled at field-sports, sang well, looked good on parade, spent his plentiful money freely, dressed elegantly, could drink anyone under the table, was handy with his fives, a sound man on the cricket field, rode his own horses to victory in regimental steeplechases and all in all was a prodigious fellow. The men loved him. It may be doubted whether the men would have thought quite so much of Jack De Baron, who was so relieved to live in an island. Yet his badinage makes him the more clubable of the two. 'I hate all kind of strictness, and duty, and self-denial and that kind of thing,' he declares, 'It's rubbish. Don't you think so?' But surely, he is reminded, one has to do one's duty. 'I don't see it. I never do mine.' But suppose it came to a battle? 'I should get invalided at once. I made up my mind to that long ago.' All very entertaining, of course, and such sentiments did much to explain why Kipling in Edwardian times was still able to write with conviction of 'flanelled fools at the wicket' and 'obese, unchallenged old things' whose inertia, resistance to change and love of past traditions had to be overcome if real Army reform were to be effected. All the more reason to praise Haldane for what he achieved.

When the Esher Report appeared Balfour was still Prime Minister. Indeed it had been he who appointed the Esher Committee to propose changes in the organization of the War Office. The essential feature of their report was that the post of Commander-in-Chief, who was responsible for policy, command and administration, should be abolished, and that these three cardinal aspects of running the Army should be separated. Policy would become the responsibility of an Army Council; administration would be delegated to District Commanders reporting direct to the War Office; and command should – a point impossible to dispute – be left to commanders. Moreover, a proper General Staff had to be established and its duties, both in peace and in war, had to be properly defined. There was one further recommendation, an important one at that, which effectively dealt with Kipling's 'unchallenged old things' – it was that an indispensable first step would be to get rid of all the generals at present holding the most senior military appointments. Balfour was wholly in agreement and lost no time in getting on with it. Eight generals were sacked. The necessary papers were issued for creating an Army Council, and the four military members appointed together with the directors who would serve under them. In addition an Inspector-General of the Forces was nominated. Lastly, and of profound importance to the formulation of strategy, the Committee of Imperial Defence was given new significance by being reconstituted and provided with a permanent secretary.* Then, as now, most strategic arguments amounted to squabbles between branches of the armed services as to which was to get the most money, and in 1904–5 the dispute was between the Army and Navy. Each maintained that the defence of the homeland lay primarily with their own service. The Admiralty and the 'Blue Water' school were convinced that a powerful navy removed any possibility of successful invasion by a foreign power.† The War Office and those who feared a surprise attack advocated a large army based on compulsory service. Balfour himself took the Admiralty view and laid down the broad policy of sea-power to protect the homeland, while the Army's principal role would be to provide forces for overseas, in particular the reinforcement of India. In May, 1905, he announced this arrangement of strategic priorities in the House of Commons, whereupon Roberts [who had ceased to be Commander-in-Chief on the War Office's reorganization, but was a member of the Committee of Imperial Defence], resigned.

As so often happens, however, pronouncements in the House of Commons were not instantly translated into effective action. There was

* The most powerful and effective one was Maurice Hankey, who held the post from 1912–38, was also Secretary to the War Cabinet and the Cabinet itself.

† There was nothing new here. During the Napoleonic Wars Earl St. Vincent said that while he did not deny the French could come, he merely maintained that they could not come by sea.

still no General Staff. The military members of the newly constituted
Army Council seemed more concerned with arguing about its com-
position and duties, even its pay, than actually creating it. Even by the
time of Balfour's resignation in December, 1905, the then Secretary of
State for War (Arnold-Foster replaced Brodrick in 1903, Brodrick
becoming Secretary of State for India, much to Curzon's displeasure as
he had never thought much of Brodrick since their having been at
Eton and Oxford together) had only just issued the Army Council's
recommendations about the formation of a General Staff. Thus it was
not until Haldane was in office that this essential step was finally taken.
Arnold-Foster's regime at the War Office was almost as controversial
and ineffectual as his predecessor's. He had proposed to divide the Army
into two separate categories – a long service force which would be
employed to serve in India and the colonies: and a contingent of short
service soldiers, who would on leaving the Colours top up the Reserve.
There would also be a small field force at home which could mobilize
quickly without calling on the Reserve. The trouble with this idea was
that it cut right across the admirable and proved system of linked
battalions, which Cardwell had introduced and which had many powerful supporters, both political and military. Another feature of Arnold-
Foster's proposals – a reduction in auxiliary forces in order to finance
his intended changes – predictably provoked eloquent protest from those
representing the Militia and Volunteers. Moreover his predecessors as
Secretary of State, both Lansdown and Brodrick, argued in cabinet
against his proposals. So it was once more a pattern of controversy,
rather than actual reform, which Balfour and his various Secretaries for
War presided over. It was to be different with Campbell-Bannerman's
administration. As the new Secretary of State for War, Haldane was
able to push through reforms extending over a number of years. He
enjoyed certain advantages. Previous dithering lent strength to his new
approach; his advocacy was formidable; the top military men supported
him, as indeed did the Prime Minister himself, for Campbell-Bannerman
was anxious properly to prepare the Army in the light of a deteriorating
situation abroad.

The essential features of Haldane's work were these: a General Staff
was at last created; the Army at home was to be reorganized to provide,
first, an Expeditionary Force of six infantry divisions and one cavalry
division, supported by appropriate artillery and administration services –
this force would be capable of speedy mobilization and be provided with
reinforcement drafts from the Reserve; second, the whole of the non-
regular contingents would be combined to form a single Territorial
Force, containing no less than 14 infantry divisions and 14 mounted

brigades, again with necessary supporting units. Furthermore, a newly formed Officers' Training Corps at schools would replace former volunteer corps. All these measures took time – most of them were implemented in three years, 1906–9 – but when in August, 1914, mobilization of the Army was actually ordered, the whole machine worked perfectly. The regular divisions were rapidly mobilized and sent to France in two weeks. Fourteen Territorial divisions were ready for home defence. And when the fighting began as it did later that month, heavy casualties which the British Expeditionary Force suffered were made up from the substantial reserves available. Haldane's contribution to the British Army's ability to fulfil the nation's undertakings to her allies had been incalculable. What is more the Army that went to France was, or so the *Official History* claimed, 'incomparably the best trained, best organised and best equipped British army which ever went forth to war'. We shall see whether this extravagant claim was justified when we follow its fortunes and misfortunes later. In the final volume of his incomparable history, Sir John Fortescue pays a proper tribute to Haldane:

A jurist of eminence and a deep student of philosophy,* he seemed to be the least fitted of men to wrestle with military problems; but he was an able administrator, and was careful to learn from others before he began himself to teach. When once he had grasped the essential details of the situation he brought a great intellect to bear upon them; and the readiness of sympathy and understanding which he showed towards his military colleagues called from them their best and most strenuous work ... the service which he wrought was of untold value to the country.

We could do now with some of these qualities and methods of working in our military ministers. Fortescue commented too that Haig considered Haldane to be the greatest Minister for War this country has ever had. He then rather curiously dissents from this view, giving it as his opinion that *Castlereagh* deserved this honour! In fact the British Army did not do very well while Castlereagh was War Minister [1805–6 and 1807–9], for it was quite unable to influence Napoleon's triumph at Austerlitz, and although there were some successes at Vimeiro and Talavera, the year 1809 saw the death of Sir John Moore and the evacuation of his army at Corunna, and Wellington's retreat to Portugal. On the other hand, the Royal Navy virtually annihilated the French and Spanish fleet at Trafalgar in 1805 with a matchless demonstration of the

---

* Haldane is said to have reduced a handful of Generals to uncomprehending silence when he replied to their questions of what sort of Army he would like: a Hegelian one.

Nelson 'touch' – thus giving some further credibility to Captain De Baron's reasoning that he was only in the army because we lived in an island. Before Haldane was beginning to effect his wholly necessary reforms in the Army, the one man who might be thought of as the only real successor to Nelson – Admiral Sir John Fisher – with the aid of his brilliant First Lord of the Admiralty, Earl Cawdor – had been planning so to strengthen and concentrate the fighting power of the Royal Navy that Germany would abandon her race to match it. Their proposed programme of laying down four dreadnoughts in 1906 and a further four in subsequent years would, had it been carried out, have given the British an unreachable lead. As it was Campbell-Bannerman did not pursue the Cawdor–Fisher programme with the result that Germany made another attempt to challenge the Royal Navy's supremacy.

This naval race was one consequence and illustration of the worsening international situation. Another was what F.L. von Jagow, German Foreign Secretary at the outbreak of the Great War, described as 'this damned system of alliances, which were the curse of modern times'. Yet there were plenty of causes for this system. For the British Army the alliance which was most to affect it was that concluded with the French in 1904. It signalled that after a long period of sitting on the fence, Great Britain finally came down on one side – the side of France. It was in helping this to come about that Edward VII made his greatest contribution to the execution of his country's foreign policy. When he visited Paris in May, 1903, he was able to render this signal service to the nation by completely winning over the French. To start with, their hostility [for South Africa and Fashoda still rankled] was both open and widespread, but the King's tact, charm and flattery caused a total volte-face. It was a remarkable demonstration of how much more a pleasure-loving man of the world, who radiated dignity, confidence and warmth, could achieve in a foreign capital than all the diplomats and officials of the Foreign Office. 'For three years,' wrote J.B. Priestley, 'his ministers and generals had been busy alienating the French, and in three days he put it all right again. There was a lot to be said, in 1903, for a King ... who had known for a long time how life can be enjoyed in Paris.' Two months later the President of the French Republic, M. Loubet, accompanied by his Foreign Minister, Delcassé, came to London. As a result the Anglo-French Arbitration Treaty was signed that autumn. The Entente Cordiale was a reality and was soon to be cemented in practical ways. Admiral Fisher's decision to concentrate the British fleet in home waters as a counter to growing German naval power was greatly facilitated by his ability to move ships from the Mediterranean because of British confidence in France's fleet there. Nor was this the only sign

1. The 1st Duke of Marlborough, 'probably the greatest British general ever to take the field'

2. The 1st Duke of Wellington 'performed one more incalculably great feat for the nation and the British Army. He invented the Tommy'.

3. The Duke of Cambridge, 'a man of limitless good intentions and sparse imaginative powers'.

4. Edward Cardwell 'did not merely enlarge the Army; he completely reformed it'.

5. Field-Marshal Viscount Wolseley, 'the very model of a modern major-general'.

6. Field-Marshal Earl Roberts, 'genial, trim and precise - blessed by the ordinary soldier'.

7. Field-Marshal Lord Kitchener, 'cold, ambitious, thorough and remote'.

8. Winston Churchill, 'the most bumptious subaltern in the British Army'.

9. General Sir Redvers Buller, 'renowned for his courage, but not for his tactical sense'.

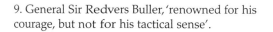

Baden-Powell, hero of Mafeking

10. Stormberg - Boers with Armstrong gun looted from British soldiers.

11. The Defence of Ladysmith.

12. Inside a Boer Laager.

13. 'The Empty Saddle'.

14. Lord Curzon.

15. Sir John French.

16. Cape Helles, July, 1915. A 60-pdr Battery in action on the top of the cliff. Up to July, 1915, there were only eight of these guns in action at Helles and by the beginning of August all but one had broken down.

17. Steele's Post, Gallipoli, held by a detachment of the 1st Australian Battalion, May, 1915.

of France's goodwill. During the Russo-Japanese War of 1904–5 –
despite the contradiction that Britain had an alliance with Japan and
France had one with Russia – French influence was significant in
ensuring that the Dogger Bank incident (the Russian fleet opened fire
in error on British trawlers off Hull) was smoothly resolved by Russian
apologies and compensation. Moreover the absurd posturing of Germany's Kaiser, William II, and his direct challenge to France in expressing his interests in Morocco, simply reinforced the ties between France
and Great Britain. If anxiety were thus partially stilled, there was plenty
to worry about closer to home.

If we now turn our eyes to the west, towards *John Bull's Other Island*,
we may remember that in the play Bernard Shaw makes the point that
there are only two qualities which matter: efficiency and inefficiency;
and there are but two sort of people: the efficient and the inefficient.
Whereas it might have been shown over the centuries that the English
were more efficient than the Irish, the latter in no way allowed this to
deter them from rebelling against the former. 'England's trouble is
Ireland's chance' had long been the cry of Irish patriots, and at the time
of England's trouble in South Africa the secret societies plotted and
planned. It only needed another opportunity, another inspiring leader,
for rebellion to break out once more. No one has summed up the Irish
problem with its implacable contradictions as they appeared to be at the
end of the last century and the beginning of this one better than James
Morris, and we may perhaps be permitted to recall his words:

> The miseries of Ireland had infected England, too, and the Irish question
> was the most crippling of all the imperial burdens. The Irish garrisons, and
> the Royal Irish Constabulary, were terribly expensive. The Irish M.P.s were
> a plague to Parliament. ... Ireland was always on the English mind, like a
> nearer Egypt. It was a backward people, properly part of the White Man's
> Burden. It was a proud and ancient people, only kept backward by oppression.
> It was a nation incapable of self-government. It was incapable of
> self-government only because it had never been allowed to try. It was
> really British anyway, and had no right to separate loyalties. It was a Celtic
> entity, different in race, custom and religion. ... It did not know its own
> luck. It had lived in tragedy for eight centuries. Free Ireland and you would
> dismember the Empire. Hold Ireland and the Empire would never be serene.

For the British Army, however, Ireland was at once a barracks, a
playground and from time to time a graveyard. Typifying it all was the
Curragh, the huge military base near Kildare, at which most British
regiments had served at one time or another, positioned more or less in
the centre of Ireland, with the barracks on one side of the road and the

race course on the other, all in a vast open plain, emphasizing to the Irish as nothing else could that here was the camp of an occupying army, made up of English, Scots, Welsh and even *Irish* soldiers in khaki, training, living, riding their horses, playing their games, and essentially there in order to see to it that Ireland remained firmly in the Imperial orbit. However calm things might have seemed on the surface, beneath it the detestation of British rule found many expressions among the rebellious Irish – the Gaelic League dedicated to restoring Celtic customs, Sinn Fein, the nationalist party established in 1905, the Irish Republican Brotherhood or Fenians who as far back as 1866 had unsuccessfully staged a revolt. Such armed revolutionary movements were wholly at odds with those more moderate Irishmen content to accept Home Rule, rather like one of the overseas Dominions, within the British Empire. Yet even so reasonable a transfer of power had no appeal to the majority of Ulstermen, to whom rule from Dublin would mean rule from Rome and who were determined to maintain and strengthen union with Britain. From this opposition to Home Rule arose the great cry Ulster Will Fight and Ulster Will Be Right, leading in turn to the so-called Curragh incident in March, 1914, when Brigadier General Hubert Gough and nearly all the officers of his 3rd Cavalry Brigade demanded an assurance that they would not be required to march north and coerce Ulster into accepting the Home Rule Bill – and got his assurance! We will look further at this affair in the next chapter. Meanwhile the irony persisted that some of the finest general officers,* private soldiers and regiments of the British Army were – Irish!

In the cavalry alone there were the 4th Royal Irish Dragoon Guards, the 5th Royal Irish Lancers, the 6th Inniskilling Dragoons, the 8th King's Royal Irish Hussars.† One of the most renowned officers of 6th Inniskilling Dragoon Guards was Captain Lawrence Oates, who found immortality with Scott in Antarctica, had shown such courage in the Boer War where he had refused to give in to a superior number of enemy ('We came here to fight, not to surrender'), successfully extracting his patrol although seriously wounded, and who excelled with horses. In particular he loved hunting and remembered his days when stationed at the Curragh: 'While out hunting yesterday I hurt my hand and although it hurt me a good deal I did not give it much more notice. This morning I find one of the bones is broken, the one leading down from the wrist to the knuckle of my little finger. I have got my left hand all done up

* Including Roberts and Wolseley, with Alexander, Montgomery and Templer still to come.
† The Regiment which General Sir John Hackett, greatest soldier-scholar of his generation, joined in 1931.

in splints and can only use my right. I am most fearfully sick about it as hunting is the only thing that makes this life endurable.' Despite his injury, however, Oates was out hunting the following day.

This emphasis on hunting aroused great variety of comment as to its value in preparing officers for war. As Lord Anglesey reminds us, Esher – whose Report did so much in reforming the Army – thought that hunting would help little when up against the highly professional Germans, who took the whole thing seriously, whereas soldiering for the British officer was a mere pastime. Curzon felt the same, deplored the fact that so few officers studied their profession or read at all. Heroism was all very well, but science was important too. French, however, pointed out that at Aldershot officers of the Cavalry Brigade would frequently give up hunting or polo in order to take their squadrons out on training exercises and even be with them in the afternoons and evenings to lecture and talk to the men. As for the men themselves there was a similar difference of view. Wavell recorded much later that in the early part of this century there was no such thing as a good soldier. Any family with a son who had joined up regarded it as a disgrace. Here he was simply echoing Kipling with his 'Tommy this, an' Tommy that, an' Chuck him out, the brute! but saviour of his country when the guns began to shoot'. Haldane, however, after two years in office as War Minister was able to point out what an excellent contribution the Army was making in providing an opening for the unemployed: 'We shall provide over 20,000 places this winter [1908], with £375,000 in food and pay for the men. That is something quite new and I am pleased.' On first taking office, Haldane had asked the all-important question: 'What is the Army for?'. If events abroad were to continue to be as dangerous as they were in the Balkans from 1912 onwards, it would not be long before Haldane, and the British Army itself, would find out.

7

THE PATH TO WAR

No objective observer could deny that Britain's obligation to defend France from attack was now [November, 1912] stronger than it had been and that Germany was responsible for this.... Haldane added [to Lichnowsky, the German Ambassador] that British opinion believed that the existing balance of forces in Europe should be maintained. It would not tolerate a defeat of France or the consolidation of all European power in the hands of a single state.

Gordon A. Craig
Germany 1866–1945

Although it was in the Balkans that the conflagration eventually began, France and Germany came near enough to war over Morocco. The crisis of July, 1911, when Germany sent a gunboat, *Panther*, to Agadir in response to France's action in suppressing a rebellion at Fez, so alarmed both Britain and France that General Wilson, Director of Military Operations at the War Office, hurried to Paris to discuss plans with General Dubail. Anglo-French conversations about military cooperation in the event of war with Germany had been going on since 1906. The French view then had been that effective cooperation would have to be properly planned beforehand. Whilst not committing the British in advance, Grey, Foreign Secretary, had agreed that military conversations should proceed between General Grierson and Major Huguet, French military attaché in London. Not much progress had been made towards agreeing precise commitments until the meeting of Wilson and Dubail in July, 1911. Then both precision and commitment led the field. Wilson put his signature to a memorandum which made it plain that should the British intervene in a war between France and Germany, an expeditionary force of six infantry divisions and one cavalry division would land in France within two weeks of mobilization, and this force, totalling some 150,000 men and 67,000 horses would concentrate in the Maubeuge area. They would be ready for battle by the day after concentration was complete.

The answer to Haldane's question: 'What is the Army for?' was becoming crystal clear. According to Wilson it was to provide two Army Corps to fight on the left flank of the French, and this answer held good right up until August, 1914, when it carried out this task with honour and distinction. The politicians still had to be convinced, however, and when Wilson returned from Paris he tried to persuade both Haldane and Grey that an absolute undertaking to support the French with all six divisions plus simultaneous mobilization was the best possible way of confronting Germany with the unattractive prospect of having to fight both France and Britain. He was able to give the Imperial Defence Committee a much needed lesson in war strategy the following month when Asquith [who had succeeded Campbell-Bannerman as Prime Minister in 1908] called a special meeting, and accompanied by Haldane, Grey, Lloyd-George, McKenna and Winston Churchill* listened first to General Wilson, then to Admiral Sir Arthur Wilson, First Sea Lord, expounding their respective views on what should be done if it came to war. These views differed profoundly. General Wilson was convinced that he was the only one present competent to have an opinion, even though he was accompanied by General Sir John French, shortly to become Chief of the Imperial General Staff. Wilson's view was that French knew nothing at all about the matter, a view certainly supported by French's subsequent handling of the British Expeditionary Force in 1914–15. As for the politicians present, they were simply ignorant – in fact Churchill had shown with a characteristic stream of minutes to Asquith on military strategy during the Agadir crisis that in his particular case this was far from being so. In any event Wilson lectured the Cabinet members as to what was likely to happen if Germany went to war with France, predicting correctly that the Germans would concentrate superior forces against the French to seek quick decision there, while holding on the Eastern front again the slow-mobilizing Russians. Additionally – and here, tutored by the French and unfamiliar with the Schlieffen Plan whose essence was a very strong right wing, Wilson erred – he expected the Germans to send no more than four divisions west of the Meuse (in fact they sent two Armies) thus wholly justifying his proposal to position the British Expeditionary Force on the extreme French left where it would be strong enough to help resist a German

* Lloyd-George was Chancellor of the Exchequer, McKenna First Lord of the Admiralty, and Churchill Home Secretary. Soon afterwards the last two changed places much to Churchill's pleasure and the Navy's readiness in 1914.

advance. Although militarily unsound, therefore, Wilson's political instinct to commit the B.E.F. was correct.

Admiral Wilson's proposals were so far divorced from the Army's as to cause astonishment and confusion among his audience. They were also so absurdly unrealistic that it was not difficult for the Prime Minister to reject them. Schooled in the ideas of his predecessor, Sir John Fisher, who had always regarded the Army as 'a shell to be fired by the Navy', Wilson suggested that the British Expeditionary Force should be landed on the northern shores of Prussia, thereby distracting sufficient German forces from the Western front to enable the French Army successfully to resist their attacks. The generals had little difficulty in arguing against such a course of action, and as a result there was agreement that the Army's role in the event of war between Germany and France would be as General Wilson had outlined. This important strategic decision had two immediate effects. Churchill became First Lord of the Admiralty in October, 1911, and was thus in a position to ensure that naval and military planning went hand in hand; and General Henry Wilson was allowed to proceed with the business of perfecting Anglo-French co-operation. He was so successful and thorough that the two General Staffs were able to plan in meticulous detail the movement of every British battalion, which trains would be provided, where everyone would be billeted, how much forage would be required, and so on. Such careful preparation was to pay high dividends. No criticism, like that levelled against the Army during the opening months of the Boer War, would be forthcoming. The sheer completeness of all necessary arrangements was to compel the admiration and astonishment of those taking part in the translation of the British Expeditionary Force from Great Britain to France.

Meanwhile although the Agadir crisis had been resolved, Germany's bellicosity had not. It is curious to recall what great misapprehensions there were in both London and Berlin as to the realities of power in their respective capitals. Kaiser Wilhelm II had always disliked Edward VII. Not only was he jealous of Edward's position as the 'uncle of Europe' and of Edward's successful tours visiting the monarchs of Austria, Russia, Italy, Spain, Portugal and the countries of Scandinavia, but he totally misunderstood Edward's role in foreign affairs, attributing to him his own personal power and so conceiving Edward to be the arch-villain in Germany's so-called encirclement. 'He is Satan,' declared Wilhelm, 'You cannot imagine what a Satan he is!' This misconception of the German Emperor's contributed to the influence wielded by the war party in Germany and so in turn strengthened the hand of Tirpitz (Secretary of State of the Imperial Naval Office) and von Moltke (Chief of the General Staff). It was hardly surprising therefore that Wilhelm II welcomed Edward's death in 1910 and the accession of George V – 'a very nice boy'. Equally damaging and misleading were the ideas held by British ministers of the powers enjoyed by their opposite numbers in Berlin. Whereas Britain's Prime Minister with his various subordinates actually controlled foreign policy and the activities of the armed forces, their equivalents in Germany did not. Military and naval chiefs in Germany were directly responsible to the Emperor. And the Emperor, whether it was a question of a great naval expansion – bound to be incompatible with any idea of rapprochement towards Britain – or the Schlieffen plan and its violation of Belgian neutrality, which would instantly invoke British support for France, would almost certainly side with his soldiers and sailors, not with his Chancellor. Yet for the British cabinet it was not easy to comprehend what a profound influence the German General Staff and Naval Staff would have over matters of foreign policy.

In avoiding war over Agadir, Lloyd-George (whose eloquence and determination as a war leader from 1916–18 was second only to that of Churchill's some twenty odd years later) had made an important contribution by his speech at a Mansion House dinner in July, 1911, which plainly warned Germany of the grave risks she was running:

> I would make great sacrifices to preserve peace. I conceive that nothing would justify a disturbance of international goodwill except questions of the gravest national moment. But if a situation were to be forced upon us, in which peace could only be preserved by the surrender of the great and beneficient position Britain has won by centuries of heroism and achievement, by allowing Britain to be treated, where her interests were vitally affected, as if she were of no account in the Cabinet of Nations, then I say emphatically that peace at that price would be a humiliation intolerable for a country like ours to endure.

Brave words, no doubt, and the immediate effects were that Germany climbed down. But this did not prevent further preparations for war from continuing. We have seen what steps the French and British general staffs had taken, but this very commitment to France brought about a reaction in this country, best illustrated by the Utopian idea that Britain should be 'allies to none and friends to all'. It was decided that one further effort should be made to reach some understanding with Germany. Some concessions as to British naval supremacy over the German fleet were even talked of. Then in February, 1912, Haldane, still War Minister, visited Berlin. Knowing the country, fluent in the language, sympathetic towards Germany in general, there could have been no envoy more likely to succeed. Yet he failed, and given the conditions which Germany insisted on for any political agreement – an unqualified promise of neutrality in the event of war betwen France and Germany – failure was inevitable. The Kaiser may have boasted that he had shown the British they could not touch his armaments, but in comforting himself that his granite attitude would induce further and more modest negotiations, he utterly deceived himself. It simply resulted in a closer understanding between France and Great Britain and an exchange of notes in which each agreed, should either be threatened by a third Power, to consult with the other about joint action. As we have seen from the words which head this chapter, the inflexible attitude of Wilhelm II and Grand Admiral Tirpitz had done no more than enhance Britain's obligation to France.

France's action in moving its fleet to the Mediterranean had enabled the Royal Navy both to concentrate its Mediterranean Fleet at Gibraltar and bring back home from Gibraltar its Atlantic Fleet. At sea Britain's position seemed secure. Moreover the Royal Navy's presence in home waters would guarantee the British Army's passage to France if General Wilson's plan for an Expeditionary Force had to be executed. In what sort of condition was the Army for its projected task after some six years under Haldane?*

The *Official History* dealing with operations in France and Belgium claimed, in a phrase already quoted on page 83, that the Expeditionary Force was incomparably well trained, well organized and well equipped. Yet it went on to point out very major deficiencies in equipment and training. These deficiencies included heavy guns, howitzers, high explosive shells, trench mortars, hand grenades, machine guns, aircraft, to say nothing of training in their use, for how could the Army train with equipment it did not possess? Moreover there had been no proper study of German tactics or weapons or doctrine. In his severe, but just, condemnation of the War Office and its military leaders, David Divine† pointed out that, looked at in the light of what actually transpired, the Expeditionary Force was in fact deficient of most of the weapons for its task. It was not merely that study of the *use* of machine guns was wholly inadequate. There were not nearly enough of them.‡ There was not only a lack of heavy guns and howitzers. No one knew how to employ them or move them about or keep them supplied with ammunition.

---

* Seely succeeded Haldane as War Secretary in 1912. Haldane then became Lord Chancellor.
† *The Blunted Sword*, Hutchinson, 1964.
‡ As late as April, 1915, Haig, then commanding 1st Army, thought the machine-gun overrated. Two per battalion were in his view enough. Later there were *sixteen*!

Motorized transport hardly existed. Cross-country vehicles were not thought of. There were no *fighting* vehicles at all.* As for shells, it was not only that a proper high-explosive shell was unavailable. There was a general and disastrous shortage of every kind of shell and no planning or resources for production. And as if all this were not enough, the British Army, in engaging to fight on the left flank of the French, was committing itself to participate in a tactical doctrine which totally ignored the lessons of the Russo-Japanese War in which the killing power of quick-firing artillery and machine-guns had robbed armies of their tactical mobility and obliged them to construct entrenched defences protected by barbed-wire entanglements. Despite repeated demonstrations of the devastating effect of fire power from fixed defences in depth, however, the French Army was governed by the law of the offensive, was wedded to the idea of mass attack, the notion that wars were won by a supreme concentrated effort at one particular point.†
Ironically enough in 1940 the German Wehrmacht showed that, given the right equipment, the right tactics and the right leadership, victory could be won this way. If leadership in the French Army, notably in the persons of Joffre and Foch, were thus manacled to false doctrine, what about generals in the British Army? Let us look at two of them, who were so profoundly to influence the affairs of the British Expeditionary Force in France and Flanders – Sir John French and Sir Douglas Haig.

That celebrated military correspondent of *The Times*, Colonel Charles Repington‡ (whom we last met as Charles à Court as one of Buller's staff officers at Spion Kop) had a curious mixture of opinions on military matters, being sensible enough on the value of aircraft and submarines, but rather surprisingly a great supporter of French and Haig in their totally outmoded theories about the superiority of 'shock action' by cavalry over the fire power of rifle and machine-gun. By 1912 French was Chief of the Imperial General Staff and Haig had the chief command at Aldershot. French's views are admirably summarised by something he had written several years earlier: 'It must never be forgotten that it is only by the employment of "shock tactics" and the superior moral of the highly trained horseman wielding sword and lance that decisive success can be attained.' Fortunately for the British cavalry he did concede that these soldiers must learn to be expert rifle shots as well. Haig had echoed French's sentiments when he reported: 'Occasions for

* In February, 1916, Kitchener dismissed a demonstration tank as 'A pretty mechanical toy', although there were those who say this was for reasons of security.
† French *dead* alone in the Great War amounted to nearly two million.
‡ In his *English History 1914–1945* A.J.P. Taylor writes that it was Repington who devised the phrase The Great War.

charging will be few, but they occur – and the results from such action will be immense. The mounted attack, therefore, must always be our ideal, our final objective.' Repington seemed to be in sympathy with both men when he declared that a cavalryman armed only with a rifle would be like a 'chicken trussed for the spit' and that the lance was an essential complement to the rifle. He also made the extraordinary statement that proper cavalry spirit scorned mathematical calculations.

There were at this time plenty of influential writers who took a far more realistic view. Among them was Robert Erskine Childers* whose book *War and the Arme Blanche* demolished the French/Haig case and insisted that training with the rifle should take absolute priority. The Marquess of Anglesey has reminded us that, in introducing this book, Field-Marshal Lord Roberts, with his indelible memories of what the Boer War had been like, turned on those who argued that lessons from this war could not be applied to future wars because things in South Africa had been abnormal. He asked a most penetrating questions – that is, were not all wars abnormal? But he went on:

> As the Boer War was the first in which magazine rifles were made use of, and as the weapon used in future wars is certain to be even more effective, on account of the lower trajectory and automatic mechanism, shall we not be very unwise if we do not profit by the lessons we were taught at such a heavy cost during the war?

He concluded that cavalry soldiers must be good shots and furthermore must be trained to fight as infantry. (There was scarcely a British cavalry regiment in the Great War or the 1939–45 War which did not do so.) Yet French and Haig stuck to their opinions. 'Both French and Haig,' wrote General Sir John Hackett in his book, *The Profession of Arms*, 'had shown marked ability as administrators, trainers and commanders of troops, with distinguished records in the South African War. Neither had the intellectual capacity to evaluate the importance of new techniques, or the imagination to break the bonds of his own experience.' Winston Churchill, who knew both men rather better than any other writer about them, makes an interesting distinction between them. He calls French a natural soldier, who although not capable of Haig's mastery of detail, yet *did* have more imagination, and would 'never have run the British Army into the same long drawn-out slaughters'. Alas, a series of such slaughters seemed to be Haig's method of waging war, summed up by his own demand that every soldier should display 'a sincere desire to engage the enemy.' Churchill's judgement is that,

---

* His best known book *The Riddle of the Sands* depicted a German invasion of Britain.

stalwart and sincere though he was, Haig was totally lacking in strategic
originality, wholly wedded to the orthodox and the conventional, utterly
without that spark of genius which is the hallmark of really great
commanders like Alexander and Napoleon.

These then were the two men who would be directing operations of
the British Army in France and Flanders. What sort of men would they
be directing? When we remember that nearly five and a half million
soldiers of the British Empire fought in France and Flanders between
1914 and 1918, it is clear that in answering the question, we have to be
selective. There is also the point that whereas the British Expeditionary
Force which began it all was composed of Regulars and Reservists, by
the end of the war it was largely a citizen Army with both volunteers
and conscripts. Nor must we forget the vital contributions made by the
Indian Army and soldiers from the Dominions. But in order to illustrate
the quality of the British infantry, bearing in mind that the Army at the
outbreak of war was composed entirely of volunteers, we may perhaps
look at one battalion – The 2nd Battalion The Cameronians (Scottish
Rifles) whose story at the battle of Neuve Chapelle in March, 1915, an
action which the battalion started with nine hundred men, and ended
with one hundred and fifty, has been so eloquently and movingly told
by John Baynes.* His portrait of the battalion in its barracks near Valetta
at the beginning of 1914 would be impossible to better. He explains that
the thousand or so officers and men were organized into a headquarters
and four companies, each of four platoons, each again of four sections,
adding – and this is a supremely important point – that although
numbers and structure have changed, the essentials remain the same
today. Above all it was self-sufficient. 'It contained all the elements to
enable it to operate independently, and yet it was commanded by an
officer who might be expected to know every man in it. It was therefore
a large and powerful body of men, but at the same time small enough
for leadership to be intimate and for most of its members to know each
other well.' It is here that John Baynes puts his finger on the enduring
strength and the absolute necessity of the British Army's regimental
system. He goes on to explain the various positions of importance in the
battalion and the personalities of those holding them at the time. He
reminds us that most of the company commanders were unmarried and
regarded the care of their men as their major interest. They identified
themselves with the efficiency and well-being of the men they
commanded. Often you would find among such officers eccentricity,
wit, kindliness, integrity and simple demands for their men to be smart,

* *Morale: A Study of Men and Courage*, Cassell, 1967.

fit and good marksmen. I have said what an exceptionally high quality British infantry battalions possessed, and in order to understand this, we may glance at a few individuals to whom John Baynes draws attention. General Sir Richard O'Connor acquired great fame in the Western Desert in 1941 and later in Normandy. As a young officer in this battalion, Baynes tells us, he had already shown signs of his future distinction:

> His main quality throughout his life has been complete integrity . . . absolutely honest, direct and without pretence . . . a very simple person, always kind, quiet and courteous, and yet with such strength of will and mind obvious in his every word and action that none would dare take advantage of his gentleness . . . Within the small world of the 2nd Scottish Rifles he was an important person, even as a subaltern. The influence of such a person, even when young and junior in rank, can be extraordinarily powerful.

Although O'Connor turned out to be an exceptionally successful commander in the Second World War, his character could be mirrored a thousand times over in his contemporaries both then and – I most firmly believe – now. Of course, in running the affairs of a battalion the officers had enormous and indispensable support from the Warrant Officers and Sergeants. How fortunate the 2nd Scottish Rifles were to have as their Regimental Sergeant Major, shortly after the Great War began, a man called Chalmers:

> Throughout his service he was the epitome of a good soldier. He possessed the dignity and quality of character which enabled him to meet his seniors and subordinates on equal footing, and to play his part in the military scheme of things without fear or favour. His complete integrity, coupled with the highest standards, which he invariably lived up to himself, made him the perfect leader.

Further down the ranks this kind of example, this devotion to the Regiment, personal discipline and insistence on the virtue of *service* for its own sake, was endlessly repeated among the N.C.O.s and private soldiers. As all of us who have been in action and in command of troops during a battle know, it is not always the model soldier in times of peace who turns out best in war. Captain Kennedy of the battalion had thought Private McHugh to be somewhat surly and resentful of orders. But how differently he showed himself to be when the guns began to shoot:

> There was no more dependable man in the platoon and no one more ready to do his full share of work and over. The smart peacetime soldier is not always the best in the trenches, whereas men like McHugh, who have shown no very great promise before, prove themselves to be possessed of wonderfully fine qualities, totally unsuspected in the quiet times of peace.

During these quiet times training for war was relatively simple. To be able to march, to shoot well, to drill, to have some mastery of tactics and field craft, to be smart and clean and disciplined – these were the watchwords. There was still plenty of time for games in the afternoons. And in the evenings, what then? We will allow ourselves one more extract from John Baynes's book:

> In those days the army carried its own life with it wherever it went, and you lived pretty much the same, whether you were in India or China or any other place. You lived between the barrack room and the wet canteen, without any social life at all. . . . There was a ritual every evening. The men would make themselves absolutely spotless – uniform pressed, boots polished, hair plastered down, bonnet on just so – as if every one of them had a girl-friend waiting at the gate. But they had no girl-friends, and they were never out of the gate. They went straight down to the wet canteen and got drunk. That was what they got dressed up for.

I hope I have not laboured this picture of life in one battalion. It is important to understand what the British infantry were like before we see them coping with the hell of Loos, the Somme and Passchendaele, and we will follow later the heroic performance of the 2nd Scottish Rifles at Neuve Chapelle. While they are still soldiering on in their barracks near Valetta, the war clouds are continuing to gather elsewhere.

In October, 1912, the first Balkan War had resulted in great successes for Greece, Bulgaria and Serbia in liberating Christians from the hated misrule of Turkey, but had also brought to a head once more the conflict of interests between Russia on the one hand, with her never-ending quest for access to warm water ports through the Bosphorus and Dardanelles, and Austria-Hungary (backed by Germany) on the other hand, determined to maintain Turkey as a counter-force against Russia and the Slavs, and to keep Serbia land-locked and weak. Germany's position was of supreme importance, for her ambitions to establish a firm position from the Baltic to the Persian Gulf (this was the real meaning of that much misused phrase *Drang nach Osten*) depended essentially on keeping Russia out of the Golden Horn. 'The conflict between the two thrusts,' wrote Sir Robert Ensor, 'the Russian north to south and the German west to east – was absolute. And it needs to be clearly grasped, because it was what motivated the war of 1914.'

The threat to British interests of the Balkan war was clear enough. If Russia went to war with the Germanic powers, France would be drawn in and thus Great Britain too. In any event, as British ministers had repeatedly declared, the prospect of a Germany, both powerful at sea and – by defeating France – upsetting the European balance, was not to be tolerated. The Foreign Secretary, Grey, in convening a peace conference in London, sought not only immediate solutions to the Balkan dispute, but also longer-term agreements which would help remove the deeper dangers of major conflict. He succeeded in neither. Although there was a temporary patching up of the Balkan states' quarrel with Turkey, they soon began to quarrel among themselves. This quarrel was interrupted in January, 1913, by the Young Turks' insurrection at Constantinople, and war against Turkey was renewed, greatly to the latter's discomforture, and by the Treaty of London in May, 1913, Turkey was obliged to cede to the Balkan States everything north of the Enos–Midia line. Crete went to Greece. But Austria and Italy obliged Serbia and Montenegro to evacuate Albania, and Serbia's insistence on compensation at the expense of Bulgaria resulted in a further outbreak of war between Bulgaria on the one hand and Serbia and Greece on the other. Initially – and here was a further lesson for the British and French armies had they cared to take notice of it – trench warfare produced little result, until the intervention of Rumania against Bulgaria decided the affair. The Treaty of Bucharest in August, 1913, enlarged Greece and Serbia at the expense of Bulgaria, which was also forced to give Adrianople back to the Turks, who had intervened at the time of Bulgaria's distress. None of these arrangements augured well for a permanent settlement. Austria so much resented Serbia's expansion that she actually proposed to her two partners in the Triple Alliance, Germany and Italy, 'a defensive attack' on Serbia. This would have been to bring the Great War forward by nearly a year, but Italy declined and there the matter rested for the time being.

Much more serious was the attitude of Germany. To those in Berlin the settlement appeared to be a further check on the *Drang nach Osten* by the imposition of a Slav barrrier between the Central Powers and Turkey. Yet Constantinople remained a sphere of German influence (at the end of 1913 General Liman von Sanders was made a Turkish Field Marshal and Inspector-General of the Turkish Army – with profound consequences for the British, Australian and New Zealand armies at Gallipoli in 1915). Germany did much more than simply lend the Turks a general officer. Convinced by 1913 of the inevitability of war between the Central Powers and the Dual Alliance of France and Russia, she took the unprecedented step of increasing the size of her standing army by 63,000 men, whereupon Russia added 130,000 to her army, and the French introduced three (it was formerly two) years' military service. 'This damned system of alliances' was becoming ever more threatening. In his brilliant *England 1870–1914* Sir Robert Ensor suggests that in taking steps to increase their regular army from 280,000 to 343,000 the General Staff in Berlin had their eyes on the summer of 1914 as the best time from their point of view for the war to start. By August of that year the German Army would be at its maximum strength, the special levy of 1,000 million marks would have been spent in equipping the Army, and there would be suitable campaigning weather both to crush France by means of the Schlieffen Plan – a six weeks' affair – *and* to turn east and deal with Russia. All very logical with hindsight, no doubt, and it was clear that Austria's aggressive policy towards Serbia was bound to cause a reaction sooner or later, but no one could have anticipated that the Archduke Francis Ferdinand would be assassinated at Sarajevo on 28 June, 1914.

Germany, France and Russia might all be increasing the size of their armies. Britain, on the other hand, proposed a 'naval holiday' – that is, Churchill suggested both in March, 1913, and again seven months later, that the four capital ships to be laid down for the Royal Navy and the two equivalent ships for the Imperial German Navy during the coming year should not be built. Germany turned down this proposal, bearing in mind perhaps that the widening of the Kiel Canal, which would allow her Dreadnought class battleships to use it between the Baltic and the North Sea, would be completed by August, 1914. Meanwhile the British Army, far from gearing itself up for war, was having a dispute with the British Government as to whether or not it would carry out its orders. It all arose when Ulstermen took a violent objection to the Home Rule Bill, which put a time limit on Ulster's right to remain outside the Dublin parliament. When the Commander-in-Chief in Ireland, General Paget, was ordered to concentrate his forces in order to reinforce the Army in Ulster should it become necessary, he instead came to London and persuaded the War Secretary, Seely, to allow those officers whose homes were in Ulster to 'disappear' should their regiments be ordered north. On his return to Ireland he not only made kown this concession, but also stated that officers not domiciled in Ulster could resign (and thereafter be dismissed) if they were not willing to take part in operations against Ulster. The result was that virtually all the officers of 3rd Cavalry Brigade under Brigadier General Gough said they *would* prefer dismissal, and many infantry formations expressed similar sentiments. The outcome of it all was that Gough obtained a written undertaking, initialled by both Seely and General Sir John French, the C.I.G.S., that he and his brigade would not be required 'to enforce the present Home Rule Bill on Ulster.' The subsequent political row was such that Seely and French had to resign, and Asquith himself, anxious not to upset the entire military hierarchy at a time when affairs abroad made it probable that the British Expeditionary Force might actually have something to do, became War Minister. The arch-villain throughout the so-called Curragh 'mutiny' had been the Director of Military Operations, General Sir Henry Wilson, another Anglo-Irishman, who despite his obligation to Government ministers had secretly been advising those very soldiers opposed to Government policy. Wilson was very adept at hunting with the hounds and running with the hare, but he was to meet his death in the end, and, as we shall see, at the hands of Irishmen. While all this had been going on the 'private armies' of both Unionists and nationalists in Ireland had been proceeding. On 24 April, 1914, Carson's Ulster Volunteers succeeded in a gun-running coup at Larne which supplied them with some 30,000 rifles and three million rounds of ammunition. Totalling perhaps some 80,000 men, they were still outnumbered by the National Volunteers of perhaps 100,000 who also succeeded in running guns into the country in July. There was, however, an important difference between these two incidents. No serious attempt had been made to interfere with Carson's operation, but both the Army and police were called out against the National Volunteers, and consequent scuffles and shooting left three Irishmen dead and nearly forty wounded. It was just one more reason for the Irish to hate, to plan, to arm and drill, to await once more the moment when England's trouble would be Ireland's chance.

England's trouble was not far off now, although the British Prime Minister, Asquith, and his senior colleagues were far from being aware of the real intentions being harboured by the military men in Berlin and Vienna. In May, 1914, their respective Chiefs of General Staff, von Moltke and Conrad von Hötzendorf, had conferred and agreed that the time for war had arrived, that delay would simply lessen their chance of rapid success. That same month the President of the United States, Woodrow Wilson, had sent his adviser, Colonel House, to Berlin, Paris and London to investigate the chances of arriving at some sort of peace arrangements. Whereas he found in Berlin an absolute determination for war among the military hierarchy, when he reported all the German preparations to Asquith and Grey, they remained entirely unconvinced of the likelihood of German aggression, putting their faith in the assurances of the German Chancellor, von Bethmann-Hollweg, and the German Ambassador in London, Lichnowsky, and totally failing to appreciate that it was not these two men who called the tune, but the soldiers in Berlin, who would almost certainly be backed by the Kaiser.

When therefore the Archduke Francis Ferdinand was assassinated on 28 June, the whole dreadful process began. Here for Austria was the excuse to attack Serbia. German support was sought and obtained. About a month after the Archduke's murder, on 23 July, Austria's ultimatum to Serbia was presented, described by Grey as the most formidable document ever addressed by one state to another that he had seen. Two days later Serbia caved in, but, bent on war, Austria rejected Belgrade's request that some points should be submitted to the European Powers for their arbitration, and began mobilization. Thereafter, despite flurries of diplomatic activity, Austria's actual attack on Serbia which began on 28 July inevitably set in train the mobilization procedures leading to general war. Great Britain's position was still equivocal, warning Germany not to rely on her neutrality and France not to rely on her support. On 31 July Russia began mobilization. Germany instantly demanded that it should cease. As Russia did not comply, the German declaration of war on Russia followed on 2 August. One day later Germany declared war against France. Britain's support of France was brought about by the German demand that Belgium allow passage of her armies. On 3 August the Belgians refused and their King appealed to King George V to intervene by diplomatic means. That same day mobilization of the British Army was authorized and Haldane himself gave the necessary orders, including those to the Reserves and the Territorial Army. At a war council also held that day, while Haldane proposed that the whole Expeditionary Force of six divisions (General Sir John French had been appointed to the command) should be sent to France, he failed to convince his colleagues, who included both Roberts and Kitchener (the latter had agreed with some reluctance to become Secretary of State for War), and it was decided initially to send only four. On the following day, 4 August, the Germans invaded Belgium, the British Government demanded withdrawal, and, as the time-limit of 11 p.m. expired without German compliance, from that time Germany and the British Empire were in state of war. In only one respect was Britain anything like ready. In July there had been a trial mobilization of the Fleet, and although they were supposed to disperse on 24 July, when the First Sea Lord, Prince Louis of Battenberg, heard of Austria's having rejected Serbia's reply to her ultimatum, using his initiative with real boldness, he cancelled demobilization of the Fleet. Churchill immediately endorsed this very proper and timely decision.

The British Army had yet to mobilize. When it did, things went smoothly and quickly, thanks to the admirable changes brought about by Haldane. In examining how the Army conducted itself during more than four years of war and hundred of battles, we must be selective and representative. By looking at two main theatres of war – the Western Front and the Middle East – it will be possible to show how the British soldier utterly redeemed what had been thought of as a poor performance in the Boer War, and we will look first at France and Flanders.

8

FRANCE AND FLANDERS

I don't know what is to be done; this isn't war.
Kitchener (of trench warfare)

One of the first things that had to be decided was what to do with the British Army. We have seen that General Wilson had made detailed plans for its despatch to France, but there had been no absolute commitment. When Asquith presided over a council of war on 5 August, therefore, it still had to be decided how much of the British Expeditionary Force should go abroad, where it should go and what it should do. On the first two questions there was much disagreement, on the last, no agreement at all. Wilson himself, present in his capacity as Director of Military Operations, regarded the other fifteen members of the council as almost entirely ignorant of what was being discussed. This was severe on the other military men there, who included Kitchener (now appointed as Secretary of War), Field-Marshal Lord Roberts, four key figures of the B.E.F. – French, the Commander-in-Chief, his Chief of Staff, Murray, and two corps commanders, Haig and Grierson, and three of Wilson's Army Council colleagues. The First Sea Lord, Admiral Battenberg, and General Sir Ian Hamilton (in charge of home defence and later to command at Gallipoli) were also there, plus the four cabinet ministers most concerned: Asquith, Haldane, Grey and Churchill. While there was general acceptance that the Territorial divisions, which numbered fourteen, could deal with home defence, thus leaving the B.E.F. free for operations overseas, there was a variety of views as to where it should go – Belgium or France? All Wilson's previous planning came to his assistance in making it plain that this planning could not be changed. All the details of railways, billets, supplies made it imperative that the whole B.E.F. of six infantry divisions and one cavalry division was depatched to take up positions on the French left at Maubeuge.

There seemed to be no immediate counter-argument, and there, for one day at least, the matter rested.

But next day at a cabinet meeting Kitchener raised objections. He had studied the Schlieffen Plan. He anticipated that a powerful right wing of the German Army would advance through Belgium to try and encircle and roll up the French Army. In that event the B.E.F. would be dangerously exposed at Maubeuge. He urged that it should go instead to Amiens and the Cabinet concurred. Whatever else might be said about Kitchener, it must be conceded that he was the only member of the cabinet or of the military experts who at this time foresaw what sort of shape the war would take. He actually declared that it would continue for at least three years and that Britain must place in the field an army of millions of men who would be required to fight a series of bloody battles on the Continent. How he arrived at this conclusion has never been clear. Grey attributed to him occasional flashes of brilliant strategic instinct, rather than some process of careful reasoning. However that may be, by insisting on it and raising the necessary armies to fight a war of this sort, Kitchener's contribution to his country's survival was incalculable. Although initially Kitchener's advice was accepted by the cabinet, Wilson had not done with it yet. A week later he called his French military friends in to argue with Kitchener that the B.E.F. had to act with the French Army to be effective at all. The overriding concern of the French was, of course, to ensure that their ally was wholly committed. Conscious of the smallness of the British contingent (this was his reason for being convinced that only by fielding large armies could Britain influence the war's outcome) – for the cabinet had also agreed that to start with only four divisions would go – Kitchener gave way after seeking the Prime Minister's approval, and the B.E.F. was instructed after all to concentrate at Maubeuge. Moreover, the fifth division was despatched on 19 August. Next day the British Army was at its concentration area and ready for action.

To understand the important part played by the B.E.F. in thwarting von Moltke's version of the Schlieffen Plan, we may perhaps first glance at how things went in broad terms from the German point of view. The essence of the original plan was speed, maintenance of momentum, a powerful right wing which would advance to the west of Paris and no irrelevant distractions elsewhere. The Germans were either unable or unwilling fully to adhere to any of these four cardinal rules. They had not calculated on Belgian resistance, yet the Belgian Army fiercely defended the Liege fortresses, losing them a vital four days; they had not expected that the British Army's support for the French would be either in time or of any significance, yet Sir John French's four infantry divisions and one cavalry division deployed at a strategically important place and advanced to Mons to block von Kluck's attempt to envelop the French 5th Army; this fatal loss of momentum caused the German High Command to abandon the letter of the Schlieffen Plan – a further enveloping movement by the right wing – and turn their thrust to the east, instead of the west of Paris, thus exposing flank and rear to a counter-attack from Joffre and Gallieni and forcing the Germans to go over to defence on the River Marne. As if this were not enough, von Moltke further breached the principles of war by failing to concentrate in the area where decision was possible – the right wing – in order to regain momentum there, and used his left wing, which should have remained on the defensive, in a strategically irrelevant attack on Nancy. Everything had gone wrong. The Marne battle was ended and the Germans withdrew to the River Aisne. Failure caused von Moltke to resign, and he was replaced by von Falkenhayn.

We cannot follow every move and every engagement of the B.E.F. during these dramatic toings and froings of the various armies, but we can at least see what they achieved at the Battle of Mons. The British 2nd Corps under Smith-Dorrien (who had taken over after Grierson's death) had deployed at Mons, both to the west along the canal to Condé and just east; on his right was Haig's 1st Corps linking up with the left of Lanrezac's 5th French Army. Their orders were to defend the line of the canal. On the morning of 23 August advancing towards them was von Kluck's 1st Army, which was observed by an aeroplane of the Royal Flying Corps*. Opposite the B.E.F. were no fewer than four German corps and three cavalry divisions, totalling some 160,000 men and 600 guns. The total strength of the B.E.F. was about 70,000 and 300 guns. The main attack by some six German divisions fell on Smith-Dorrien's corps of two divisions. In her remarkable account of what happened in *August 1914* Barbara Tuchman has described the opening encounters:

> At 9 a.m. the first German guns opened fire on the British positions, the attack falling first upon the salient made by the loop of the canal. The bridge at Nimy at the northern-most point of the salient was the focus of the attack. Lunging at it in their dense formation the Germans offered 'the most perfect targets' to the British riflemen who, well dug in and expertly trained, delivered fire of such rapidity and accuracy that the Germans believed they faced machine-guns. After repeated assault waves were struck down they brought up more strength and changed to open formations. The British, under orders to offer 'stubborn resistance', kept up their fire from companies in the salient growing smaller with every half hour. From ten-thirty onwards

---

* In 1914 the R.F.C. had 63 aeroplanes.

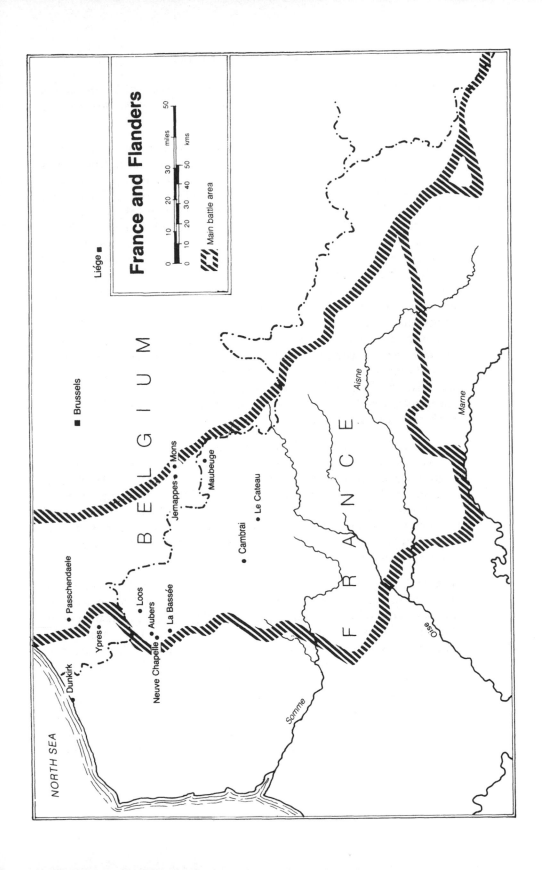

France and Flanders

Main battle area

the battle was extended along the straight section of the canal to the west as battery after battery of German guns, first from the IIIrd and then from the IVth Corps, were brought into action.

During the afternoon the intense German pressure on ever smaller British numbers forced withdrawal to a second line of defence a few miles further back, and Smith-Dorrien's earlier preparation of the canal bridges for demolition was seen to be wholly justified. There was, however, difficulty in destroying two important bridges at Jemappes and Mariette, because there were no detonators to set off the charges. At the first the gallantry of a sapper corporal and private not only rectified this error, but won them respectively the Victoria Cross and Distinguished Conduct Medal. At Mariette another V.C. was won by Captain Wright, but the bridge still failed to blow up. Happily the Germans did not take advantage of their opportunity to pursue the retiring British. The effect of this successful resistance by Smith-Dorrien's Corps on the B.E.F.'s Commander-in-Chief, French, was initially that he would continue to stand on the defensive, but news that Lanrezac's 5th Army was to retire obliged French to conform and the retreat from Mons began. In a curious way that the British Army was to perpetuate for other inconclusive engagements still to come, the Battle of Mons became a legend. As Barbara Tuchman puts it:

> As the opening British engagement of what was to become the Great War, it became endowed in retrospect with every quality of greatness and was given a place in the British pantheon equal to the battle of Hastings or Agincourt. Legends like that of the Angels of Mons settled upon it. All its men were valorous and its dead all heroes. The deeds of every named regiment were chronicled down to the last hour and bullet of the fight until Mons came to shine mistily through a haze of such gallantry and glory as to make it seem a victory.

The myth was to be repeated twenty-six years later when Gort succeeded in extracting another B.E.F. from another wavering French front in another battle of withdrawal to a place called Dunkirk. Meanwhile in August, 1914, the retreat from Mons went on, checked for a time at the battle of Le Cateau on 26 August and then resumed. There was little contact with the advancing Germans for two reasons. First the German Army was more concerned with moving forward than engaging the 'contemptibly little' British Army; secondly, and this showed how completely the French policy of drawing in the British once and for all was succeeding, because the B.E.F. was obliged to conform to the movements of the French Army. Any idea of an independent role for the B.E.F.

was at an end, and when Joffre determined on a counter-offensive against the advancing Germans, the British were obliged to conform. This countermove began on 5 September, by which time there was a thirty-mile gap between von Kluck's 1st Army, once more moving west to meet French advances from Paris, and von Bülow's 2nd Army engaged by the French further east. Into this gap the B.E.F. slowly and cautiously made its way, with hardly any contact except a few cavalry skirmishes, until on 9 September the German armies conducted a general withdrawal to the River Aisne. Then all manoeuvre and mobility virtually ended. The Germans, A.J.P. Taylor tells us, had unwittingly 'stumbled on the discovery which shaped the first world war: men in trenches, with machine guns, could beat off all but the most formidable attacks. The Allied advance ground to a halt. On 16 September French issued his first instructions for trench warfare.'

Professor Taylor goes on to explain that when the B.E.F. was moved to Flanders with the idea of outflanking the Germans, it simply collided head on with the German Army trying to do the same to the Allies. The result was the ghastly first battle of Ypres, in which concentrated attacks on narrow fronts, with constant reinforcement of failure, led first to the B.E.F.'s practically running out of supplies and ammunition, then a German breakthrough, which they failed to exploit (a pattern repeatedly to be reproduced during the next three years – particularly by the British), this gap effectively blocked by French reserves, and finally, after the battle had lasted for a month – from 12 October to 10 November – deadlock, with the British in possession of a salient leading to two further battles of Ypres, even more costly, disastrous and indecisive than the first. Worst of all, as Professor Taylor summed it up, 'the first battle of Ypres marked the end of the old British army. The B.E.F. fought the Germans to a standstill, and itself out of existence. More than half of those who crossed to France in August were now casualties; one in ten had been killed [three-quarters of them at Ypres]. The high command and the staff officers survived. The old army was gone past recall.'

The British soldiers had lived up to Ludendorff's declaration that 'they fight like lions'. The British generals had endorsed Colonel Hoffman's rejoinder that they were 'led by donkeys'. Between August and November, 1914, one British army had been all but destroyed. Before the generals could destroy another, they would need some more soldiers. And Kitchener was busy making sure that there would be plenty of them. Before we see how he set about it and with what results we may perhaps recall the impression he made upon one of these new soldiers – J.B. Priestley:

I saw him only once but had a close view of him. This was early in the Great War when I was a private soldier in the first New Army he had raised, often known as the 'first Hundred Thousand'. We were stationed in Aldershot and one day the whole division was drawn up on parade, outside the town, to be inspected by Kitchener. We waited for hours, and it rained all the time, so long and so hard that the blue dye began to run out of our absurd forage caps. And then at last there he was, glaring at us rank by rank – a huge figure with an outsize purple-swollen face – no, not the result of drink, because he was then strictly teetotal – and through this unmoving mask the strange eyes moved, stared, glared. I must confess that to me, just turned twenty, standing there rigid, with blue rain running down my face, feeling, as I was often to do in the army, idiotic, he seemed a monster. But he was not a monster. Grimly devoted to duty, ready to work day and night, he could be tough and rough, but there was no deliberate cruelty working in him.

The response to Kitchener's recruiting appeal: 'Your Country needs YOU' was striking. Convinced as he was, when everyone else expected a short war, that Britain would need to deploy millions of soldiers to fight for years in bloody Continental battles, he had on becoming Secretary for War pressed initially for conscription. Accepting Asquith's opinion that it was not politically prudent, he turned his attention to voluntary recruiting instead.

We may perhaps remind ourselves that at the outbreak of war the Regular army totalled about 160,000 men, and we have seen that of this number more than half made up the six infantry divisions and one cavalry division of the B.E.F. ready for instant despatch overseas. There were four more regular divisions in India and the colonies, but these would not be available until the colonies themselves had raised sufficient forces to replace them. There was also the Indian Army, and we will look at their contribution to the struggle against Germany shortly. There was no hesitation among the imperial volunteers from the Dominions. Australia, New Zealand and Canada instantly responded to what one young man from Melbourne,* who was to be killed in France in 1915 called 'the bugles of England blowing o'er the sea'. All three sent their expeditionary forces to Europe within a month or two of the war's beginning. Even South Africa despatched troops to Europe, as well as rounding up the German forces in south-west Africa. The whole British Empire was at war with Germany. The loyalty, devotion to duty and sacrifice so consistently shown by volunteers from Britain's far-flung colonial possessions, taking part in a war which was essentially about the balance of power in Europe and of little relevance to their own

* J.D. Burns.

remote countries, was at once staggering and unifying. The tragedy of it all has been movingly summed up by James Morris:

> The imperial soldiers found themselves transported, all too often, from their own sunlit spaces to the mud and drizzle of Flanders and France, where they floundered and died, were gassed or mined or mutilated, shivered in the unaccustomed cold or miserably ate their alien rations, year after year, trench after trench, sadness after sadness to the end.

Back at home there were the fourteen Territorial divisions and a further fourteen cavalry brigades, raised essentially for home defence, without an overseas service liability, administered by the County Associations. There were also some 300,000 reservists, composing both a Special Reserve designed to reinforce Regular Army units and a National Reserve to keep the Territorial Army up to strength. Kitchener decided that he would raise a completely New Army of seventy divisions with a strength of one and a quarter million men. He was determined first of all that this new army should be quite separate from the Territorials. Not only did he under-estimate their quality, but he wished to avoid what he foresaw as influence from County Associations in trying to get appointments for their own nominees. Moreover he wanted these new divisions to be created, so to speak, in his own image. It would be an Army created by him, with all the appeal of something new, unconfused by existing plans, which would be designed to bear Britain's share of the fight against Germany and above all would be under his own direct control at the War Office. In launching his recruiting campaign Kitchener aimed, to start with, at one hundred thousand volunteers. The response must have astonished even himself.* The very first week ending on 5 September produced 175,000 men. By the end of that month, three quarters of a million had signed on. Voluntary recruitment lasted until March, 1916, when it became compulsory. In these eighteen months two and a half million men enlisted. How was this New Army to be trained, equipped and prepared for battle? There were many senior military men, who were not only opposed to the idea because it cut into the immediate needs of the B.E.F. in France, but because they believed such new armies could not be effective in the field until far too late. Henry Wilson, now Deputy Chief of Staff with the B.E.F. with a particular duty of liaising with the French, poured scorn on the whole concept, calling Kitchener's 'preposterous and ridiculous army of 25

---

* A.J.P. Taylor reminds us of Rupert Brooke's poem, *Peace*, embodying this response:

> Now, God be thanked Who has matched us with His hour,
> And caught our youth, and wakened us from sleeping.

corps . . . a laughing-stock of every soldier in Europe', pointing out that the Germans had spent forty years raising such an army with conscription thrown in, and now Kitchener proposed to do it in a year or two by voluntary methods. He put his finger closer to what mattered, however, when he wrote:

> Under no circumstances can these mobs now being raised, without officers and NCO's, without guns, rifles, or uniforms, without rifle-ranges or training grounds, without supply or transport services, without *moral* or tradition, knowledge or experience, under no circumstances could these mobs take the field for 2 years.

Yet Kitchener persevered. Desperate diseases had to be relieved by desperate appliances. Improvisation was the order of the day. He kept some 500 officers of the Indian Army who were at home on leave, called back retired officers and non-commissioned officers, made use of what regulars could be purloined from the B.E.F. With these he would be able to instil some of the basic principles of soldiering into his new intakes. While it was true that there were inadequate supplies of rifles, ammunition, clothing and so on, factories would be set up and meanwhile purchase from overseas would supplement what was available and was being produced at home. Barrack accommodation was expanded by making use of buildings not normally allocated for this purpose, empty married quarters were converted, tented and hutted camps created, buildings requisitioned, soldiers were billeted on families, the whole country responded to the exceptional need for recruiting centres and all the clerical and administrative work involved in accepting the huge numbers of volunteers who came forward. As for what Henry Wilson called *moral* (he meant what we now spell morale) one of the most important of all decisions made at this time was not to raise *new* regiments, but to expand the two-battalion regiments which already existed under the Cardwell system. In this way it was possible to build on centuries of military tradition, records of gallantry, comradeship and achievement, sources of regimental devotion to the Colours, a heritage of unfailing pride, spirit and strength.

The speed of organizing all these men into formations was remarkable. As early as the second week of September, 1914, Kitchener's first 100,000 had created six new divisions, which as that distinguished Canadian historian, George H. Cassar, has explained in his brilliant study of Kitchener, were numbered 9th to 14th (the B.E.F. was now composed of eight regular infantry divisions). All in all Kitchener raised thirty new divisions, and no doubt would have raised many more had it not been for his death by drowning when the cruiser *Hampshire* hit a mine off the Orkneys in June, 1916. His achievement was unique, not only in itself, but because he was probably the only man in England who both foresaw the need for these huge armies and had the ability to force such drastic measures through. By the spring of 1915 – thus again proving Henry Wilson wide of the mark – the new divisions of Kitchener's armies were in France and soon afterwards to take their place in the trenches. 'They proved,' writes Professor Cassar, 'as brave and stubborn as British soldiers of any period. They were pitted not against equally improvised formations but against the most highly trained and formidable troops on the Continent. Time and again they returned, after sustaining losses on a scale unparalleled in war, with an ardour and fighting spirit barely diminished, to attack once more. Here was the greatest display of inborn martial qualities that mankind could show.' Bearing all this in mind, Cassar was right to subtitle his biography of Kitchener: *Architect of Victory*. Before we see how both the remnants of the Regular Army and Kitchener's new armies were slaughtered in the pitiless war of attrition to end all wars of attrition, we will turn briefly to see what contributions to the Western Front were being made by the Indian Army.

Two Indian infantry divisions had arrived in France as early as September, 1914. After a month or so of training they were put into the line to relieve II British Corps. Some fought in the Neuve Chapelle sector, others at Ypres. As Philip Mason has so eloquently recorded,* although Indian soldiers were highly trained for war, it was war of a very different sort from the wet, cold and flat country where they now found themselves. Skirmishes, ambushes, the endless sniping and fanatical bravery of the North West Frontier tribesmen – all these were familiar to them. Trench warfare, the mud, continuous damp chill, shells, machine-guns, inadequate weapons, the impossibility of replacing casualties, particularly the British officers who knew them, their language and their ways – all these were bewildering , but did not seem to detract from the sheer fighting qualities of Sikhs, Dogras, Pathans and Punjabi Muslims. 'The devil knows what the English had put into those fellows,' wrote one German soldier in a letter home after enduring an attack on his trenches. 'With a fearful shouting thousands of those brown forms rushed upon us ... At a hundred metres we opened a destructive fire which mowed down hundred but in spite of that the others advanced ... in no time they were in our trenches. ... With butt ends, bayonets, swords and daggers we fought each other and we had bitter hard work.' Perhaps the most remarkable story which Philip Mason tells of this

* *A Matter of Honour*, Jonathan Cape, 1974.

phase in the bitter fighting round Neuve Chapelle and La Bassée concerns the relatively little known Garwhalis, whose 1st and 2nd Battalions were brigaded with the 2nd Leicesters, a brigade which was awarded three out of five Victoria Crosses won by Indian soldiers in France. Everyone who knew them spoke highly of the Garwhal men. Their record was uniformly good, and the Corps Commander under whom they served, General Sir James Willcocks, recalled that their fighting spirit and discipline were such that they all at once won a place of being 'in the very front rank of our best fighting men'. The Commanding Officer of the Leicesters alongside whose Regiment they fought was equally extravagant in his praise. Their morale and prestige were permanently high because they always performed well. Quick to adjust to totally strange conditions, there were times when they saw even more quickly than their British counterparts what sort of tactics were required to recapture trenches taken by the Germans. Eschewing a frontal attack which he rightly judged would simply mean mounting casualties, their Commanding Officer chose a flank attack, and 'bombed their way along the whole length, capturing over a hundred prisoners, and this became the standard practice'. One of their junior N.C.O.s, Naik Darwan Sing Negi, although wounded three times and covered in blood, persevered until the attack was over. He was awarded the V.C. All this was taking place during the early days of trench fighting in October and November, 1914, before the front stabilised. The Garwhalis were to distinguish themselves again in March, 1915, when the first great British offensive of the war was launched at Neuve Chapelle, but before we see what happened both to them and to the 2nd Scottish Rifles, whom we met earlier at their peace-time station in Malta, we must see how it came about that Sir John French, still in command of the B.E.F. at this time, decided to go over to the offensive at all.

The real trouble facing the British as 1914 ended and 1915 began was that no one had any clear idea as to what was to be done to defeat the Germans. The French might be anxious to liberate national territory, but Kitchener believed the German defensive lines to be impregnable to frontal assault. There were innumerable suggestions about using British sea power in an indirect approach which might obtain a foothold here and there (in the next chapter we examine how tenuous and tragic the Gallipoli* foothold turned out to be), but could hardly seek decision with the bulk of the German Army. In the end it was not the result of any grand strategic plan that Haig's 1st Army attacked at Neuve Chapelle; it was done in order to gratify both French's and Haig's desire to justify

---

* Turkey had entered the war on Germany's side in October, 1914.

their own positions, to show their French allies they were doing something, and to bring off a tactical coup.

Field-Marshal Sir John French wanted the bulk of Kitchener's new armies to be put under his command. Not only would this greatly enhance his own importance, but he believed – and in this respect he was right – that the decisive theatre for the employment of British military strength would be northern France. In order to bring about what he desired, however, and sure of his subordinates' support, he had to do something. In February, 1915, he noted that 'a vigorous offensive movement by the forces under my command should be planned and carried out at the earliest possible moment'. Conveniently for him, but not, as it transpired, for the soldiers required to launch it, Haig had already worked out a plan to attack the German positions at Neuve Chapelle. French adopted it. There were some favourable circumstances which justified a degree of optimism on Haig's part. But, as so often in the future, promise was not fulfilled by performance. Haig's advantage in numbers was enormous. This was made plain by 1st Army's Special Order of the Day dated 9 March, 1915, which announced that 48 battalions were going to attack a German position held by a mere three battalions. Moreover this position formed a salient sticking out towards the British lines, with flimsy entrenchments and a mere dozen machine-guns, and, perhaps most significant of all, any substantial German reserves would be unlikely to make their presence felt for about 48 hours after the initial assault.

We will not follow the dreadful catalogue of mistakes and missed opportunities which marred the whole operation. It is enough to say that the British broke through the German lines, but before the follow-up battalions could exploit this initial success, the Germans had blocked the gap. In *The Donkeys*, Alan Clark describes the events of 10 March, 1915, as being of special interest historically simply because it was one of the very few occasions when a proper hole was made in the German defensive line (Loos in September, 1915, and Cambrai in November, 1917, were the only two others), but ' the complete failure to exploit it in a vigorous and urgent fashion was due to concern – which may well be felt to have been unwarranted – at two checks which had been administered on the extreme flanks of the break-through'. Clark goes on to explain that on the left of the enemy salient, that is the northern sector, two particular German machine-gun positions had not been neutralized because of a blunder in the artillery programme, so that when it was assaulted by the 2nd Battalion, the Middlesex Regiment, they ran into sustained fire which literally wiped out the battalion. On their right were our friends in the 2nd Scottish Rifles who suffered from flanking fire almost as badly. John Baynes has described in terrible detail what it had been like for those who took part:

> Nobody had seen the ground over which they were advancing. A few officers had seen the short stretch up to the first hedge, but none had seen further than that. The officers had seen air photographs and made sketch-maps before the attack, and had undoubtedly briefed their men as well as they could. But by 9.30 a.m. practically every officer had been killed or wounded, and the N.C.O.s who took their place had to go on memory. ... Added to this was the difficulty of not knowing what had happened to other members of the battalion, nor to the flanking battalions. ... The general noise, the constant sound of rifle and machine-gun fire from all sides, and the sudden bursts of shells, were all upsetting to those trying to struggle across the slippery, icy fields. Worse than all this was the shock of seeing so many others killed and wounded ... just as they needed directions and encouragement more than ever before these men of the 2nd Scottish Rifles did not know where to turn. Time and again the pattern of command changed as officers and N.C.O.s were killed. The extraordinary thing is that in spite of all these elements of chaos the attack continued and retained a certain cohesion.

John Baynes continues with his account of the battalion's action, pointing out that at 9.30 a.m. that morning by which time most, but by no means all of the grievously numerous casualties had been inflicted, there must have been as many as four hundred killed and wounded soldiers lying in a space not more than 200 yards by 100. He adds that great imagination is needed to form a picture of such slaughter. No one depicted the horror and futility of trench warfare better than Siegfried Sassoon, and although his poem *Counter-Attack* was written of a different battle, we may try to fill this gap in our imagination here and now:

> The place was rotten with dead; green clumsy legs
> High-booted, sprawled and grovelled along the saps;
> And trunks, face downward, in the sucking mud,
> Wallowed like trodden sandbags loosely filled;
> And naked sodden buttocks, mats of hair,
> Bulged, clotted heads slept in the plastering slime.

What was left of the 2nd Scottish Rifles went on. Further advances, more casualties, consolidation in a former British trench and 'Ruined House', sergeants in command of companies, some hot food, perhaps three hundred men left of the 700 or so who went over the top that morning. While the British High Command reinforced failure, but failed to exploit success, the soldiers of the Scottish Rifles endured four more days of it before they were relieved. In command, the only officer left who had not been killed or wounded, was Second-Lieutenant Somervail; the splendid R.S.M. Chalmers had survived it all; and one hundred and forty-three others. The whole operation had been a fiasco, except for the courage and high morale of the soldiers. At the cost of some 600 officers and over 12,000 men, the British Army had captured a useless shattered salient about two miles wide and a little more than half a mile deep.

The comment made on it by Haig's intelligence officer, Charteris, was that it had made the French think highly of our Army. The comment made much later by Liddell Hart, who himself suffered in the Great War, was that the British High Command totally failed to see the lessons of Neuve Chapelle – first, that the narrower the front was on which an attack was made, the easier it would be for the Germans to concentrate against and close it; second, that it was not the length and volume of artillery bombardment which mattered so much as the speed with which it was followed up by the infantry, together with the absolutely overriding need for maintenance of momentum once any sort of breach of the enemy's defences had been made. But the mistakes made at Neuve Chapelle were to be repeated time after time. How did the British Army put up with it? I can reply in three words, endurance, performance and perseverance owed their origin and their survival to the *the regimental system*. As John Baynes puts it: 'The front-line soldier in a good infantry battalion in 1915 was primarily concerned with getting on with his job of defeating the Germans, and had little time to indulge in reflections on the ultimate value of what he was doing. In his mind the Germans were going to be defeated by his own battalion; whether Devons, Middlesex, Scottish Rifles or what you will. Some of the officers might discuss occasionally the competence or otherwise of higher formations and Generals, but all their real interest was centred on the battalion. The biggest thing of all was that the battalion should do well; this bound all ranks together as nothing else could.' How wholly this sentiment was reflected by the Garwhalis, whom we met earlier, by their performance during the Neuve Chapelle action. The 2nd Battalion took their objectives in a style immortalized by Rifleman Gobar Sing Negi, who, having taken command of his platoon when its commander was killed, went on to lead his men into trench after trench with bomb and bayonet. His posthumous V.C. was the third of the five awarded to the Indian Army in France.

The sheer vacancy of the British High Command's mind is admirably demonstrated by the *Official History's* comment that, despite the failure of Neuve Chapelle, all the senior commanders agreed that for the next offensive, undertaken in cooperation with the French Army against Aubers Ridge in May, 1915 [by which time German use of poison gas had added to the dangers and burdens to which Thomas Atkins was subjected], the tactics would be the same all over again, 'but much more successful because we have learnt its lesson and shall know what to avoid this time'. But they had not learned anything, and the German Chief of General Staff, Falkenhayn, while acknowledging the bravery and endurance of British troops, was confident that they could achieve nothing decisive against the German Army because they 'have proved so clumsy in action'. Yet Allied military doctrine stuck to the absurd notion that attrition was the key to success. The attack at Aubers might have failed with heavy losses. No matter! They would plan another attack. This time Kitchener himself must bear some of the responsibility, for although in July, 1915, he had complained to Robertson (C.I.G.S. 1915–1918) that all the assurances of Joffre and Sir John French about pushing the Germans back by their attacks earlier that year had resulted in heavy losses and no gains, by August he held a different view. The failure of the Dardanelles campaign (which we look at in the next chapter) and the reversals suffered by Russia had persuaded even Kitchener that more had to be done to help the French, even if it meant further risk of heavy infantry casualties. The battle of Loos on 25 and 26 September started with an assault by the 1st Division (the British offensive was in general support of Joffre's attacks in Champagne and Artois where the French Army in all suffered one and a half million casualties), and, like so many other similar operations, it met with initial success in penetrating the first lines of German trenches, followed by failure to exploit quickly, exhaustion, mounting losses, deadlock. It was a familiar pattern, and once again showed that once the first momentum of an attack had faltered, as falter it always did as soon as the Germans realized what was happening and took appropriate countermeasures, any renewal of the attack, that is to say a reinforcement of failure, simply resulted in more and more losses with nothing to show for them. So it was at Loos, and we may now take a look at the second day when for the first time two Divisions, 21st and 24th, of Kitchener's New Armies went into action. They were required to assault the so-called German 'Second Position' which was astride two villages and a Hill 70 Redoubt, giving the German machine-gunners the overwhelming advantage of enfilade, that is flanking, cross-fire across the Loos valley itself.

It was, as Alan Clark wrote, like the Charge of the Light Brigade all over again, although in much slower time and a hundred times worse. After a wholly inadequate artillery programme which inflicted no damage on the Germans at all, thousands of British infantrymen, massed

together, advanced across open country towards the intact defences of
the German lines. The German machine-gunners waited until the
advancing infantry were about a thousand yards away, and then opened
fire. Never before, one German regimental diary recorded, had there
been such a target. Never before had the machine-guns done their work
so effectively. The entire field in front of them was covered with enemy
soldiers deliberately moving towards them in ten columns, each in
extended line, and the Germans simply raked these columns with such
appalling effect that the dead and wounded went down hundreds at a
time. Yet some came right up to the wire entanglements, which were
too strong to be cut and too high and wide to be climbed. Another
German war diary noted that the English advanced as if it were a field-
day manoeuvre, but the flanking machine-gun fire and artillery shells
riddled the ranks and destroyed complete battalions. The whole affair
lasted three and a half hours until at length, despite incredible courage
and perseverance, having endured terrible losses (of the roughly ten
thousand soldiers in the attack, 385 officers and 7,861 men were lost),
the pitiful survivors made their way back to their own trenches. The
Germans called the battlefield *Leichenfeld von Loos* – the field of corpses –
and as the remnants crawled or stumbled back 'no shot was fired at
them from the German trenches for the rest of the day, so great was the
feeling of compassion and mercy for the enemy after such a victory'.
Yet the spirit of Kitchener's volunteers for his New Army was such that
when the Corps Commander, General Haking, visited the survivors and
asked what had gone wrong, he received the astonishing reply that they
would do better next time. If, after nearly a year of trench warfare, this
was the best the British Army's generals could do, there would not be
many next times to conjure with. In 1916 and 1917, however, as we
shall see, the generals became even more profligate with the lives of the
gentlemen in khaki.

Of course, it was not always like the carnage of Loos for those British
soldiers who manned the trenches. A special correspondent from *The
Times*, who visited the front lines shortly beforehand, wrote of 'trench
staleness' and of the need for literature to cure 'mind-rust induced by
monotony':

The world war in the West has become a parish pump war. The business of
war today is the most infinitely complicated business in the world, and just
as in a highly specialised manufactory the individual workman may spend
his whole life upon one particular piece of work and never gain any comprehensive knowledge of the whole process necessary to the completion of
the finished manufacture, so the overwhelming majority of our soldiers, both

officers and privates, are limited to a comparatively narrow round of routine work.

This, of course, has been true to a very great extent of all modern warfare, but it is especially true of our months-long war of positions. A battalion may march from billets to the trenches and from the trenches back again to the billets many times in succession without ever being called upon to take part in any more active operations. For weeks together the private soldier's view of the countryside may be limited to the sandbagged trench he is occupying, so much of the German parapets and the intervening barbed wire entanglements as can be seen through a periscope, the sun-baked sides of the communication trenches, and the relatively restricted area into which he is periodically withdrawn to rest.

Just so! 'Three quarters of a soldier's life,' said Rosenstock-Huessy, 'is spent in aimlessly waiting about.' Better that, however, than indulging in the sort of offensive, mounted entirely to please the French, that Kitchener's New Army had undertaken at Loos. The battle which lasted until mid-October cost the British 50,000 casualties in all, and it cost Sir John French his job. Haig had long been intriguing against him, and in December replaced him. With Haig as Commander-in-Chief of the British Army in France and Robertson as C.I.G.S. – and Robertson had made it a condition of his accepting the appointment that *he* would determine strategy and decide how to conduct the war – it was clear that these men would see to it that the main theatre of war would be France and therefore it would be in France that the bulk of the British Army would fight. All this greatly weakened Kitchener's position, which had already been gravely damaged by dithering over the Dardanelles campaign. Another casualty of this ill-fated attempt to turn the Central Powers' flank was its most ardent advocate, Winston Churchill, who resigned as First Lord of the Admiralty in November, 1915 and then sought solace by commanding a battalion in the trenches, where we will visit him shortly.

The new year brought about another great change for the Army. In January, 1916, Asquith gave in to political pressure for the introduction of conscription and the Military Service Act was passed. As A.J.P.Taylor has so forcibly pointed out this measure did not at once increase the number of men available for military service. Rather it reduced this number, for whereas those working in essential jobs like manufacturing munitions and mining coal could not be prevented from volunteering, they could not be conscripted. It had been thought that between six and seven hundred thousand so-called 'slackers' would be rounded up for compulsory service. The authorities found instead that about three-quarters of a million men claimed exemption on one ground or another. It would not be until the battles of 1917 that the huge numbers of conscripted men would make their presence felt, but by the summer of 1916 the volunteers who had responded to Kitchener's* call had built up Haig's army to a total of almost sixty divisions, enough for Haig, who believed that if sufficient weight of artillery were applied, a hole really would be made in the German defences, allowing the infantry to follow on and clear up, leaving it to the cavalry – this was a cherished* dream of Haig's – to break through and crack about in open country. It was going to be the first really 'big push' by the British Army, and in Haig's view perhaps the last, as he had succeeded in convincing himself that a major offensive could win the war. The place eventually chosen for this battle was – the Somme!

In spite of Robertson's intentions that he would call the strategic tune, in fact it was Joffre who did so, and he wanted the attack to be a joint operation involving both armies and therefore at the junction of the two, the Somme. Haig would have preferred an attack in the north where there was at least some possibility of turning the flank of the German defences. No such opportunity offered itself where the British and French armies joined hands.

The Somme offensive was an unmitigated disaster. Haig's tactics were based on a totally false conception – moreover one that had already been shown as false by previous offensives – that is to say a prolonged and powerful artillery bombardment would so destroy the German defences and defenders that it 'would leave nothing alive', so allowing the infantry to follow up and capture their objectives without a fight. In fact even after a week of pounding, the artillery shells did not even cut the German wire, had no effect whatever on the deep dugouts occupied by the German machine-gunners, and simply provided them with additional craters to which they deployed when the guns lifted, and so found themselves admirably placed to deal with the slowly advancing British infantry, mowing down line after line. It was on the first day of the battle, 1 July, 1916, that the British Army suffered more casualties in one day than it ever had before, nearly 60,000 in all, of which one-third were killed. A padre at a Casualty Clearing Station noted in his diary for that day:

---

* Kitchener was drowned on 5 June, 1916, when the *Hampshire* hit a mine, giving rise to Lord Northcliffe's comment that Providence was after all on the side of the British Empire. Lloyd George became Secretary for War on 4 July, three days after the battle of the Somme began.

We got back for a late breakfast and soon the wounded by German shells came in, then all day long cars of dying and wounded, but all cheerful for they told us of a day of glorious successes. They are literally piled up – beds gone, lucky to get space on floor of tent, hut or ward, and though the surgeons work like Trojans many must yet die for lack of operation. . . . We have 1,500 in and still they come, 300–400 officers, it is a sight – chaps with fearful wounds lying in agony, many so patient, some make a noise, one goes to a stretcher, lays one's hand on the forehead, it is cold, strike a match, he is dead.

After two days of it, the padre records:

Now I know something of the horrors of war, the staff is redoubled but what of that, imagine 1,000 badly wounded *per diem* . . . Oh, if you could see our wards, tents, huts, crammed with terrible wounds – see the rows of abdominals and lung penetrations dying . . . in strict confidence, please, I got hold of some morphia and I go back to that black hole of Calcutta and use it or I creep into the long tents where two or three hundred Germans lie, you can imagine what attention they get with our own neglected, the cries and groans are too much to withstand and I cannot feel less pity for them than for our own.

Thirteen British divisions had gone 'over the top' on that first day and for the 60,000 casualties had perhaps gained a mile of strategically useless ground. Yet Haig persisted. Another major assault was mounted at dawn on 14 July. The same futile tactics were employed. The German machine-gunners were again enabled to spray targets which were impossible to miss. Even when some of the leading German trenches were overrun, the success was not exploited. The German counteraction simply meant that wave after wave of British infantrymen were slaughtered and the few survivors were back in the trenches they had left that morning by early afternoon. It seemed to be an unchanging pattern, in A.J.P. Taylor's phrase: 'brave, helpless soldiers, blundering obstinate generals; nothing achieved'. But Haig would not give up.

    In September he even tried using the new tanks, but on far too small a scale to have any effect, other than to throw away the benefit of surprise which their employment in mass might have had in contributing to a real breakthrough and a decisive victory. By mid-November, at a total gain of some five miles, when the Allied losses totalled more than 600,000 [420,000 British, 200,000 French] and some 450,000 German casualties had been inflicted, the whole thing had bogged down in mud. Kitchener's New Army had been virtually destroyed. 'Not only men perished,' wrote A.J.P. Taylor. 'There perished also the zest and idealism

with which nearly three million Englishmen had marched forth to war.'
In reviewing Tim Travers's book *The Killing Ground*, Brian Bond sums
up the total lack of harmony between the High Command who made
the plans and those required to carry them out:

> The whole chain of command proved too cumbersome to take advantage of
> the fleeting opportunities that did occur, for example at Montauban on July
> 1. Too often the front line units were given impossible tasks against uncut
> wire and machine-guns, their protests ignored and their commanders made
> scapegoats after costly failure. . . . After the initial failures, Haig and G.H.Q.
> could think of no alternative but repeated attacks against the German lines
> in the hope that the enemy's reserves would be exhausted and his morale
> would crumble . . . what was really needed was a fundamental change in
> strategy and tactics.

One of those who condemned Haig's premature and abortive use of
tanks was Winston Churchill. 'The ruthless desire for a decision at all
costs,' he wrote, 'led in September to a most improvident disclosure of
the caterpillar vehicles.' Churchill had never been slow in coming
forward with powerful advice on tactical and strategic matters, and six
weeks *before* the Somme offensive started, he had warned the House of
Commons about the dangers of such futile waste. He had by this time
served on the Western Front himself as a battalion commander and had
written to his mother describing his feelings:

> Commanding a battalion is like being captain of a ship. It is a vy searching
> test and a severe burden. Especially so when all the officers are young & only
> soldiers of a few months standing: & when a hundred yards away lies the
> line of the German army with all its devilments & dodges. One would not
> have thought it possible a year ago to put a battalion thus composed in the
> line. But they will give a good account of themselves & no part of the front
> will be better guarded.

Churchill proved a brave and successful Commanding Officer of the 6th
Battalion, The Royal Scots Fusiliers, while making sure that his supplies
from home [he asked his wife to send stilton cheeses, hams, sardines,
beef steak pie and other things, signing himself 'Your loving and
devoted – greedy though I fear you will say, W.'] were adequate. Some
of his brother officers deplored the nerve-racking experiences of going
into no-man's land with him. 'He was like a baby elephant out in no-
man's land at night,' wrote Hakewill Smith. 'He never fell when a shell
went off; he never ducked when a bullet went past with its loud crack.
He used to say after watching me duck: "It's no damn use ducking; the
bullet has gone a long way past you now".' Churchill was determined

to share his men's dangers, make them feel he was with them in everything, stimulate their courage and never let them down. He had plenty of narrow escapes, he even commanded his brigade for a time when the Brigadier General was away, and was highly critical of the Army's administration, which in his view totally lacked drive. The sacrifice of brave and conscientious infantry soldiers would, he argued, never be adequate for fighting a war which depended on brain-power and mechanical devices. He felt deeply for his men, forced to live in the trenches under such harsh conditions, exposed to needless death, in danger of being worn down by despair. He did all he could to lighten their burden, and reserved his anger for those in authority. In a phrase reminiscent of King Lear* he wrote to his wife: 'By God I wd make them skip if I had the power – even for a month.' His mind was never far from his great longing to return to politics. He urged his wife to keep in touch with Lloyd George, whom he saw as the key to his own future position. The amalgamation of the 6th and 7th Battalion of the Royal Scots Fusiliers seemed a sensible time to leave the trenches, as his own command disappeared. Even though offered a brigade by Haig, he strongly felt that he could do most for the war effort by returning to Parliament. His proper war station was there. When he left the Battalion in May, 1916, the Adjutant, speaking for all the officers, made plain what it had meant to them all to serve under his command and how they regarded his going as a personal loss. Yet Churchill's return to England did not herald an instant revival of his political fortunes. In regarding Lloyd George as a key figure for the future, however, he was not wide of the mark.

The great political issue of the day was, of course, conduct of the war. Churchill, back in the House of Commons in May, 1916, was foremost in condemning premature offensives in France:

> Many of our difficulties in the West at the present time spring from the unfortunate offensive to which we committed ourselves last autumn. . . . Only think if we had kept that tremendous effort ever accumulating for the true tactical moment. . . . Might we not then have recovered at a stroke the strategic initiative without which victory lags long on the road? Let us not repeat that error. Do not let us be drawn into any course of action not justified by purely military considerations. The argument which is used that 'it is our turn now' has no place in military thought.

Yet these arguments had prevailed, and Haig, full of confidence, had

---

* I have seen the day, with my good biting falchion,
I would have made them skip.

destroyed the best part of Kitchener's New Army on the Somme. Lloyd George, having taken office as War Minister just after the Somme offensive began, and anxious to enjoy credit for its success, was even as late as August and September, 1916, still championing Haig and Robertson. But when it all went wrong he was foremost in turning against them. How to do better? That was the question, and Lloyd George thought he had the answer – a War Council of three with himself in charge. All this led to such a controversy between Bonar Law (leader of the Unionist, i.e. Conservative, Party), Cecil, Chamberlain and Curzon on the one hand, and Asquith on the other that both Lloyd George and Asquith resigned, and, as subsequently Asquith refused to serve under Bonar Law, it was Lloyd George who in December, 1916, became Prime Minister, heading a coalition government and forming his own war cabinet – himself, Bonar Law, Henderson (Labour leader), Curzon and Milner. There was no place for Churchill. Indeed one of the conditions of the Unionists' joining the government was that Churchill should be excluded. Another one was that Haig should remain as Commander-in-Chief in France.

One of the great contributions which Lloyd George made in the strategic running of the war was his insistence in April, 1917, against the wishes of Carson, First Lord of the Admiralty, and Jellicoe, First Sea Lord, on introducing the convoy system. The difference it made was dramatic. Instead of 25 per cent of shipping being lost to U-boats before convoys started, only one per cent were lost from all causes. In winning this battle with the Admiralty, Lloyd George had engaged in violent conflict with the Admirals. He did not wish to indulge in a similar confrontation with the Generals, so that when Haig unfolded one more plan for winning the war, a gigantic offensive in Flanders designed to break out of the Ypres salient, advance to the Belgian coast, outflanking and rolling up the German defences, despite his misgivings, Lloyd George was persuaded by the joint compliance of Smuts (now a member of the War Cabinet), Curzon, Bonar Law and even Robertson, the C.I.G.S. (despite his private doubts), to allow Haig to have his way. Apart from the total unsuitability of the Flanders plain for an operation of this size, a place which was mainly renowned for past failures and which rain and heavy bombardments would simply turn into an impassable sea of mud – all this apart, no one, least of all Haig, had yet devised a formula which would guarantee an initial breakthrough of the German defences, upon which everything else depended*. So on the last day of

---

* Although at Vimy Ridge in April 1917 the Canadians had shown how to capture an objective with precision and certainty.

July, 1917, began the tragic and futile third battle of Ypres, known better as Passchendaele, a relatively unimportant objective in the latter stages of the battle. The battle lasted in all about three months. Floundering through seas of mud the British Army succeeded in gaining some four miles of tactically useless ground which rendered the salient more vulnerable than ever. Official figures as to British losses vary according to source from 250,000 to 324,000. Germans, of course, were killed too, but for every two German soldiers that died, the cost had been three British.

The tragedy of Passchendaele has been quite unforgettably re-depicted by Lyn Macdonald*, who in an article in *The Times* published in 1987, seventy years after the battle, summarised the grand sweep of its design and the appalling horror of its reality. The tiny and shattered village of Passchendaele was in itself insignificant. It simply happened like many other places to overlook the Ypres salient in British hands and therefore became an objective. Its capture was the futile climax of a three-months-old battle, whose purpose had been to push some thirteen miles beyond the Ypres salient, take Antwerp and Zeebrugge from the rear, and by totally outflanking the German Army's position in Belgium, roll it up and force the Germans back to the Rhine. Passchendaele itself was to be taken within a day or two. In the event it took a hundred days less a few hours, and by the time it had been taken, the butcher's bill totalled a quarter of a million casualties, and the whole purpose of the operation had long been forfeited. The fact is that the German defences were well nigh impregnable, with row after row of concrete pillboxes housing machine-gun emplacements. Lyn Macdonald explains that the two-week long preparatory bombardment simply churned the land over which the troops had to advance into a kind of bogland of craters and little mounds. This part of Flanders was, in any case, reclaimed bog. Even before the rains started – and from the beginning of August onwards it rained more or less continuously – the soldiers were being asked to advance through liquid mud. Lyn Macdonald writes:

> The attack was launched at dawn on July 31. After the capture of the first thinly held outpost lines, floundering forward into machine-gun fire that spat from the slits of a thousand concrete strongholds, the troops were shocked to discover that they were storming a citadel.

The deaths were not all caused by enemy fire. Soldiers who fought the battle remembered that all around them were nothing but dead bodies and exploding shells and flying bullets. The only refuge was a shell-

---

* *They Called it Passchendaele*, pub. Michael Joseph, 1987.

hole, and here as likely as not another and even more terrible death awaited them. They would sink up to the shoulders in the mud, impossible to rescue. One man of the Suffolks pleaded with those coming to his rescue to shoot him. 'The more we pulled and the more he struggled the further he seemed to go down. He went down gradually. He kept begging us to shoot him. But we couldn't shoot him. Who could shoot him? We stayed with him, watching him go down in the mud.' And for what? For Passchendaele? Lyn Macdonald goes on:

> There at least, the planners reckoned, the troops could stand on higher, drier ground for the winter and would be poised to advance for the breakthrough in the spring. To the tank crews bogged down in the swamp, to the infantry slogging inch by inch up the grisly ridges, to the gunners labouring to drag the guns forward through the slough, to the signallers struggling to lay the wires that were cut to pieces as quickly as they spooled them out, even Passchendaele a mile or so away seemed as unattainable as the mountains of the moon. For the rest of their lives the men who came out of the battle remembered it with horror.

This was the place they called Passchendaele, and despite later on in November an unexpected breakthrough by the Royal Tank Corps at Cambrai, this time using their tanks *en masse* – so unexpected in fact that no arrangements to exploit success had been made (and all the ground gained was soon recaptured by the Germans) – Haig's war-ending offensive of 1917 had resulted in total failure. Before long it would be the German's turn to attack with very different consequences and some severe shocks for the Allies. We may perhaps note before turning to this that by the time of Haig's abortive third battle of Ypres, it was clear that Churchill had backed the right horse. In July, 1917, Lloyd George had asked him to rejoin the Government as Minister of Munitions.

The war still had one year to run. Earlier in 1917 there had been some events of enormous strategic moment. In March, 1917, the Russian revolution had more or less removed the Eastern threat to Germany. In April another but more distant threat appeared when the United States declared war on Germany. And of profound importance to the British conduct of war, then and in the future, in October, 1917, Trenchard created the Royal Air Force and the myth – which cost us dear in the second war with Germany – that air power could by itself win wars. At the beginning of 1918 Haig demanded another 600,000 men. For the time being he got 60,000 – higher priority being given to the other armed services, the merchant fleet, mining and war production. He thereupon longed to milk the huge British armies in the Middle East, whose campaigns in Turkey, Mesopotamia and Palestine we will examine shortly. In February, 1918, Lloyd George at last got rid of Robertson and Wilson was appointed C.I.G.S. in his place. Haig remained at his post, and was shortly to have much to think about, as, on 21 March, Ludendorff launched the great German offensive designed to divide the French and British armies and seize the Channel ports. He succeeded in neither objective but Haig's Special Order of the Day, 13 April, showed how serious the situation was. The British Army had been driven back forty miles in disarray and actually faced defeat. It was addressed to All Ranks of the British Army in France and Flanders:

> There is no other course open to us but to fight it out. Every position must be held to the last man: there must be no retirement. With our backs to the wall, and believing in the justice of our cause, each one of us must fight on to the end. The safety of our homes and the freedom of mankind depend alike upon the conduct of each one of us at this critical moment.

Foch was appointed Commander-in-Chief of the Allied Armies, Haig's Army was reinforced to the tune of half a million men, some from the Middle East, some from home, the American contingents were rapidly building up to some thirty divisions, and by July the German effort was exhausted. Thereafter the initiative passed once more to the Allies, never again to be forfeited. In August and September they were attacking all along the line. Moreover, the Central Powers were helpless to stem events in the Balkans and in Syria. Ludendorff, who by this time wielded virtually supreme power in Germany, insisted on the German Government's seeking an armistice. On 23 October Germany accepted President Wilson's Fourteen Points. A week later Turkey surrendered. On 3 November Austria-Hungary did the same. Four days after that the German armistice delegation asked Foch in the famous railway carriage at Rethondes for an armistice and the terms were made known to them. On 9 November Kaiser Wilhelm II took refuge in Holland and abdicated. On 11 November the armistice was signed. Winston Churchill's Regiment, the 4th Hussars, had been in France and Flanders throughout the war, and its Commanding Officer, Lieutenant-Colonel Laing, recalled the comment made by some of his Old Contemptibles when the Armistice was announced: 'There was nothing in the way of cheering or any demonstration. The men merely dismounted and sat on the side of the road, and pulling out a cigarette proceeded to light it.' The only comment they made, said Laing, was : 'Well thank God that's over.' Another more ominous comment, however, had been made by a battalion runner in the List Regiment when he heard the news of Germany's surrender in hospital: 'Everything went black before my eyes

as I staggered back to my ward. . . . The following days were terrible to
bear and the nights still worse. . . . During these nights my hatred
increased, hatred for the originators of this dastardly crime.' As Chancellor of the Third Reich and Supreme Commander of the Wehrmacht,
the former List Regiment *Meldegänger* Adolf Hitler was to indulge his
hatred to the full.

During this war to end war the British Army had expanded from a
small all-volunteer force of less than quarter of a million (excluding the
Indian Army and other Dominion and Colonial forces) to one of millions
of both volunteers and conscripted men. Nearly one million had been
killed; a further two million had been wounded, and as far as France
and Flanders went, the Army had been required to indulge in an
unending series of costly and usually disastrous attacks. The British had
certainly fought like lions, and they had certainly been led by donkeys.
Yet attrition had in the end won the day. It does little to justify the
ways of the generals to the men under their command. One of the most
telling indictments of the British High Command was levelled at them
by a Canadian soldier, W.G. Smith, who became a battery sergeant-
major and who is quoted by Alexander McKee in his excellent study of
Vimy Ridge. 'The battle arrangements were purely criminal,' he wrote,
'time and again perpetually the same mistakes. Butchering the poor
bloody infantry and knocking the light artillery to pieces. The generals
could be excused for First Ypres, Loos or Givenchy, they had to learn
their trade, the same as we did, but to continually repeat those mistakes
stamps them as fools who should have been court-martialled, not honoured.' Mr Smith went on to say (and here he echoes Winston Churchill's
despairing doubt that the British soldiers in Singapore and Tobruk in
1942 'won't fight') that 'You cannot kill 700,000 stallions of the best
breed, out of a small country, and then expect the nation to hold up. . . .
Haig and his commanders dissipated and destroyed the finest army
Great Britain ever did, or ever will, put into the field. The army of 1918
was not a shadow of the army of 1916. I believe this deterioration was
shown in the mass surrenders of Burma, Singapore, Tobruk. I think
our people of 1914–1918 would not have quit so easily. It seems to
represent lack of faith in leadership – or maybe the young men of 1940
were smarter than we were; they would not die needlessly.'

These sentiments are in great contrast to what Jeanne MacKenzie has
to say in her book sub-titled *A Tragedy of the First World War** in
which she traces the lives and deaths of eight young men:

---

* *The Children of The Souls*, Chatto & Windus, 1986.

Brought up at the end of one century in the belief that they had a vocation of leadership in the next, the children of the Souls exemplified the attitudes of a generation that volunteered in the wave of euphoric patriotism that swept over Britain in the summer of 1914 – and sent the entire subaltern class to its death. What made them go with songs to the battle, and bear its horrors with unexamined stoicism, was a profound belief that the gentlemanly values were still the values of chivalry, that there were such things as debts of honour and that they had to be paid, and that no man had the right to ask another to do something he would not give the lead in doing himself.

One of these young men was the Prime Minister's son, Raymond Asquith, an officer with the Grenadier Guards who in June, 1916, wrote to Diana Manners (who later married Duff Cooper) from the trenches in France:

I have lived for a week almost entirely in muck... the most accursed unholy and abominable place I have ever seen, the ugliest, filthiest most fetid and most desolate – a wood where all the trees had been cut off by shells the week before and nothing remained but black stumps of the most obscene height and thickness – craters swimming in blood and dirt, rotting and swelling bodies and rats like shadows fattened for the market moving cunningly and liquorishly among them, limbs and bowels nesting in the hedges and over all the most supernaturally shocking scent of death and corruption that ever breathed o'er Eden. The place simply stank of sin.

Raymond Asquith was killed in action with the 3rd Grenadier Guards on 15 September, 1916. Some of his friends faced death elsewhere – notably in Gallipoli.

9

WAR AGAINST ISLAM

Oh Muslims! Embrace ye the foot of the Caliph's throne and join in the *jihad*, the Holy War. Warfare is ordained for you. Your enemies will not cease until they have made you renegades from your religion if they can. Drive them out! If they attack you, slay them! Such is the reward of unbelievers.

SULTAN MEHMED V November, 1914

It has all too frequently been the case that the British, when taking on some huge Continental armies, have put their faith in sea power, and rather than emulate those European nations whose sole idea of strategy was the massed attack – and in any event initially lacking the means for such emulation – have sought instead the open flank. In November, 1914, when deadlock on the Western Front had already laid its puzzling restraints on British strategists, who at all costs wished to avoid wasting millions of lives recapturing French territory (but nevertheless, as we have seen, went on to do so) and when Turkey had entered the war on Germany's side, once more the appeal of the so-called indirect approach to these strategy makers was strong. 'They sought a field of action,' wrote A.J.P. Taylor, 'where the Germans could not get at them, and forgot that then they would not be able to get at the Germans. If this field of action were outside Europe, so much the better: it would bring territorial gains for the British Empire.' In short, decision on the Continent would be pursued in theatres far distant from the Continent, if possible against an inferior foe and with all the enormous advantages offered by sea power in the way of choosing time, place and concentration of effort. During a meeting of the newly formed War Council on 25 November, Maurice Hankey, the Secretary, noted the views of the First Lord of the Admiralty on the dangers presented by a large Turkish Army which was moving south through Palestine and would before long be poised to mount an attack on the Suez Canal:

> MR CHURCHILL suggested that the ideal method of defending Egypt was by an attack on the Gallipoli Peninsula. This, if successful, would give us control of the Dardanelles, and we could dictate terms at Constantinople. This, however, was a very difficult operation requiring a large force.

Russia's plight after her armies' defeat at Tannenberg was an added reason for intervention against Turkey, as the Russian Commander-in-Chief, Grand Duke Nicholas, had appealed to the Allies for assistance in their struggle with Turkey, but it was not until January, 1915, that the War Council made up its mind to mount an attack on the Dardanelles and even then it was initially to be done without the participation of the British Army.

It came about like this. On 1 January, 1915, the British Ambassador in Petrograd, Sir George Buchanan, had telegraphed to the Foreign Secretary, Grey, relaying the Grand Duke's request that some sort of demonstration against the Turks, whether naval or military, should be made in order to draw off some of the Turkish forces operating in the Caucasus and so ease the Russians' position. Grey consulted Kitchener, who in turn consulted Churchill, asking if a *naval* demonstration could be made at the Dardanelles, because 'We have no troops to land anywhere,' and 'We shall not be ready for anything big for months'. Thereupon Churchill signalled on 3 January to Vice-Admiral Carden, commanding the R.N. squadron blockading the Dardanelles, and asked whether it would be practicable to force the Dardanelles 'by ships alone', if necessary using old battleships and in view of the strategic stakes accepting serious losses. Carden's reply, received on 5 January, stated that, whereas he did not believe the Dardanelles could be rushed, he did consider that by using large numbers of ships and extended action they might be forced. After further consultation Churchill telegraphed to Carden again next day asking for details of what force would be needed and how it would carry out the operation.

Before a reply was received deliberations by the War Council had revealed other important views – first, Sir John French's belief that the German defences in France were impenetrable, yet that no attempts should be made in other theatres until the impossibility of a break-through on the Western Front had been further proved. Kitchener, however, still had his eye on the Dardanelles, with its potential for establishing communication with Russia and bringing in some of the Balkan powers against Germany. In response to Hankey's contention that, by successfully breaching the Dardanelles, sea power could make itself felt in Central Europe by advancing an army along the Danube into Austria, Kitchener – having formerly denied the existence of *any* troops – offered the entirely intuitive opinion that 150,000 troops would be enough to capture the Gallipoli peninsula. At this time Churchill was still thinking in terms of action in Northern Europe, particularly the Baltic and Borkum, but Vice-Admiral Carden's reply to his signal, which reached the Admiralty on 12 January, had a profound effect. It was nothing less than a detailed plan to force the Straits by ships alone, thus relieving the pressure on Russia, turning the Central Powers' flank, ensuring that the southern Balkan nations would rally to the Allies, and all without removing any troops from the Western Front. No wonder it was so appealing! No wonder it was adopted! At the War Council next day, 13 January, one of the conclusions endorsed was that 'the Admiralty should also prepare for a naval expedition in February to bombard and take the Gallipoli peninsula, with Constantinople as its objective'.

The necessary preparations therefore got under way, but it was not long before Kitchener began to have doubts about the soundness of a purely naval expedition. Having been alerted to the dangers by a member of his intelligence staff, Captain Deedes, who knew Turkey and its armed forces, Kitchener agreed on 16 February to make available the 29th Division and it was further accepted by the War Council that the Australian and New Zealand (ANZAC) troops in Egypt could be moved to Lemnos to support the attack if needed. All this meant that, instead of the operation being a purely naval one, it was now taking on the character of a joint naval and military affair, a development greatly welcomed by Churchill. It meant too that henceforward rapid and fruitful cooperation between Churchill and Kitchener would be indispensable. This was asking too much. Moreover, Fisher, First Sea Lord, was intensely concerned that any dissipation of the Royal Navy's strength in the North Sea would seriously endanger the country. To Churchill's fury and consternation, Kitchener dithered, at one moment agreeing to the despatch of the 29th Division, the next withdrawing this agreement. Finally he decided not only to send this division but also General Sir Ian Hamilton, who had been his Chief of Staff in South Africa. On 12 March, 1915, Kitchener told Hamilton: 'We are sending a military force to support the Fleet now at the Dardanelles, and you are to have command.' It would include the Royal Naval Division, units from the Indian Army, French divisions and the ANZACs. But first the Royal Navy was, after all, to have a go with ships alone.

On 18 March the combined fleet (four French ships took part, in addition to some dozen R.N. battleships) under command of Admiral de Robeck attempted to force the Straits. The battle lasted all day and ended in absolute triumph for the Turkish defenders. Despite an intense

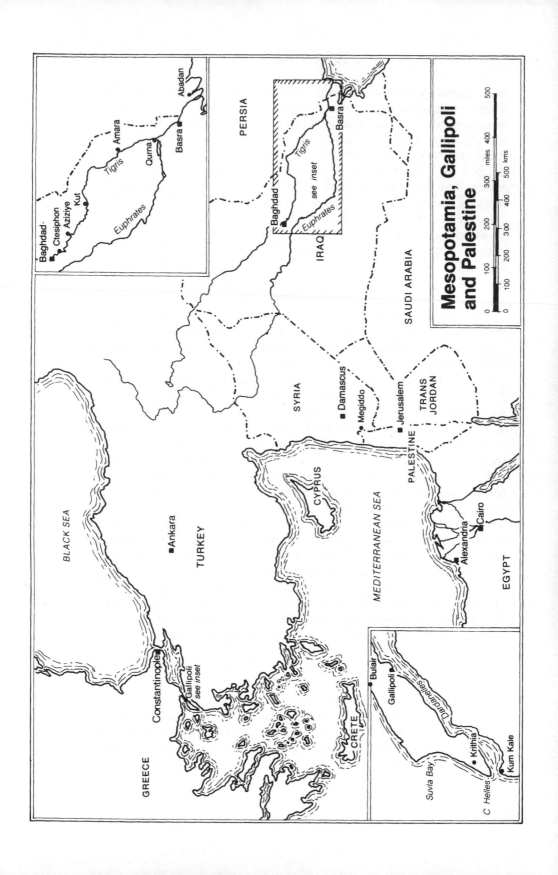

Mesopotamia, Gallipoli and Palestine

GREECE

BLACK SEA

TURKEY

■Ankara

Constantinople

Gallipoli
see inset

CYPRUS

MEDITERRANEAN SEA

CRETE

PALESTINE

Damascus
Megiddo
Jerusalem

SYRIA

TRANS JORDAN

Cairo

Alexandria

EGYPT

SAUDI ARABIA

PERSIA

IRAQ

Baghdad

Basra
see inset

Tigris

Euphrates

Inset (top left):

Baghdad
Ctesiphon
Aziziye
Kut

Tigris

Amara

Qurna

Basra

Abadan

Euphrates

Inset (bottom right):

Bulair

Gallipoli

Dardanelles

Suvla Bay

Krithia

C Helles

Kum Kale

Scale:

500
400 miles
300
200
100
0

500 kms
400
300
200
100
0

pounding of the Turkish forts, only four guns were destroyed out of nearly 180 deployed to defend the Dardanelles. Not a single one of the 400 mines was cleared. Three battleships were sunk and three more disabled. 'When it proved,' wrote James Morris, 'that the mystique of the Royal Navy could not force a passage through the Dardanelles, the great ships, turning heavily in the narrow waters of the straits, abandoned the assault and disappeared to sea, where presently the Turkish lookouts on the heights could see their dark silhouettes and billowing smoke-trails scattered among the islands of the archipelago.' Hamilton, who had witnessed the assault, signalled to Kitchener:

> I am most reluctantly driven to the conclusion that the Straits are not likely to be forced by battleships as at one time seemed probable and that, if my troops are to take part, it will not take the subsidiary form anticipated. The Army's part will not be a case of landing parties, for the destruction of forts, but rather a case of a deliberate and progressive military operation carried out in force to make good passage for the Navy.

Kitchener concurred and Hamilton interpreted his concurrence as a clear directive that he was to take the Gallipoli Peninsula. To prepare for it he took his army to Alexandria in order to reorganize and then return to effect landings in some three weeks time. Meanwhile the Turks – for all Allied hope of surprise had long since disappeared – reinforced Gallipoli threefold, bringing the garrison up to a strength of six divisions. Behind the Turks was the organizing and training genius of General Liman von Sanders and the tactical brilliance of Mustapha Kemal. Thus the British Army, already committed to a war of attrition on the Western Front, was about to indulge in an amphibious assault on unreconnoitred country defended by rather more soldiers than Hamilton to start with had at his own disposal. It was not precisely a recipe for success.

Apart from Hamilton himself – whom Robert Rhodes James has described as an attractive, intelligent and sensitive man, who, however, 'lacked that element in a commander which is so difficult to define with exactitude, that inner confidence, that basic common sense, that understanding of reality ... that mental and moral toughness ...' – there were some memorable people about in the Gallipoli campaign. One of them, of course, was Rupert Brooke, who on his way to the Dardanelles wrote that he had never been so happy in his life, and, alas, before he could, like Hamlet, 'prove himself most royal, had he been put upon', found himself some corner of a foreign field. The corner turned out to be in the olive groves of Skyros, where he was buried by such heroes as Bernard Freyberg (under whose command I served and whom I was honoured to meet during the second contest in Italy in 1945), Oc Asquith, Charles Lister and Patrick Shaw Stewart, whom James Morris called the most gifted man of his generation, and who wrote of Brooke that he supposed God's passion for picture-making had to be gratified by such a death – 'It's very like Byron, really. . . . He will be a great legend now and have a great fame: it is everything to know that his poetry is good enough to read on its own merits.' There were other men there who were to achieve great literary fame, among them John Masefield, A.P. Herbert and Compton Mackenzie. There was also another Herbert – Aubrey – *The Man who was Greemantle*, John Buchan's romantic hero, who shortly before the Army departed for this ill-fated adventure wrote from Lemnos:

> Here we are off at last. Bands playing, troops cheering, the wind blowing and the sea shining. Well it's the way to begin an odyssey, and I start upon it with a real thrill. I don't feel as if it was real men and friends I was going to meet. The whole thing is so incredibly unreal. We are like ghosts called upon to make a pageant on the sea. Every way one turns, from the African savage on shore to the Etonian fop, to the wooden horse of Troy or to the wily Greek of this place, it is all a dream.

It was a dream shortly to be shattered. Right at the outset there was dissension among the senior commanders as to what should be done. Whereas Hamilton wanted the main effort to be on the Gallipoli Peninsula itself, that is the European part of the Dardanelles, with the ANZACs landing south of Suvla Bay and 29th Division either side of Cape Helles on the southern tip, Birdwood, commanding the ANZACs, favoured the Asian shores where there would be so much more room for manoeuvre, while Hunter-Weston (29th Division) was much concerned at the severe restriction of beaches at Cape Helles. Hamilton had his way and, apart from diversionary landings by the Royal Naval Division at Bulair and by the French at Kum Kale on the Asiatic shore, the two main efforts were at Helles and south of Suvla. The whole plan had major defects. Secrecy did not exist. Everyone knew the expedition's destination. Moreover there was a totally unwarranted assumption that all that was needed was to get ashore, and then, since the Turks were negligible, the rest would look after itself. Administrative support was wholly inadequate. Above all there was, to anticipate a phrase to which Montgomery became addicted, no master plan. Despite these drawbacks, both the ANZACs and the 29th Division got ashore. But the Turks' reaction under von Sanders, and more particularly Mustapha Kemal who was in command of the battle against the ANZACs, was swift and resolute. Hamilton's troops were simply pushed backed and pinned to the shore. So bad was the ANZAC situation that Birdwood recommended evacuation. Hamilton, while taking no grip at all of the battle during the first day (25 April), refused to consider it and simply ordered the two positions, near Suvla and at Helles, however precarious, to be held. Let us visit each place, firstly V beach at Cape Helles in the company of James Morris who wrote so eloquently about it; secondly the ANZACs with Aubrey Herbert who was there. It was the ghastly shambles at V beach, Morris explained, that was characteristic of the entire campaign:

> There the landing was to be made immediately below the village of Sedd-al-Bahr, where a mediaeval castle stood at the water's edge like a memorial to more ancient battles. A collier, the *River Clyde* [3,900 tons], was to be beached to act as a large landing craft, and from its hull, it was hoped, 2,000 men of the Munster Fusiliers and the Hampshire Regiment would move across lighters to the beach, and so up the bluffs that rose, steep but not high, immediately behind. The assault went in silently at 6.20 a.m. . . . Gently and quietly, in perfect silence, the *River Clyde* ran herself ashore beside the castle, towing her lighters, and at the same time a flotilla of boats approached the beach with a battalion of the Royal Dublin Fusiliers. Everything was silent. The place seemed deserted, or stunned by the awful bombardment. . . .
>
> The moment the boats grounded a vicious fusillade of machine-gun and rifle fire fell upon them, from hidden positions in the escarpment . . . Boat after boat was riddled with fire, the soldiers jumping overboard, slumping over the gunwales, screaming or leaping terrified into the water. Boats full of dead men drifted away from the beach, or lay slowly tilting in the water, and a slow crimson stain of blood spread out to sea. Only thirty or forty survivors, scrambling up the beach, reached the cover of a ridge of sand, where they huddled helplessly beneath the bullets raging over their heads. . . .
>
> When the sally-ports of the collier were flung open, and the Munsters and Hampshires sprang out, they were met with a blast of fire like the smack of heat on a tropical day. They died almost as fast as they appeared, blocking the doors and gangplanks, falling into the sea: only a handful floundered ashore and took shelter with the Dubliners in the lee of the escarpment. The whole beach now was littered with corpses – 'like a shoal of fish', said the Turkish commander.

It soon became apparent that, far from a great strategic coup, turning the flank of the Central Powers and finding an alternative to the dreadful and pointless carnage of trench warfare in France and Flanders, the British Army had merely found another theatre of war in which to indulge in this same futile slaughter. Hamilton seemed incapable of anything but ordering fresh attacks, to which the Turks responded with counterattacks.

In the south attempts to reach Krithia resulted in the loss of nearly 7,000 men for a gain of six hundred yards. Hamilton demanded reinforcements. At ANZAC the conditions were so appalling that Aubrey Herbert, fluent in Turkish, was trying to arrange a truce so that each side could bury their dead. On 24 May it took place and Herbert recorded in his diary:

> We walked from the sea and passed immediately up the hill, through a field of tall corn filled with poppies, then another cornfield, then the fearful smell of death began as we came across scattered corpses. We mounted over a plateau and down through gullies filled with thyme where there lay about 4,000 Turkish dead. It was indescribable. One was grateful for the rain and grey sky. The smell was appalling. . . .
>
> The dead fill acres of ground, mostly killed in one big attack, but some recently. One saw the result of machine-gun fire very clearly; entire companies annihilated – not wounded, but killed, their heads doubled under them with the impetus of their rush and both hands clasping their bayonets . . .
>
> The burying was finished some time before the end. There were certain tricks on both sides I think. . . . At 4 o'clock the Turks came to me for orders . . . I retired their troops and ours . . . I told them that neither side would fire for twenty-five minutes after they had got into their trenches . . . At last we dropped into our trenches glad that the strain was over.

It was not only the soldiers who were casualties. Failure at Gallipoli caused Fisher to resign as First Sea Lord. The Unionists who joined Asquith's government insisted that Churchill – regarded by many as the architect of the Gallipoli adventure and thus a natural scapegoat – should go. He thus lost the Admiralty (to Balfour) and went to the Duchy of Lancaster. But Hamilton was reinforced, and in August another great effort at Suvla Bay was made with the elderly and incompetent Stopford nominally in command. The troops got ashore, the Turks occupied the hills dominating the landing places, more trenches were dug, the supporting ANZAC attack almost, but not quite, broke through the Turkish lines, then furious counterattacks under the personal leadership of Mustapha Kemal threw back the British and ANZAC troops. Once more stalemate, but the fault was not with the troops. It was with the generals, and notably with Hamilton, who, as the *Official History* justly put it: 'lacked the iron will and dominating personality of a truly great commander . . . He left too much to his subordinates and hesitated to override their plans, even when in his opinion they were missing opportunities.' He paid the price, was recalled in October, 1915, replaced by Monro (who immediately recommended evacuation of the entire expedition), and was never given another command. In mid-December the Suvla and ANZAC beaches were evacuated, three weeks later the Helles beaches. This was the most successful part of the whole enterprise, for it was all done without loss. Yet of the half million Allied soldiers who took part in the campaign, losses overall, including sickness, had been almost half. 25,000 had been killed, three times as many wounded, more than 10,000 were missing. And all for what? It had simply demonstrated that the German Army on the Western Front could not be outflanked by Mediterranean adventures (although the lesson was to be once more largely ignored in the Second World War) and therefore lent great power to those like Haig and Robertson who insisted that in France and Flanders alone decision could be attained. Yet, as James Morris wrote: 'Long after the Empire had ended altogether, Britons would remember the names of Gallipoli and the Dardanelles'. Patrick Shaw Stewart, who was with the Royal Naval Division and one of the last to leave Cape Helles, summed up the whole thing like this: 'The landings, the early attacks, the August push, the stagnation, the storm, the cloud-bursts, the heat, the cold, the flies, the smells and the puddles: I know them all and one day I shall write a supreme history with appendices on each of the Aegean islands.' Alas, he did not for he was killed in action on the Western Front, still with the Royal Naval Division, in January, 1918. Had he written his supreme history, he might have acknowledged that the Gallipoli campaign had at least been a *glorious* failure for the British Army and the ANZACs. Our next glance at war against the Turks includes a humiliating capitulation which marred an operation undertaken not for any necessary strategic objectives, but to gratify the appetite of thwarted personal ambition.

At the beginning of November, 1915, Asquith, speaking of the campaign in Mesopotamia, told the House of Commons: 'I do not think that in the whole course of the war there has been a series of operations more carefully contrived, more brilliantly conducted, and with a better prospect of final success'. By final success Asquith meant the capture of Baghdad. Yet within a month the British army, commanded by Major-General Charles Townshend, was doomed – besieged at Kut. The Mesopotamian campaign began in November, 1914, with an operation designed to protect Persian Gulf oil by securing the oil refinery at Abadan from any possible Turkish attack. This was done by seizing the port of Basra – rapidly and successfully achieved by three British–Indian brigades. By 9 December both Basra and Qurna were in British hands and for all intents and purposes the troops had done what was required

of them. The oil supply was secure. Turkish counterattacks, launched
in April, 1915, were beaten off without difficulty, and there the matter
might have rested but for the influence of the Viceroy of India, Lord
Hardinge (Persian Gulf affairs were supervised from India, not Britain),
the Indian Political Service officer on the spot, Cox, and the newly
arrived General Sir John Nixon. To these former players of the Great
Game, wedded to the so-called Forward Policy and intoxicated by the
idea of capturing the supposedly great and exotic prize of Baghdad, the
idea of pushing on offered substantial political and strategic advantages.
In fact there was no realistic strategic spur 'to prick the sides of their
intent, but only vaulting ambition which o'erleapt itself' – and fell!
Worse still, no proper administrative build-up or proper preparations
for a further advance were made. Besides, it was appalling campaigning
country. James Morris describes it like this:

> Much of it was empty desert, inhabited by lawless predatory Arabs who
> loathed nearly everyone, the rest wide and foetid fen, inhabited by amphibi-
> ous marshmen who detested everyone else. The irrigation works of the
> ancients had long since crumbled, and the long years of Turkish rule had
> left only decay and depression. There were no paved roads, no railways.
> Such towns as existed were hardly more than excretions of mud, like piles
> of rubbish in the wasteland, relieved only by the minarets of shabby mosques,
> or the lugubrious walls of forts. In the summer it was indescribably hot, in
> the winter unbearably cold. In the dry season everything was baked like
> leather, in the wet season 10,000 square miles were flooded, the waters
> gradually oozing away to leave malodorous wastes of marsh. Fleas, sand-flies
> and mosquitoes tormented the place.

It was into this country that Major-General Charles Townshend led his
6th (Poona) Division at the end of May, 1915, with a view to taking
Amara, some 75 miles north up the Tigris river. It was done more by
dash, improvisation and relentless pursuit than tactical skill. Townshend's infantry was embarked in small boats, the guns were carried in
barges supported by small warships and mine-sweeping launches. As
the Turkish island defences were met they were deluged by fire from
this amphibious force which then attacked with bayonet-bearing infantry. The Turks simply retreated or surrendered. As the water got
shallower and fewer boats could be used, Townshend, with paddle-
launches towing barges and a mere company of infantry, was hot in
pursuit, leaving his main forces far behind, and by 3 June this first part
of the operation was all over. A garrison of some 2,000 Turks surrendered
to a handful of British–Indian soldiers under command of a corporal.
If ever there were a time for pausing, consolidating, reorganizing and

reinforcing, it was now. Townshend's troops were exhausted, sick, ill-supplied with necessities like fresh food and medical equipment, and well below strength. Townshend himself had been forced to take sick leave, and on his return in September was doubtful about the wisdom of advancing still deeper into enemy territory with relatively small forces, and already there was talk of substantial Turkish reinforcements, particularly divisions from Gallipoli [where, since the failure of the British August attacks, there had been far less activity]. The Turkish veterans of Gallipoli would be a different proposition. But General Nixon's confidence and ambition knew no bounds. It was Baghdad on which he had set his sights, and, as there was no restraining hand on the bridle from either London or Simla, Townshend was ordered to push on. His forces took Kut-el-Amara at the end of September, and here again was a moment to pause, re-group, reinforce, prepare (however cautious a general Montgomery may have been, his maxim of 'no advance without security'* was sound). But no such strength of character or leadership was forthcoming, and still further north Townshend's men went. Later in October he overcame a Turkish force in Aziziye, halfway between Kut and Baghdad, giving rise to Asquith's ill-chosen prediction in the House of Commons, but at Ctesiphon, where the Turks had deployed their veterans well dug in behind barbed wire entanglements, his division met a first, and fatal, setback. Only eighteen miles from Baghdad, his gallant, but sick and depleted, division made one more great effort. They took the first lines of Turkish defences, manned by 20,000 soldiers, compared with Townshend's 12,000. Townshend lost more than a third of his force, and at this point realised that his exposed and vulnerable position could not be sustained. He determined on withdrawal to Kut. Pursued by greatly superior Turkish forces, by 8 December, 1915, Townshend's troops – there were in all some 13,000 British and Indian soldiers with 40 guns – were besieged. The siege was to last for nearly five months.

During the retreat to Kut the soldiers had behaved magnificently, as the *Official History* recorded:

The troops were very tired ... the force stumbled on, only half awake ... all ranks were thankful to lie down and sleep on the road in column as they were. But even sleep was difficult, as the cold was intense and there was no food. For over twelve days, General Townshend's force – largely composed of young soldiers – had been fighting, marching, or working continually,

---

* The motto was not original, having been, according to James Morris, invented by the Jewish force which served under Allenby in Palestine.

frequently without sufficient food or water and deprived of sleep. This forty-four mile march ... carried out in thirty-six hours was therefore a severe test.

It was just another instance of what the British or Indian soldier, no matter what the blundering of his generals might bring about, was capable of doing.

There were more such instances during the several attempts to relieve Kut, among them an attack by the 1st Punjabis on the Turkish defences at Shaikh Saad, about thirty miles south of Kut. But the Turks were far too well dug in with excellent fire support, the totally flat country afforded no cover for tactical movement and the weather in late January, 1916, with continuous rain had caused extensive flooding. This particular attack cost the battalion half its strength, and once more the arrangements for the wounded were wholly wanting. One of the Regiment's officers, Major Evans, wrote of the appalling suffering, the wounded left lying out in the open in freezing rain and dying of exposure. However hard the brave medical orderlies worked, they simply could not deal with the numbers requiring attention. Those who were picked up were then subjected to long agonizing journeys in carts without springs only to arrive at dressing stations which were themselves a horror of inadequacy and disorder. All in all the operations to relieve Kut cost nearly 25,000 men. At Kut itself conditions, bad enough to start with, – no sanitation, filth, poverty, squalor, not enough food or water, men dying from sickness, morale crumbling – deteriorated from week to week, month to month, until inevitably by March the talk was of surrender, and Townshend himself, beginning now to blame the higher command for all his misfortunes, decided that he could not hold out much longer than mid-April. The surrender when it came on 29 April was accompanied by a communique from Townshend, telling his men that they had done their duty and could be proud of themselves. General Khalil Bey, the Turkish commander, courteously returned Townshend's sword, but despite all the formality and ceremony the fact remained that more than 10,000 British and Indian soldiers had capitulated as a result of a strategically irrelevant operation at a time when things were going badly elsewhere. Townshend spent his captivity comfortably in a villa in Constantinople. More than fifty per cent of his men died, either on the terrible march from Kut to Baghdad and then on to Turkey or in dreadful prisoner of war camps. Yet Aubrey Herbert who was prominent in arranging the surrender terms thought he had negotiated reasonable conditions, since the Turks held all the cards. He was, however, mistaken in putting any faith in their ideas of honourably keeping their word.

Herbert recalled his meeting with Khalil; with him were Colonel Beach and Captain T. E. Lawrence:

> At last we came to Khalil's camp, a single round tent, a few men on motor cycles coming and going, horses picketed here and there. ... Khalil throughout the interview was polite. He was quite a young man for his position, I suppose about thirty-five, and a fine man to look at – lion-taming eyes, a square chin and a mouth like a steel trap.

Herbert extracted all sorts of promises about care of the British wounded and exchange of prisoners, even about lenient treatment of Kut's Arab population, but all to no avail. The Kut Arabs were subjected to a full measure of Turkish cruelty – hanging, torture, beggary. No boats were provided to transport British prisoners, and the consequent march to the north, during which they were starved and beaten, bears comparison with Japanese treatment of Allied prisoners in Burma in 1942. Aubrey himself returned to England via Egypt and then went to Salonika, where 200,000 British troops were to be tied up ineffectually, succumbing largely to malaria rather then enemy bullets. Lawrence had other fish to fry, and this time was enabled to stage further encounters with the Turkish Army which made him a legend. It was part of the third effort of the British to get the better of the Turks and this time was crowned with startling success. Much of this success was because the man in supreme command was Allenby – 'The Bull'. By the time Allenby arrived in Egypt in June, 1917, the disaster of Kut had been redeemed by General Maude's properly prepared and deliberate advance on and capture of Baghdad, but what Allenby had in mind was the defeat of the Turkish armies in Syria, and the liberation of Jerusalem and Damascus.

Allenby was perhaps the last British soldier to employ cavalry in a wholly traditional way, in large numbers and with total success. Once more manoeuvre came into its own. His campaign in Palestine and Syria lasted a year. His army was drawn from almost everywhere in the Empire. Apart from British regiments, there were the heroic ANZACs, units from as far afield as Singapore, South Africa, the West Indies, Egyptian troops, horse, foot and guns from the Indian Army, and of course the Arabs themselves rising in revolt against their Turkish masters – the guerrilla campaign conducted by Lawrence and others having a profound effect on Turkish communications and morale. But it was Allenby's genius for planning, for bluff, for concentration at a decisive point, for switching his spearheads of advance and for sheer speed that confounded the Turks time after time as his armies constantly outflanked and destroyed them. By Christmas, 1917, he had captured

Jerusalem, entering the city, as James Morris put it, 'more as a pilgrim than as a conqueror. The troops who lined the dusty road to the walls were dressed in their battle-frayed khaki, and so was the general himself. ... To most people there he undoubtedly represented not so much Christianity, or even the Allied cause, as the British Empire. . . . Emerging into the bright sunshine Cromwell's descendant, at the head of the armies of the Empire, entered the Holy City. He is said to have remembered the moment always as the climax of his life.' Yet more triumphs awaited him. In September, 1918, at the battle of Megiddo, Allenby defeated the last of the Turkish armies opposed to him. By this time he had almost half a million men under his command, and by entering Damascus in the following month, he virtually brought the Syrian campaign and the Ottoman Empire to an end. It says much for Allenby that he was able to recognize the guerrilla-organizing genius of Lawrence and, despite his suspicions that Lawrence was something of a charlatan, had the vision and confidence to back him. Churchill, always seeing war as a great romantic adventure, was lavish with praise of Lawrence. In *Great Contemporaries* he wrote of both Lawrence the soldier and 'his audacious, desperate, romantic assaults ... Grim camel-rides through sun-scorched, blasted lands, where the extreme desolation of nature appals the traveller ... with infinite privation men on camels with shattering toil carried dynamite to destroy railway bridges and win the war ... Lawrence rousing the fierce peoples of the desert, penetrating the mysteries of their thought, leading them to the selected points of action and as often as not firing the mine himself'. As for *Seven Pillars of Wisdom* Churchill regarded it as unsurpassed as a story of adventure and war, as a portrait of the Arab, ranking as one of the truly great pieces of literature in the English language. Yet Lawrence could have done little without Allenby's support. In the smoking room of the Cavalry and Guards Club hang pictures of many field-marshals, among them French, Haig, Birdwood and Allenby. Of them all Allenby was by far the greatest general, even though, as A. J. P. Taylor pointed out, the Syrian campaign did little to damage the Germans. Nor did other so-called 'side-shows' like Salonika where over half a million Allied troops, including 200,000 British were more or less held in thrall by the Bulgarian army, so robbing the Western Front of the strength to inflict more damage on the Germans. Nevertheless a month after Allenby's capture of Damascus, Ludendorff finally pronounced the game over and persuaded the German government to make peace. For the British Army it would mean drastic reductions in size and deployment, and for some a longed-for 'return to real soldiering'.

10

BETWEEN THE WARS

In the mid-1930s the Army was indeed pathetically unprepared to participate in a European war; even the leading regular infantry divisions [there were only five] were lacking in vital weapons, stores and specialist personnel, while not a single armoured division yet existed. Moreover, so far from the small available forces at home being concentrated and organized for a European emergency, the Abyssinian crisis led to a significant and, as it proved, permanent reinforcement of the Middle East.

Brian Bond

There was a certain pleasing irony about the supposedly war-mongering Winston Churchill (in 1915 he had referred to 'this glorious delicious war') being appointed War Minister in January, 1919, shortly after the war against Germany had ended. Indeed he himself had had doubts about accepting the post, asking what was the use of being War Minister without a war, and receiving the cutting rejoinder from Bonar Law that he would never have been offered the position had there been a war. What many of Churchill's colleagues at that time failed to discern was his resilience and realism. Even at that time his insistence on magnanimity in victory was as plain as his former defiance in defeat, and he threw his weight behind those who sought some measure of reconciliation in dealing with the Central Powers. And despite his eagerness to support the Tsarist forces who were still engaged against the Red Army with further British commitment, he was quick to recognize that no such wish existed among the soldiers longing for demobilization, and thereupon took steps to speed up their return to civilian life. But these sensible measures in no way affected his suspicions and hatred of Bolshevism. 'He saw all acts hostile to Britain,' wrote Piers Brendon, 'whether in Ireland, the Middle East or India, as part of an international revolutionary conspiracy directed against the victorious empire.' We may perhaps glance now at what the British Army was up to in those wholly diverse parts of the Empire.

In Ireland we must go back first to the rising of Easter, 1916. Although conscription had been introduced in 1916, it did not apply to Ireland, and although, as we have seen, there were many Irish regiments engaged in battles as far apart as Gallipoli and Flanders, there were also large numbers of both Ulster Volunteers and Irish Volunteers, armed, drilling and, in case of the latter, seeking opportunity for open rebellion. Sir Roger Casement had even tried to recruit a legion of Irish soldiers from prisoner-of-war camps in Germany to fight against the British. He was unsuccessful, but plans were nevertheless made to stage a rising on Easter Sunday, 1916, with military support to be supplied by the Germans. When Casement returned to Ireland by German submarine on Easter Friday, he was without any German help and was almost at once arrested. The rising for Sunday was called off, but in spite of this a small group of Irishmen took possession of the Dublin General Post Office and declared an Irish Republic. Fighting began between the Irish nationalists and the British Army. Casualties on both sides were heavy – a hundred British soldiers and 450 Irishmen were killed. The remaining rebels surrendered when the Post Office had been destroyed a few days later. The men who had signed the declaration of independence, together with Irish Volunteer commanders (except de Valera), were shot. All subsequent attempts by Asquith, Lloyd George, Carson and Redmond to set up Home Rule for Ireland, less the six counties of Ulster, failed. An Irish Republic would have to wait, but the Irish Nationalists grew stronger. After the war, with Churchill at the War Office, the Irish Republicans launched their campaign of violence, and one of the measures taken to combat terrorism was a form of counter-terrorism in the shape of the notorious 'Black and Tans'. The Irish 'troubles' were characterized by brutality on both sides. The Irish Republican Army, which at any one time could call on perhaps 5,000 men for 'active service' (a phrase again familiar to us in the 1970s and 1980s) were fighting against what they thought of as British occupation. They would collect together in small groups to attack an Army convoy to seize arms or would stage an assault on an isolated police station, not wearing uniform, but usually identifiable by their trench-coats, and then after the raid was over, disperse again to their homes or hiding places. The British Army deploying against the I.R.A. was some 50,000 strong, the Royal Irish Constabulary perhaps 10,000, and in the same way that we have seen recently in Ulster anti-guerrilla tactics had to be acquired and practised. There was no question of pacification or the restoration of law and order. The thing just went on,* hardly helped by the Black and Tans or the Auxiliary Division, whose activities simply increased resentment, hatred and bitterness. Through it all there was still the problem of Loyalist Ulster.

In 1921 the C.I.G.S., General Sir Henry Wilson (assassinated by the I.R.A. in the following year in London) had given it as his view that to subdue Ireland would demand the deployment of an Army of 100,000 specially recruited soldiers to indulge in full-scale war. Lloyd George, urged by Smuts and strongly supported by King George V, sought reconciliation, and after protracted negotiations and endless dis-agreements, even more fighting between the various representatives of Sinn Fein and the I.R.A., the Treaty establishing an Irish Free State of 26 Counties (that is excluding Ulster) was accepted by both the Irish and the British in December, 1922. British troops left Ireland the same month, and some of the most famous fighting regiments of the British Army ended their history. This same year saw further Army cuts for other reasons.

'When the Great War was over,' wrote Jock Haswell, 'Britain as usual rewarded her soldiers by immediately dismantling the huge machine created to win it, and sending back into civilian life the great wealth of loyalty and talent which the citizen army had brought to every arm and department of the service.'† In one respect, however, a permanent link was forged for all those who had served. Whatever criticism there might have been for Earl Haig's conduct of war, there was only praise for his creation and organization of the British Legion, still thriving today with its Clubs country-wide and its funds annually augmented by the Poppy Day appeal with memorial services held everywhere on each November Sunday nearest to Armistice Day, 1918. Apart from this the British Army once more retired behind its barrier of separateness and became once more a kind of Imperial policing force. The Geddes 'axe' of 1922 reduced its size still further and caused a number of famous regiments to amalgamate, so that we find such names as the 4th/7th Royal Dragoon Guards, three new Regiments of Hussars – 13th/18th, 14th/20th and 15th/19th, whose combined battle honours more or less catalogue British military history – and even Lancers – the 16th/5th and the famous 'Death or Glory' 17th/21st – for all the lessons of machine-guns and barbed wire had still not done away with either the horse or the lance. Indeed as late as 1925 we find Field-Marshal Earl Haig writing that, although he was all in favour of aeroplanes and tanks, they were but

* About 700 Irishmen were killed and a similar number of policemen and soldiers.
† *The British Army: A Concise History*, Thames & Hudson 1975.

accessories to the man and the horse, and 'I feel sure that as time goes on you will find just as much use for the horse – the well-bred horse – as you have done in the past'. Certainly in Hitler's war the Wehrmacht found extensive transport use for horses, right up until the end – but they were not always well-bred.

Even though Britain reassumed its almost total indifference to defence matters and an Army career was thought of as an agreeable sporting and social background for officers and a means of relief from unemployment for the rank and file, yet now and again the activities of the British or Indian armies struck the headlines and engraved another date, another incident, on the nation's history. One such affair was the terrible massacre at Amritsar in 1919, which Churchill called something without parallel in Britain's Imperial history, an event 'of singular and sinister isolation'. At that time, with nationalist feelings riding high in India, there had been rioting and deaths at Amritsar. Public meetings had been forbidden. When, in defiance of this order, hundreds of people assembled in the confined space of the Jallianwalla Bagh, a sort of public garden in the centre of the city, with only few narrow exits, the local commander, Brigadier General Dyer, felt it necessary to reassert the Raj's authority over the political demonstrators, among whom tension was so charged and emotion so inflamed that they would be unlikely to listen to reason. Indeed they were far too occupied listening to the oratory pouring from the mouth of the speaker addressing them. The arrival of British armoured cars, Gurkha and Baluchi soldiers with British officers in command, and their deployment at one end of the square went almost unnoticed. But not for long, as James Morris has so strikingly described:

> When the orator looked over his shoulder, and saw the soldiers kneeling there, he shouted to the crowd not to be alarmed – they would never shoot – they only had blank cartridges. Hardly had he spoken than a command rang out, and the impassive Gurkhas, obedient as machines, began to shoot at point-blank range into the crowd. The panic was frightful. People fought each other to get to the gates. They scrabbled at high walls, they trampled one another down, they rushed this way and that, they tried to hide, to take shelter behind each other, to lie flat on the ground. The Gurkhas were unmoved. Loading in their own time, they aimed especially at the two exits at the bottom of the garden until the gates were jammed with dead and wounded Indians, and nobody else could escape.

It only went on for about six minutes, but in that time nearly four hundred people (some sources say 800) had been killed and 1,500 wounded. Dyer himself was obliged to resign and, despite support from many quarters, spent the rest of his life brooding about whether he had been right or wrong. Although Gandhi recognized at the time of Amritsar that the British could not be turned out of India by force alone, the event so reinforced his and his followers' determination to pursue a path, any path, to ultimate independence that from this time forth, the British position in India was a holding one, conviction and initiative largely gone. Yet despite the inevitability of change, the Indian Army was still to perform great deeds of military prowess and incalculable political significance for the King Emperor and the British Empire.

Elsewhere the British Army's activities had been less spectacular and more effective. At Chanak in September, 1922, General Harington, by his cool generalship and disobedience to orders, (Lloyd George, backed by Birkenhead and Churchill – then Colonial Secretary – instructed Harington to send an ultimatum to the Turks, now led by Mustapha Kemal Pasha; Harington preferred firm negotiation) had averted war. In his book about the *Chanak Affair*, David Walder gave us an affectionate and accurate portrait of the Army of the Black Sea, as it was called. He pointed out that in spite of what had happened in France and Flanders, the horse – as Haig had been the first to assert – still had a powerful position. Apart from the cavalry regiments themselves, the artillery was largely horse-drawn, some by teams of Clydesdales; the Royal Army Service Corps went about its business of distributing supplies with horse-drawn wagons; even infantry battalions had their own horses to move their vehicles about. Rifles, machine-guns and pistols were all of the 1914 pattern. Even uniforms were the same as before, including the sun helmet introduced by Wolseley. As David Walder explains, there were reasons for all this:

> This was essentially an army coming back to peacetime habits, dress and attitudes of mind. Hence there was a quite definite drive, as always after any war, to return to the pre-war style of military behavior ... although the British army was beginning once again to insist on punctilious ceremonial and general 'spit and polish', which had received a nasty knock in the mud and lice of the Western Front, comparatively this was the most efficient army in the Middle East. Better trained, better disciplined, well fed and well cared for medically ... its morale was high.

One of the reasons for this high morale was that General Harington insisted on proper care and guidance for the soldiers. He went to extreme lengths to ensure that their life was as agreeable as possible, organizing sport, guiding their behaviour in alien surroundings, watching their health, and above all winning their loyalty by his sincere and simple approach. If Chanak brought distinction to General Harington and further fame to the British Army, however, the same could not be said for

Lloyd George, whose policies here had antagonised the Conservatives – Bonar Law going as far as saying that the British could not act alone as the policemen of the world – and resulted in their withdrawal from Coalition and a decision to fight independently the forthcoming general election. Lloyd George resigned and never held office again. The next Prime Minister to hold office for any appreciable length of time was Baldwin, and in his 1924 administration, which lasted for five years, Winston Churchill was Chancellor of the Exchequer. Now more concerned with holding down expenditure on defence than he had been when heading the Admiralty or the War Office, Churchill hit upon the device of reviving the so-called ten years' rule, which Lloyd George had invented in 1919, that is that the service chiefs should base their policies on the notion that there would be no major war within the following ten years. It was conveniently a rule which was permanently renewable, and was in fact repeatedly renewed until finally abandoned in 1932.

In his brief Premiership, Bonar Law had revived the Committee of Imperial Defence to supervise the direction of British defence policy. Baldwin presided over it from 1925, and took advice from the newly constituted Chiefs of Staff committee, which – unlike now – had no supra-service chairman. The chair was taken by whichever of the three chiefs of staff was senior. This system robbed it of any likelihood that impartial strategic advice would be forthcoming. Each service chief was concerned primarily with his own service. Thus the battle for resources was waged between them, and, at a time when defence expenditure was being reduced year by year, there was little opportunity for forging a coherent defence policy. The Royal Navy was concerned principally with maintaining its fleet of battleships, including parity with the United States of America, an absurdity in the sense that under no conditions could America be seen as a possible enemy, but an excellent excuse for the Admirals to retain their beloved warships.

The Royal Air Force under the fatherly hand of Trenchard embraced the theory that air power alone could win wars, and that therefore superiority in the air was of prime importance. A requirement of some fifty squadrons was laid down, but happily for Britain this theoretical requirement was not translated too soon into practice. Had it been, the outbreak of the war in 1939 might have seen the R.A.F. equipped already with out-of-date bombers and fighters. Overseas, the R.A.F. had shown, in quelling a revolt in Iraq by the simple expedient of bombing villages of the tribesmen who were rebelling, how much more cheaply and quickly they could do it than by mounting a full-scale punitive expedition with troops.

As for these troops themselves, it was the Army, as A. J. P. Taylor

18. The Somme, 1916. 'The British Army suffered more casualties in one day than it ever had before'

19. Sir Douglas Haig with Mr Lloyd George, France, September, 1916. With them are M. Thomas and General Joffre.

20. The Arras offensive, April 1917. Mark II tank ditched crossing a captured communication trench.

21. Australians passing along a duckboard track through the devastated Château Wood in the Ypres Salient.

22. British troops in a captured trench on the Ancre, 1917.

23. German trench mortar being prepared for action.

24. Waiting for the breakthrough - Scots Greys near Montreuil, May, 1918.

25. Battle of St Quentin Canal. Mark V tanks going forward with 'cribs' to enable them to cross the Hindenburg Line. Bellicourt, 29 September, 1918.

26. (*Above*) 'Behind the Turks was the tactical brilliance of Mustapha Kemal'.

27. (*Above right*) 'Of them all Allenby was by far the greatest general'. He is seen here with the King of Montenegro.

28. (*Right*) Lawrence of Arabia.

29. 'The whole retreat towards Dunkirk turned into an epic'. Troops returning from France, June, 1940.

30. Mr Churchill in the uniform of the RAF with his Chiefs of Staff. *Left to right*: Air Chief Marshal Sir Charles Portal, Admiral Sir Dudley Pound, Churchill, General Sir Alan Brooke and Lord Louis Mountbatten.

31. The Western Desert Tanks.

32. The Western Desert Artillery.

33. The Western Desert Infantry.

34. The Western Desert Repairs.

emphasized, which was the principal sufferer during the period of the ten years' rule from 1922 to 1932. 'With a great war ruled out, there was nothing for it to do, except to guard the air bases from which the R.A.F. dominated the Middle East, or occasionally to quell civil disturbances at home and abroad.' There was no great revolution in tactical doctrine or new equipment or training. The tank was largely forgotten about or ignored. Haig's insistence on the importance of the horse might not have commanded much support from those who really thought about defence [and we will see shortly what thinkers like Liddell Hart and others were saying and writing]. The horse's social prominence, however, was as great as ever. The theories of mechanized armies, which, in a phrase used by Hitler before his rise to power, would 'regain the superiority of free operations', and become the dominant feature of land warfare, were simply pushed aside. Although the British Army may have largely neglected either to develop or acquire new weapons and equipment, however, it was something of a comfort to know, as Professor Taylor reminds us, that much of its annual income was spent on improving the living conditions of the ordinary soldiers.

For those English men and women who had no direct contact with the British Army for reasons of family or environment, the image of the soldier was often carved by contemporary fiction or the cinema. In the third volume of his Imperial classic, *Farewell the Trumpets*, James Morris has recalled for us what a powerful influence novels like *A Passage to India* or *Kim* had on the public mind. They were not primarily about the Army, more about the British position in India which was only maintained because of the Army, and in Kipling's case usually portrayed the soldier in a flattering, but not over-romanticised, light. Indeed it is often the 'native', like Gunga Din, who wins the highest praise. When it came to the cinema, who can forget Gary Cooper in *Lives of a Bengal Lancer* – however divorced the film was from the book Yeats-Brown had written? It somehow stimulated a satisfaction and pride in the courage and good humour and devotion to duty of the soldier, vicarious though these feelings may have been. Who did not enjoy John Clements' receiving, redeeming and returning *The Four Feathers*? Was it illusion? Reality differed.

Reality was illusion of a different sort, a refusal to take necessary steps to protect the realm, a taking of refuge in such comforting ideas as the 'indirect approach' (that is reliance on relatively small intervention on a flank by wielding Britain's traditional sea power and so avoiding direct confrontation), and thus accepting a 'limited liability' of solely Imperial reinforcement – all of which were devices to persuade the policy makers that there was no need and indeed no strategic justification for undertaking a commitment in the one theatre – Europe – where commitment was indispensable. Although Baldwin had declared in 1934 that Britain's defensive frontier lay on the Rhine, no attempt was made to turn this prescient observation into hard defence policy. During this time between the wars the writings of Liddell Hart, who later became a kind of unofficial adviser to Hore Belisha (Secretary for War 1937–1940) and thus had much influence on the making of policy, were notable both for their foresight and their ambivalence. In the first place, as early as the mid-1920s he was advocating the formation of a 'New Model' army whose essential character would be mechanization – tanks, motorized infantry to carry them into battle and supported by motor-borne guns. He was anticipating the Wehrmacht's doctrine of *Blitzkrieg* when he wrote:

> Once appreciate that tanks are not an extra arm or a mere aid to infantry but the modern form of heavy cavalry and their true military use is obvious – to be concentrated and used in as large masses as possible for a decisive blow against the Achilles' heel of the enemy army, the communications and command centres which form its nerve system. Then not only may we see the rescue of mobility from the toils of trench war-warfare, but with it the revival of generalship and the art of war, in contrast to its mere mechanics.

This was a remarkably far-sighted estimate of what generals like Guderian, von Manstein and Rommel were later to do. But in advocating a return to the traditional maritime strategy and the 'indirect approach', Liddell Hart was on less sure ground. He might argue that 'an examination of military history points to the fact that in all the decisive campaigns the dislocation of the enemy's psychological and physical balance has been the vital prelude to a successful attempt at his overthrow', that this dislocation was always the result of a strategic indirect approach, and that 'no general is justified in launching his troops to a direct attack upon an enemy firmly in position' – but his argument fell down when confronted with Napoleon's success at Austerlitz, Ludendorff's offensive of March, 1918, and, although it came much later, the celebrated victory of Montgomery at El Alamein. Moreover, although Wellington's Peninsula campaign was important, it only succeeded because the Russians, Austrians and Prussians had knocked the stuffing out of the Grande Armée [a pattern that was to be repeated with the Italian campaign of 1943–1945], while Gallipoli had been a costly failure.

Michael Howard really had the last word on it all when he wrote that the maximum support available to a Continental ally applied at the nearest possible point was fundamental to British strategy. Any peripheral adventures were essentially secondary and simply made possible by wielding sea power. But *decision* could only be achieved in Central Europe. This had certainly been the case in the Great War. It was to be repeated in the war against Hitler's Third Reich. Yet as late as February, 1938, long after the Rome–Berlin Axis had been established – in October, 1936, after Italy had swallowed Abyssinia, Germany had re-occupied the Rhineland and was about to bully Austria into the *Anschluss*, indeed in the very same month that Hitler had begun to exercise supreme command of the *Wehrmacht*, and shortly after he had declared to his military chiefs his intention to overthrow both Austria and Czechoslovakia – at this very time we find the C.I.G.S., General Ironside, noting in his diary:

> We have no Continental commitment now. I told the Commanders' Conference that our wretched little Corps of two divisions and a mobile division was unthinkable as a contribution to an Army in France. Nothing behind it either. Let us make Imperial plans only. After all, the politicians will be hard put to refuse to help France and Belgium when the 1914 show begins again.

Thus we have the curious circumstance of the General Staff recognizing that, if it came to war in Europe, the British Army would have to go and help, but that nothing should be done to plan for or prepare for such a contingency. This absurdity was fully appreciated by the Director of Military Operations, General Pownall, who lost no time in making it plain to Hore Belisha, when he first discussed the problem with the War Minister early in 1938, that the Army must be got ready for its inevitable European role, or 'the troops would go untrained and ill-equipped for the purpose – with dire results'. How had this total unpreparedness of the Army for its most probable role in war come about?

By the end of 1934 it was plain to all those who were prepared to see it that the principal threat to Britain was from Germany, and that a policy of disarmament and collective security, although having the virtue of economy, was in all other respects a recipe for disaster. Baldwin therefore decided that while the supremacy of the Royal Navy should be maintained, it would also be necessary to build up the Royal Air Force to a position of at least parity with Germany. But, as A.J.P. Taylor so bluntly explained, as economy was still the order of the day, this meant that the Army was once again at the end of the queue for defence resources. 'There was,' he writes, 'to be a "limited liability" army, fit only for colonial defence.' But, he goes on to explain, something unprecedented occurred in March, 1935, when the National Government, still at this time headed by MacDonald, published a *Statement Relating to Defence*. Designed, largely by both civil servants and military

heads, to make politicians and the public wake up to the dangers with
which Japan, Italy and Germany were confronting the world, and
declaring that Britain must put her faith and effort, not in collective
security, but in armed force, it was largely ineffectual. And the international reaction to what was actually being done by the European
dictators did little to deter Hitler and Mussolini from taking further
risks and embarking on new adventures.

After Hitler's announcement in March, 1935, that a new German
Army based on conscription and totalling thirty-six divisions was to be
created, together with the revelation that the *Luftwaffe*, which already
had a thousand operational aircraft, would be further expanded, the
conference at Stresa attended by the British, French and Italians in
April may have produced plenty in the way of words, but nothing in
the way of action. Apart from reiterating their allegiance to the Locarno
Treaty (which in 1925 had guaranteed both the Franco–German and
the Belgian–German borders), the only significant steps taken to check
aggression were the pacts concluded for mutual aid by the French
and the Soviet Union, and between the Russians and Czechs. Hitler
meanwhile made one of his speeches to the Reichstag, deploring war,
appealing to the Western democracies longing for peace and offering to
limit German naval strength to thirty-five per cent of the Royal Navy.
Britain's readiness to be deceived was illustrated by the signing of just
such a naval treaty in June, 1935. One of the lone voices in Britain to
condemn appeasement was that of Winston Churchill, who, out of office
since 1929, had been consistently campaigning for rearmament. He had
made it clear that ever since the Stresa conference, Italy's preparations
to embark on the conquest of Abyssinia had been apparent and that
even if Britain attempted to persuade Mussolini that such a course of
action would result in her hostility, it would do no good because
'Mussolini, like Hitler, regarded Britannia as a frightened, flabby old
woman ... incapable of making war'.

In the event Italy attacked Abyssinia in October, 1935, but the feeble
response of the League of Nations in merely applying sanctions did
such damage to the reputations of France and Britain that Hitler soon
embarked on his own policy of aggressive expansion, confident that
there would be no interference. First came the re-occupation of the
Rhineland in March, 1936. It was a major gamble, for Hitler had only
a few brigades and, had the French Army moved against him, he would
have been obliged to withdraw. The French did nothing except reinforce
the Maginot Line, and the Führer had triumphed not only over the
Western democracies, but over his own General Staff whose timidity
had urged against the move in the first place. The Spanish Civil War

gave both the Germans and the Italians a unique opportunity to try out
new weapons and new tactics, again without any material interference
by France and Britain. The whole strategic balance in Europe was being
altered. Germany's occupation of the Rhineland, as Churchill predicted
in the House of Commons, would enable her to build up defences in
the West – the so-called Siegfried Line – and thus present a double
danger, first freedom to strike in the East, second the ability to repeat
the deadly thrust through Belgium in the West should it come to war
there. Later that year two further steps were taken by Hitler. In August,
1936, Ciano, Italian Foreign Minister and Mussolini's son-in-law, had
discussions in Berlin at which the Führer emphasized that the stronger
Germany and Italy became, the more likely it was that some accommodation with Britain would be reached. Nor did he conceal his contempt for the British Government. 'Today she is governed merely by
incompetents.' Formerly, when led by adventurers, she had created a
world empire. Following these discussions, the second move was the
actual signing of the October Protocols, setting up the Rome–Berlin
Axis.

When, in November, 1937, Hitler gathered his Commanders-in-Chief
around him and explained his blueprint for *Lebensraum*, and in particular
the acquisition of Austria and Czechoslovakia, he had already seen what
that peerless combination – the *Panzer* and the *Stuka* – could do in
action. During the Spanish Civil War one of the key features of *Blitzkrieg*
tactics, instant support of forward troops by both fighting and transport
aircraft, had been demonstrated with startling success. (Ironically the
British and French military leaders drew precisely the opposite conclusions, which were profoundly mistaken ones – Gamelin, the French
Chief of Staff maintained that tanks would never break through as
anti-tank guns would always stop them, while the C.I.G.S., Deverell,
regarded German tanks as fit only for the scrap-heap.) Hitler's planning
directives specifically referred to the employment of Panzer Armies for
the 'elimination' of Austria and Czechoslovakia. His whole discourse
was one of cynical calculation.It was a question of how to obtain the
largest gain at the smallest cost. Of course, there would be opposition;
of course, there would be risk. France and Britain were 'hate-inspired
antagonists', and even though weak, had to be reckoned with. What
would the great powers actually do? Hitler found little difficulty in
persuading himself that they would do nothing. Italy would be too much
concerned with Britain and France. Russia would have her eye on Japan.
Any concerted action was far from likely. The will to resist was lacking.
In any event, risk or no risk, Austria and Czechoslovakia must be
conquered and at lightning speed, *blitzartig schnell*.

And so they were! The *Anschluss* was effected with minimum fuss and with the rather useful lesson that many of the *Panzers* broke down en route, so that proper measures to ensure this did not recur could be taken. On 14 March, 1938, Hitler entered Vienna in triumph. On the same day Churchill told the House of Commons:

> The gravity of the event of March 12 cannot be exaggerated. Europe is confronted with a programme of aggression, nicely calculated and timed, unfolding stage by stage, and there is only one choice open, not only to us but to other countries, either to submit like Austria, or else take effective measures while time remains to ward off the danger, and if it cannot be warded off to cope with it. . . . A long stretch of the Danube is now in German hands. This mastery of Vienna gives to Nazi Germany military and economic control of the whole of the communications of South-Eastern Europe, by road, by river, and by rail. What is the effect of it upon what is called the balance of power? . . .
>
> Czechoslovakia is at this moment isolated, both in the economic and in the military sense. . . . How many potential allies shall we see go one by one down the grisly gulf? How many times will bluff succeed until behind bluff ever-gathering forces have accumulated reality? Where are we going to be two years hence, for instance, when the German Army will certainly be much larger than the French Army?

His warnings went unheeded. Hitler went on with his plans to 'smash Czechoslovakia'. It is true that Chamberlain returned from Munich at the end of September, 1938, talking of 'peace with honour' and 'peace for our time', but the fact was that the Sudetenland had been handed over to Germany (and by March, 1939, the German Army had poured into Bohemia and Moravia), honour had been forfeited, and, far from peace, all that Britain had gained was a little time to get ready for war. This time something was actually done.

Although aircraft production and radar cover greatly increased during the year between Munich and the outbreak of war, while the Royal Navy began its preparation for a Far Eastern fleet in addition to maintaining its superiority over the German and Italian navies, the principal effect of Chamberlain's determination to become more powerfully armed was felt by the Army. The generals had always disliked the doctrine of 'limited liability' which virtually robbed the Army of any significant role in a European war, and they now insisted that an Army fit to wage war on the Continent was indispensable. It was therefore agreed by the Government to set a new goal of six regular and twenty-six Territorial divisions. Two other recommendations made by the Army chiefs – that some move towards conscription would be needed to meet the new target and that a Ministry of Supply should be set up to cope with contractual, development and production arrangements for all the extra weapons to equip the enlarged Army – were for the time being shelved by the Government. There had already been a degree of mechanization. As early as 1928 two cavalry regiments, 11th Hussars and 12th Lancers, had been converted to armoured cars, and then in 1935 it had been decided to rearm eight more cavalry regiments with light tanks, one of them being Churchill's regiment, 4th Hussars, to whom he announced during a visit:

> Whatever be the weapons which are given to the 4th Hussars, the regiment will play the same tune on them and will carry the same old traditions, whether it be the sabre and the wheel into line for the charge, whether it is as mounted infantry, as rifle-armed cavalry or, as you are now, a mechanized unit.

It would not be long before they were in a position to start playing – rather jangled – tunes on their new weapons, together with all the other mechanized cavalry regiments, which by September, 1939, had together with the Royal Tank Corps been formed into the new Royal Armoured Corps. Six months before this Chamberlain had 'guaranteed' Poland and in April the two steps which the Army hierarchy had been pressing upon the Government – compulsory military service and forming a Ministry of Supply – were taken. In the following month Hitler was telling his generals that Poland had to be isolated and attacked at the first suitable opportunity, and that although there would be war, it would be necessary to avoid *simultaneous* conflict with the principal Western powers – France and Britain. He went on to outline how France would be defeated, by a wheeling movement towards the Channel ports, not the encirclement of Paris, and explained that there would then be no need to invade Britain – her supplies would be cut and capitulation would follow. Hitler had one more strategic coup up his sleeve before his armies actually invaded Poland – the signing of the Nazi–Soviet Pact on 24 August, and a week later the appropriate frontier incidents were provoked, the Führer signed his Directive No 1 for the Conduct of the War which ordered the German Army to begin its attack on Poland at 4.45 am the following morning. Two days later, there having been no response to the British ultimatum, Britain declared war on Germany, the French following suit. As in the previous war the entire British Empire found itself at war within a few days. Eire, as expected, remained neutral. The most important development in London was that Churchill became First Lord of the Admiralty. Winston was back.

The B.E.F. under Lord Gort made its somewhat sluggish way to

France with four infantry divisions – the armoured division was not ready – but nothing like the exact and complete preparations which existed in 1914 had been made. The fact was that the British Army was totally inadequate in size, in equipment, in doctrine and in training to indulge in what turned out to be a global war. Fortunately there was to be a short breathing space of 'phoney war' until the Wehrmacht's Panzers and Stukas cut the French Army to pieces and drove the British Army back to Dunkirk and evacuation. We will accompany the gentlemen in khaki theatre by theatre (rather than in strict chronology) – first in France and Norway; then the Middle East; next defeats in the Far East; the slogging match in Italy; Normandy to the Baltic; finally triumphs in Burma. The road to victory was, as Churchill promised, to be a long and hard one.

11

FINEST HOUR

From the way you're carrying on, anyone would think you'd won the
bloody war. The sooner you realize you nearly lost it, the better.
Now you're going to learn to be proper soldiers.

Sergeant-Major to Dunkirk veterans

There was no grand Anglo-French strategy for the conduct of the war.
The first eight months from September, 1939, to May, 1940, have been
called *Sitzkrieg*, and this really is what it was, sitting down and waiting
to see what would happen, the French Army manning the Maginot
Line with a few half-hearted patrols into German territory, the British
Expeditionary Force slowly building up its strength and digging some
inadequate defensive positions on the Franco-Belgian frontier. If there
was little strategic thinking at Gort's headquarters or by the French
Commander-in-Chief, Gamelin, there was plenty being done by Hitler
and his staff (which we will examine shortly) and also by the newly
appointed General Officer, Commanding-in-Chief, Middle East, Arch-
ibald Wavell. Although this is to anticipate subsequent events, it is
important to understand here and now that the strategic importance of
the Middle East and the Mediterranean was appreciated by the British
government and as a result both naval and military forces were being
assembled there. Wavell's appreciation, made as early as August, 1939,
was that, whereas Germany would seek to dominate eastern and south-
eastern Europe, Italy would attempt to do the same in North Africa and
the Mediterranean. Control of the Mediterranean would therefore be
an indispensable feature of British strategy, not merely to defend British
interests and positions in the Middle East, but to be able to take the
offensive against both Italy and Germany. To Wavell all this meant
that his task was to secure Egypt and the Canal, control the Eastern
Mediterranean, clear the Red Sea and eventually develop operations on

land in Europe against the Axis powers. It was not until Italy declared war – on the collapse of France – that Wavell began to put all these ideas into practice. When he did he met with some startling successes and some equally dramatic reverses.

In the spring of 1940 reverses were to be the order of the day, and the first one suffered by the British Army was in Norway. Hitler had planned for some time to occupy Denmark and Norway in order to forestall any British action there, secure Swedish ore for Germany and to provide further bases for his Air Force and Navy to conduct operations against Britain. On 8 April Hitler launched his invasion. Surprise, speed and sheer military skill paid great dividends. Denmark was overrun and all the important Norwegian ports were captured by the Germans. British intervention was a catalogue of confusion, contradictory orders and failure. Although Narvik was captured after six weeks of fighting, it was taken only to be evacuated again, while the two principal landings at Namsos and Aandalsnes aimed at Trondheim fared even worse. The British Army was having its first lesson on the impossibility of conducting amphibious operations without enjoying two of the conditions essential to such operations – absolute clarity and coordination between the various services and complete air and naval superiority. Of course there were gains too, in that the German Navy had suffered heavy losses – three cruisers and ten destroyers, together with three other battleships disabled. But the fact was that in this first encounter with Germany's armed forces, and in circumstances where it might have been supposed that the Royal Navy's strength and traditions would be decisive, the British Army had been put ashore, only to be beaten and chased out again. Not only had the Germans demonstrated how effective air power could be when properly used in conjunction with land forces. The German Army itself had shown how excellently trained and led it was. Churchill summed it all up like this:

> At Narvik a mixed and improvised German force, barely six thousand strong, held at bay for six weeks some twenty thousand Allied troops, and though driven out of the town lived to see them depart. The Narvik attack, so brilliantly opened by the Navy, was paralysed by the refusal of the military commander to run what was admittedly a desperate risk. The division of our resources between Narvik and Trondheim was injurious to both our plans. . . . At Namsos there was a muddy waddle forward and back. Only at Aandalsnes did we bite. The Germans traversed in seven days the road from Namsos to Mosjoen, which the British and French had declared impassable. . . . We, who had command of the sea and could pounce anywhere on an undefended coast, were outpaced by the enemy moving by land across very large distances

in the face of every obstacle. In this Norwegian encounter, our finest troops, the Scots and Irish Guards, were baffled by the vigour, enterprise, and training of Hitler's young men.

In *The Gathering Storm* Churchill emphasizes that in their struggle with the Royal Navy, Germany all but destroyed its own, for, in June, 1940, after the Narvik evacuation had been carried out, all that the *Kriegsmarine* could effectively put to sea were seven warships – three cruisers, two of them light, and four destroyers. This was to have a profound influence on the aftermath of the British Army's next confrontation with the Wehrmacht. Indeed, together with the Royal Air Force's performance, it was to ensure that the invasion of Britain could not be undertaken and that the struggle against Germany could be carried on. Had it not been for another supremely important consequence of the Norwegian campaign, who knows what course the war might have taken? But Chamberlain fell and Churchill became Prime Minister on 10 May, the very day that the Germans began to destroy both the French Army and the French people's will to fight.

If we are to understand how it was that the Wehrmacht overcame the French Army like a summer's cloud, we must understand too both the character and the strategic ideas of Gamelin, Supreme Commander of the French Armies. He was 68 years old. In the Great War he had commanded a division and served on Joffre's staff. He was dedicated to the preservation of French manpower and French territory. His entire strategic thinking was defensive. Having at first dismissed the whole concept of blitzkrieg – the notion of concentrated armoured forces supported by aircraft breaking through and then widening and deepening their penetration to disrupt the entire enemy's army – he then countered its swift and devastating demonstration in Poland by saying that it could not happen in France. His idea of exercising command was to tuck himself away in a remote headquarters at Vincennes without radio communication, and then delegate the crucial north-eastern front to General Georges. He even believed that the German Army would be labouring under a severe disadvantage because none of its generals had held that rank during 1914 to 1918. He put his faith in the Maginot Line and his conviction that the main German attack, when it came, would be through Belgium. This conviction was reinforced by the capture of German documents at Mechelen in January, 1940, purporting to show that operational plans for invading Holland and Belgium were valid. But by this time Hitler was thinking very differently.

As early as October, 1939, Hitler had put the cat among the German generals' pigeons by proposing to von Brauchitsch (Army Commander-in-Chief) and Halder (Chief of the General Staff) that the main thrust should be to the south of Namur directed at Amiens in order to 'cut off and annihilate the enemy'. He followed this by suggesting that one of the main *Schwerpunkte* should strike through the Ardennes to Sedan and on further west from there. These ideas sprang from the dazzling prospect of being able to break through a weak French centre and thereby destroy the whole French Army with paralysing velocity and strength. It was all a piece of his favourite tactical theories of over-whelming speed, surprise and concentration which would decide the campaign with a single lightning stroke. It was the very antithesis of limited, frontal attacks against the main enemy defences. Fortunately for the Wehrmacht, Hitler's concept was strongly supported by such men as von Manstein, von Rundstedt and Guderian – even Halder, once convinced, bent all his brilliant organizational energy into turning operational concepts into sound plans – and the upshot of it all was that when the final directive was drawn up the main effort would be in the centre. In the north von Bock's Army Group B, with 29 divisions including three panzer divisions, was to be a kind of bait to persuade the French and British forces into Holland and northern Belgium; in the south Army Group C under von Leeb would threaten the Maginot Line; while von Rundstedt in the centre would have 45 divisions in his Army Group A, including *seven* panzer divisions, to blast his way through the Ardennes, bounce his way over the Meuse between Dinant and Sedan and race on to the Channel ports. While all this planning was being perfected, Gamelin was making his own master plan, which could hardly have suited the Germans better. He would deploy his hundred or so divisions to form a strong right flank based on the Maginot Line and a strong left flank for the Dyle–Breda position in Belgium. The British Expeditionary Force (by May, 1940, it totalled a dozen nominal divisions) would largely be employed with this left flank. The Allied centre opposite the Belgian Ardennes would remain understrength, despite General Georges's objection that the whole German plan to attack through Belgium might be a piece of colossal bluff, so facilitating an enemy breakthrough in the centre. Alistair Horne summed up the strategic opportunity thus open to the Germans: 'What a standing temptation the spectacle of this French line, then, so weak in the centre, might present to an opposing captain of audacity and genius!'

The British Army's part in the whole affair was essentially subor-dinate. Lord Gort, who commanded, was a proper fighting soldier, but had little notion of armoured warfare. Indeed the B.E.F. contained only one tank brigade. What is more, although Gort was fully aware of the restraints placed upon him by being obliged to conform to the French supreme command, his loyalty to unified action and his instinctive obedience to higher authority placed him in a most difficult position. One of Gort's Corps Commanders, General Sir Alan Brooke (who was to win the everlasting admiration and gratitude of the nation for his performance as C.I.G.S.) thought little of his Commander-in-Chief's comprehension of strategic issues. He thought of him as 'a queer mixture, perfectly charming, a very definite personality, full of vitality, energy and *joie de vivre* and gifted with powers of leadership, but he fails to be able to see the big picture'. Yet, as David Fraser in his masterly biography of Alanbrooke points out, when things went badly wrong 'it was Gort's decision, and Gort's alone, which in May, 1940, was to save the B.E.F. Unsupported, to some extent in defiance of his formal instructions, backing his hunch about the futility of further reliance on Allied plans, he saw one thing might be done: the Army might be saved to fight again. He acted on that insight and showed unflinching willpower in so doing. Gort's skill in the handling of a large army, or the planning for it, may be questioned. There are, however, many occasions in war when will is more important than skill. At a vital moment Gort showed will, and many were thus saved for ultimate victory.'

How did the British Army get into such a pickle that the only thing which really concerned its Commander-in-Chief was how to save it from extinction? When the German bait was dangled by their anticipated invasion of Holland and Belgium on 10 May, the French 7th Army and the B.E.F. duly moved north to their positions on the River Dyle, thus evoking from Hitler the comment that he could have wept with joy, so completely had the Allies done what he was hoping they would do. The whole campaign was over in a matter of four weeks. First Holland was overwhelmed and capitulated, while the main German thrust by Army Group A to the Meuse and beyond was successful beyond all expectations. Guderian's Corps had established bridgeheads over the Meuse by 13 May; three days later he was allotting his three panzer divisions routes to flood through a fifty-mile gap in the French defences, and despite a temporary hold-up – on 16 May Hitler actually ordered the advance to halt as he was worried about the southern flank – he surged on, reaching St Quentin by 18 May, Amiens two days later, while on the 21st the leading elements of 21st Panzer Division were at the Atlantic Coast. In the wake of this devastating onslaught by von Rundstedt's Army Group was the hapless General Corap's 9th Army, which simply disintegrated. In Vercors' words, 'The whole retreat towards Dunkirk turned into an epic, but it was a sombre epic. The disaster was immeasurable. The French Army was smashed to pieces, cut to shreds by the tanks, nailed to the ground by the enemy's Stukas. A hundred miles from the front dazed soldiers were still streaming back.' The Belgians gave up on 27 May, the B.E.F. uncomfortably sandwiched between Army Group B in the north and the main *Schwerpunkt* of Army Group A was obliged to fall back on Dunkirk [from which, together with many French soldiers, they were evacuated on 4 June] and by 16 June the French themselves had surrendered. Italy, anxious not to be deprived of such apparently easy pickings, had declared war on 10 June.

The B.E.F. had, however, given a good account of itself in a number of battles, and in one with Rommel's 7th Panzer Division near Arras, General Martel's force, made up from 1st Army Tank Brigade and 151st Infantry Brigade, fought so well that Rommel thought the entire British B.E.F. was engaged. The scrappiness of the action is made plain by Sergeant Hepple of the 7th Royal Tank Regiment in describing his encounter with groups of Germany infantry and anti-tank guns:

> Near the main road west of Achincourt we came under anti-tank fire and received three hits. The effect was that of hitting a large stone at speed, and the track on the right-hand side was seen a yard or two in front of the tank. Two more shots followed, and then the guns were silenced by our fire, and that of the I tanks.... We were subjected to intense rifle fire for some minutes, and then left alone, apparently in the belief that we were all killed. After five or ten minutes about thirty to fifty Germans were congregated in groups on the road and to the right of us. We estimated the range of each group, and then opened fire. Many of the enemy fell, but some doubtless were unhurt. Later an abandoned anti-tank gun, about 800 yards to our right front, was re-manned, but was seen to be deserted after we fired upon it.

Such minor and uncoordinated actions could not prevent withdrawal to Dunkirk. Churchill, never bolder than when faced with a seemimgly hopeless situation, was unable to bolster French morale or persuade them to counterattack. By 19 May Gort had begun his preparations to withdraw to the coast. Although Ironside tried to persuade him to mount a counter-attack southwards, as the bulk of the British forces were engaging the Germans on the line of the Scheldte, such a move was out of the question. Gort was determined to save the British Army. Weygand had replaced Gamelin, but was equally ineffectual, and by 27 May Gort was ordered by the Government to evacuate the maximum force possible. Churchill had already made it clear to French Ministers that, whatever they did and whatever happened at Dunkirk, 'we shall fight on for ever and ever and ever'. In the end the miracle of Dunkirk saved nearly 340,000 men, of whom about 220,000 made up the British Army. Only some 70,000 men had been lost, but nearly all the B.E.F.'s guns, tanks and major equipments had to be left behind. In a last attempt to support the French Churchill despatched General Sir Alan Brooke with two divisions to France in June, but they too had to be evacuated. Together with troops from the rear areas a further 200,000 Allied soldiers returned to Britain. 'The grand total of men brought back to Great Britain during the battle of France,' records A. J. P. Taylor, 'was 558,032, of whom 368,491 were British.' The Army would be able to fight again. In a broadcast on 2 June Anthony Eden had declared that the 'British Expeditionary Force still exists, not as a handful of fugitives, but as a body of seasoned veterans. The vital weapon of any army is its spirit. Ours has been tried and tempered in the furnace. It has not been found wanting. It is this refusal to accept defeat that is the guarantee of final victory.' Characterizing this spirit, standing supreme above his fellow men, intoxicating the world with his oratory and almost single-handedly inspiring the nation to live and revel in its finest hour, was the Prime Minister, Mr Churchill. No one has drawn so striking or so true a portrait of him at this moment in Britain's history than Sir Isaiah Berlin:

> In 1940 he assumed an indomitable stoutness, an unsurrendering quality on the part of his people, and carried on. If he did not represent the quintessence and epitome of what some, at any rate, of his fellow citizens feared and hoped in their hour of danger, this was because he idealised them with such intensity that in the end they approached his ideal and began to see themselves as he saw them: 'the buoyant and imperturbable temper of Britain which I had the honour to express' – it was indeed, but he had a lion's share in creating it. So hypnotic was the force of his words, so strong his faith, that by the sheer intensity of his eloquence he bound his spell upon them until it seemed to them that he was indeed speaking what was in their hearts and minds. Doubtless it was there; but largely dormant until he had awoken it within them.

So there is, therefore, some justification for Piers Brendon's claiming that it was Churchill's oratory that was his greatest single contribution to the war, that he had galvanized his people by the power of rhetoric alone. Yet it was, of course, far more than this. Churchill himself conceded that rhetoric could not guarantee survival. Constant activity, eternal vigilance, the undimmed offensive spirit, defiance in spite of all the odds, fertility of imagination, spurring all manner of people into action, boldness, above all – leadership – these were the ingredients of survival. And as a war leader Churchill was unique. Despite some will-o'-the-wisp notions, he was a master of strategy. He really believed he understood the business of war, and with reason. What other Prime Minister (and Minister of Defence) had fought on the North-West

Frontier, charged at Omdurman, stood on the bloodied heights of Spion Kop, commanded a battalion in the trenches, been First Lord of the Admiralty and Secretary for War, voraciously studied the technicalities of ships, aircraft and guns, thought, written and debated about war for nearly half a century? The only other Prime Minister ever to have been a professional soldier was the Duke of Wellington. Despite this background, or perhaps because of it, in June, 1940, Churchill did not harbour a very high opinion of his generals. He thought them far too negative and obstructive to the ideas with which his own mind was teeming. With General Ismay at the head of his Defence Office, Churchill bombarded the Chiefs of Staff and others with his schemes for action, both defensive and offensive. As early as 18 June, 1940, two weeks after Dunkirk, he was demanding to know what General Paget, Commander-in-Chief, Home Forces, was proposing to do about forming Storm Troops:

> We have always set our faces against this idea, but the Germans certainly gained in the last war by adopting it, and this time it has been a leading cause of their victory. There ought to be at least twenty thousand Storm Troops or 'Leopards' [they were later called Commandos] drawn from existing units, ready to spring at the throat of any small landings or descents. These officers and men should be armed with the latest equipment, tommy guns, grenades, etc., and should be given great facilities in motor-cycles and armoured cars.

Nor did Churchill stop at aggressive defence measures. No sooner had the British Army been turned out of France then he wanted to mount 'a vigorous, enterprising and ceaseless offensive against the whole German-occupied coastline', raiding deep inland, destroying vital installations, 'butchering' Germans and then 'bolting'. He therefore required the Joint Chiefs of Staff to make their proposals for raising Commandos from the Army and Royal Marines, for forming parachute troops up to a minimum strength of five thousand, for organizing espionage and intelligence arrangements and transporting tanks to the beaches. He told Mountbatten to turn the south coast of England into a springboard for attack. All these ideas, streaming from his ever-active mind in chits, as often as not marked 'Action This Day', and being instantly followed by discussions with his military chiefs, at which he mercilessly harangued them (sometimes suggesting that with the example of Admiral Byng before them it might be a good thing to shoot a few generals) – all this gave new life to the machinery directing the war. Churchill's drive and vitality somehow revitalized the whole machinery responsible for running the country and the war – 'it was as though the machine had overnight acquired one or two new gears, capable of far higher speeds than had ever been thought possible'.

Some of the generals who had returned with the British Army from Dunkirk, however, were to command Churchill's lasting respect and admiration, among them Sir Alan Brooke (from November, 1941, C.I.G.S. to the great benefit of the Army and the nation) and two major-generals, Harold Alexander and Bernard Montgomery. They had both commanded their divisions with coolness and skill. They both knew how to get the best out of their soldiers. And what soldiers they were! Here is John Mannion of the 2nd Battalion, East Yorkshire Regiment which was in one of the brigades of Montgomery's 3rd Division, manning the perimeter at Dunkirk:

We had withdrawn past Nieuwpoort on May 30, and were getting a fair amount of stick from Jerry. We were all young, fit and strong, well trained and well disciplined and confident that we could take on anything that Adolf sent against us. Right until the evacuation we were firmly convinced that we were drawing the enemy into a trap and that sooner or later we would turn on him and give him such a dose of his own medicine as would settle his hash once and for all.

I was with the drummers of the A.A. Platoon for the protection of Bn HQ at the Coxyde crossroads. Sgt Pip Jacobs told me and old soldiers Thomas and Wilson, both ex-drummers, to make our way to a nearby farmhouse, to establish ourselves on the upper floor and, with a Bren gun I was carrying, endeavour to quieten those Jerries nearest to our position. I had used up my ammunition and, on the way to the farmhouse, I picked up some ammunition and cigarettes which I found lying about. I knocked a hole in the farmhouse roof and thoroughly enjoyed, for a change, blasting away at Jerry, though I must admit he sent a certain amount our way. Years later I was discussing this incident with Pip Jacobs and he said, 'Yes, of course, I remember it; you silly twit you were firing tracer and Jerry stonked hell out of us!' Well, at that particular period, beggars couldn't be choosers . . .

We went onto the beaches and we marched and marched; trudged would be a better word, as those who have marched on sand with weapons and equipment will agree . . . We marched for an hour or so with little interference when suddenly all hell seemed to be let loose. We hardly knew what hit us. The Guards up ahead got it first and our share rapidly followed. La Panne was well alight and shells were exploding all over the place. I flew into the sea, hoping that any shrapnel would be stopped by the water and not by the body beautiful . . . We stayed put for that night. Next morning some went on to Dunkirk town which seemed to be completely ablaze. There was no question of rejoining the Battalion; individuals and units were inextricably mixed. In any case, I saw little point marching and decided to take my chance where I was. I glanced out to sea, and through the mist or fog I saw some sort of long boat drifting inshore ... we made a dash for it, fortunately reaching it as the water reached our necks ... there were by now plenty of willing helpers to get me aboard and, eventually, we found ourselves joined by some 90 others. Soon we were picked up by the Minesweeper *Strive* and my adventures for the time being anyway were over.

Such were the men who returned from Dunkirk and slowly but surely were reorganized, first of all to resist the threatened invasion of these shores and then to get the Army ready for war elsewhere. While the evacuation from Dunkirk was under way the Chiefs of Staff were deciding that although the target of 32 divisions would be stuck to (this figure excluded a further 23 divisions from the Dominions and India), they could not be fully equipped before 1942, and that war would therefore have to be waged by bombing and by subversion, together with the ever-present hope that Germany's economic position would so decline during the next year or so that a great battle on the Continent as in the previous war would not be necessary. Meanwhile General Sir Alan Brooke, now appointed Commander-in-Chief, Home Forces, got on with the business of equipping and training the Army, noting in his diary that, although he was short of trained formations, he did not consider the position hopeless. He organized exercises designed to harden the men and sort out competent commanders. It was not only the British Army that he could call on in late 1940 and early 1941, but also General de Gaulle's French forces, the Poles under Sikorski and the Canadian Corps.

In the event these armies were not required to fight in defence of Britain's shores. Although Hitler issued a War Directive for Operation *Sea Lion*, the invasion of England, conditions to make possible such a venture were never forthcoming. He himself had described it as 'an exceptionally bold and daring undertaking' and had laid down that the Royal Air Force would have to be so morally and materially reduced that it would be unable to deliver any significant attack on the invading German forces. The Battle of Britain saw to it that no such reduction was made, and two days after the R.A.F.'s great victory on 15 September, 1940, Hitler cancelled *Sea Lion*. He would, like Napoleon, seek decision elsewhere. If Hitler could not get to grips with the British Army, the British were similarly unable to get at the Germans. There was, however, another theatre of war, another centre of gravity (which Churchill had been bold enough to reinforce even while invasion threatened), suddenly by Italy's joining in the conflict turned into an area of active operations –

the Middle East. It is to East Africa, the Western Desert and the Mediterranean that we can now turn our attention and see what the far-sighted Wavell, whom we met at the beginning of this chapter, was getting up to.

12

REDEMPTION IN AFRICA

We never went West of Gezira,
We never went North of the Nile,
We never went past the Pyramids
Out of sight of the Sphinx's smile.
We fought the war in Shepheard's and the Continental Bar,
We reserved our punch for the Turf Club lunch
And they gave us the Africa Star.

This agreeable jingle of the 'gaberdine swine' – the staff officers of General Headquarters, Middle East, in Cairo – was often seen to be self-deprecatory, for the tunics of these officers were sprinkled with D.S.O.s and M.C.s long before the Africa Star was issued in 1943 when the North African campaign, with its seesaw of fortunes, its colourful personalities, its reputation of being 'a gentleman's war', *Krieg ohne Hass* (war without hatred) was the way Rommel put it, the fame of the 8th Army and the birth of the Montgomery legend – when all this had passed into history.

Perhaps most important of all for the British Army was that in Africa it began to redeem itself. The Desert Rats became world-famous, the 7th Armoured Division a household word. Churchill talked of them as being 'lean, bronzed, desert-hardened and fully mechanized'. But it was not only the British themselves who shared this special place in the history of war by virtue of serving in the desert. Five years after the war was over, General von Ravenstein, who commanded 21st Panzer Division, spoke of the staunch comradeship with which warriors of the African campaign greeted each other, whether they were from England, Scotland, Germany, Italy, India, South Africa or New Zealand. They were, he said, brave and chivalrous soldiers, who had and still respected each other, bound together by strong, invisible links, recalling a fight that was fierce, but fair. Some of the formations which fought in the desert figure large not only in their own histories, but in those of their allies and enemies alike. Who can forget, who has read of them, the fame and fortunes of such divisions as 15th and 21st Panzer, Ariete, 90th Light, the Highland Division, the New Zealanders, 6th Australian, 4th Indian or 7th Armoured? These last two were there at the beginning and at the end. A historian of the former recalls his first meeting with the latter:

They took the road so many came to know so well, turning north at the Pyramids across a hundred miles of hard sand to the causeway over the magenta lagoons behind Alexandria, thence west through the rolling dunes, which skirted the bright thunderous Mediterranean, past scattered date oases and fig plantations, until beyond the dusty hamlet of Burgh el Arab the road rose to the crest of the dunes and along the easy valley inland a train snorted up to a sun-bitten drought-stricken halt whose name (which did not matter then) was El Alamein. Forty miles farther on at El Daba Divisional officers met for the first time the bronzed and cheerful officers and men of 7th Armoured Division, who had kept watch for years in the sandy wastes; who knew more about the desert and its ways than anyone alive; who, having taken as their emblem the Libyan jerboa, were destined to be known as The Desert Rats as long as memory remains.

Thus 4th Indian Division came to a battlefield on which it was destined to find fame. The Western Desert, between the Nile Delta and the Gulf of Sirte, once a naked and desolate expanse, was no longer empty upon the maps. British officers in search of adventure and against the day of battle had charted its maze of age-old trails, had plotted its contours and defined even its most insignificant features. Of the traditional soft burning sand of the Sahara, they had found little, save in the Great Sand Sea far to the south. But there were vast stretches of hard sand and of stony ground raddled with black basaltic slabs; there were bony ridges and ribbed escarpments and deep depressions; there were flat pans which held water after the rains, where gazelles cropped the coarse grass in midsummer. There were wadi-fed flats which sprang overnight into flowery glory in spring; there were endless undulating sand and gravel dunes whose crests marched in rhythm, like waves at sea.*

Here then was the battlefield described in almost lyrical language. Why was it so important for the British Army to have it and make use of it? We have seen what Wavell had to say about the need, not merely to defend his Middle East base, but to take the offensive against the Axis

---

* G. R. Stevens, *Fourth Indian Division*, Maclaren & Sons.

powers from it. On becoming C.I.G.S. General Sir Alan Brooke echoed Wavell, declaring his conviction that every effort should be made to conquer North Africa as soon as possible, so that the Mediterranean could be opened (and thus make real savings in one of the Allies' vital commodities – *shipping* – without which a real assault on Hitler's *Festung Europa* would never be possible) and so that offensive operations against Italy could be mounted. Churchill himself was never in doubt about the absolute indispensability of the Middle East as a base for the waging of war. Indeed he had taken grave risks in reinforcing it at a time when the invasion danger to Britain itself had not disappeared. In April, 1941, when the Desert Fox, Erwin Rommel, had brought a new dimension to desert battles and shown what bold leadership from the front, deploying mixed groups of panzers, anti-tank guns, artillery and armoured infantry in lightning exhibitions of fire-power and manoeuvre, could do to overwhelm the slower thinking, more conventional British, so concerned was the Prime Minister that he insisted on further reinforcing the Middle East 'whose loss would be a disaster of the first magnitude to Great Britain, second only to successful invasion and final conquest'. It was not to be thought, he wrote, that British forces would wish to survive such a disgrace as to be expelled from Egypt. Not only was it essential to hold Egypt. The Germans had to be beaten and expelled from Cyrenaica. In the end they were, but what a long and hazardous game it was! We may perhaps think of the battle for North Africa as having five phases.

It took the British Army the best part of three years – from September, 1940, when the Italian 10th Army lumbered reluctantly across the Egyptian frontier, until May, 1943, when Alexander was able to announce that the campaign was over – to defeat the Italians, held together both militarily and morally by the small but skilful Afrika Korps under its brave and brilliant commander, Rommel. For most of these three years the Wehrmacht was engaged in a life and death struggle with the Red Army, while the battle of supplies – which was the key to success in the desert fighting – was nearly always being won by the British. Indeed the British were supported throughout by a powerful and secure base, excellent intelligence, continuous reinforcement, assured and abundant supplies, plentiful, although not always, superior weapons, strong and active Royal Navy and Royal Air Force units, and intact lines of communication. Why then against an enemy which was either half-hearted or inferior in numbers did it take them so long? Initially the answer is that although the British regiments were lacking in neither courage nor determination and although they found it easy enough to defeat the Italians, they were not good enough to beat the

Germans. We may perhaps illustrate this by examining the five phases: first in late 1940 and early 1941, O'Connor turned the Italians out of Egypt, captured their army and conquered Cyrenaica; then in the spring of 1941 Rommel brought blitzkrieg to the desert and turned the British out again; (between January and May, 1941, General Platt and General Cunningham successfully defeated the Italian forces in East Africa, largely with Indian, South African and African troops); in the third phase Auchinleck pushed Rommel back with the *Crusader* battles from

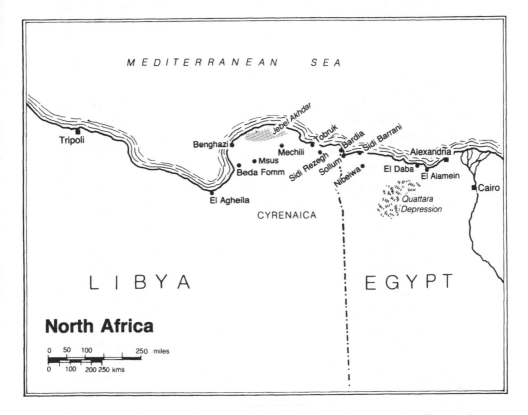

November, 1941, to January, 1942; within a few months Rommel enjoyed his most startling successes, captured Tobruk (a bitter blow for Churchill – 'Defeat is one thing; disgrace is another') and threatened Egypt itself at Alamein; the final phase began with the arrival of Alexander and Montgomery; then came the latter's relentless battle of attrition at Alamein, followed almost at once by the Allied landings in French North Africa and between them the slow grinding of Rommel's *Panzerarmee* into retreat and subjection.

It was here therefore that the British Army learned its business. It was after all the only theatre where British troops were engaging Germans on land (including a somewhat unpalatable taste of it in Greece and Crete, where as so often elsewhere in the past they were put ashore only to be faced with impossible odds, beaten in the field and then either evacuated or imprisoned), and as the *Official History* pointed out it was also here that 'the techniques of land warfare were kept constantly up-to-date, the intimate tactical cooperation of land and air forces evolved and perfected, and the conduct of large and intricate landing operations put to the practical test'. It was moreover a proving ground for British generals, and Churchill kept on changing them until he found the ones he wanted. At the start of the campaign he had been delighted with Wavell's offensive, *Compass*, during which General O'Connor had won a signal victory. His first success was at the Battle of Sidi Barrani where he employed 4th Indian and 7th Armoured Divisions completely to outflank the Italian defences in their various encampments, taking them by surprise first at Nibeiwa and in the space of an hour capturing 4,000 prisoners, 23 tanks, numerous guns and lorries, all at trifling loss to the British and Indian troops. He then went on to deal with the rest of the Sidi Barrani camps, disrupting two entire Italian corps, taking in all some 40,000 prisoners, 73 tanks and 237 guns at a price of about 600 British casualties. Exploiting this coup by pushing further west with the 6th Australian Division along the coastal route and with 7th Armoured Division racing across the desert in a series of left-handed hooks, O'Connor proceeded to capture Bardia (which yielded a further 40,000 prisoners, nearly 500 guns, 127 tanks and 700 lorries), then on 22 January, 1941, Tobruk and yet another great haul of captive men and material. Finally came a brilliant climax designed to destroy the rest of the enemy's army – the Australians continuing to advance along the coast road and 7th Armoured Division, led by the famous 11th Hussars with 2nd Rifle Brigade and three artillery batteries, sweeping over the desert via Mechili and Msus to Beda Fomm to close the trap and cut off the retreating Italians:

> It was then that the 11th Hussars showed what all their training in the desert had made them capable of. They had no maps, but by the time the main body reached Antelat their leading patrols had already cut the coast road. By midday on 5th February Colonel John Combe had established his whole force astride the enemy's withdrawal routes near Beda Fomm. What is more he had got there in front of the Italians, but only just, for two hours later leading elements of the garrison retreating from Benghazi came into sight. Numerically the odds were uneven to the point of absurdity. Benghazi's

garrison was 20,000 or so and included many regiments of tanks and guns. Combe had fewer than a regiment's worth of guns and at that stage no tanks at all, since 4th Armoured Brigade, albeit making all the speed it could, was hours behind. His total force numbered less than 2,000. Combe's concern, however, was not that he had so many of the enemy to take on; it was that they might slip past him to the south before 4th Armoured Brigade came up. He resolved to fight astride the road.

The battle began when one of the Rifle Brigade companies and C Squadron, 11th Hussars, supported by the R.H.A. batteries, opened fire on the enemy vanguard. Although the company was in a defensive position, it could not by virtue of size alone extend across a broad front, so that C Squadron moved further south to dissuade the Italians from an outflanking movement. They resorted therefore to frontal attacks on the Rifle Brigade. These attacks failed. More difficult to cope with were the hundreds of prisoners who wanted to surrender.

About three hours after the battle started, Combe's force was glad to see 4th Armoured Brigade's leading tanks. It was the 7th Hussars, and they appeared most appropriately to the left and rear of the leading Italian columns. Their commanding officer had not time to waste on complicated operation orders. With the one word, 'Attack!', even that almost superfluous, he launched his regiment at the enemy. The effect on thousands of Italians, on their guns, petrol lorries, civilian refugees and so on of the wholly unexpected appearance of two squadrons of Hussars charging at them with guns blazing may perhaps be imagined. Panic spread among the soldiers, fire among the trucks. Destruction and prisoners multiplied. Only nightfall prevented the whole thing being finished there and then.

Holding the ring at night was not easy for the small British force, but it was done. Next day the growing Italian strength produced sharper fighting, and they made many an attempt to break their way through with tanks and infantry. But 7th Armoured Division held on, and in doing so knocked out nearly 100 Italian tanks. Again night fell and again the Italians made what was most dangerous of all for so tenuous a trap – strong night attacks by mixed teams of all arms. No less than nine times the Rifle Brigade repelled the enemy, and still they did not give up. At dawn, mustering all the tanks they had got left, about 30, the Italians made a last push to force their way through. This too was held, and at that the entire army surrendered.

It had been that rare thing, the classic armoured pursuit, a battle of annihilation. As O'Connor was later to report: 'I think this may be termed a complete victory as none of the enemy escaped'.*

Certainly the British Army had redeemed itself. But this victory, com-

* From the author's *Battle for North Africa*, Batsford, 1969.

plete though it was, did not finish the game. It was simply the first of
the shuffling to and from Benghazi that was to be a feature of the desert
war for two more years. O'Connor's campaign had lasted two months,
from December, 1940, to February, 1941, and two British divisions had
destroyed an Italian army of 10 divisions, capturing 130,000 prisoners,
400 tanks and 800 guns and advancing 500 miles into enemy territory.
O'Connor wanted to go on to Tripoli, but was prevented by the demands
for succouring Greece (Hitler having sent a German Army there to
rescue the Italians from a further rebuff) and the fears that even if he
might advance that far, it would be impossible to maintain an army
there at the end of such long and vulnerable lines of communication.
The Royal Navy and Royal Air Force were busy elsewhere and already
overstretched. Moreover Rommel had arrived in Tripoli on 12 February
with the Afrika Korps, at that time, it is true, containing only one
German division, which although called 5th Light was very powerful in
reconnaissance, artillery and anti-tank units (including the dreaded
88mm gun) and had 5th Panzer Regiment with 70 light tanks and 80
Mark IIIs and IVs. Formidable too was Fliegerkorps X which had
deployed 50 Stuka and 20 fighter bombers in support of Rommel's
operations. The British were about to learn that their tactics and equipment and generals might do well enough against the Italians, but against
the Germans it was going to be a different story.

Some parts of the story, however, were for the ordinary British soldier
much the same. For them the desert war was, in a telling phrase coined
by Fred Majdalany, almost a private one. If you found yourself with your
regiment 'up in the blue', values changed. All life's normal environments
were absent. There were no trees or houses, villages or towns, usually
only one road, no people, no pubs, no girls. Other things mattered –
things like water, petrol, tea and the blessed brew-up, letters and parcels
from home, cigarettes, whisky, going on leave to Alexandria or Cairo.
Life was hard, but fair, although there was no shortage of discomforts.
The flies were legion and could be a torture; intense heat could be
exchanged for numbing cold; gyppy tummy could mean numberless
excursions with a spade; desert sores could become putrid; the *khamsin*,
the all-penetrating sand-storm, so called because it was supposed to last
for fifty days in the early part of the year, could almost bring everything
to a standstill. And the ever-present consciousness that the Afrika Korps
was probably not far off, led by Rommel, who became almost a heroic
legend to the British soldier, because of his dash, his chivalry and his
habit of leading from the front. Yet no one who served in the desert
would have wished it otherwise, would have wanted to miss so exciting,
comradely, almost romantic an experience. Churchill, every ready with

the haunting phrase, got it right once more when he said that if a man were to be cross-examined later as to his war-time doings, it would be enough for him to reply that he had fought with the 8th Army.

There was even a kind of special code of behaviour, which tried to lay down what might and might not be done in making life more tolerable for desert comrades. Thus you were required to ensure that none of your actions endangered others – no fires after sunset; respect for his slit trench; no borrowing of water or petrol; no rubbish left behind which would breed flies; no question of asking him to do things which were for you to do; no idle talk; no helping yourself to his cigarettes unless plentiful enough to be spared; no criticism of his commanders (your own commanders were fair game). Above all to those sharing in this great adventure – for that is how it was looked upon – be courteous, hospitable and helpful. It was a sum of fellowship in the desert, to be applied without exception. Not a bad code, if we think about it now, and one that could be beneficially applied today in many walks of life other than soldiering.

At the end of March, 1941, Rommel began his first offensive with the idea of recapturing Cyrenaica, and so rapid and successful was his advance that Churchill cabled Wavell in some alarm, sensing that the desert flank – 'the peg on which all else hung' – was in jeopardy and urging Wavell to chop off the enemy's head if he stuck it out too far. How different was the reality! Rommel simply rolled up the British positions, capturing several generals, including O'Connor, outflanked and invested Tobruk, and even crossed into Egypt itself at Sollum. The whole thing was typical of Rommel's lightning methods. Not content with leaving operations to his subordinate commanders, he would fly over the leading elements in his light aircraft, and then drop clear and concise orders to them, such as: 'Mechili clear of enemy. Make for it. Drive fast, Rommel.' He then decided to drive up to the front, where 5th Light Division was in the lead and take over direction of the operation himself. It was a method of command which seemed to have little appeal to British generals, who were more inclined to sit back at their headquarters, having issued orders, and then await events. Rommel preferred to exert direct influence on what happened himself. In two weeks he had reconquered Cyrenaica and was trying to take Tobruk.

All this so concerned Churchill that he took the bold step of des-patching the *Tiger* convoy of 238 tanks and 43 Hurricane fighters to Alexandria through the Mediterranean, having made it plain to the Chiefs of Staff that the fate of the entire war in the Middle East – with the huge stakes of the Suez Canal's future, the Egyptian base itself, the cooperation of American shipping in the Red Sea – might turn on the arrival of a few hundred armoured vehicles. He also made it plain to Wavell what he would then expect of the use of these tanks – 'no German should remain in Cyrenaica by the end of the month of June'. Once the tanks were safely there both he and the Chiefs of Staff kept up the pressure on Wavell, a signal to him at the end of May laying down that, since German occupation of Crete enabled the Axis to open sea communication with Cyrenaica via Western Greece, this route had to be interfered with. This in turn meant getting Malta to resume its disruptive operations on Axis shipping. Therefore, to help Malta, airfields in Eastern Cyrenaica had to be recaptured. Thus Rommel's forces there had to be engaged and destroyed. It was all very logical. The only trouble was that when Operation *Battleaxe* was launched in mid-June, it quickly became plain 'that the means and methods that had done so well against the Italians were not good enough against the Germans'. Rommel, master of the spoiling attack, was also skilful in his defensive arrangements, demonstrating a tactical point that the British Army never quite seemed to grasp – how effectively tanks could be employed in a defensive battle in close cooperation with anti-tank guns, particularly when these latter happened to be 88mm. They took heavy toll of the cruiser tanks of 7th Armoured Brigade and the Matildas of 4th Armoured Brigade. C Squadron of 4th Royal Tank Regiment fought bravely on until all but one of their tanks had been ripped apart. Even the one surviving tank did not give up, but joined the Cameron Highlanders in their attempts to hang on in defence of an escarpment which they had captured. Yet without either sufficient anti-tank guns or armoured support they could not do it.

Having held the British attacks, Rommel then proceeded by a series of rapid and unexpected shifts of weight further to outmanoeuvre and dismay his enemy, so that *Battleaxe* lost all momentum and ended with far heavier casualties for Western Desert Force – about 1,000 men and 100 tanks – than for the Germans. The British still seemed not to have grasped the way the Afrika Korps operated. Rommel's panzer groups had a clear doctrine that their tanks were there to destroy the enemy's infantry and soft vehicles, and that it was the job of their own anti-tank guns, notably 88mm and 50mm, to take on British tanks. Moreover a fundamental feature of the German method was to operate in closely and permanently integrated groups of tanks, infantry and guns. There was no comparable teamwork on the British side, and all too often armoured and infantry brigades would fight separate battles.

The failure of *Battleaxe* so disappointed and exasperated Churchill that he determined on a change of Commander-in-Chief. Wavell was relieved by Auchinleck. He had done some remarkable things while in command – the triumph of East Africa, his first offensive which destroyed a complete Italian Army, the tragedies of Greece and Crete, remaining unruffled as fortune turned upside down, and winning golden opinions from Rommel, who thought of Wavell as the only British general in the Middle East with 'a touch of genius' and from his devoted and loyal subordinate Bernard Fergusson, who looked upon his chief with deep affection and had predicted in 1939 that Wavell would prove himself one of the great commanders of history. He did, but the sad thing was that he never got on with Churchill, despite their having much in common – their deep interest in history and literature, their fascination with strategy and military matters – for with the Prime Minister Wavell seemed dull and taciturn, and looking as the former unkindly put it 'like the Chairman of a golf club'. It was not long before Churchill began to bully Auchinleck too. The new Commander-in-Chief, however, insisted upon certain conditions before launching his winter offensive to turn the Germans out of Cyrenaica once more and relieve Tobruk. He demanded time, reinforcement and preparation, got them all and did not embark on Operation *Crusader* until November, 1941. There were by this time many circumstances in his favour. Tobruk was tying down four Italian divisions and three German battalions. The savaging of Axis supply convoys from Malta and elsewhere was having serious consequences – 35 per cent of supplies and reinforcements despatched to North Africa were lost in August, 63 per cent in October. Moreover the newly named 8th Army had two powerful Corps – 30th which was strong in armour, 13th with such famous formations as 4th Indian and the New Zealand Divisions. Fresh from his triumphs in East Africa, General Cunningham was in command of 8th Army. He planned a battle which would oblige Rommel to do what he, Cunningham, wanted him to do. It turned out otherwise.

There were four main phases of the battle. First, three British armoured brigades advanced with the idea of concentrating at Sidi Rezegh and drawing Rommel's panzers forward to their destruction. Instead the British brigades got the worst of the encounter. Next Rommel put himself at the head of the Afrika Korps and made a dash to the frontier, which together with his tank losses so dismayed Cunningham that he recommended breaking off the battle. Auchinleck properly insisted on continuing with the offensive in order to force Rommel back to his supply bases. It worked, but because be believed Cunningham was now 'thinking defensively', Auchinleck relieved him and appointed Ritchie in his place. The third phase saw more heavy fighting at Sidi Rezegh, and then finally Rommel cut his losses and withdrew to Agheila. So confused had some of the fighting been that

some of those doing it had little idea of what was really going on. Robert
Crisp of the 3rd Royal Tank Regiment gives us the feeling of what it
was like:

> From that moment on I can truthfully say that none of us had more than
> the vaguest idea where we were from day to day and hour to hour or what
> was happening either to our own forces or the enemy's. The campaign swung
> violently from one end of the desert to the other. One morning we would be
> southwest of Sidi Rezegh; the next afternoon we would be well east of the
> point at which we had spent the first night after crossing the Wire. That I
> had actually seen the rooftops of Bardia that second afternoon was an
> unbelievable dream, part of another unreal existence. There was no such
> thing as advance and retreat. We roared off to areas of threat or engagement
> depending on the urgency of the information. We chased mirages and were
> chased by mirages. Every few hours a landmark or a name would punch our
> memories with an elusive familiarity, and we would recall a forgotten early
> incident or a battle fought there days before that was now part of a past so
> near in time but so distant in event.
>
> We went without sleep, without food, without washing or change of
> clothes, without conversation beyond the clipped talk of wireless procedure
> and orders. In permanent need of everything civilized, we snatched greedily
> at everything we could find, getting neither enjoyment nor nourishment.
>
> The daily formula was nearly always the same – up at any time between
> midnight and four o'clock; movement out of the leaguer into battle positions
> before first light; a biscuit and a spoonful of marmalade before the flap of
> orders and information; the long day of movement and vigil and encounter,
> death and the fear of death, until darkness put a limit to vision and purpose
> on both sides; the drawing in of far-flung formations; the final endurance of
> the black, close-linked march to the leaguer area; the maintenance and
> replenishment and order groups that lasted till midnight; the beginning of
> another 24 hours.

Such were the impressions of one British officer. It had become clear
that the British 8th Army had not yet got two vital things right. They
did not seem able to master the control of large forces in fast-moving
operations. This was the first thing. The second one was in part the
cause of the first. Command arrangements were faulty, not only in
mechanics, but in personalities too. Auchinleck had sacked one Commander 8th Army in the middle of the battle and appointed another.
Before long he was to do the same again in circumstances far more
dangerous and difficult. Indeed, had it not been for the fortunate
strategic condition that by mid-1942 Hitler was so obsessed with the
German Army's struggle in Russia that he could spare little thought

and certainly no extra panzer divisions for Rommel, even the staunch Auchinleck might have failed to save Egypt from the Desert Fox, riding high after his bouncing of Tobruk and harrying a 'brave but baffled' 8th Army back to the relatively narrow front and partially prepared defences of El Alamein.

Although Auchinleck could draw some comfort from the results of *Crusader* – he had relieved Tobruk, inflicted a sort of reverse on Rommel and reoccupied Cyrenaica – there were disquieting developments too. Japan's entry into the war in December, 1941, altered the whole course of the war and stretched British resources as they had never been stretched before. Major reinforcements of land, sea and air forces on their way to the Middle East were diverted to the Far East. Auchinleck even had to accept *reductions* in his existing force levels. Meanwhile, because of a German build-up of their naval and Luftwaffe strength in the Mediterranean, some much-needed supplies of tanks, guns, ammunition and petrol were reaching Rommel. Malta, that thorn in the Axis supply lines, had largely been neutralized by Kesselring, who then made the fatal error of releasing four squadrons of fighters and bombers at the very moment Malta received some Spitfire replacements. None the less, when Rommel launched his counter-attack from Agheila in January, 1942, he swept 13th Corps aside. It was in any event far too dispersed. General Tuker, who commanded 4th Indian Division, explained that there was no principle of mutual support between divisions and no firm base behind which formations could rally for coordinated defence in depth. Rommel was able to report to Hitler that during the January–February fighting 'the British 8th Army was so severely beaten that it was incapable of further large-scale operations for months afterwards'. Worse was to come, however, for when Rommel renewed his offensive in May, 1942, he overcame the British in their Gazala positions, drove them back to Alamein, captured Tobruk with some 50,000 men and huge supplies of petrol and vehicles, and so convinced Mussolini that he was about to drive on to Egypt that the Duce made plans to enter Alexandria riding on a white charger. But Auchinleck, this time dismissing Ritchie and assuming command of 8th Army himself, so conducted what has sometimes been called the first battle of Alamein that even though the British Army was at bay, Rommel's rush was successfully stemmed. Once it had been, Churchill went himself to Cairo, and this time appointed what became a winning team – Alexander as C.-in-C., Montgomery in command of 8th Army.

To these two Churchill gave a clear and simple directive – to take or destroy Rommel's Army together with all its material. They did eventually do so, but it took them eight or nine months plus the intervention of another Allied Army, this time containing United States forces, which landed in French North Africa. Montgomery was just the man for 8th Army. Brimming with confidence, gifted with an ability to make his intentions and requirements absolutely clear, a superb public relations man, an energetic trainer and organizer, a great booster of morale, and with the ruthless determination to see a battle of attrition (the set-piece attack was his metier, as his phrase 'no more manoeuvre; fight a battle' indicated) through to its bitter conclusion, he also enjoyed huge advantages. Among them were great superiority in weapons, men and supplies; a powerful Desert Air Force; the incalculably good fortune of *Ultra* intelligence, so that he knew all about Rommel's movements, designs and difficulties; the total backing of his military and political chiefs; and plenty of *time* for preparation. It was hardly surprising, therefore, that when Rommel, in what might almost be thought of as a last, fine, careless rapture launched the Afrika Korps at the strong, deep and ready defences of Alam el Halfa, Montgomery easily saw him off, and commented that next time it would be his service, with the score one love in his favour. That time came in October, 1942, with the renowned battle of El Alamein.

This battle, which Rommel called one without hope, was supported by unprecedented weight in artillery and R.A.F. support, and featured immense superiority in tanks, guns and anti-tank guns. Rommel's Panzerarmee was simply crushed by his enemy's weight. There were five phases: first, the break-in on the night 23/24 October; then what Montgomery called 'crumbling operations' on the 24th and 25th – on this day Rommel returned from sick leave; the third part featured Rommel's counter-attacks for the next two or three days, when Montgomery was forced to think again (his so-called master plan triumphed in the end only because he had sufficient reserves to vary it – even Churchill in an agony of impatience asked Brooke, the C.I.G.S., during this pause if the Army had not got one single general who could win one single battle); fourth was Operation *Supercharge* on the night of 1/2 November with a new point of concentration which so wore down the German and Italian defences that they could no longer prevent a break-out; and finally the break-out itself from 3 to 7 November. On the following day, 8 November, the Anglo-American forces of Operation *Torch* landed in French Morocco and Algeria. Rommel knew then that there was no future in Africa for him any more. His way of life there had fallen into the seer, the yellow leaf.

Before we follow him to the end of the game, however, we may perhaps visit two British regiment during the battle of Alamein, one at the outset, another near the end. The first story is told by H. P. Samwell,

at the time a platoon commander of the Argyll and Sutherland Highlanders, who found himself in action for the first time during the break-
in, the night of mines and wire:

> The line had broken up into blobs of men all struggling together; my faithful
> batman was still trotting along beside me. I wondered if he had been with
> me while I was shooting. My runner had disappeared, though; and then I
> saw some men in a trench ahead of me. They were standing up with their
> hands above their heads screaming something that sounded like 'Mardray'.
> I remember thinking how dirty and ill-fitting their uniforms were, and smiled
> at myself for bothering about that at this time. To my left and behind me
> some of the NCOs were rounding up prisoners and kicking them into some
> sort of formation. I waved my pistol at the men in front with their hands up
> to sign them to join the others. In front of me a terrified Italian was running
> round and round with his hands above his head screaming at the top of his
> voice. The men I had signalled started to come out. Suddenly I heard a
> shout of 'Watch out!' and the next moment something hard hit the toe of
> my boot and bounced off. There was a blinding explosion, and I staggered
> back holding my arm over my eyes instinctively. Was I wounded? I looked
> down rather expecting to see blood pouring out, but there was nothing – a
> tremendous feeling of relief. I was unhurt. I looked for the sergeant who had
> been beside me; he had come up to take the place of the one who had fallen.
> At first I couldn't see him, and then I saw him lying sprawled out on his
> back groaning. His leg was just a tangled mess. I realized all at once what
> had happened; one of the enemy in the trench had thrown a grenade at me
> as he came out with his hands up. It had bounced off my boot as the sergeant
> shouted his warning, and had exploded beside him. I suddenly felt furious;
> an absolute uncontrollable temper surged up inside me. I swore and cursed
> at the enemy now crouching in the corner of the trench; then I fired at them
> at point-blank range – one, two, three, and then click! I had forgotten to
> reload. I flung my pistol away in disgust and grabbed a rifle – the sergeant's,
> I think – and rushed in. I believe two of the enemy were sprawled on the
> ground at the bottom of the square trench. I bayoneted two more and then
> came out again. I was quite cool now, and I started looking for my pistol,
> and thinking to myself there will be hell to pay with the quartermaster if I
> can't account for it. At the same time I wondered when I had got rid of my
> stick, as I couldn't remember dropping it. I felt rather sad; it had been my
> constant companion for two years at home. I had walked down to the pictures
> with my wife and had put it under the seat, and on leaving I had forgotten
> it, and had had to disturb a whole row of people to retrieve it. I started then
> to wonder what my wife was doing at that moment.

Such had been a gallant infantry soldier's first encounter with the enemy, and because of actions like his platoon's Montgomery's break-in was successful. So was the break-out, but not before comparably brave performances by a famous cavalry regiment, the 3rd Hussars, commanded then by Sir Peter Farquhar, who recalls being instructed by Montgomery to push on with his regiment towards the Sidi Rahman track to hold the door open for 1st Armoured Division. While accepting the order, Farquhar felt bound to point out that it was suicidal. 8th Army Commander replied that it had to be done and that he was prepared to accept 100 per cent casualties in tanks and men. Farquhar admired this frank, tough answer, reflecting that there was in that case no more to be said. His regiment, together with others of 9th Armoured Brigade, carried out their duty with great gallantry, suffering heavy losses – 9th Armoured Brigade in fact lost 75 per cent of its tanks and 50 per cent of its tank crews. Farquhar gave orders for 3rd Hussars to advance on the right of the Wiltshire Yeomanry at 6.15 on the morning of 2 November and at first things went well. Then, silhouetted against the dawn light as the leading squadrons reached the Rahman track, they became easy targets for the German anti-tank guns and were heavily engaged. They seemed to be almost surrounded by enemy guns, but like their ancestors at Chillianwallah (where the 3rd Light Dragoons, as the Regiment was then called, redeemed an otherwise disgraceful performance by the British cavalry in the Sikh war of 1849) they pressed on relentlessly. At one point Farquhar found his regiment was reduced to seven tanks, and was obliged when his radio broke down to go round on foot giving his orders. What mattered was that 3rd Hussars and their Yeomanry companions held the door open long enough for the 2nd Armoured Brigade to come up, fight its way forward, widen the gap and enable the breakthrough to take place. The veteran New Zealand commander, General Freyberg, told Farquhar that his regiment was magnificent, that the Hun was beaten and now was the time for pursuit. Pursuit after Alamein turned out to be a dull and measured affair, but this did not alter the crucial importance of victory, victory which at such a time and in such circumstances was all important. The *Official History* recorded how wholly welcome was the communique of 4 November that Axis forces were in full retreat. Churchill went so far as to have the bells rung, calling it 'A glorious page in British military annals'. Moreover the British Army had found a battle winner at last, and Fred Majdalany paid a proper tribute to Montgomery when he declared that at a time when the world's future was in the balance Montgomery 'rallied his country's soldiers as Churchill had rallied its people'.

There was still much to be done. The 1st British Army in Algeria was receiving a proper blooding, and the first difficult steps of Anglo-

American cooperation were being taken. The Americans suffered a serious set-back at Kasserine where Rommel, once more donning his Napoleonic long-boots, gave them a shock. The British 6th Armoured Division played a significant role in helping to restore the situation. Slowly, but surely, Rommel's Panzerarmee was being crushed and stifled by 8th Army advancing from the east and 1st Army from the west, and, even though Hitler, indulging in one of his favourite gestures of refusing to acknowledge military realities and so reinforcing failure, poured more troops and equipment into Tunisia, removed Rommel, who again was unwell and had lost his touch, by May 1943 the thing was over and some 250,000 German and Italian troops were in captivity. Alan Moorehead, one of the really great war correspondents, described some of the last moments when 6th Armoured Division broke through to Hammamet:

> They roared past German airfields, workshops, petrol and ammunition dumps and gun positions. They did not stop to take prisoners – things had gone far beyond that. If a comet had rushed down that road, it could hardly have made a greater impression. The Germans now were entirely dazed. Wherever they looked, British tanks seemed to be hurtling past. Von Arnim's guns would be firing south only to find that the enemy had also appeared behind them – and over on the left – and on the right. The German generals gave up giving orders since they were completely out of touch and the people to whom they could give orders were diminishing every hour. In what direction, anyway, were they to fight? Back towards Zaghouan? Towards Tunis? Under the German military training you had to have a plan. But there was no plan. Only the boats remained – the evacuation boats which had been promised them. The boats that were to take them back to Italy. In a contagion of doubt and fear the German Army turned tail and made up the Cape Bon roads looking for the boats. When on the beaches it became apparent to them at last that there were no boats – nor any aircraft either – the army became a rabble. The Italian Navy had not dared to put to sea to save its men. The Luftwaffe had been blown out of the sky. In other words, the Axis had cut its losses and the Afrika Korps was abandoned to its fate.
> On May 10th I set off up the Peninsula through Hammam Lif to see one of the most grotesque and awesome spectacles that can have occurred in this war – an entire German army laying down its arms.

Such was the completeness of the victory wrought by the British Army – with, of course, infinite aid from the Royal Navy, the Royal Air Force and numerous allies. The fighting men had done their stuff. Nor should we forget the indispensable part played by those supporting them, as General Surtees so eloquently expressed it:

In the rear services let tribute first be paid to troops in their tens of thousands – to the driver trundling his truck through hundreds of miles of nothingness day after day, cursing his 'V' cigarette, consoled by his brief 'brew-up' of tea; to the private cockily controlling a gang of skilled Egyptians in a workshop; to the sergeant confidently carrying out a charge which in England would have been given to an officer assisted by senior non-commissioned officers.

For Churchill it had been the redemption of his strategy. It was he above all who had been the architect of victory in North Africa. It was after all the one place where British troops were engaging the German Army, so we may understand his passionate concern with winning. Now that it had happened, he asked himself, what should we do with our victory? One thing was certain. In no circumstances would he allow 'the powerful British and British-controlled armies in the Mediterranean to stand idle'. We shall see in a later chapter how they were employed. But first we must pay a visit to another theatre where more or less everything was going wrong.

13

DEFEAT IN THE FAR EAST

The city of Singapore must be converted into a citadel and defended to the death.... Our whole fighting reputation is at stake and the honour of the British Empire.... There must be no question or thought of surrender.

Churchill

The greatest humiliation suffered by the British Army during the Second World War was not being chased out of Europe by the Wehrmacht nor being chased round the Western Desert by Rommel. It was not even the premature capitulation of Tobruk. It was the surrender of Singapore to the Japanese. And as James Morris pointed out 'the fall of Singapore presaged unmistakably the end of Empire itself'. It was on 7 December, 1941, that Japan attacked the United States at Pearl Harbor and the United Kingdom in Malaya and Hong Kong, thus bringing about a truly world war, for a few days later Hitler declared war on the United States. Why he did so without first wringing from Japan an absolute undertaking to mount an instant offensive against the Soviet Union – particularly when we remember that December, 1941, was the very month when the Wehrmacht's assault on Russia was faltering, when the hitherto victorious German Army wavered, and feelings of desperation and despair were being harboured by general officers and ordinary soldiers alike – must remain one of the mysteries of history. It can only be explained by Hitler's conviction of his own destiny to decide the fate of the world, his eagerness to punish the United States for their open support of Britain and his confidence that America was a decadent, unmilitary democracy which would quickly succumb to the Master Race. Nevertheless, it set the stage for Allied Grand Strategy, and when Churchill, Roosevelt and their respective Chiefs of Staff met in Washington in that same month, they drew up a blueprint for the

prosecution of the war which in essence was that Japan would be denied
the means to wage war while the Allies would concentrate on Germany's
defeat, tighten the ring round her by giving support to Russia, strengthening their position in the Middle East and obtaining possession of the
whole North African coast.

Such strategic guidelines were small comfort to the British and
Dominion soldiers in Hong Kong and Malaya, who were quickly overwhelmed by the Japanese. In the case of Hong Kong no one had any
doubts about the outcome, although as Churchill put it 'the finer the
British resistance, the better for all'. When we consider the odds, their
resistance was all that could have been expected. The Japanese deployed
three divisions and had total air supremacy. The British mustered six
battalions, including two Canadian, some volunteers and a few guns.
After fighting a delaying action on the mainland in order to effect
demolitions at Kowloon, the garrison withdrew to the island itself and
continued the fight, sustained no doubt by one of the Prime Minister's
characteristic telegrams, assuring the defenders that their efforts against
such a barbarous assault would add yet another glorious page to British
military history. Their defence could not last long. On 18 December
the Japanese made their first landings and by numbers alone forced back
the garrison. There were many examples of great bravery, including
that of Brigadier Lawson, a Canadian, who personally took charge of
the hand-to-hand struggle outside his headquarters when they were
overrun. He and his men were killed. Further appeals from Churchill
to prolong the fighting as long as possible did not go unheeded, and by
their resistance soldiers, sailors, airmen and civilians alike won what
Churchill called 'lasting honour'. But the inevitable capitulation came
on Christmas Day.

In Malaya too things were going badly. On 8 December the Japanese
had made landings in the north-east at Kota Bharu, Singora and Patani,
and a few days later had expelled the defenders and captured airfields.
They had also fought a successful battle at Alor Star on the west side
of the peninsula and by 17 December had taken Penang, capturing
numerous small craft which enabled them to conduct a series of small
amphibious outflanking movements as they advanced further and further
south. Moreover, the British, Indian and Australian troops, basing their
defensive tactics primarily astride the roads, seemed quite unable to
counter the speed and improvisation of their enemy who used bicycles
to push their way forward along jungle and plantation tracks, outflanking
the British time after time. By the end of December the Japanese had
reached Ipoh near the west coast and Kuantan in the east. With three
divisions now in action and strongly supported by their air force, they

were poised to force the British further and further south. It did not take them long to drive the British out of Malaya altogether. There was a battle at Kampar in early January and another one at Segamat-Muar in mid-January. The Japanese had every advantage. They were reinforced by a further two divisions, they had command of the air, able both to assault our positions frontally – employing the Imperial Guards Division and with many tanks – and at the same time conduct outflanking operations by sea. By the end of the month the Army Commander, General Percival, made the important decision to retire to the island of Singapore itself. In describing the short and futile battle for Malaya, Churchill drew attention to the heavy advantages which the Japanese enjoyed. They were skilled in jungle warfare; they had made careful studies of the terrain and the conditions; they had prepared the way by infiltrating agents and assembling reserves of bicycles; they were masters of the air; they had infinite adaptability; they were now about to demonstrate that the supposed impregnability of Singapore and the hitherto tradition of European invincibility were hollow myths. Although the British managed to withdraw strong forces into Singapore and even reinforce it with the 18th Division, neither the will nor the skill to resist the Japanese were present. The condition of the British Army in Singapore was one not of defiance, but of dissipation. 'It might be a hundred thousand men,' wrote Churchill, 'but it was an army no more.'

Much of this is explained by the nature of the battle for Malaya. In his fine study of the Indian Army Philip Mason* takes as an example the performance of 12 Brigade, part of the 11th Indian Division. He points out that the troops, whether British or Indian (12 Brigade contained the Argylls and the 5th/2nd Punjabis), were wholly unprepared for the sort of fighting they now faced. They had neither the weapons to counter the numerous Japanese tanks not the training and expertise to operate swiftly and lightly equipped in the jungle. The Japanese, however, had a practised and perfected drill for jungle fighting, engaging and pinning any opposition they met frontally, then outflanking it by going through the jungle and establishing blocks *behind* the force still being engaged. Or, if this were not possible, simply effecting further landings from the sea, where, as in the air, they were masters. Moreover, the Japanese were masters at travelling light. Apart from bicycles they had light carts to carry rice and ammunition enough for several days. The whole idea that Singapore could not be approached by a full scale army overland was blown away after a few days of battle. Yet the

*A Matter of Honour, Cape, 1974.

performance both of individual soldiers of the 5th/2nd Punjabis and the battalion as a whole was superb:

> On Christmas Day Sepoy Shiv Ram, a Dogra, volunteered to cycle in civilian clothes through the screen of Japanese patrols and get information. He understood the penalty if he was caught; this was before it was known that the Japanese frequently treated any prisoner in the same way as a spy. Shiv Ram carried out his mission successfully in spite of meeting two Japanese patrols; he went again and was able to indicate the exact time and place of a Japanese attack, which was repulsed with heavy loss. He was awarded the Indian Order of Merit.

Philip Mason tells us also of one platoon commander in the battalion, Jemadar Mohammad Hassan, whom the orders to retire earlier than originally planned did not reach. Undismayed, he remained in position and continued the fight, until, after realizing that the rest of the battalion had withdrawn, he succeeded in battling his way back to his battalion, taking some stragglers from another unit with him. For this brave action he received the Military Cross. Throughout all this fighting, it must be remembered, there was almost no time for food or rest. The men were more or less continually in action and most of the time under attack from the air. There was no sign of the Royal Air Force. Under such circumstances, morale is not easy to sustain, yet the battalion, much reduced in numbers, fought on. On 7 January two companies found themselves subjected to prolonged attacks by Japanese tanks. They managed to destroy some with mines and antiquated anti-tank weapons, but more and more tanks appeared. 'It was men against machines – and the enemy were able to bring up fresh infantry every thirty-six hours and launch them against troops who were utterly exhausted, outnumbered, outweaponed, outorganized, outplanned.' By the end of January when the remnants of the battalion were withdrawn to Singapore, they were down to 80 men, and although reinforcements from India arrived, there was no time to train or organize before the tragedy of Singapore put them all into captivity.

Before all the troops had withdrawn to the island, Churchill had cabled to General Wavell (now Commander-in-Chief, India, but also with the responsibility for the South-western Pacific, including Burma, Singapore and the Dutch East Indies) asking what would happen if such withdrawal were necessary, how many troops would be needed for its defence, how would landings be prevented, would fortress cannon be able to dominate siege batteries, in short was everything being prepared? Wavell's reply was hardly sanguine, pointing out that until lately the whole defensive system had been based on repulsing seaborne attacks and not to deal with an assault from the Johore Straits on the northern side of the island. Moreover the fortress cannon were unsuitable for counter-battery engagement. Much would depend, Wavell concluded, on the situation in the air. From all this Churchill understood that no proper measures had been taken by any military commanders since the war with Japan had started to prepare Singapore against an attack from the north. So much for the hope expressed by Sir Shenton Thomas, Governor of the island, to General Percival that he would chase the little men off. The fact was that even while the Japanese were rapidly advancing down the Malayan Peninsula, no one in Singapore was taking the thing seriously. As James Morris has reminded us, when the Army talked of constructing some defensive positions on the Golf Club, they were informed that the Club committee would have to consider the matter before any decision could be taken. 'The muddle was terrible. Military clashed with civilian, commander with commander, outdated orders were scrupulously obeyed, initiatives were smothered in protocol and convention.' Despite all Churchill's talk of defence to the death and the Empire's fighting reputation and honour, the result of Japanese shelling and bombing, their crossing the Johore Strait on 8 February – they attacked the weakly held north-west of the island, the main defences being in the north-east – and the threat by General Yamashita to mount annihilating attacks, was that, on 15 February, General Percival, convinced that of his alternatives – counter-attack or surrender – only the second was practicable, gave in. James Morris summed it all up like this: 'Asians were never to look upon Englishmen in quite the same way again. The Royal Navy had failed; the British armies had been out-classed; white men had been seen in states of panic and humility; the legend had collapsed in pathos – or worse still, bathos, for the generals were second rate, the songs were banal, the policies were ineffective and even the courage was less than universal.' Yet despite it all, despite so ignominious a reverse for British arms, and the disgrace which it brought, despite even further failure, retreat and defeat in Burma, it was here that the British won back honour and esteem.

The Japanese invasion of Burma lasted from January, 1942, until May when the monsoon put paid to further advances. There was never any chance that the British would be able to defend Burma successfully. In the first place they had always assumed that, because of the moun-tainous country to the east and north, any attack would come from the south or from the west. The Japanese chose otherwise. In the second place there were not enough troops, and those that were there had inadequate training and equipment. Thirdly the British, Indian and Chinese troops seemed unable to find an answer to the Japanese tactics, which had proved so successful in Malaya, of frontal engagement, followed by wide outflanking movement which then established strong positions *behind* the defenders. By 20 February the three British–Indian brigades of 17th Division were obliged to retreat to the Sittang river, if they were not to be surrounded and defeated in detail. It was here that one of the most controversial incidents of the retreat took place. In what is perhaps the best-written book about the war by any general, *Defeat into Victory*, William Slim explained the appalling dilemma faced by the Divisional Commander, Jackie Smyth VC (of whom another great soldier-writer, James Lunt, recorded at the time that he was 'a soldier's general', and on whose conduct he later modelled himself), when he was woken in the middle of the night 22/23 February to be told that, while one of his brigades was safely across the bridge – the *only* bridge – over the river, and his other two brigades were still fighting their way to it, Japanese forces had now inserted themselves in between and might at any moment capture the bridge and open the way for them to stream on to Rangoon. Smyth ordered that the bridge be blown. It did not save Rangoon. But, as Slim pointed out, however easy it might be to criticize such a decision, no one not faced with comparable circumstances can understand the weight which a commander bears at so critical a time. Slim called it the decisive battle of the first campaign, and in order to get the feel of what it was like for those who were there, we may perhaps recall his summing up of the consequences of Smyth's decision:

> The sound of the explosion was a signal for a sudden lull in battle. Both sides knew what it meant: the Japanese that however fiercely they attacked they could not capture the bridge; the British that they were in desperately hard case. With a final effort they broke through to the bank. In horror they saw the broken bridge; it was hopeless to attempt to get vehicles or guns across. These were, as far as possible, destroyed, and men and officers individually and in parties stripped themselves and took to the water. A few managed to cross with their arms on rough rafts or petrol tins; the majority had to swim for it, helped only by bamboos. It was impossible for any man, even a powerful swimmer, burdened by equipment or arms to get over. Numbers were drowned; some were shot while crossing. By the afternoon of the 24th, all that had reached the west bank out of the eight battalions that had been cut off was under two thousand officers and men, with five hundred and fifty rifles, ten Bren guns, and twelve tommy-guns between them. Almost all were without boots, and most were reduced to their underwear.

Despite all the efforts of General Alexander, who had been sent out by Churchill to take charge, Rangoon was abandoned on 7 March, and indeed Alexander and his forces moving north to Prome were fortunate to get away, only doing so because the Japanese commander blocking that route rigidly adhered to his orders to rejoin the main Japanese advance to Rangoon. 'The loss of Rangoon,' wrote Churchill, 'meant the loss of Burma, and the rest of the campaign was a grim race between the Japanese and the approaching rains.'

It was Slim who had commanded the Burma Corps during the retreat. He was unable to prevent the Japanese from cutting the Burma Road, that vital link between Lashio and Chungking. There seemed to be no stopping the Japanese advance. By late March they had pushed the Chinese out of Toungoo and were advancing against the British at Prome. A month later the Chinese had been turned out of Burma – some into China itself, some under the American General Stilwell into India astride the Irrawaddy. The British under Alexander and Slim had withdrawn to Kalewa. The final retreat from there to Imphal, where the routes into India could be blocked, was, under the full fury of the monsoon, an incalculably miserable affair. Slim described it like this:

> Ploughing their way up slopes, over a track inches deep in slippery mud, soaked to the skin, rotten with fever, ill-fed and shivering as the air grew cooler, the troops went on, hour after hour, day after day. Their only rest at night was to lie on the sodden ground under the dripping trees, without even a blanket to cover them. Yet the monsoon which so nearly destroyed us and whose rain beat so mercilessly on our bodies did us one good turn – it stopped dead the Japanese pursuit. As the clouds closed down over the hills, even their air attacks became rare. . . .
>
> On the last day of that nine-hundred-mile retreat I stood on a bank beside the road and watched the rearguard march into India. All of them, British, Indian, and Gurkha, were gaunt and ragged as scarecrows. Yet, as they trudged behind their surviving officers in groups pitifully small, they still carried their arms and kept their ranks, they were still recognizable as fighting units. They might look like scarecrows, but they looked like soldiers too.

This was in mid-May, 1942. When, some two months earlier, Slim had received his instructions from Wavell and been told that his task, like Alexander's, would not be easy, he had asked Wavell why Singapore had fallen. 'He looked at me steadily for a moment and then told me.' Slim does not say what Wavell said, but we may infer that some doubts were cast on the fighting spirit of the British Army, doubts which had certainly been expressed by Linlithgow, Viceroy of India, and even by Churchill himself. We will leave to a later chapter how the British soldier totally redeemed his reputation in Burma, as we have seen he did in North Africa, and quite apart from the main operations of Slim's 14th

Army, we shall meet such remarkable men as Orde Wingate, Bernard Fergusson and Mike Calvert, to say nothing of Spencer-Chapman in Malaya and Tom Harrisson in Sarawak. But first we must return to Hitler's *Festung Europa*.

14

THE D-DAY DODGERS

O Death be kind to the swaddie
The man with the load of bull –
Be kind to the muscled body,
Thumbs up and belly full.

Browned off with the bints and boozing,
Sweating on news from home,
Bomb-happy and scared of losing
This tent of flesh and bone ...

Jocelyn Brooke

The 8th Army went to Italy because it was there, that is because the 8th Army was standing victorious on the shores of North Africa, and Italy, with Sicily as a stepping stone, was just across the water from Tunisia and Malta, ready, willing and eager to stop fighting the Allies and end their alliance with Germany. While both the British and the Americans agreed that a cardinal feature of their joint strategy to crush Germany first would be a cross-Channel operation aimed at the heart of the Third Reich, there was considerable disagreement as to timing. At first the Americans wanted to do it in 1942, but soon were convinced by the British that the *only* feasible operation in 1942 would be the landings in North-West Africa. Their reluctance to accept this view was reinforced by their being obliged also to accept that mounting *Torch* in Morocco and Algeria would in effect mean that there was no question of invading North-West Europe in 1943 either, and that *Round-Up*, as this latter plan was then named, would have to wait until 1944! Such considerations did not dismay Churchill who was consistently an ardent advocate of the idea that, by moving northwards into Europe from Africa, further opportunities would be created. He had always held the view that invading North-West Africa would not prejudice the subsequent thrust across the Channel. It would complement it. In all his astonishing surveys of strategic options and forecasts of how things might develop, none was more prescient than his minute written in mid-1942, explaining how the right wing of a Second Front – that is in North-West Africa – could support and be supported by the left wing, which would be the cross-Channel invasion:

> The flank attack may become the main attack, and the main attack a holding operation in the early stages. Our second front will in fact comprise both the Atlantic and Mediterranean coasts of Europe, and we can push either right-handed, left-handed, or both-handed, as our resources and circumstances permit.... In so vast and complex a scene above all it is specially desirable to have options open which allow of strategic manoeuvres according as events unfold.

From this concept emerged the so-called Mediterranean Strategy, which was discussed and finalised by the Allies at their Casablanca conference in January, 1943, at a time when the North African campaign still had a few months to run and it was necessary to decide what to do when it was successfully concluded. The British Chiefs of Staff were in no doubt that of the two broad policies – either to concentrate resources in the United Kingdom with a view to the cross-Channel operation and abandon Mediterranean prizes, incidentally giving the Germans respite by lengthy inactivity; *or* to pursue now the offensive in the Mediterranean with a view to invading France in 1944 and bringing certain relief to the Russian front – the second was the correct one. At Casablanca it became plain to the Allies that if they were to exploit their victories in North Africa and make use of the substantial armies there in such a way as to bring relief to the Russians, knock Italy out of the war and cause the Germans to dissipate their resources by defending the southern part of the European fortress, there was really no alternative but to land these armies somewhere on the northern shores of the Mediterranean. Where was still a question. Italy, Sardinia, Corsica, the eastern islands or mainland? In the end the Allies chose the easiest option – Sicily – but, as Michael Howard has emphasised, at the time the landings there were made on 10 July, 1943, it had not yet been decided where they would go next. There was also the question of what the Italians and the Germans would do and whether getting involved on the Italian mainland would not commit the Allied armies to a campaign in difficult, easily defended country, and thus eat up Allied resources to an extent disproportionate to the distraction imposed on the enemy.

In the event the invasion of Sicily brought about the fall of Mussolini,

the defection of Italy from the Axis and the rapid German occupation
and control of Italy down to a line well south of Rome. During the six
weeks which elapsed between Mussolini's overthrow on 25 July and the
Italian Armistice on 8 September, Kesselring deployed sixteen German
divisions, disarmed the Italian Army and began to prepare the formidable Gustav Line across the country, based on a feature immortal
in the history of the British Army – Monte Cassino. The fears of a long,
protracted campaign on a relatively narrow front, leaving only one
alternative to frontal attacks – amphibious landings, with assault shipping always at a premium – over country characterised by repeated
mountain ranges and rivers, with rain and impassable mud for most of
the year, where the advantages of Allied air power and armoured strength
could not be exploited, against fanatically brave and skilful German
veterans, with little hope of breakthrough or decisive manoeuvring and
the prospect of ending up trying to storm the Alps – all these fears were
about to be realised. Nevertheless the battle for Italy brought further
honour to regiments of the British and Indian Armies, to say nothing
of the Canadians, New Zealanders and countless other Allies, including
powerful American divisions, and we may perhaps now illustrate this
by examining some of the actions the D-Day Dodgers took part in.

Fred Majdalany, who fought as an infantry officer in North Africa,
Sicily and Italy, who knew a great deal more about war than most and
who wrote about it almost better than anyone else, put his finger
unerringly on what battles were like in general for the ordinary infantryman and more particularly what shape they tended to take in Italy.
He explained first of all how complex battles are – 'a patchwork of tiny
operations carried out by groups largely unaware what similar groups
on their left and right are doing' and certainly not caring greatly. A
battle could go on for weeks or months, as it did for example at Cassino.
Even in the middle of such a battle, some parts of an infantry battalion
will be resting or enjoying good meals cooked by the battalion cooks
and sent up in the so-called 'echelon' trucks. It was never easy to define
just when one particular battle began or another one broke off, although
in the case of Cassino – about which Majdalany wrote so movingly and
realistically – this was clearer simply because of the all-dominating
nature of the Monastery and the Hill itself. For those of us who read
later in the newspapers about a battle we had taken part in, what was
described was usually quite foreign to our own recollection of it. 'It is
difficult for Trooper Jones to grasp that on that unhappy morning when
all but two tanks in his squadron were knocked out, he was part of a
"great armoured breakthrough"'. It is no easier for a lonely platoon
commander, recollecting in tranquillity a shambles in which his company

commander dispatched him into the night without any clear orders about what he was to do, to realize that he was nevertheless an important contributor to a "three-point thrust".'

To most of us who took part in the Italian campaign it seemed an endless repetition of trying to get forward against obstacles, whether natural ones like rivers, mud and mountains or those arranged by the Germans, such as mines, anti-tank guns, mortars and blown bridges. The country was simply made for defensive operations. 'No sooner has one river or mountain barrier been crossed than another bars the way. Plains are few and far between and too small for the decisive use of tanks. A defender can fight an unlimited number of delaying actions from one end of the country to the other. ... Strategically Italy might be a soft underbelly [the expression used by Churchill to describe Anglo-American intentions to Stalin]: tactically it was a scaly pachydermatous backbone.' So, as Majdalany put it, a pattern of operations developed which was constantly repeated by the Germans and which, it seemed, could go on being repeated without end:

> The Germans would hold a position for a time until it was seriously contested: then pull back a mile or two to the next defendable place, leaving behind a trail of blown bridges, minefields, and road demolitions. There was always a new defendable place at hand. The Allied armies would begin with a night attack – ford the stream or river after dark, storm the heights on the far side, dig themselves in by dawn, and hope that by that time the Sappers, following on their heels, would have sufficiently repaired the demolitions and removed the obstacles to permit tanks to follow up and help consolidate the new positions. The Germans, watching these proceedings from the next vantage point, would attempt to frustrate them by raining down artillery and mortar fire on their own recently vacated positions.

It was all too easy, especially when some of the German divisions were such battle-hardened and well-led formations as 1st Parachute and 90th Panzer Grenadier. Of course, not all the advantages were with the Germans. The Allies had almost total air superiority. Not that it availed them much beyond being able to launch important, but not decisive, landings at Salerno and Anzio, and indulging in the morale-raising, but tactically fruitless, bombing and destruction of the Monastery at Monte Cassino. The scale of the campaign may perhaps be judged by the numbers engaged and the casualties on either side. In order to put the thing into perspective we may recall that in Italy the contest was being waged by something like twenty divisions on either side, whereas in Russia Hitler had deployed some 185 divisions. Perhaps half a million German casualties were inflicted, 300,000 on the Allied side. That there were not more for the Allies, who were constantly attacking, owes much to the skill and effectiveness with which they deployed and used their considerably greater strength in artillery. However difficult the naturally defensive country was for tanks and infantry, it did not prevent the Royal Regiment of Artillery from giving such continuous and accurate support and thereby saving many Allied lives.

The Italian campaign may be said to have had five parts: first the capture of Sicily which began on 10 July, 1943, and lasted thirty-eight days. There had never been much doubt about its result, given the huge Allied air and naval superiority, and their ability to reinforce at will. There were also invaluable lessons for future operations – how to handle great armadas of warships and transports; the business of getting troops ashore in their landing craft, and supporting them with fire power from air and sea, together with supplying them across beaches; how to use airborne troops most effectively (in Sicily nearly everything had gone wrong, with the parachutists being dropped prematurely or miles away from their target); the tricky matter of coordinating Anglo-American joint operations and their command, particularly when faced with such *prima donna*-like generals as Montgomery and Patton. But Sicily was taken, together with many Italian prisoners; most of the Germans got away, having shown how skilfully and effectively they were able to conduct defensive operations in ideally suited terrain. It cannot be said that this lesson was properly taken in by the Allied strategic planners. The subsequent battle for Italy itself, which lasted about a year and ten months, may be divided like this. From September, 1943, to January, 1944, there was the initial invasion across the Straits of Messina and landings at Salerno, followed by advance to the winter line; then the battle for Rome until the beginning of June, 1944, including the epic, bloody struggle for Cassino and the near disastrous landings at Anzio – designed to relieve the fighting at Cassino, but in the end saved by it; next the advance from Rome up to the Gothic line and the failure to break through it during the Autumn months of 1944, capped by another winter of watching and waiting; until finally in the Spring of 1945 the Allies attacked across the Senio driving all before them and accepting the surrender of a million German soldiers, about a week before another surrender at Lüneburg Heath on 8 May, 1945.

Throughout it all the strategic arguments persisted, Churchill always eager to bring off some great coup in Italy with armies which were still predominantly British or British-controlled, the Americans far more concerned with what was happening in North-West Europe (both before and after D-Day) and even insisting on the almost pointless invasion of southern France by robbing Italy of divisions which might have turned the scale there more quickly. Commanders came and went. Montgomery, never at his best in Italy, went after the Sangro had been reached, for his all-important task in planning and conducting the invasion of Normandy; Alexander had already assumed the supreme command, bringing his charm, reputation and optimism to bear on the strains created by such an egoistic and conceited American general as Mark Clark, who handled his army in such a way as to draw the maximum credit to himself; Oliver Leese who succeeded Montgomery in command of the 8th Army, but showed little drive in directing its activities; McCreery, who displayed such courage and grip at Salerno and who conserved and prepared the 8th Army for the triumph of its last battles. And on the German side the ruthlessly competent Kesselring who would *guarantee* success in defending certain lines for certain times, and was ably served by his subordinates von Vietinghoff, von Mackensen and von Senger und Etterlin, all brave, experienced commanders. How successful they were may be illustrated by recalling how the British Army got on against them during two parts of the campaign – Cassino and the Gothic Line. For the first we will allow Fred Majdalany to tell us what the battlefield looked and felt like:

> From the crest above the village we could look down over the whole of the Cassino battlefield. Even at a distance, and to eyes not unused to destruction, the ruins of Cassino were awe inspiring. This was indeed a stricken town. Not a single whole building remained, only fragments of wall and heaps of rubble. These jagged fragments of buildings had a ghostly, slightly obscene quality that is hard to describe; it was like a forest of stalagmites. Cassino in destruction was different from all other places.
>
> Away to the left ran the thin streak of the Rapido River, stretched like a steel cord across the entrance to the Liri Valley. The fortifications on its far bank linked up with the mountain range which began behind Cassino, and became higher as it went east till it culminated in the towering peak of Monte Cairo, over five thousand feet high, and the anchor of the Cassino defence system.
>
> Stark and clear now was the one that was the most important of them all – Monastery Hill. Having seen the country we could properly understand now the difficulties of this battle that had been going on for nearly four months. The Monastery, converted into a fortress and securely planted on the crest of the precipitous rocky slopes of Monastery Hill, commanded a perfect view of every single approach to the Liri Valley, through which an army marching on Rome must pass. This amazing viewpoint – from which the German artillery was so accurately directed for so long – was protected on its eastern side by the mountains and to the west by the narrow but fast-flowing Rapido,

and the steel and concrete defences behind it. It was obvious now why the Monastery had become the bogy of every operation.

It was not just the British who tasted the bitterness of the battle for Cassino. In Alexander's final offensive, *Diadem*, which began on 11 May, New Zealanders, Indians, Canadians, South Africans, Americans, Frenchmen, Poles all took part, as well as British soldiers. It was the Poles who took Cassino at last, the French Goumiers who outflanked the German Gustav and Hitler Lines, the Americans who surged forward from the Anzio beachhead. Two weeks after this final battle began the 5th and 8th Armies were driving north in accordance with Alexander's plan to encircle and destroy the German 10th Army. Only General Mark Clark's vanity, which caused him to alter his line of advance in order to be the captor and liberator of Rome, saved the Germans, who withdrew successfully to live and fight many another day. To get the feel of what it had all been like, we must return to Fred Majdalany, whose battalion was holding the line before the final offensive took place:

When the right-hand company reported two green Very lights no one paid very much attention. Sentries were always reporting lights. Sometimes the lights were there and sometimes they weren't. Being a sentry sounds simple enough, but it is one of the most thankless and wearing duties of the infantryman. For two hours at a stretch he must strain at the darkness with his eyes and his ears. He is alone with the dark, the cold and his thoughts. Unless you have done it you cannot imagine how slowly the two hours drag themselves out. It is possible, especially when you have had a long spell in the line, to see lights which aren't there. In any case, Very lights are relatively commonplace. They are a routine item in the frontline night.

Then there was the clatter of machine-gun fire from the direction of the right-hand company. Not the random bursts that both sides exchanged every day and every night but a purposeful and sustained fire from several guns. Three minutes later the company reported that Point 593 was being attacked. This was one of the key hills. The Northamptons and ourselves held the near side of it; the Boche were on the other slope. It was a pretty congested hill. Neither side had to travel very far to attack the other.

Being attacked by night is particularly unnerving because you cannot tell if there are twenty of the enemy or a whole battalion. If two machine-guns can infiltrate through your positions and open fire from behind, the most dogged temperament finds it hard to resist the impression that it is surrounded. We had ourselves on several occasions successfully employed this technique and taken a large number of prisoners at the cost of very few casualties.

There was nothing for it but to 'Stand to' and await developments. There were no further signals. There was a great deal of firing, and a good many flares and Verys were going up. It might be the start of an offensive – or it might be a fighting patrol. At any moment we expected to hear our machine-guns get to work – if it was a big attack they were bound to go for the ridge overlooking us. Messages were flashed to the mortars and the guns to stand by ready to bring down fire on all the SOS targets. The tension of total alertness temporarily eclipsed one's tiredness. Nobody spoke, unless it was to pass a message on the telephone or the wireless. You just stood or leaned or sat motionless – and fancied you could hear your heartbeats.

Then the firing seemed to die down slightly – or was it that you wanted it to die down? No, it was definitely easing off. Nobody said anything, but everyone simultaneously sensed the easing of the tension. People began to talk again. They made the rather forced little jokes which always follow a period of fear. We still had no idea whether the attack had been made by twenty or two hundred. Twenty minutes later we heard that it had in fact been made by twelve men. One of them had been wounded and taken prisoner. He said it was a fighting patrol of twelve. Its object had been to get a prisoner. One suddenly felt very, very tired.

This somewhat lengthy extract from *The Monastery* sums up what it was like to be an infantryman of the British Army in Italy in 1944. Later that year when the battle for Rome had been won – and eclipsed by the Normandy landings – 8th Army had closed up to the so-called Gothic Line which ran through the Apennines roughly from Rimini on the east coast to Pisa on the west, an attempt was made to break through that line, descend into the Po Valley and defeat the German Army once and for all. It was early September when 1st Armoured Division commanded by Major-General (later Field-Marshal Sir) Richard Hull was instructed to effect this breakthrough, and the Regiment in which I had the honour to command a troop, the 4th Hussars, in which Churchill had served in the 1890s and of which he was Colonel, was in the van. Indeed the squadron I belonged to was in the lead – not because we had initially been chosen for this honour by the Commanding Officer, who at first appeared to have more confidence in his two more senior squadron leaders, but because these two squadrons had somewhat ignominiously been led by these two officers into a bog – and my own troop was actually at the head of it all. Furthermore, as the map-reading was not easy, I had positioned myself and Sherman tank at the absolute spearpoint of this mighty armoured instrument, poised to rush headlong into the Po Valley and roll up the 'Teds'.* Our first contact with the enemy was

* The British soldiers in Italy often referred to the Germans in this way – the Italian word for German being *tedesco*.

just south of Coriano and several days later we were still trying to fight our way forward, having lost five officers, thirty-five men and nine tanks, while the Germans steadily reinforced the Coriano position. We had achieved nothing. The trouble had been, as so often before and since with the British Army, that there was no proper coordination between tanks, infantry and artillery. Tanks had been invited to advance unsupported against enemy defensive positions, which were models of concealment, well-sited anti-tank guns, tanks and artillery/mortar observation posts. But worse was to come, far worse, for another cavalry regiment, the Queen's Bays, on 20 September, when they were asked to attack an objective, again without infantry support, which was heavily defended by German anti-tank guns. The Bays' own account of it goes like this:

> We knew that we should not get far even if we could spot the guns that had already fired. There were probably more and after realizing what was coming the enemy had probably whipped up some more tanks to oppose us. While we waited for the word to go, we looked at the ground we had to advance over. There wasn't a stitch of cover anywhere that a tank could get hull-down behind and fire, not a single fire position between us and the objective. We could see the latter plainly about 2,000 yards ahead with a few trees and farms scattered about on it. We looked at likely places that might conceal enemy positions and started shooting with everything we had. Then we started to advance. . . .
>
> The shelling in the hollow ceased, and the Germans began to bring their attention to bear on the latest development. . . . The express trains* started up again with increasing ferocity. Armour-piercing shot seemed to come from all directions [most of it was coming from the Bays' left *rear* which emphasises the absurdity of the manoeuvre] – some, the bad shots, passed overhead, others hitting the ground with colossal force and kicking up earth and stones in front of the tanks. As they halted to fire, to locate the opposition, the tanks were knocked out one by one. Most of them burst into flames immediately. A few were disabled, the turrets jammed or the tank made immobile. As the survivors jumped out, some of them made a dash across the open to get back over the crest among our own infantry, but they were almost all mown down by German machine-gun fire. The craftier men lay flat or dived into small hollows in the ground and lay immobile, waiting until they could get back under cover of darkness. All but three tanks of the two squadrons that took part in the attack were destroyed, and many gallant officers and men were killed in action that morning.

It has often been said by infantrymen that they would never have liked

---

* For the tank crew an armour-piercing shot going by sounded like an express train.

to have been cooped up in tanks (and tank crews have expressed equal dislike of walking about the battlefield as infantry do) and this account of so tragically disastrous and unnecessary an action helps to explain it. A scapegoat was, of course, found – not the Corps or Divisional Commander, however, whose collective responsibility it really was, but the Brigade Commander (who, it is agreeable to record, since he had vehemently opposed the operation, subsequently became a full General and did much for the British Army when he was Adjutant-General).

So the slow, slogging advance of the 8th Army continued. Attempts to break the Gothic Line bogged down in the autumn and winter rains. Respite, and further training, manning the Senio winter line, plans for a great spring offensive, and at last on 9 April, 1945, the last battle for Italy began. Just over three weeks later it was all over, and, as General McCreery explained, the enemy armies were defeated south of the Po. For those of us who took part in the pursuit, having crossed the Po, it was a glorious experience to be concerned more with getting enough maps than ammunition, but it had only been achieved after nearly two years of bitter, bloody fighting against not merely a skilful, well-equipped and determined enemy, but often against the hard unyielding nature of the country itself, with mountain, river and weather so welding together that it seemed to be the elements themselves that the British Army was taking on. 'In this battle,' wrote McCreery, 'as always, the decisive factors have been the magnificent fighting qualities of our soldiers and good junior leadership.' He was right. Generalship alone could not win battles. Had it all been worth it? Had the Italian campaign achieved what it set out to achieve? Opinions vary. But in the round the campaign had been inevitable, given the circumstances of finding large Allied armies victorious on the shores of North Africa, armies which *had* to engage the Germans quickly or fail to bring any relief to the hard-pressed Russians or facilitate the vital task facing Allied soldiers about to invade Normandy. There may have been disappointments. All the extravagant talk about advancing through the Ljubljana Gap and capturing Vienna came to nothing. But as a proper finale to the Mediterranean strategy, designed to draw German forces away from both the Russian front and later Normandy, the Italian campaign did what it set out to do.

Throughout it all the British soldier cheerfully accepted the appalling conditions under which he had to fight, discovered, as one member of the S.A.S. put it, that Italian wine and women were a marked improvement on the North African variety, and like the Two Types, so graphically depicted by Jon, made the best of being a D-Day Dodger. And from those who succeeded in dodging D-Day, we may perhaps now turn to those who did not.

15

D-DAY TO V.E. DAY

We shall have to send the soldiers into this party 'seeing red'. They must see red. We must get them completely on their toes, having absolute faith in the plan; and imbued with infectious optimism and offensive eagerness. Nothing must stop them. Nothing. If we send them into battle in this way – then we shall succeed.

Montgomery

Many soldiers of the British Army had to wait until 6 June, 1944, to get into action. But when they did the action was fierce enough to satisfy anyone's taste for war. The invasion beaches, the battle for Caen, Operation *Goodwood* (Montgomery's attempted break-out in July), Arnhem, the bitter Rhineland fighting, crossing the Rhine – there was something for everybody, the renowned airborne forces, the armoured regiments, the ubiquitous artillery and unobtrusively valiant sappers, all the vast and indispensable administrative machine, and of course for the poor bloody infantry. In a remarkable book published in 1948 Alexander Baron* tells the story of a battalion, imaginative in name, but real enough for all that, which for four and a half years prepared itself for the great day and then took part in what was perhaps the most important battle fought by the British Army in the whole Second World War, and certainly Montgomery's *chef d'oeuvre* – the battle for Normandy. For those who were part of an infantry battalion during the war, whether in England waiting for the invasion or elsewhere, whether veterans of battle or not, Baron's story will ring wholly true. He describes the endless routine of training and marching, weapon drill and lectures, people coming and going, fights in and out of pubs, football, going on leave, moving from one camp to another, new machine-guns being

---

*From the City, from the Plough, Cape.

issued, practised with and mastered, the NAAFI, dances with local girls, rumours about the Second Front. All the familiar regimental characters are there – the kindly, competent Commanding Officer, who loves the battalion and is generally loved by them; a fanatical unbalanced company commander, glorifying war, springing unnecessarily violent tests on sentries and longing to win the DSO; the sound experienced platoon sergeant who served in the desert and Italy, and while conscientiously devoted to duty, is not particularly relishing the prospect of more action; the old soldier from Ireland, knowing his weapons, knowing his rights and knowing the weaknesses of NCOs; the private soldier, drunk, dirty, ill-disciplined, *enfant terrible* of the battalion, who when it comes to battle is fearless and successfully takes on an enemy machine-gun post by simply walking towards it and silencing it with a grenade. And the battalion's soldiers as a whole, brought up to war strength by the beginning of 1944, welding themselves into a formidable team, marching, manoeuvring, shooting, being subjected to cold, fatigue and hardship, taking tough assault courses in their stride, were becoming as proud of themselves as the Colonel was of them. They would need to be good in view of what Montgomery had in mind for them. Yet this time nothing was going to be left to chance. The planning was meticulous, the intelligence gathering was comprehensive, the deception measures were masterly and the sheer preponderance of both fighting strength and logistic resources was overwhelming. For the assault there were available no less than 1,200 warships, 1,600 transports, 4,000 assault and landing craft, 13,000 aeroplanes, and armies totalling between three and four million men There were also the so-called Mulberry artificial harbours to facilitate rapid build-up and an oil pipe-line to pump supplies under the sea.

Knowing by now as the Allies did what the power of the Wehrmacht was like, how skilful, brave and determined the German soldiers were, how excellent their weapons and formidable the commanders, they knew too that they would need all the strength they could muster. Field-Marshal von Rundstedt, who had been recalled by Hitler to be his Commander-in-Chief, West, had some 60 divisions to defend about 2,000 miles of coastline (in June, 1944, there were more than 200 German divisions on the Eastern Front, and, as we have seen, about 20 in Italy). There could therefore be no question of defending everywhere in strength and depth, and von Rundstedt's broad policy was to be strong in important, vulnerable areas, to deny the ports through which the Allies would reinforce, and to have powerful armoured counter-attack forces ready to move rapidly with air support to enemy bridgeheads. It was an admirable theory. In practice it could not be done, for the requisite panzer and Luftwaffe units did not exist in sufficient numbers. Nevertheless, von Rundstedt was supplied with one asset, who, however much the General Staff might have disapproved of him, made a world of difference in preparing for the invasion in the short time left to him from February, 1944, onwards. This asset was another Field-Marshal – Erwin Rommel. *His* ideas were very different. He maintained that every advantage must be wrung from so formidable a defensive obstacle as the sea, so that invasion could be defeated on the beaches. He held the view that, once ashore, Allied forces would be so powerfully supported by air supremacy that German mobile reserves designed to intervene would never get to the scene of action. Therefore the enemy had to be annihilated before he ever reached the main battlefield. The invading troops had to be stopped in the water.

Rommel was a general whom every proper soldier must admire because he always matched his words with action. In the relatively short time he had – and the thought that he could have been appointed to command in the West after his return from Africa in March, 1943, must give us pause – Rommel deployed every kind of ingenious device for making the Allies' task more difficult – underwater explosives, millions of mines on the beaches, steel and concrete protected guns, pillboxes, wire, machine-guns, the 88mm anti-tank guns which he had employed with such devastating effect in the desert. To deter airborne landings he arranged for the flooding of low-lying ground and where there were suitable dropping zones he had posts driven into the earth and booby trapped. His whole defensive strategy depended on having as much fire power in the shop window as possible, for obstacles, however sophisticated, are not much use unless covered by fire. Being convinced that all would turn on the first 24 hours or so, for he believed that once the Allies were firmly ashore they would be very difficult to dislodge, he wanted as much panzer strength up in the front line as he could put there. But in this he was strongly opposed by the commander of Panzer Group West, Geyr von Schweppenburg, who wanted to keep his main forces in reserve until the main Allied landings had been located. The whole question was referred to Hitler, who backed neither General fully, so that Rommel did not get his panzers in sufficient strength forward, nor Geyr a powerful and properly supported reserve. Compromise proved fatal. There was another area in which Hitler compromised, again greatly to the Allies benefit. A great deception operation had been mounted to convince the Germans that the main landings would be made east of the Seine in the Pas de Calais area, and so convinced did the Germans become that the entire 15th Army was stationed well to the north-east of Normandy. The one man to guess correctly where the landings would be effected was the Führer himself and certain reinforcements to the Normandy area were made, much to the consternation of Allied intelligence staffs. Happily, Hitler did not fully back his intiuition, partly no doubt because he wished to protect the V weapon sites in the Pas de Calais sector.

All the work which Rommel had been doing to make landings from the sea more difficult had demanded a response and here the ingenuity of Major-General Sir Percy Hobart was given free rein and produced such admirable antidotes as DD tanks to swim ashore, tanks with flails to set off mines, flame-throwing tanks to reduce strongpoints and 'Bobbins' to lay down a firm carpet on soft ground so that the normal fighting tanks did not get bogged down. Of course, the assault when it came was to be from the air and sea, airborne troops to be dropped the night before the seaborne attack, to seize vital bridges, occupy and hold important ground and knock out coastal batteries which could interfere with the armada of ships carrying the soldiers first to the positions where they transferred to assault craft, then on from there to the beaches. What was it like on the day?

An officer of the South Lancashire Regiment remembered getting up at 3 o'clock in the morning of 6 June, having breakfast at 4 o'clock and almost at once seeing a destroyer on the flank of the landing ship go down, sunk by a torpedo. As this member of Montgomery's great Army surveyed the ocean and saw it covered with Allied shipping his confidence was restored. He and his men got into their assault craft without trouble and in spite of a heavy swell began their run-in to the beach in company with the rest of the flotilla. The clouds of dust caused by naval bombardment which rose from the beaches so obscured them that he was unable to make out whether the point where they were about to land corresponded with the oblique photographs they had so often studied. They had studied the matter of underwater obstacles too, but on actually coming level with them they were surprised to find them so tall, so high out of the water, and as the boat crews weaved between the pickets and the rails with mines on top of them, it seemed 'like groping through a grotesque petrified forest'. On the beaches themselves the noise was continuous – mortar fire, machine-guns, tanks and 88mm guns. The battalion fought a series of small, yet desperate, actions mainly to overcome the various strongpoints and pillboxes which opposed them. Many officers were killed, including the Colonel who, in order that he could be easily recognised, carried a small flag of the battalion colours – too easy a target for snipers. Once the beaches had been cleared, the battalion was to rendezvous at Hermanville. First to get there was the Battalion HQ, more conventionally later arrivals at the objective, and by H + 4 hours the battalion, despite its losses, had dug in round the village, ready for the expected counterattack which in this case did not come. So, all along the Normandy beaches, similar stories were being told. By the evening of D-Day over 150,000 men had been landed. Not all of them got away with not being counterattacked.

A captain of the 12th Parachute Battalion, which had landed during the night before D-Day to secure a tactically important feature, had been despatched with a dozen men to form a reconnaissance screen, and he recalled as dawn broke how quiet everything seemed, with no enemy to be seen. Above, the Spitfires circled, and well behind him the rumble of battle told him about the struggle for the beaches. Yet just in front of the positions he and his men had taken up, concealed in slit trenches with camouflaged steel helmets and blackened faces, a farmer led his horse and cart. But by 1030 the enemy had found them. Infantry and SP guns appeared, the guns firing straight into their position, the infantry beginning to work round to their right flank. After failing to bring down the supporting fire he called for, and seeing the enemy fire reduce his effective strength to three men, the captain chose discretion, evacuated his position and withdrew to the main battalion area. He then had the satisfaction of noting that the two enemy SP guns following up were quickly knocked out by his battalion's anti-tank guns, that the attacking infantry withdrew and that the battalion position held firm. A few days later the bridgehead had been consolidated and by 20 June Montgomery had 20 divisions ashore.

Shortly before this and as the Allies were strengthening their hold on Normandy, the commander of an artillery battery had what he called a 'bloody day'. After hours of exhausting activity and thousands of shells fired, he was fixing up the night tasks and enjoying a glass of whisky with one of his Forward Observation Officers, sitting on the bonnet of his jeep, when they heard a plop and a whine. At this stage in the war such noises were not listened to with curiosity alone. Hurling themselves to the ground, the battery commander escaped unhurt, his FOO received a large piece of shrapnel in his leg; the whisky bottle, two glasses, even the jeep, itself were written off. At least, they reflected, it had not been an 88mm whose shells arrived before you heard the plop.

All did not go according to plan, although Montgomery subsequently claimed that everything had proceeded exactly as he had foreseen. Broadly, the master plan worked − that is, after securing the lodgement area, the British would engage and hold the main German strength against them on the left, particularly the panzer divisions, so allowing the Americans to push forward and break out on the right, the western, flank. In this way, more or less, the battle developed. Yet Caen, an objective for the first day, did not fall until after mid-July when Montgomery launched his armoured divisions in Operation *Goodwood*, hoping that they would break through the German defences in the area Bourguebus-Vimont-Bretteville and destroy the enemy there. So skilfully had Rommel made his dispositions, however, and so well did Sepp Dietrich's 1st Panzer Army conduct itself, that Montgomery's armour did not break through. They did what was necessary in so concentrating German strength against them that in the following month the Americans did at last break out. Rommel played no part in this battle himself. He had been wounded in an air attack on 17 July, the day before it started. He was finished with Normandy and before long finished altogether, for the Führer, whose fury after the unsuccessful attempt to assassinate him on 20 July knew no bounds, implicated him in the plot and forced his suicide. Not for the Desert Fox an honourable death in action, but squalid murder by the man he had served so well. He will always be admired by British soldiers for his dash, his chivalry and his habit of leading from the front, a method of command which seemed to have little appeal to most British generals.

The British Army's conduct of *Goodwood* was a classic example of their faith in the eventual triumph of hope over experience. Time after time in the past armoured regiments had advanced against the Germans without the close support of infantry. They had done it in the Western Desert, they had done it in Tunisia and they had done it in Italy. The result was always the same – heavy casualties and no decisive results. Yet they did it again in Normandy, and as a consequence lost large numbers of tanks and lives without gaining their objective. Once again the Germans, this time initially in the person of Colonel von Luck and his battle group, showed how relatively small numbers of tanks, anti-tank guns and infantry, with call on artillery and mortar fire, could defeat greatly superior strength of armoured forces even though powerfully supported from the air. It was done by bold and skilful manipulation of fire power and clever use of ground. *Goodwood* ground to a halt and with it any hope of a British breakthrough.

Yet *Goodwood* was not the only occasion when Montgomery, master of attrition and the set-piece battle, allowed himself the luxury of an adventurous fling. There was also Arnhem in September, 1944. By then the Normandy battles had cost the German Army over 2,000 tanks and assault guns and the best part of 20 infantry divisions. Falaise, Avranches, Mortain and Patton's drive to the east had taken their toll. Yet somehow the bustling Model, summoned from the Eastern Front to replace von Kluge, had stitched the thing together, withdrawn the remnants of the German Army across the Seine and imposed delay on

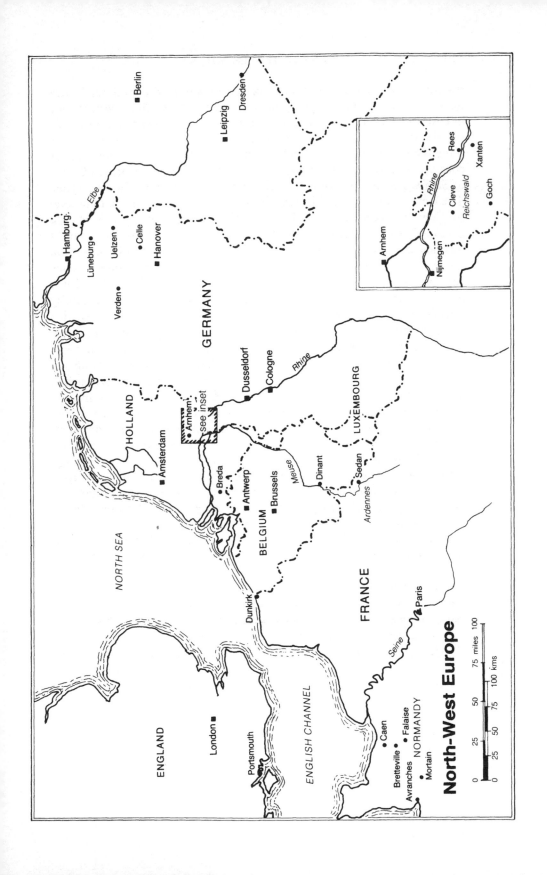

North-West Europe

ENGLAND

NORTH SEA

ENGLISH CHANNEL

London ■

Portsmouth ●

Dunkirk ●

Caen ●
Bretteville ●
Falaise ●
NORMANDY
Avranches ●
Mortain ●

Seine

Paris ▲

FRANCE

Sedan ●

Ardennes

Dinant ●

Meuse

Breda ●
Antwerp ■
Brussels ■

BELGIUM

LUXEMBOURG

Amsterdam ■

HOLLAND

Arnhem
see inset

Dusseldorf ■
Cologne ■

Rhine

GERMANY

Verden ●

Lüneburg ●
Uelzen ●
Celle ●
Hanover ●

Hamburg ■

Elbe

Berlin ■

Leipzig ■

Dresden ■

Inset:

Arnhem ●

Nijmegen ■

Rhine

Cleve ●
Rees ●
Xanten ●

Reichswald

Goch ●

0   25   50   75 miles 100

0   50   100 kms

the Allies. Eisenhower had taken over command of the land battle and his policy was one of advancing on a broad front, the most certain way of ensuring decision nowhere. Montgomery condemned the policy. 'To get decisive results,' he wrote later, it was essential to concentrate somewhere 'left, centre, or right, whichever the supreme commander considered most suitable. It was as simple as that, and the British Chiefs of Staff supported my view. But the American Generals did not agree. The Germans recovered.' In fact Eisenhower did agree to what General Sir John Hackett called in his brilliantly composed book *I Was a Stranger** (by far the best thing he has done) 'a bold plan by which it was hoped to bring the war in Europe to an early end. The intention was to lay an airborne carpet northwards across three river lines at once and then wheel the following armour and infantry righthanded down into the Ruhr ... The two southernmost crossings were successfully consolidated. The most northerly and most hazardous, where the British 1st Airborne Division with the Polish parachute brigade was set down near Arnhem on the Lower Rhine, was not.' He explains that the Germans succeeded in holding the ground forces despatched to join up with this lightly equipped force and that such heavy attacks were then made on it that, without reinforcement, the issue was not in doubt. 'In the end the remnant of the 1st Airborne Division was withdrawn across the river, two thousand men out of ten, leaving the badly wounded with the enemy.' His own brigade suffered badly, he himself was seriously wounded, and it is in this book that he gives so eloquent and moving account of how he was cared for by the Dutch and eventually escaped back to England. He says little of the battle itself, but the heroism of the British parachute troops in what can truly be called an epic battle lives on in many a Regimental history and many a film, one of which was based on Cornelius Ryan's *A Bridge Too Far*.† We may perhaps get the feel of what it was like at Arnhem bridge itself from his book:

> At the Arnhem bridge the massive defiance by the valiant few was nearly over. At dawn the Germans had renewed their terrifying bombardment. In the morning light the stark pitted wrecks that had once been houses and office buildings were again subjected to punishing fire. On each side of the bridge and along the churned, mangled ruins of the Eusebius Buiten Singel, the few strongholds that still remained were being systematically blown apart. The semi-circular defence line that had once protected the northern approaches had almost ceased to exist. Yet, ringed by flame and sheltering

* Chatto & Windus, 1977.
† Hamish Hamilton, 1974.

behind rubble, small groups of obstinate men continued to fight on, denying the Germans the bridge.

Only the rawest kind of courage had sustained Frost's men up to now, but it had been fierce enough and constant enough to hold off the Germans for three nights and two days. The second Battalion and the men from other units who had come by twos and threes to join it [a force that by Frost's highest estimate never totalled more than 600–700 men] had been welded together in their ordeal. Pride and common purpose had fused them. Alone they had reached the objective of an entire airborne division – and held out longer than the division was meant to do . . .

But now the time of their endurance had nearly run its course. Holed up in ruins and slit trenches, struggling to protect themselves and cellars full of wounded, shocked and concussed by nearly unceasing enemy fire, and wearing their filthy blood-stained bandages and impudent manners like badges of honour, the Red Devils knew, finally, that they could no longer hold.

It had been gallantry of the highest order. But alas, it had not brought the war to an early end. Indeed greatly to the surprise of almost everyone, including the German Army itself, Hitler was shortly to indulge in one last offensive, a final throw by the Supreme Commander willing to gamble everything in a last desperate fling. In the middle of December, 1944, he launched a counter-offensive in the Ardennes. Although it achieved some initial success the attack was blocked by courageous, uncoordinated groups of American soldiers, the heroic defence of Bastogne, the grip established by Montgomery on the northern shoulders of the so-called Bulge, the intervention of Patton's 3rd Army and the overwhelming air power of the Allies. Hitler thereby squandered his last reserves, and as Montgomery put it, 'after the battle the Germans gave no serious resistance'. This was hardly accurate, as the hard-fought Reichswald battles indicated, to say nothing of the Rhine crossing itself. Montgomery was more accurate when he declared that the battle of the Ardennes was won principally because of the American soldier's fighting qualities, although even this admission did little to soothe the ruffled feathers of American generals who had earlier been infuriated by Montgomery's press conference at which he called the Ardennes 'a very interesting battle' and implied that his own grip of the situation was what had saved it. The British were engaged in the battle too, but not heavily.

The Third Reich was now falling apart. In January, 1945, Stalin launched his greatest offensive of the war, with 180 divisions, including 4 Tank Armies, each of which contained 1,200 tanks. The Eastern

Front collapsed like a house of cards. By February the Russians were threatening Vienna and Berlin; in March both the American and British armies crossed the Rhine. It would not be long before the Red Army linked up with the Western Allies on the Elbe, but before they do, we might glance at two late actions of the British Army, one in the Reichswald, another during the Rhine crossing. In the battles for clearing up to the west bank of the Rhine, Montgomery's Army Group was given the sector from Nijmegen to Düsseldorf, and as part of that operation 30 Corps, commanded by Horrocks, had to deal with the Reichswald. The country was hardly conducive either to comfort or to mobile operations. Horrocks's Corps had to attack between two rivers, the Meuse and the Rhine, ground liable to flooding when the dykes were cut; the Reichswald itself with its narrow rides had to be crossed; the Germans had had plenty of time to prepare their defences and had heavily fortified both Goch and Cleve, natural battlements at the eastern exits of the Reichswald; as if this were not enough when the attack started it both thawed and rained. It was 9 February, 1945.

Sir Martin Lindsay commanded 1st Battalion, The Gordon Highlanders, in the attack and remembered well how, soon after the battalion had got under way, the whole momentum of the advance was stopped by enemy mines and machine-gun fire. He admirably conveys the utter fog and confusion of a battle:

> Just as we got there we were ambushed. There was a burst of Schmeisser in front, and the sharp explosions of one or two German grenades. Immediately five or six Germans came to life in trenches on either side of the path. They must have been asleep, for one-third of us had already passed them. There was an instantaneous crash of automatic fire from the column and every one of them fell riddled with bullets. It was all over in about two seconds, and our only casualty was MacPherson, slightly wounded in the leg. Actually it was a most efficient performance on our part, but all I thought at the time was: 'God, how bloody! Ambushed before we've even started, this is going to be the bloodiest show that's ever been' ...
>
> Every hundred yards took us about fifteen minutes, and the confusion was indescribable. I found myself scrambling along with Porter, at the head of his platoon, he in front with an automatic very much at the ready, and me close up, keeping direction with a compass ... All we could do was push on slowly, climbing over tree trunks and branches or crawling under them. 'What an awful balls-up of this I've made,' I thought to myself, having lost all control. 'It's going to be a ghastly failure' ... [we] were in the middle of a minefield ...
>
> There was another loud bang and one of them fell down, badly injured.

35. (*Above*) Field-Marshal Earl Wavell - 'the only British general with "a touch of genius"'.

36. (*Above right*) General Alexander in North Africa. He was later to use his 'charm, reputation and optimism' to good effect in Italy.

37. (*Right*) Field-Marshal Rommel, the Desert Fox, with Field-Marshal Kesselring.

38. Field-Marshal Slim, author of 'perhaps the best-written book about the war by any general'.

39. Orde Wingate (*right*) 'was perhaps the most remarkable of all'.

40. British troops manhandling a gun into position, Burma, 14th Army, 1944.

41. D-Day, 6 June, 1944.

42. Normandy, 16 June, 1944. HM King George VI and General Sir Bernard Montgomery talking to officers on the beach.

43. The Battle for Caen: British troops pinned down during the struggle for the city.

44. British vehicles and armour waiting to cross one of the six bridges over the Orne at the start of Operation *Goodwood*, 18 July, 1944.

45. Korea: 'C' Squadron, 8th Hussars, and men of the Gloucestershire Regiment before the attack on Hill 327.

46. Malaya: 'Everything stinks of rotting vegetation. You are always wet through'.

47. 'A disaster for British policy and prestige'. Men of 3 PARA at El Gamil airfield, Port Said, during the Suez operation, November, 1956.

48. 'Adaptability afforded by helicopters'. An AB 205 being unloaded in Dhofar.

49. 'Peace-keeping operations by UN forces'. Ferret scout cars of 'A' Squadron, 5th Royal Inniskilling Dragoon Guards on patrol in southern Cyprus.

50. Victory in the Falklands was achieved by determined political and military will and 'yomping'.

51. 'The seemingly endless Ulster commitment'. Soldiers of the 1st Battalion, The Prince of Wales's Own Yorkshire Regiment, in Portadown.

52. Troops clearing a Taleban held compound in Helmand Province, Afghanistan.

It now took a long time to get out the two wounded men with every footstep being prodded first. Danny had ceased to be talkative, and I learned that he had received a lot of wood splinters in the back of the head, as Porter had in the face. When the stretcher party had left, the Canadian pioneer sergeant prodded his way up to me and led me safely out of the minefield by planting my feet precisely in his footsteps.

During this battle, D Company, which Lindsay had been with, lost all its four officers. In assessing the respective danger, or what he called unpleasantness, of soldiering in this campaign, Lindsay put the job of the sappers highest, next the infantry who were called upon to fight so continuously, and third airborne forces – because they had long rests between operations – and tank crews, who were not in action as frequently as infantry. This last point would probably have been endorsed by a member of the 4th Royal Tank Regiment, however unpleasant a time he had of it during their drive forward through Hochwald to Xanten:

> Our objective was the high ground to the north-east of Sonsbeck – the last important high ground before the Rhine. Soon after 1400 hours the leading squadron moved into battle and a running fight started which lasted without a break until 0630 the next morning. At first the main opposition came from German SPs, cunningly hidden. They took a lot of shifting and knocked out several tanks, killing a squadron leader amongst others, before they were knocked out in their turn. We took as our axis a road with a farm astride it every two or three hundred yards. Each farm was strongly defended by the Boche. We soon settled down into a set drill which each time ended in a mad rush by our infantry into the blazing buildings. The German gunners had a field day indeed. From their positions on the high ground they could see the movement of every tank and vehicle. Accurate and heavy fire took a distressingly large toll of our men, particularly of tank commanders who often had to be out of their tanks talking to the infantry. The steadiness and persistence of our infantry friends under this withering fire, and without the armoured protection we had, won our special admiration that day.

Having cleared the Germans from the west bank of the Rhine, the Allies now had to cross it and this Montgomery did on the night of 23 March. As was customary with him the assault conformed to the basic rules of being tidy, elaborate, fully prepared and supported by massive fire power. Among those who crossed that night was our friend Martin Lindsay and his Gordon Highlanders. He recalled that it was a splendidly clear night with a moon, the loading area full of buffaloes, the amphibious river-crossing craft, the men filing up to them, mortars smacking down but mercifully not hitting any of his men, an absolutely continuous bombardment by their own guns of enemy positions on the far side, a sheep and lambs suddenly trotting past the soldiers, all of whom got over the river in less than two hours. This had been easy enough. Fighting on the other side was not:

> By the evening the enemy had been pushed back to quite a small area, about 200 yards by 200 yards, at the very east end of the town [Rees]. B Company was trying to clean them up, as indeed they had been for the last three or four hours, while A and D Companies and the Black Watch to the north were acting as stops to prevent their breaking out. These Hun parachutists were very tough. They had been chased out of France, Belgium and Holland, into Germany, back over the Rhine, and now street by street across Rees into a corner. Yet they were still fighting it out.

Shortly after this the remaining Germans surrendered. A week after crossing the Rhine, Montgomery had 20 divisions and 1,500 tanks under his hand ready to advance, both to complete the northern part of encircling the Ruhr and to gallop from there across the Westphalian plain to the Elbe. Eisenhower's broad plan was to close up to the Elbe to link up with the Russians there at Leipzig-Dresden, to join hands further south as well and prevent the establishment of a National Redoubt (in fact a myth), while further north the Elbe would be crossed in order to drive to the Baltic coast and prevent the Russians advancing into Schleswig-Holstein towards Denmark. This latter task fell to the British 2nd Army which advanced swiftly and successfully. They captured Celle on 12 April, Uelzen three days later. The full horrors of Belsen concentration camp were revealed – 10,000 unburied dead lying about, thousands of decomposing bodies in pits, and 40,000 living but starved men, women and children. Turning north the British pressed on, reaching the Elbe in the Hamburg–Darchau area, capturing Verden on 17 April and Lüneburg next day. Hamburg itself was not entered until 3 May, by which time the battle for Berlin was over, the Führer dead, and the end of war in Europe, V.E. Day, only five days off. A young officer of the 11th Hussars, Richard Brett-Smith, remembered how his regiment led the famous Desert Rats, 7th Armoured Division, into Hamburg:

> There was something unnatural about the silence, something a little uncanny. As we drove up to that last great bridge across the Elbe, the final obstacle that could have held us up so long, it seemed impossible that we had taken Hamburg so easily. Looking down at the cold grey waters of the Elbe swirling far below, we sensed again that queer feeling that came whenever we crossed an enemy bridge, and it would have been no great surprise if the whole

structure had suddenly collapsed ... But no, it did not blow up ... we were across the last obstacle, and there were no more rivers to cross ... There was a lot of clicking of heels and saluting, and in a few moments Hamburg, the greatest port in Germany, had been surrendered ...

The end of the German Army was indeed a wonderful and astonishing sight. We had long guessed how disorganized the enemy was, and that his administration had broken down, but even so, the sight we now saw was stranger than we had ever expected. Thousands of infantry, *Luftwaffe* men, SS men, anti-tank gunners, *Kriegsmarinen*, Hungarians, Rumanians, ambulance men, Labour Corps men, *Hitler Jugend* boys, soldiers of every conceivable age and unit, jostled one another in complete disorder ... down every road the *Wehrmacht* struggled to give itself up, its pride broken, its endurance at an end.

So the British Army had arrived in Germany and was in occupation of the north German Plain. It had come to stay, and we shall see later how the British Army of the Rhine soldiers on there, very different in numbers, in equipment, in housing, in function and in recruitment, but – *Gott Sei Dank* – very much the same in regimental organization and in spirit. In achieving this satisfactory conclusion to so long and hard a struggle, the British Army had, as Churchill had promised, fought in France, fought on the beaches and landing grounds, fought in the fields, in the streets and in the hills. As a result of its efforts and those of its Allied comrades in arms, the German Army had been defeated in the field. So had the Japanese Army, and it is to General Sir William Slim and his Fourteenth [the Forgotten] Army that we must now return to see how he set about and achieved the reconquest of Burma.

16

VICTORY IN THE FAR EAST

If five hundred Japanese were ordered to hold a position, we had to kill four hundred and ninety-five before it was ours – and then the last five killed themselves.

Slim

There could be no better lesson for the aspiring commander of today than to study and understand the three great difficulties confronting General Slim when he took over the 14th Army and how he tackled them. In his own account of the battles for Burma* he lists them as supply, health and morale. The first was solved by exploiting, improving and adding to all the existing means of communication – railways, rivers and roads – and developing a new system altogether, which was essential both for supplying China and so keeping China in the war and for enabling the deep-penetration Chindit forces of Wingate and others to fight – supply by air. Between India and Burma there were virtually no communications. They had to be built. Slim has called the road construction from Dimapur to Imphal and then down to the Burmese frontier an extraordinary feat of engineering. 'There was something splendid in its sweep through jungle, along mountain flanks and over torrents. Day and night without a break thousands of lorries swung round its curves, and ground in low gear up its gradients. Then from this main artery, at Imphal, branched off that crazy road to Tiddim, 180 miles away in the Chin Hills, zigzagging up cliffs, meandering through deep valleys, soaring again literally into the clouds. The making of this road was hardly a more wonderful feat than keeping it open against the spates, subsidences and the great landslide of the monsoon.' It was not only roads which had to be constructed. More than two

*Defeat into Victory, Cassell, 1956.

hundred airfields were built, pipe-lines laid, ports' capacity multiplied, the railways improved and their capacity quadrupled. It was all a triumph of planning and perseverance. And the variety of supplies necessary to keep operational an Army of well over half a million men, with different foodstuffs for, say, Indian and British soldiers, ammunition for infinitely varied weapons, petrol, boots and clothing almost defies description.

Without supplies the Army could not fight, yet at one stage it seemed to General Slim that, with a casualty rate from sickness of about twelve in every thousand *every day*, his Army was melting away. Sickness arose from several diseases – malaria was the worst, then dysentery, skin troubles and jungle typhus. In 1943 the ratio of men evacuated for sickness compared with wounds was 120:1. Four remedies were applied; the latest medical techniques were introduced; cases were treated in forward areas; serious casualties were evacuated by air; and morale, the third great problem, had to be put right. What Slim had to say about this is so perceptive and so lastingly relevant to the foundation of morale in the British Army that it is worth recalling it in some detail. He maintained first of all that the different elements contributing to high morale were spiritual, intellectual and material, and that their importance was in that order. Thus, there had to be some great purpose, which had to be gained by means of action and that what each man did towards this purpose mattered. Further, it was necessary that the thing *could* be done and that the outfit he belonged to was effective. Confidence in the leadership was essential, so that no matter how hard and dangerous fighting might be, there would be no chucking away of lives. Finally, weapons and equipment had to be good, while conditions in general had to be made as tolerable as they could be. In putting all these ideas into practice Slim spent much time talking to his men, and everyone spent a lot of time training. In jungle warfare, whether a huge campaign like the one in Burma or a relatively small-scale operation in Borneo during the so-called 'confrontation' of Indonesia, the key to success is proper patrolling. It was entirely necessary that the British and Indian soldiers should be confident that they could dominate the jungle, so, as Slim put it, they could 'get the feel through the army that it was we who were hunting the Jap, not he us'.

We will not follow the campaign in detail. Very broadly the British stood on the defensive in 1943, although there was the Arakan offensive, which did not succeed and from which Slim learned how the training and tactics of his British, Indian and Gurkha soldiers must be changed to counter Japanese methods. Patrolling would have to become bold, wide, cunning and offensive. In the second Arakan campaign, mounted

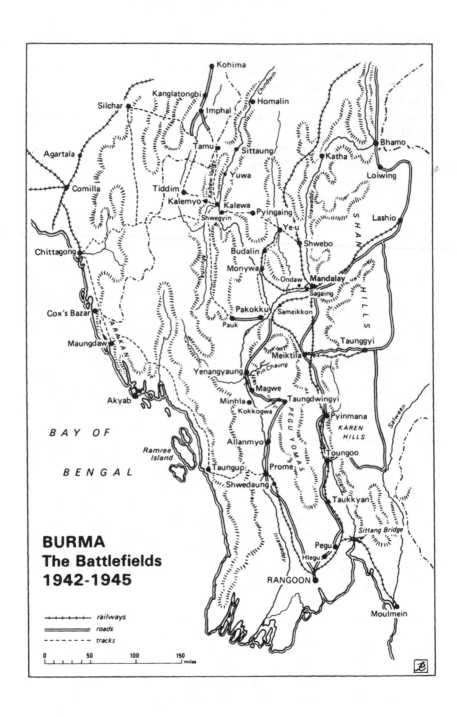

BURMA
The Battlefields
1942-1945

railways
roads
tracks

0   50   100   150
                      miles

towards the end of 1943 and lasting until the following March, things went better, and when we follow the activities of a junior NCO in the 1st/11th Sikhs, we may understand why:

During the attack on India Hill, a feature near Buthidaung, on March 12th 1944, Naik Nand Singh was leading his section towards a Japanese position. His was the leading section of the leading platoon of C Company. India Hill was a knife-edged ridge covered with jungle and the exact layout of the Japanese position could not be seen. In fact, it was held by about forty Japanese, placed singly in holes or in trenches that took two men each. There was only one way to get near the position, by a narrow track; as Nand Singh's section reached the crest they came under heavy rifle and machine-gun fire and every man but Nand Singh fell. But he went straight at the nearest trench and though hit by a fragment of grenade he sprang into the trench and bayonetted both occupants. There was another trench of the same kind close by and Nand Singh jumped out of his trench and dashed towards it. He was hit again and knocked down but he got up and hurled himself into the second trench, killing the two occupants of that too. He went on and took a third trench. The rest of the platoon then moved up and took the position, killing 37 of the 40 men holding it. Nand Singh won the V.C.

The major campaign which followed and lasted until July, 1944, included the strategically crucial battles of Kohima and Imphal which turned the scales. The 14th Army, with British, Indian and Australian divisions, decisively defeated the Japanese, and India was saved. By this time British air supremacy, which not only removed enemy aircraft from the scene, but enabled massive air supply to keep isolated groups of Allied soldiers operational, was a major contributor to success. Much of the fighting was fierce and close-quarter, for example the hand-to-hand engagement astride the Deputy-Commissioner's tennis court at Kohima, where, as James Morris has told us, the war memorial marks the site of the battle, with the tennis court lines still drawn in white. Slim himself called it all a 'prolonged and hard-fought battle [which] swayed back and forth through great stretches of wild country; one day its focal point was a hill named on no map; the next a miserable unpronounceable village a hundred miles away. Columns, brigades, divisions, marched and counter-marched, met in bloody clashes, and reeled apart, weaving a confused pattern, hard to unravel.' The Japanese fought with their customary contempt for death, seeming able to go on without food or supplies or hope. Conditions were appalling, but the pursuit of the defeated Japanese went on even though the monsoon was raging, and the tracks were so slippery and muddy that it sometimes took more than an hour for unladen soldiers to cover a mile, and on one occasion 'half a company took ten hours to carry two stretcher-cases four miles'. The fanaticism of the Japanese soldiers is illustrated by our soldiers' finding them dead from starvation or being posted in possible tank crossing places with bombs which they were then required to detonate as the enemy tank passed over them. But what mattered was that Slim's 14th Army had won, and now it seemed the reconquest of Burma would be only a matter of time.

Contributing greatly to the gradual assertion of their superiority was the astonishing work of Wingate and his Chindits, with men of the calibre of Bernard Fergusson and Mike Calvert. Of all the remarkable men to emerge and take high command of bold, imaginative and effective military measures, Orde Wingate was perhaps the most remarkable of all. Churchill called him 'a man of genius who might have become a man of destiny', a description which almost precisely fits Lawrence of Arabia, whose kinsman he was. Wavell, who gave Wingate such unwavering support, also attributed him with military genius, and pointed out how thorough and complete all his planning, training and administrative affairs were. And Bernard Fergusson, who commanded one of the Chindit columns with such gallantry and success, wrote of Wingate; 'No other officer I have heard of could have dreamed the dream, planned the plan, obtained, trained, inspired and led the force. There are some who shine at planning, or at training, or at leading; here was a man who excelled at all three, and whose vision at the council-table matched his genius in the field.'

The simplicity of the idea – planting relatively small bodies of troops astride enemy communications and supplying them by air, so that their ability to harass and disrupt the enemy's activities could be prolonged – was reinforced by Wingate's insistence on standards of perfection. Like his patron, Wavell, he insisted on unpredictability – a doctrine that never had greater relevance to the British Army than it recently has had in Northern Ireland. As he developed his ideas and the range of his operations, his brigades would establish 'Strongholds' which were themselves defensible and from which columns would set out to harry the enemy. Bernard Fergusson has described how his brigade and Mike Calvert's were to support each other in an operation designed to block the railway which the Japanese were using to supply their forces fighting Stilwell's Chinese. Calvert's brigade flew to its landing area on time, but Fergusson was delayed by a long march in to his Stronghold, and no sooner there than required to go and take Indaw airfield from the enemy. Things went wrong and he certainly had his share of ill-luck:

So secret had been the plan that a Column of another Brigade, passing through a neighbouring area towards a different objective, gave out in all innocence to every village through which it passed, as its cover plan, that it was on the way to attack Indaw. This information reached the Japs, and they at once sent forward troops in the direction from which in fact I was approaching. Secondly, the Column that was to come in from the south, having decided to bivouac for the night, suddenly found itself astride a motor-road unmarked on the map. . . . They were in the process of unloading their animals, and their muleteers therefore had no hold of their mules' headropes, when three lorry-loads of Japanese troops drove to their own surprise into the middle of the circle that was about to be the Column's bivouac. They opened fire, the mules stampeded, casualties were inflicted on both sides; and when it was all over the Column had lost all its heavy weapons and most of its mules, and its commanding officer had been wounded. . . . Thirdly, I had failed to appreciate for the second time in two years that we would be operating in an area which was short of water.

Such were the vicissitudes of operating deeply behind enemy lines. Fergusson pointed out that although men could go for long periods without food, in the heat conditions of Burma they had to have water. Neither men nor mules could be restrained when water suddenly appeared or was scented. His problems were solved by air supply. Before this operation was over, Fergusson heard that Wingate had been killed in an air crash. 'Here,' he wrote, 'was the biggest blow of all.' But Wingate's ideas, his ideals and his reputation live on. There were other heroes in his mould – Tom Harrisson (who in 1963, while still Curator of Kuching Museum, was so generous in the advice he gave me, when I was commanding the forces in West Sarawak against Indonesian incursions) dropping into Sarawak by parachute and organizing the tribes for guerrilla action against the Japanese – in the long houses you can still the heads taken by Dyaks; and Freddy Spencer-Chapman, for whom the jungle of Malaya was neutral, but who made sure that with his Force 136 (some of whose Chinese members were so troublesome to the British a few years later) he killed as many Japanese as possible – in two weeks he and his patrols accounted for 1,000 enemy soldiers and blew up thirty bridges. He was a man out of Britain's imperial past, and as James Morris put it, 'he had tried himself to the utmost, in exploits of astonishing courage and endurance, and stripped and scoured by the war, allowed to kill in a legal cause, he had, like many an imperialist of previous generations, found his metier!'

However inspiring, exciting and enviable such exploits may have been, they were sideshows and the real business was still being conducted by Slim and his 14th Army. Their reconquest of Burma has been called by Jock Haswell 'one of the most difficult and brilliant offensive campaigns in the whole history of the British Army', and by March, 1945, Slim had virtually destroyed the Japanese position in Burma, crossed the Irrawaddy, recaptured Mandalay and Meiktila, and obliged the enemy to leave Rangoon. By May the campaign was over, but not the war. Happily the need to invade Malaya and re-take Singapore was done away with by atomic weapons' destruction of Hiroshima and Nagasaki, weapons which were within a dozen years to have so profound an effect on the size and recruitment of the British Army. Mountbatten, Supreme Allied Commander in South-East Asia, received the surrender of the Japanese command in Singapore, a role he carried out with characteristic grace and style. The 'Armies of the Rising Sun' were finished, and the humiliation of Singapore's surrender was avenged, and indeed, as the war finally ended, the British position in the world seemed to have been wholly restored. It was not so, of course, as James Morris has reminded us. 'With imperial armies deployed across the world, with a Royal Navy of 3,500 fighting ships and a Royal Air Force of unparalleled prestige, in theory the British Empire was a power as never before. . . . And if it was illusory, if the British victory was a defeat disguised, if the propagandists had given the people some false ideas about themselves and their prospects, if the Empire was not so united and powerful as Churchill suggested, if the grand euphoria of 1945 was all too soon to dissolve, still there was much to be proud of. They had stayed the terrible course, start to finish.' It was only of the British people and the British Army that it could be said that they had fought it from start to finish and emerged victorious. Field-Marshal Slim, as he was by the time he published the book, ended it by hoping that it would leave above all the impression that the war in Burma had been a *soldiers'* war. 'There comes a moment in every battle against a stubborn enemy when the result hangs in the balance. Then the general, however skilful and far-sighted he may have been, must hand over to his soldiers, to the men in the ranks and to their regimental officers, and leave them to complete what he has begun. The issue then rests with them, on their courage, their hardihood, their refusal to be beaten either by the cruel hazards of nature or by the fierce strength of their human enemy. . . . To the soldiers of many races who, in the comradeship of the Fourteenth Army, *did* go on, and to the airmen who flew with them and fought over them, belongs the true glory of achievement. It was they who turned Defeat into Victory.'

So the Second World War ended. Some 300,000 servicemen had been killed. For the British Army, however, the fighting did not end. The savage wars of peace were about to get under way again. But this time it would not be part of what James Morris called an imperial progress. It was to be an imperial retreat. Kipling, poet of Empire, was always the best portrait painter of the British soldier and before we leave those who helped to win the war which undermined their own country's greatness, we may perhaps recall Kipling's words, composed to honour the efforts which soldiers had made in a former war, but wholly fitting for this one too:

> They have learned great faith and little fear and a high heart in distress,
> And how to suffer each sodden year of heaped-up weariness.
> They have borne the bridle upon their lips and the yoke upon their neck,
> Since they went down to the sea in ships to save the world from wreck.

17

KEEPING THE PEACE – WITH GUNS

As long as we rule India, we are the greatest power in the world. If we lose it we shall drop straight away to a third-rate power. . . . Your ports and your coaling stations, your fortresses and your dockyards, your Crown colonies and protectorates will go too. For either they will be unnecessary, or the toll-gates and barbicans of an Empire that has vanished.

Curzon

For centuries the British Army had been garrisoning and policing the Empire with a view to enlarging it or at least hanging on to what we had got. Now the Army garrisons were still there and were to have much policing to do, but most if it was done with a view to handing power over to those who were generally thought of as 'nationalists'. Many of the leaders of these so-called nationalist movements had Communist leanings. The guerrillas who had fought with Spencer-Chapman against the Japanese in Malaya, the Burmese Defence Army which had turned against the Japanese, were Communist-inspired. Men like Kenyatta, Nkrumah and West Indian political agitators had been politically indoctrinated in Moscow. Even in India Communist propaganda was circulating in condemnation of imperialism and advocating revolution. India was one of the first to go, quickly followed by Burma and Ceylon. There was much bloodshed in the last year before partition, but the blood was either Muslim or Hindu. 'Violence erupted on a scale never known in British India before,' wrote James Morris, 'even in the Mutiny. . . . Whole communities were massacred. Entire train-loads of refugees died on the tracks, to the last child in arms. In the Punjab gangs of armed men roamed the countryside, slaughtering columns of refugees, and thousands of people died unremarked in the streets of Amritsar, where the death of 400 had horrified the world twenty-five years before.'

Mountbatten, last of the Viceroys, persevered, doing what could be done with a Boundary Force to keep the peace. But 'the British Army was steadily and unostentatiously withdrawn: one by one, the regiments left the soil of India, embarking on their troopships at Bombay while the bands on the Apollo Bunder played Auld Lang Syne'. No longer would it be necessary for Thomas Atkins to speak his atrocious Hindustani and put his best foot first when marching from one station to another:

> It's none so bad o' Sunday, when you're lying at your ease,
> To watch the kites a-wheelin' round them feather-'eaded trees,
> For although there ain't no women, yet there ain't no barrick-yards,
> So the orficers goes shootin' an' the men they plays at cards ...
> So 'ark 'an 'eed, you rookies, which is always grumblin' sore,
> There's worser things than marchin' from Umballa to Cawnpore;
> An' if your 'eels are blistered an' they feels to 'urt like 'ell,
> You drop some tallow in your socks an' that will make 'em well.

All that was finished, and there would be no Burma girl either, sitting and waiting for the British soldier when he took the road to Mandalay once more. But he would still be going east of Suez and let us go with him now for the first and (except for something much closer to home which we must look at later) the longest of internal security campaigns, which kept him busy for the best part of twelve years. On the way to Malaya with the various regiments that took part, regiments still largely composed of national servicemen, the troopship will pass or call in at ports and places where other garrisons soldiered on or would need powerful reinforcements for further wars of counter-insurgency – Gibraltar and Malta, peaceful enough now, but the latter still scarred from its vital role in war; Cyprus, soon to be the scene of another bitter struggle; Palestine where the British had failed to mediate between Arab and Jew and in May, 1948, had washed their hands of the problem which many accused them of having created; Suez and the Canal Zone, temporary home for many more national servicemen, getting their knees brown, leaving to the Egyptians and then briefly returning in one of the most controversial and damaging military adventures ever undertaken by the British; Aden, a mere coaling station once, later an important piece in the Middle East power game; into the Indian Ocean, leaving Kenya, where we shall meet the Mau Mau gangs in due course, well behind us; calling in at Ceylon, which became a Dominion in this same year; and so on to disembark at Singapore, spend a few days at Nee Soon camp before taking the train or driving the lorries and armoured cars up country to various parts of Malaya, where the Malayan Races

Liberation Army* – better known to the security forces as CTs (Communist Terrorists) were making their bid to take the country over. It is 1948, and the long, long war is just getting under way.

What became known in Malaya as The Emergency began in the middle of 1948. Chin Peng had fought with the British in Force 136 during the war. He and some of his men had actually taken part in the Victory Parade in London. From being a member of the war-time Malayan Peoples' Anti-Japanese Army, he had been made Secretary General of the Malayan Communist Party in 1947, and had initiated a campaign of urban strikes and riots in an attempt to gain further support for the party. But he soon saw that these measures were arousing hostility rather than recruits, and so he determined upon a campaign of armed rebellion. Prospects were more promising by returning to the jungle and then exploiting the discontent of half a million Chinese squatters who scraped a living from land near the jungle's edge. From such people, recruits could be enlisted, money extorted and information gained. At the outset Chin Peng's army of guerrillas numbered perhaps 10,000, of whom rather less than one third were organized into some ten regiments of fighting men based in the jungle, and constantly moving from camp to camp to avoid detection. His plan was to mount a campaign of terror – murder, coercion, economic disruption – from a number of secure jungle bases and then expand areas of control until eventually he would establish authority over the whole country. The non-combatant guerrillas, about 7,000 of them, made up a Self-Protection Corps whose job it was to mix with the population, get information, money, food, weapons, recruit more support, and generally provide back-up for the active bands of terrorists. It was a complex and country-wide underground network and nearly all its members and support came from the Malayan Chinese.

There were, broadly, four parts to this long drawn out counter-insurgency war from the British point of view. First from 1948 to 1950 the Army and Police conducted a kind of holding operation under the direction of the Malay Federation's Commissioner of Police. There was compulsory registration and control of firearms. Great sweeps were made through the jungle to locate bandit camps and kill their occupants – usually ineffectually. Smaller operations based on better information were mounted and some success achieved. Suspects were detained. Much of the military activity was in the form of reaction to the terrorists' activities. But taken as a whole the Security Forces' efforts obliged the guerrillas to abandon the idea of establishing liberated bases. On the

---

* When the campaign began the guerrilla forces were named the Malayan Peoples' Anti-British Army, simply substituting the word British for Japanese.

other hand the terrorists could still count on considerable support from the squatters. The second phase, which began in 1950, was far more methodical. General Briggs, who had been appointed Director of Operations, set up a Federal War Council, which controlled proper Emergency machinery in every State and District, each of which had its own triumvirate of police and military commanders under the senior officer of the Administration to coordinate and direct operations.

But Briggs did much more than simply bring a proper organization into being. He struck shrewd blows at the whole Communist Party's organization. Those members of the Self-Protection Corps who could be identified were arrested and interned. Then a great move to interfere with all the support given to the bandits by squatters was taken. His plan set about re-settling all the half million squatters into new villages which were protected by newly raised Home Guard units. By the end of 1951 these measures were having their effect, and the terrorists were faced with the alternative of either further coercion, which would turn the population against them, or serious dwindling of support in the form of food, money and information. As in all operations of this sort everything depended on good intelligence, and on the whole the best information was made available to the side which was expected to win. Isolate the terrorists from their means to wage guerrilla warfare, and you were on the way to ending the Emergency. Yet the terrorists still enjoyed many, and some spectacular, successes. The murder of Sir Henry Gurney, British High Commissioner, in an ambush resulted in the appointment of General Sir Gerald Templer to replace him in February, 1952. Templer would combine in his own person supreme civil and military power, and thereupon embarked on a strategy which not only intensified the battle to isolate the guerrillas, but launched a civil aid programme and gave promises of political independence. In this way the hearts and minds of the population were courted and won. This third phase, which lasted from 1952 until 1957, under Templer and others gradually eliminated most of the Communist terrorists, saw the growing declaration of 'White' areas free from terrorist influence, and established self-government for Malaya. Last stage of all from 1957 to 1960 consisted of a general mopping-up operation; Chin Peng and his remaining followers retired from the game and found refuge in jungle camps on the borders of Malaya and Thailand.

To do all this had demanded immense numbers of soldiers, police and local defence forces. They numbered a quarter of a million at the height of the affair. There were about 25,000 British soldiers, many more from Australia, New Zealand, East Africa and Fiji. Gurkha battalions were numerous and were uniquely good at jungle fighting. The

Singora

THAILAND

Kota Bharu

Alor Star

KEDAH

Sungei Patani

PENANG

KELANTAN

PERAK

TRENGGANU

Taiping

Sungei Siput

Kuala Kangsar

Chemor

Ipoh

The
Dindings

Kampar

PAHANG

Kuantan

SELANGOR

Kuala Lumpur

NEGRI

SEMBILAN

Segamat

MALACCA

Muar

JOHORE

Johore Bahru

Singapore

Malaya

```
0      25      50    miles   100
0    25    50    75   100 kms
```

Malayan Scouts were formed by Mike Calvert and provided a nucleus for the re-emergence of the S.A.S. Regiment. Between them they killed a thousand terrorists. Every sort of regiment of the British Army served in Malaya during the twelve-year war – infantry battalions, artillery, engineer and cavalry regiments all took to 'jungle bashing', having acquired their own instructors at the Jungle Warfare School. Auster aircraft flown by Army pilots helped to identify positions, direct artillery fire and supply patrols. The Royal Navy helicopters took part, and pointed the way for their subsequent invaluable use in campaigns still to come. My own regiment, the 4th Hussars, was there and I had the good fortune to be commanding a squadron. We did not only patrol the roads and tracks with our armoured cars, and escort convoys and V.I.P.s, but took to the jungle on foot in frequent operations to seek out bandits or acquire information. On one occasion I received the curt, but clear, instruction to travel down the railway line between Ipoh and Chemor with seven or eight men in two little jeeps fitted with wheels matching the rail gauge to clear the line of mines and an ambush party of guerrillas who had shot up the night train to Taiping. A simple enough order, I reflected. As we set off, a last minute caution to be careful and to report if I were ambushed was given. Away we went, the leading jeep about 50 yards in front of mine, headlights on as it was a dark, cloudy night, guns at the ready, all round look-outs, the radio operator with me. All serene for a few miles, then suddenly as we were passing through a steep cutting, the somewhat eerie sound of wheels on tracks was shattered by a prolonged burst of automatic fire, which seemed to spray both jeeps. Lights off, we pressed on for a hundred yards, halted, dismounted, and, leaving a sentry with each jeep, now closed up together, doubled back to the ambush area. Some of us crawled to the top of the northern bank from which the shooting had seemed to come, and with our Sten guns fired somewhat blindly at – what? Shadows, trees, the undergrowth; certainly no sinister figures were to be seen. My sergeant gave me a grenade, and moving back to the other bank, I drew the pin and flung it as far as I could towards where we thought the firing had come from. A violent explosion, then silence, except for the chattering of insects. There was no question of pursuing anything in total darkness. We rallied at the jeeps, unwittingly walking over wires and explosives attached to the railway line (which we did not discover until the morning when they had to be defused and removed). The leading jeep had bullet holes in the body, but happily nobody had been wounded. I reported on the radio that we had been ambushed and were proceeding to Chemor, which we reached soon afterwards without further incident. At the station there we rendez-vous'd with armoured cars and armoured personnel carriers, and on the way back to Ipoh, stopped to search a village opposite the ambush site. No one there, no one knew anything or had seen anybody. We reported the railway line clear, only to be informed at breakfast time by the police that it wasn't clear. The engine driver had seen the explosives. Out we went again, this time by train, with an explosives expert. We removed fuses, took away the explosives and wires, again reported all clear. The night train to Taiping got under way at last, some twelve hours late. All in all a tiny, unimportant incident, yet characteristic of the disruption to normal life that such trivial guerrilla action could cause.

It was not the only time we made use of the trains in our operations. Soon after this, I was sent for by the local military commander, told of a reported bandit camp, containing half a dozen terrorists, in the jungle between Ipoh and Sungei Siput, a renowned area for terrorist activity, where numerous squatters provided them with the support they needed. It was important to try and conceal our intentions in order not to frighten the bandits away before we got near their camp. This meant having an approach which could not be seen too readily and reported. The road and track approach would have been an instant give-away. Twice I went up in an Auster to survey the surrounding country and decide both where to put the ambushing 'Stops' out and which way to advance with the main flushing party. The railway line passed about five miles from our target. We requisitioned a train for what was ostensibly a routine changeover of personnel between Ipoh and Kuala Kangsar, and before dawn one morning set off. At pre-planned places the train halted to let off first the blocking party under command of one of my troop leaders, who was to be given a certain time to get into position, then later my own larger group which would advance to the patch of jungle, reputed to house the camp. It all went according to plan, and my most vivid memories are of the sharp cracks made by all of us as we made our way through a bamboo plantation – it was impossible to move through this area silently – and the surprise of observing one of my sergeants suddenly shouting in pain, halting, stripping off his jungle green shirt, to reveal red ants crawling all over his back and chest. We got into position, I established a small headquarters, the blocking party reported over the radio that they were in position, the flushing group – who were understandably concerned that they would not be shot by the blockers – moved in. There was no shooting at all. There was no game, in fact. The birds had flown, but there were unmistakable signs of a camp, and we had in this first shot at *ulu* bashing gained a little experience.

Some months later after endless patrolling, support for the local

Gurkha battalion, the clearing of squatter camps and more sorties into the *ulu*, we suffered our first casualties, when an armoured car and A.P.C. patrol ran into a strong ambush (which had been laid to destroy a convoy of lorries) on the steep, winding, jungle-overhung track to the north-east of Sungei Siput. One officer and six men of Ours were killed, others wounded, but so well did they fight back that they accounted for sixteen bandits. Never before had the C.T.s been worsted in an ambush.

From time to time we were asked to undertake more light-hearted operations. The colonel sent for me one day and told me to take my squadron at once to Sungei Patani in Kedah and report to the commander of a Gurkha battalion. We would then go south to sweep the Dindings and search for a bandit gang that had been unpleasantly active. Some sort of cover plan was needed to divert attention while the main force was unobtrusively getting into position. I was therefore given a dual task – to support the main operation and to execute the deception plan, which was to take two troops and ostentatiously occupy the island of Pangkor, a small, beautiful island, about six miles by three, lying opposite and two miles from the small port and fishing town of Lumut in the Dindings. I mustered my force early one morning and, sending an officer ahead to requisition three launches, we set off in our armoured cars, pennants flying, to Lumut, where we boarded the three launches. Standing on the bridge of the centre launch, accompanied by my Sergeant-Major, I felt something of the destroyer captain's piratical dash. I made the proper signal and off we went, the launches leaving a fine wake behind them. Soon after, we landed at three separate jetties, and I despatched the two troops to the northern and southern ends of the island, while with my small headquarters I made for the beautiful bay on the west coast. It was idyllic. As I lay on the beach after a brisk swim, I watched the Malabar fishermen pulling in their great nets and chanting their calypso-like songs, and reflected that but for the Dindings operation, which shortly I would have to get on with, I would never have come to this beautiful island. The troopers of my squadron who had taken part in the invasion of Pangkor never forgot it. They would often ask when they would be taking part in another so indisputably successful operation – all objectives captured and no casualties.

Of course, the armoured car regiments like mine did not do the real work. This was done by the infantry who lived in the jungle for long periods, had to get to know how to move through it silently, how to build bashas of tree branches and leaves, what could and could not be eaten, how to combat the blood-sucking leeches, how to set up an ambush and patiently, motionlessly, wait for it to be sprung. They had to be able to recognize, often with the help of expert trackers, when booby traps had been set by retiring terrorists. For many of them the jungle was not, as Spencer-Chapman had called it, neutral. That most valiant of defence correspondents and chronicler of his own adventures, Tom Pocock, remembered a talk he had with a young officer of The Queen's Own Royal West Kents, who described his dislike of the jungle:

> It's the perpetual gloom and the smell of corruption that is so awful. Everything stinks of rotting vegetation. You are always wet through; it rains like hot pennies six times a day and the leaves never stop dripping. In dense secondary jungle it is good going to cover a hundred yards in a hour and you cannot see the enemy an arm's length away. But most terrifying of all is at night, when you are one of a patrol's four sentries. It is the blackest darkness and you can make no noise and certainly not communicate with your neighbours, twenty-five yards away. There is an intense loneliness. What I loathe most and have never got used to, is living like an animal; wet, filthy and hungry. But an even worse fear is that I might let my men down; that keeps me going.

Tom Pocock went on to say that this young officer dreamed above all of getting some dry socks. In all the ambushes he had laid, sometimes for several days and nights, only once had he seen anyone who might remotely be the enemy, not bandits carrying guns, but a small family group including young women, who although with no obvious right to be where they were, seemed innocent enough. It was the only time he had such a contact, and so uncertain was he about them that he decided not to give the order to fire and let them go past.

Frank Kitson, renowned exponent of counter-insurgency operations, whom we shall meet again in Kenya, Cyprus and Oman, tells a different story in his book *Bunch of Five*,* when after exhaustive intelligence gathering, watching the pattern of local activities and some appropriate deception measures, two men of his Rifle Brigade company lay in ambush one September morning of 1957 in the state of Johore:

> Corporal Bryan was a burly Englishman, steady as a rock. Rifleman Henry came from the West Indies. He was small and dark, a great favourite with the other men and one of the best shots in the company.
>
> According to Jonathan's [platoon commander] calculations a terrorist was likely to appear to within fifty yards of their ambush position at some time between 7 a.m. and midday. He would be there to talk to the tappers who were working on the rubber trees. A great deal of skill and effort had gone into the making of these calculations, but it would all be in vain if Bunny Bryan and Egbert Henry proved unequal to their task.

* Faber & Faber, 1977

The job which these two men had got to do also required a high degree of skill and effort. They would have to lie absolutely still for several hours despite the goading of the mosquitoes, the irritation of the undergrowth and the slowly moving shafts of sunlight which baked first one part of their body and then the next. They could not wipe away the sweat or move their stiffening limbs because tappers were working within a few yards of their position. At the same time they had to remain on a razor's edge of alertness because the target, if it came, might only present itself for a few seconds. Furthermore both Bryan and Henry had lain in ambush on numerous occasions in the past without ever seeing a terrorist and this made it even more difficult to maintain the intense degree of readiness required ...

Henry became aware that something unusual was happening. One of the tappers had stopped work and was talking to another man. He could hardly see them, but they were walking fast through the trees. He got a glimpse of them for a moment and got the impression that the other man was wearing a khaki uniform. Judging by their course, he would see them once more for a split second between two bushes slightly to his left and then for rather longer in a wider gap to his front. The next glimpse convinced Rifleman Henry that a terrorist was about to appear in his sights.

Deep down in most people lies the natural computer of the primitive hunter, rusty and disused. In Henry's case it had been brushed up and exercised by many hours of practice on the jungle range. As a result, information regarding distance, angle, speed and light was processed automatically, his rifle came into the aim; there was a loud crash which echoed around the trees and the target fell to the ground and lay there concealed in the long grass.

It was a minor affair, Frank Kitson recorded. But it was nevertheless wholly illustrative and an important achievement – a total vindication of the discipline, patience, training and practice which the battalion's commanders had insisted on month after month. The dead terrorist was identified and led to further useful deduction as to what the gang to which he had belonged might be up to next.

In the 1950s the British Army was engaged not only in wars involving withdrawal from Empire. There was also a full-scale war in Korea during which the British and their U.N. Allies fought against the North Korean Army and the Chinese. Korea, like Waterloo, was a damn'd serious business, but unlike Waterloo it was not won by the British and their allies. The result was a draw. When the North Koreans mounted their attack across the 38th Parallel on 25 June, 1950, they took the South Koreans and Americans by surprise and, to start with, carried all before them, until the Americans succeeded in establishing a defensive perimeter round Pusan in the south-east of the country. In September a bold amphibious landing by the 10th United States Corps at Inchon reversed the position, so that the 8th U.S. Army was able to relieve Seoul, cross the 38th Parallel and advance north. By October United Nations troops had reached the Yalu River on the Chinese border. Massive Chinese intervention then drove the United Nations forces back again, and from April, 1951, until July, 1953, when an armistice was finally signed, the war became a slogging artillery duel with both sides dug in with huge trench systems reminiscent of the Great War and a similar sort of stalemate.

The British Army's part in it all was both honourable and costly, and they were joined by Canadians and Australians to make up the 1st Commonwealth Division. In particular the British infantry once more won lasting fame for their gallantry and skill. On 27 April, 1951, there appeared in *The Times* an article telling the story of 1st Battalion, The Gloucestershire Regiment, which while serving in the line with the British 29th Brigade, endured the Chinese assault for some three days. It was called the battle of the Imjin River, and the Commanding Officer, Lieutenant-Colonel Carne, was subsequently awarded the Victoria Cross in recognition of the heroism displayed by himself and his battalion. The article, which was headlined *Gloucesters Bear the Brunt*, reads:

> When the Chinese waded across the shallow Imjin river on Sunday night the brunt of their attack fell on this battalion. Cut off, surrounded, without food or water, it fought for 80 hours.
>
> The Royal Northumberland Fusiliers, on their right, went to their help – still with the roses in their helmets with which they had been celebrating St. George's Day – but the Chinese drove in between them. Throughout Monday night the Chinese attacked on every side, screaming, blowing bugles, ringing bells, and clashing cymbals. But the Gloucesters held them and fought back, giving not an inch of ground.
>
> A battalion from the Philippines fought fiercely in an attempt to break through to their relief, but failed. On Tuesday afternoon a column of British tanks similarly failed. The officer commanding the Gloucesters thereupon sent for his company commanders and ordered them to break out with their men as best they could. The battalion commander*, the chaplain, and the medical officer stayed behind with the wounded.
>
> One company decided to fight its way north and then west. An Associated Press correspondent, flying over the enemy lines, saw them walking north through the mountains, straight into the Chinese lines. He said that some of

---

* In fact the battalion commander quite properly broke out with a small group of Battalion HQ but was later captured.

them escaped to safety, but nobody knows how many. Others were eventually rescued by a tank column which broke through from the south.

That was how it appeared to a correspondent reporting at the time of the battle. The tanks which had helped belonged to the 8th King's Royal Irish Hussars, and in their history's account of the battle it is made clear how difficult it was to counter the Chinese tactics of continual infiltration and penetration between the British infantry positions. Having crossed the Imjin in great strength during the moonlit night of 22 April, they made their way right up to and round the forward British defences. Even the gun positions of 45th Field Regiment found themselves under enemy rifle fire. C Squadron, 8th Hussars, under command of the gallant Henry Huth, made a desperate bid to relieve the hard-pressed Gloucesters, but the battalion was completely surrounded. This squadron also assisted the Royal Ulster Regiment to defend their sector of the front, but again the Chinese got round behind. Thus the pattern of the battle was one of continuous Chinese masses pressing forward through and round the dispersed British defences, until on 25 April the 29th Brigade was ordered to withdraw. During this phase of the battle C Squadron was again continuously in action trying to delay the advancing Chinese long enough for the infantry battalions, which were not – like the Gloucesters – surrounded, to move back to the relative security of the main supply road. They were also able to help by carrying wounded infantrymen out of the battle after all tank ammunition had been fired off. Right until the end Henry Huth and a few other tanks engaged the advancing enemy to give the infantry time to get back to safety. In three days fighting more than a thousand men had been lost. Only four officers and thirty men returned from the Gloucesters, but the regiment had added even more renown to its honourable record – two V.C.s and two D.S.O.s were among the many gallantry awards they received. In C Squadron, 8th Hussars, apart from Henry Huth's D.S.O., three Military Crosses and two Military Medals were won. *Imjin* is one of their principal battle honours.

One of the main points made by Max Hastings in his masterly *The Korean War** is how reluctant the Americans were to dismount from their lorries and move off the roads in order to fight in the hills and so dominate the battlefield. It was a lesson the British had learned in Burma, in a different way in Malaya, and were to apply again in other counter-revolutionary wars, including Kenya where in 1952 the Mau Mau began their revolt accompanied by peculiarly loathsome practices. Like most rebellions against colonial authority the one in Kenya was

* Michael Joseph, 1987.

about land and power. The Kikuyu tribe believed that land had been stolen from them by the European settlers and they not only wanted it back, but they also wanted better conditions of land tenure, increased wages and a share of political influence. The so-called Kikuyu Central Association had become the Kenya African Union with Jomo Kenyatta at its head. Some of its members advocated violence to achieve their aims and the Emergency really began when the Mau Mau – as the dissidents were known – organized themselves into gangs and began their campaign of murder and intimidation. These gangs, each some 200 strong, totalled perhaps 15,000 at their maximum strength, and were supported by even more dissidents, who were organized in Committees and provided supplies, recruits and money to the gangs. The gangs themselves operated from bases in the Aberdare Forest and the Mount Kenya Forest. The security forces opposing the Mau Mau gangs were made up of various military units – The King's African Rifles, battalions from the British Army and a Territorial battalion of local residents, perhaps 10,000 soldiers in all, together with the Kikuyu Guard and Kenya Police, which numbered some 50,000. The Emergency lasted four years and in this time it is believed that about 11,000 members of the Mau Mau gangs were killed as opposed to two and a half thousand loyalists, mostly African.

Frank Kitson is critical of the way in which the British Army set about conducting its counter-insurgency operations and in particular he points out that to start with there was no proper understanding of how to build on what he calls 'background intelligence' so that the soldiers in a given area could discover the pattern of insurgents' behaviour there, and then take the necessary steps to deal with them. In Kenya, as in Malaya, the bands of guerrillas in forest or jungle were dependent on support from the people living outside these hiding places and had to emerge to make contact with them. It was this need that Kitson studied and exploited. As a member of the intelligence staff in Kenya he took the imaginative and courageous step of creating 'counter-gangs', that is supposedly Mau Mau gangster teams, which operated in the forests exactly like the men they were hunting. He explains how his methods led to success:

Many Africans were only too eager to help us destroy Mau Mau if they could do so without being discovered. An effective method of using such people was to get the police and army to cordon an area where Mau Mau were particularly active and round up every single person. At the same time we would collect together a few of the people who wanted to help us and who had knowledge of the area in which the round-up was taking place, and clothe them from head to foot in huge hoods with holes for the eyes. We then brought them to the cordon and made all those who had been rounded up pass in front of them. When one of our hooded men recognized one of these men as Mau Mau he told us what he knew about him. If two or three hooded men, who were often not even known to each other, said the same thing, we arrested the person and interrogated him. A big operation of this sort lasting all day might result in our catching fifty or sixty prominent supporters and a handful of forest gangsters who were visiting them. It was in fact another method of turning background information, that is to say our knowledge of one-time Mau Mau supporters who wanted to help us, into contact information.

Such methods were often far more fruitful than large-scale sweeps through forest areas by soldiers and police, although occasionally, of course, such patrols would contact a gang of terrorists, and then by rapid reinforcement get some kills or captures. But it was very much a hit-and-miss affair, rarely based on hard information. The Army was too ready to expect precise details of where the enemy were and what they were going to do next, details that the intelligence staffs were unable to provide. Kitson's whole idea was that by building up a record of gang policies and likely future plans, there would emerge a pattern of behaviour which could be exploited. In describing two different operations mounted in the Kiambu District, Kitson showed in his *Bunch of Five* how a plan based on information obtained by his pseudo-gangs could be infinitely more successful than one designed simply to comb an area where terrorists were thought to be. The latter, involving four battalions and lasting three weeks, was in his judgement 'a colossal and expensive failure like all other big operations mounted in similar circumstances'. Soon afterwards a very different kind of activity produced good results. Based on evidence gathered from a dead-letter box that a gang would be visiting a particular area to contact its supply group, and introducing a new technique of clearing thick cover by arming thousands of women with pangas and surrounding an area with armed Kikuyu Guard, some excellent results were obtained. Kitson describes how the action developed:

> The next contact was rather more exciting and occurred about an hour and a half later. This time three terrorists were involved. They had evidently been falling back before the oncoming line of cutters, but had got worried when they heard chopping behind them as well. They decided to open fire at the cordon and dash through it . . .
> Eric and I were standing about two hundred yards away when the terrorists opened fire. Immediately the women hurled themselves to the ground and

the terrorists jumped up to break the line. But ranges were short and there were plenty of Kikuyu Guard around. A moment later all three were down and we ran forward to prevent the women from chopping up the bodies.* By this time we had armed ourselves with sticks and we managed to keep the girls at bay. It was as well that we did so because two of the three were important men, one being the gang leader himself, a fact which made us all feel that the operation had been worth while.

In fact this was by no means the end of the business. By the time the operation was called off in the evening eighteen terrorists had been killed and we were all exhausted. The greatest surprise came when the body which I had picked up in the morning turned out to be none other than the senior gang leader from Kiambu District.

So military successes based on proper intelligence, combined with progressive political advances, had their effect. The military campaign which made use of internment, proper protection of loyalist elements, isolation of revolutionary cells and committees from one another, and attacks on the forest gangs brought the Emergency to an end. Proper organization of intelligence had been a major factor in its resolution, and remains the common thread of all such situations. Getting the people on your side is in the end what determines the outcome of counter-insurgency campaigns. It had been a slow and painful affair in Kenya. It was something that was never achieved in Cyprus.

EOKA† began its campaign of violence on 1 April, 1955, by exploding bombs aimed at military installations in Cyprus. This Greek-Cypriot rebellion against the British was designed to forward their idea of *enosis* (union with Greece), and was led by Archbishop Makarios, Ethnark of Cyprus, and Colonel Grivas, a former officer of the Greek Army. Caught between the Turkish Cypriots' refusal to contemplate *enosis* and the Greek Cypriots' insistence on it, the British Army found itself once more struggling with the problem of internal security. Field-Marshal Harding had been appointed Governor, and with 12,000 soldiers, rising later to 17,000, combed the Troodos mountains in a drive to capture Grivas. He was nearly caught, but not quite. The British need to hang on to Cyprus had been enhanced by its becoming their main Middle East base after the evacuation of the Canal Zone in Egypt. In trying to find some compromise between British and Greek-Cypriot require-ments, Harding tried negotiating with Makarios early in 1956, but the talks failed, and the Archbishop was sent to the Seychelles. The pattern of violence initiated by the EOKA gunmen was especially brutal, cow-

* Not for humanitarian reasons, but for identification.
† National Organization of Cypriot Fighters.

ardly and almost calculated to destroy any sympathy with the Cypriot-Greek cause that might have existed. As Tom Pocock wrote of the British deaths: 'Shock was heightened by contrast, for the killings were often performed before scenery that had seemed beautiful, reassuring or domestic ... the boy on his way to the bathing beach; the middle-aged man watering his roses; the footballers blasted by a bomb; the couple shot on a picnic; the RAF man, turning to fetch a mug of water for the Greek-Cypriot, who then shot him dead; unarmed Servicemen shot while shopping.' It was a grim picture.

Some of the concern for what was happening in Cyprus itself was relieved by a far greater tragedy and fiasco brought about by Nasser's nationalization of the Suez Canal in July, 1956. Eden's determination to bring about Nasser's downfall led to one of the least edifying incidents in British imperialistic adventures. Collusion with the French and Israelis, a shabby pretence at taking action to prevent war, a false undertaking to hand the Canal over to the United Nations, an ultimatum to Nasser – the most popular Arab leader ever to have appeared – all followed by somewhat clumsy, indecisive military action simply shocked and antagonized Britain's friends and enabled the Russians, engaged in suppressing a Hungarian rising with unparalleled ferocity, to threaten the descent of missiles on London unless the invasion force were withdrawn. American financial pressure exerted by the wholly unsympathetic Eisenhower administration left the British with no choice but to give way. It was not so much a disaster for British arms (for the soldiers, notably the Parachute Regiment, had fought gallantly and effectively enough) but for British policy and prestige. James Morris characteristically summed up the position:

> The invasion force, laboriously assembled and poorly equipped, did indeed invade Egypt, capturing Port Said and advancing down the canal. The Egyptian air force was virtually destroyed by attacks on its airfields, and scurrilous leaflets, ludicrously inciting the Egyptians to rebel against their leader, were dropped in the streets of Cairo. The Israelis occupied the east bank of the Canal, the British and French pushed southwards to occupy the west bank. But in no time the British lost their resolution, as the terrible truth dawned upon them that they could no longer behave imperially. The whole world was against them, even their oldest friends, and even in Egypt it seemed, the most despised of their dependencies, they could no longer honour their own convictions. Even a Wog had a voice at the United Nations now, and all the splendours of the past, assembled in such pitiful pastiche in the familiar waters of the eastern Mediterranean, could not save the British from ignominy. The invasion force was withdrawn, and the imperial ghosts turned uneasily in their graves.

Perhaps worst of all from the British soldiers' point of view, it was an operation in which they themselves did not believe. They had been asked to take part in many unlikely, even desperate, ventures before, and had accepted them all with their own brand of humour, tolerance of hardship and danger, and a conviction born of patriotism and confidence that what they were doing was in some curious way proper and justifiable. But about this campaign there had been none of that. Even when assembling in Britain for the voyage to Malta or Cyprus, the mood of many of the soldiers had been that of dubious discontent with the whole enterprise. '- - - - Nasser!' had appeared chalked on the sides of the trucks taking them to the docks. There had been a kind of half-hearted disbelief in the justice, fairness and even the purpose of the thing. This scepticism did not rob the soldiers, most of them still national servicemen, of their discipline and dignity in battle. But the spirit of doing something almost noble in a just cause, a belief in the inevitable rightness and success of the undertaking, a cocky cheerfulness, which had so typified Thomas Atkins in past affairs – all these were missing.

Not long after the Suez débâcle, Eden's fall and his replacement by Macmillan, something occurred of profound consequence both to the Army and to the nation. The Sandys Defence White Paper of 1957 announced that National Service would be ended, phased out over the following few years. What Trevor Royle in his book about the experience of national service called *The Best Years of Their Lives* would not therefore be enjoyed by British youth after the onset of the 1960s. We will look later at the All Regular Army, which was able to turn its attention to becoming a more efficient, tighter force of professional soldiers, relieved of the task of training endless drafts of civilians who did their two years service and then departed. Yet this long association which the twenty-year experience of a citizen army had brought about between the Regular Army and the sometimes reluctant heroes ensured a future understanding of one another, an abolition of the gap dividing military and non-military which was to have incalculable social benefits. This reduction in the Army's size also resulted in the disappearance of many renowned regimental titles. Numerous amalgamations of cavalry regiments either resulted in fractional (but happily not fractious) unions, such as the 9th/12th Royal Lancers, or in new names without numbers like the Queen's Own Hussars; while the infantry battalions found themselves grouped together in so-called 'large regiments' like the Royal Anglians, the Green Jackets or the Royal Regiment of Fusiliers – later to be organized into Divisions (Scottish, Queen's, Light, Prince of Wales's, King's and, of course, Guards). But one thing did not change, and provided no one is allowed to interfere with it in the future, never will change – the special pride in and spirit of each individual battalion or regiment – which is the unique and infinitely precious strength of the British Army, one of the constant and wholly admirable themes coursing throughout this brief survey of a century's action. Despite all these ups and downs, the regimental system – envy of less happier lands – survived and flourished. Meanwhile, in the late 1950s, while all these changes were getting under way, internal security operations continued.

In Cyprus the campaign went remorselessly on. Even though the soldiers (and *police*, whose courage and enterprise were examples to anyone wearing uniform) had their successes against the mountain gangs, which never numbered more than a thousand armed men, a third of whom were hard-core skilled, ruthless fighters, who would not hesitate to shoot British soldiers' wives in the back when out shopping, there were always more recruits, and the widespread support of EOKA gunmen by nearly all Greek-Cypriots never wavered. It was only when Makarios renounced *enosis* and was prepared to settle for Cypriot independence that a solution emerged. In February, 1959, agreement was reached by Britain, Greece and Turkey – which Makarios accepted – that the island would become independent, but that Britain would maintain two sovereign base areas at Episkopi and Dhekelia. In his admirable *East and West of Suez* Tom Pocock, who was frequently in Cyprus during the troubles and, as was customary with him, took more risks than most soldiers, recorded that the Governor, Sir Hugh Foot (Lord Caradon) who had succeeded Harding, was optimistic about the future of Cyprus as he boarded a destroyer off Famagusta. He rejected the pessimistic predictions of those who said 'the island will go down in a sea of blood and hate'. Despite the later peace-keeping operations by U.N. forces, including contingents provided by the British Army, despite even the Turkish invasion of Cyprus in 1974 and their occupation of its northern parts, who would say, looking at other areas of the former British Empire, that Foot was wrong? As he and his wife left Government House, Makarios, the first President of an independent Cyprus, inspected a guard provided by Wavell's regiment, The Black Watch. Tom Pocock records that His Beatitude's congratulatory message to the guard commander was that it had been an excellent turnout. Cyprus still provides a welcome alternative to BAOR and Northern Ireland for the British Army. The two sovereign base areas are still there and we continue to supply troops to the U.N. Peacekeeping Force.

This was all going on west of Suez. For those who had been shipped 'somewheres east of Suez' even more exciting and demanding activities

were in progress for some special members of the Army. Even for the
élite of all élites, the SAS Regiment, the capture of the Djebel Akhdar
in the Oman must, whiles memory holds a seat in this distracted globe,
be remembered in its history. The year was 1958, the circumstances
that the position of the Sultan of Muscat and Oman, with whom Britain
had a treaty, was being challenged by Talib, who had raised an army of
Omanis and made himself an independent and powerful master of
central Oman, with the seemingly impregnable Djebel Akhdar at once
a symbol and a centre of his authority. The Sultan, having neither the
financial means to recover his authority by bribery nor the military
strength to do it by force, turned, as so many oriental despots in the
past had, and so many in the future would still do, to the British Army
to get him out of trouble. After a great deal of preliminary operations
to acquire intelligence and deceive the rebels as to what the British
intended to do, an assault on the Djebel itself – 6,500 feet above sea
level, surrounded by mountain peaks rising to 10,000 feet, accessible
only by tracks and narrow passes, almost designed for ambush, with
high, inhospitable ground dominating every side – was made by the SAS,
led by its Commanding Officer, Lieutenant-Colonel Deane-Drummond,
and with such renowned figures as Johnny Watts and Peter de la Billière
there too. They succeeded in reaching the summit by a demonstration
of what supreme physical and mental toughness could achieve. Once
there they were supplied by the RAF, who also harassed the rebel
positions with air strikes. Large hauls of weapons, ammunition and
documents were made, Talib's rebel gangs melted away, and the whole
challenge to the Sultan's authority was for the time being at an end.

While all these adventures were in progress, life in the British Army
of the Rhine pursued its leisurely course of manifesting Britain's commitment to NATO. To keep an Army of some 55,000 permanently in
Germany, with appropriate RAF support, was a new commitment and
looks like being an indefinite one. As such it is to be welcomed by those
who wish to see the Army preserve its structure, its capability and above
all its regiments. In the later 1950s manoeuvring in Germany reached
a new pitch of extravagance and extensiveness. Several armoured divisions at a time would 'swan' across the Hanoverian plains, fighting each
other in mock battles of unparalleled severity, making or breaking the
reputations of aspiring commanders, and almost exhausting the patience
of the Westphalian farmers. But the real action was elsewhere, fortunately at that time sufficient to provide a welcome change from serving
in such cantonments as Hohne or Osnabrück or Münster. The skirmishes
of counter-insurgency operations went on. It was largely a rear-guard
action now, even though some of the campaigns could be counted as

successes in that power was handed over in an orderly fashion. As we have seen the British Army was in action in Malaya still, in Cyprus, in Kenya, in Southern Arabia. And while the 1950s persisted it was still an Army largely made up of national servicemen which was doing it all. In the next decade, there would still be plenty of fading imperial adventures to indulge in. But by then it would be done by professionals.

18

THE PROFESSIONALS

The British Army, though small, can do anything and go anywhere.
Arnold White

Accompanying this suggestion as to what the average Englishman thought about the Army, Arnold White, in his *Efficiency and Empire*, published in the 1890s, gave other examples of the Englishman's creed, equally distinguished by an arrogant assumption of superiority and equally shown to be false during the coming two decades. They included such familiar sentiments about one Englishman being able to beat two foreigners, that we were the most enlightened people in the world and that the Empire, quite apart from being incomparably great, was not subject to decay because it was free from militarism. Whether those members of the 'Volk' who suffered in Kitchener's concentration camps or were penned in by the lines of block-houses, the Tibetan lamas brushed aside by Younghusband as he led his bayonets to Lhasa, or the Amritsar agitators shot down by Gurkha riflemen, would have endorsed this view about freedom from militarism may be doubted. There was, however, some reason to acknowledge that the British Army could go more or less anywhere, thanks to the Royal Navy, and do more or less anything, even if in the case of South Africa it took a very long time. It was undeniably small – in its peace establishment. But it was backed up by an Indian Army of comparable size. Each was about 200,000 strong, and deployed or deployable all over the world.

By the 1960s the Indian Army had long since ceased to serve an Empress or Emperor. Only the peerless Brigade of Gurkhas survived as part of Britain's Army. Yet as far as the Army's size and its recruitment were concerned, things had come roughly full circle since the 1890s. Once more a small, professional, all-volunteer Army of about the same strength as in 1890 was in being, but *not* deployed all over the world.

It was still in the Far East, in the Middle East, in the Caribbean; there were still troops in Cyprus, in Gibraltar, in Malta, even in Libya; there was a garrison in Hong Kong, there were soldiers in Aden, the strategic reserve, stationed at home would, with the help of the Royal Air Force, mount exercises in many parts of the Commonwealth; there was above all a powerful, well-equipped and highly trained British Army of the Rhine, where some 55,000 soldiers lived, worked, married, exercised and fulfilled Britain's treaty obligations. Let us pay a visit to some of these gentlemen in khaki, and start where in fact they had for a time changed the khaki drill they had worn in Aden and Sharjah for suits of jungle green, more appropriate for the jungles and rivers and long houses of Borneo.

The Borneo campaign was in many ways one of the most satisfactory to be conducted by the British Army during the gradual withdrawal from Empire. There was plenty to do; it lasted long enough (about three and a half years) for many regiments to be involved, but not too long to become tedious; there was lots of variety and excitement, not too many casualties (some 114 Commonwealth soldiers were killed, 180 wounded, while the Indonesians lost more than 1,600); it vindicated once and for all the use of helicopters in such operations, and ended in complete success. The whole thing started with the Brunei rebellion of December, 1962, which was quickly suppressed by a joint force of Gurkhas, Royal Marines, The Queen's Own Highlanders, and my own regiment, now The Queen's Royal Irish Hussars. Most of the rebels were accounted for, forty odd killed, several thousand captured, although a few hundred fled to the jungle. But it was plain to British intelligence that the principal threats to Sarawak, North Borneo and Brunei – one internal, one external – were still to come. President Sukarno of Indonesia had long opposed the formation of Malaysia (planned for September, 1963) and in declaring his policy of 'confrontation' he intended to disrupt it by incursions into the three parts of British Borneo mentioned above from Kalimantan or Indonesian Borneo. These incursions would be made by regular Indonesian troops and by the remnants of Azahari's Brunei rebels. At the same time the so-called Clandestine Communist Organization, recruited from the Chinese minority – very roughly one third of the million and a half population of British Borneo – and numbering anything from ten to twenty thousand would constitute the internal threat. By early 1963 the British had deployed troops in West Sarawak, Brunei and North Borneo (now Sabah), and the famous anthropologist and curator of Kuching museum, Tom Harrisson, whom we last met raising the Dyak tribesmen against the Japanese, had a call on his former followers whom he had once more alerted. Harrisson's

Force numbered several thousand and, quite apart from their fighting and tracking abilities, they were invaluable in providing intelligence. Overseeing all this military activity was the renowned jungle warfare expert, Major-General Walter Walker.

As Commander British Forces West Sarawak I had what sounded like huge responsibilities and what was a very small force to discharge them. From my headquarters in the Police compound at Kuching I was required to preserve the integrity and security of the 1st, 2nd and 3rd Divisions of Sarawak, a vast area with almost 750 miles of border with Kalimantan. To carry out this task I had a mere 300 or so soldiers – one armoured car squadron of my own regiment; a company of infantry, supplied by the Royal Marines, a few administrative troops, two Auster light aircraft, a squadron of the SAS Regiment, and two naval mine-sweepers. The continuous acquisition of intelligence was, of course, a vital ingredient of the whole operation, and this was done in several ways. The SAS deployed deeply, integrated with friendly tribesmen at key river junctions and villages (long houses), conducting their sur-veillance and information-gathering, and reporting with their excellent communications both to their own headquarters and to me. The rest of the force, while securing certain important communication centres, conducted an endless and comprehensive programme of patrolling – by road, by river, for Sarawak is a country of rivers, using long boats and the R.N. minesweepers, and on foot, penetrating deep into the jungle. By using the light aircraft, as well as boats and Land Rovers, I was able to go everywhere and see everything myself. To increase our capability we began to re-establish the Sarawak Rangers (who had been used in Malaya itself during the Emergency) and by all this patrolling we hoped to reassure the local people, gather more intelligence and attempt to deter those who might be planning to turn the potential external or internal threat into a reality. General Walker embarked on his 'Hearts and Minds' campaign of further assistance and support to the Sarawak tribesmen, with medical supplies, radios, movement of people and goods, in his drive to win their loyalty and allegiance. Having consulted Tom Harrisson (who, perhaps because of his profound knowledge of the country and peoples and our relative ignorance, had a very low flash-point of temper losing) and also the police and civil administrators of all three Divisions, having also toured my parish, it was glaringly plain that if there were incursions by the Indonesians across the border or some internal flare-up, the only way to react with real speed would be with helicopters. At my next meeting with General Walker I bid for some. He was wholly understanding, but having only a few at his disposal, felt he must keep them centrally under his own hand. It was not long before events obliged him to relent.

On Good Friday, 12 April, 1963, while I was shaving in my room in the Sarawak Steamship Company's villa, which we used as a mess, Captain Rodney Martin not only burst in – he was clearly bursting with news. It seemed that a group of about thirty guerrillas (as yet unidentified – later it turned out that they were Indonesian regular soldiers) had crossed the border at Tebedu, a village some forty miles south of Kuching, had killed a few policemen (one enterprising constable had escaped with his life by concealing himself in the tank on top of a water tower), and generally looted and terrorized the place. What, Captain Martin wanted to know, were my instructions. Having made sure that the proper messages had already been despatched, I asked him to assemble my subordinate commanders in my office in thirty minutes, and – so that there would be something fitting to record for the *Regimental Journal* – asked that my breakfast should be served at my office too. The situation at Tebedu was quickly restored by a troop of Royal Marines, but a journey which could have been measured in minutes by helicopter took ten times longer on the poor, twisting jungle track. The Tebedu incident in itself was not very important. It was what it heralded. Confrontation was no longer an idle threat. The battle for Borneo, albeit fairly low-key, had begun.

It was in the end serious enough, however, to require the deployment of more than 15,000 soldiers in Borneo, a relatively simple exercise given the continued existence of the Singapore base with its powerful naval and air forces. The build-up to this level was gradual, and began as a result of intelligence I received soon after the Tebedu raid. Having finally persuaded General Walker to let me have some helicopters (detached from HMS *Bulwark* and magnificently flown and maintained by the Royal Navy) we were able greatly to expand our patrol activity, and by appearing here, there and everywhere make it seem that every platoon was a company, every troop a squadron. But the information coming in from SAS patrols, from special signal units listening to Indonesian transmissions and from police sources indicated that more guerrilla raids were imminent. Moreover, some of the natives were restless, and there were disquieting signs that the Clandestine Communist Organization would shortly be making a move. If these two threats developed simultaneously, it would be hard to keep control of the huge area constituting Sarawak's 1st, 2nd and 3rd Divisions with a mere handful of troops. After discussions with the police and the Governor, I despatched a message to the British Commander-in-Chief, Singapore, recommending that a brigade should be sent to West Sarawak at once to guarantee its security. Messages of this sort are customarily

received by staff officers and commanders, whose programmes at the
polo and golf clubs are thus disagreeably interrupted, with a good deal
of scepticism. But happily General Walker trusted my judgement, and
next day a posse of generals arrived in my office, courtesy of the Royal
Air Force, to discuss the matter. It was agreed that 3rd Commando
Brigade, Royal Marines, would arrive in West Sarawak as soon as HMS
Bulwark, other naval vessels and the RAF could get it there. It was not
before time. Shortly afterwards Indonesian incursions greatly increased.
So began a gradual escalation of military activity on either side, the
Indonesians employing more and more regular units, the British
strengthening their forces in response.

As always in such affairs the principal burden fell on the infantry –
the Gurkhas playing their very special part – and many regiments did
their six-month tour of operations, some from Malaya, some from Hong
Kong, some from Britain: the Parachute Regiment, the Green Jackets,
the Brigade of Guards, and many others, supported by helicopters,
armoured cars, the gunners and sappers, all the logistic people, plus
massive, continuous aid from the Royal Navy and Royal Air Force.
Tom Pocock admirably describes his visit to a typical scene of action in
deep jungle near Long Semado where the Royal Leicestershire Regiment
had fought a sharp engagement with the enemy:

> The helicopter flew high over jungle that was ruffled by hills, then ridged
> by ranges of mountains, rising above misty valleys, following each other like
> waves. At last we sank towards a clearing in the trees, felled to make a landing
> site near the tribal settlement of Long Semado, where other helicopters had
> just landed the Leicesters, fresh from the battlefield. They were all vol-
> unteers – for conscription had ended in 1960 – and many were not yet twenty,
> but they bore themselves with an extraordinary degree of nonchalance. Their
> green combat dress was dark with sweat, but they were freshly shaven; strings
> of bright Kelabit beads were strung round their necks and at the belts of
> several hung *parang* swords. When asked about the battle, they described it
> as young men in Leicestershire might have talked about their part in a hard-
> played football match, but without boastfulness, or any apparent sense of
> surprise at finding themselves so engaged in such a place.
>
> Their story was simple, brave and brutal. It had been known that the
> Indonesians were over the border and an alarming report reached the Leices-
> ters' patrol base from the Border Scouts that an abandoned camp had been
> discovered in the jungle; no ordinary camp, however, for this could have
> been occupied by 500 men. Undeterred, the platoon commander, Second-
> Lieutenant Michael Peele, six months out of Sandhurst, led his twenty-five
> men to the site and followed tracks, only a day old, that led from it to another,

slightly smaller camp, also abandoned. Another fresh trail led from this towards the border and the Leicesters followed it, their Border Scouts now lagging behind, until they sighted another camp ahead of them and saw that this one was occupied. Peele guessed that he might be outnumbered by, perhaps, ten to one, but, hoping that surprise would shorten the odds, ordered his men to drop their packs and divided them into two groups, one to assault, the other to work its way round to the far side of the camp to ambush any retreating enemy. But before the cut-off party was in place they were seen by a sentry, the alarm sounded and Peele gave the order to charge. Firing from the hip, they rushed the camp and, for fifteen minutes, a furious battle was fought among the trees. Then, suddenly, it was quiet; the enemy had disappeared; all but seven, who lay dead. The Leicesters searched the camp, collecting half a ton of modern weaponry and stacks of documents and maps. The odds had not been quiet as fearsome as they had expected; they had only been outnumbered by two, or three, to one.

As they stood in groups, talking and drinking cans of fizzy lemonade, or leaned against trees, reading letters from home that had arrived in my helicopter, their *sang froid* was even more impressive than their account of the small, complete victory. It was something I was to encounter repeatedly along the frontier.

General Walker was not content simply to react to and destroy Indonesian raids into British, or rather by now, Malaysian Borneo. He was determined to take the fight into enemy territory, that is to seize the initiative, cross into Kalimantan, find out where the Indonesian camps were, what routes they were likely to use to the north and generally disrupt their activities. These so-called 'cross-border operations' paid huge dividends and were executed not only by the SAS, but by Gurkha and other British battalions. 'We are changing our role to recce and offensive operations in Kalimantan,' wrote the Commanding Officer of 22 SAS Regiment, explaining also that Border surveillance would be taken over by a Parachute Regiment, including the Gurkha Parachute Company.

'We are allowed 5 miles for *attributable* operations,' he went on, 'that is we can bash anything up to this range. "A" Squadron should have five patrols for cross-border ops by end of month. . . . Gurkhas killed at least twelve at Nantukor in a really good deliberate attack on their base.' The extension of these 'Claret' operations enabled General Walker and his successor to dominate the border areas. By the autumn of 1965 it was clear that Sukarno's policy of confrontation had failed. His subsequent flirtation with Communist leaders in his own country led to civil war and his overthrow by the Army. General Suharto took over in the

spring of 1966 and a few months later made peace with the Malaysian
government. It was the British Army that had saved Malaysia from a
danger which threatened to strangle it at birth. Their tactics, combining
the acquisition of good intelligence, strong patrol bases, aggressive
patrolling and ambushing, cross-border operations, exploitation of the
splendid mobility and adaptability afforded by helicopters, sound use
of artillery, a hearts and minds campaign which guaranteed the tribes'
support – all these had prevailed against an enemy not lacking in courage,
skill or perseverance. In this campaign the British regiments had been
accompanied by their comrades from Australia, Singapore, New Zealand
and Malaysia itself, together with the brave and brilliant Gurkhas and
the local scouts raised, trained and supervised by the SAS. It had in
short been a success. The same could not be said of Aden.

It is important, as we move to southern Arabia, to distinguish between
Aden and the Dhofar. In the first of these the British conducted a
campaign, which, despite all the skill and courage of the regiments
involved (who can forget, for example, the re-occupation of Crater by
the Argyll and Sutherland Highlanders under the admirable leadership
of Lieutenant-Colonel Colin Mitchell?) was doomed by lack of political
will, and resulted at length in a hesitant and humiliating relinquishment
of colonial rule – thus confirming Curzon's prediction that with India
lost 'your ports and your coaling stations, your fortresses and your
dockyards, your Crown colonies and protectorates will go too'. In the
second we have a very different story, in which a patient and eventually
triumphant exercise in winning the hearts and minds of the tribesmen
turned them away from armed Communist-led insurrection, and back
to allegiance to Oman's Sultan. In any counter-insurgency operation,
one of the first essentials of government is to convince the waverers that
it is going to win. If the people are so convinced, it is likely that their
support will be forthcoming. Without this support, there is no possibility
of the government's enjoying control of the population, and in order to
eliminate subversion, such control is indispensable. We have seen how
this worked in Malaya and in Borneo. Frank Kitson has pointed out
that 'few individuals can possibly support a government which is obvi-
ously going to lose, even if they sympathize with its policies and detest
those of the insurgents'. If withdrawal of colonial authority is inevitable,
then two conditions must precede it – absolute destruction of the
subversive movement and indisputable establishment of independent
authority powerful enough to destroy any renewal of subversion. In Aden
the British made the unredeemable error of ignoring these requirements.
Having announced their intention of withdrawing from the country in
1968, when it became independent, the British simply made it plain that

sooner or later the insurgents would get control. It was, Julian Paget wrote in his *Last Post in Aden*, 'a disastrous move from the point of view of the Security Forces, for it meant that from then onwards they inevitably lost all hope of any local support'. In other words, the hearts and minds campaign had been thrown away before it had even been conducted.

We need not follow this almost purposeless campaign in detail. The Emergency was formally declared in December, 1963, and ended only with the final British withdrawal in November, 1967. Yet it is memorable for a number of events and people. There were really two uprisings to deal with – one among the Radfan tribesmen of the Protectorate, another from the urban guerrillas of Aden itself. Neither was winnable, unless the British had declared their intention, and provided the resources to turn intention into feasibility, to stay indefinitely. Yet the performance of British soldiers in the scorching arid mountains of the Radfan, soldiers drawn from many regiments, or in the mean alleyways of Crater and the Sheikh Othman, is beyond praise. So is the courage and example shown by men like Jack Dye, commanding the South Arabian Army, permanently on the edge of mutiny, or members of the SAS doing their undercover work in urban Aden, or Colin Mitchell's Highlanders fastening so tight a grip on Crater that terrorist activity declined almost totally. And to those of us who were there at one time or another, the fascination of that least glamorous of colonies somehow imposed its grip.

The barren rocks of Aden when first sighted are unprepossessing enough. But drive up the Dhala road towards the frontier with North Yemen, fly over the Radfan mountains in an Auster aircraft, looking down on that grim, dry, inhospitable country, visit a frontier fort, meet and talk to the proud, independent and fanatically brave tribesmen, and you are instantly taken back to the bold, romantic days of Empire when there was 'neither East nor West, Border, nor Breed, nor Birth'. You really did feel yourself to be almost at the ends of the earth. But it was all illusion. The reality was that the Peoples' Democratic Republic of Yemen emerged, and became at once a lackey of the Soviet Union and a base from which to launch a major effort to subvert and unseat the Sultan of Oman. We will see later how this effort was defeated, but we may take leave of Aden by recalling James Morris's picture of how the British quit one of the original acquisitions of Empire, with guns at the ready until the very last moment:

Step by step they withdrew from the city to the harbour and the airfield, and while the Royal Marines kept the indigenes at bay, a stream of aircraft flew off the last of the imperialists. Offshore two carriers, a depot ship and a submarine waited; helicopters clanked heavily around the harbour; at the airfield transport planes arrived in a ceaseless flow from Cyprus, refuelled again and took off with their loads of refugees. Gradually the British perimeter contracted, closer and closer to the shore, while outside it rival groups of Arab guerrillas sniped, looted and skirmished. The High Commissioner flew off in a helicopter to the carrier *Eagle*. The last commandos raced for their helicopters. The last flag was lowered. The last flotilla of the Royal Navy, its crews smartly lining their decks, its radars twirling, sailed away from Steamer Point into the Red Sea.

Behind them the guerrillas fell upon the abandoned stores and barracks, swarmed up the steps to Government House, and shot at each other from rooftops.

Such was the scene in November, 1967, as the British left Aden. The Dhofar war belongs to the 1970s, and we will look at it in the next chapter, but before leaving the 1960s, we must say goodbye to the man whose activities have more than any other dominated this story of the British Army, the man who began his career as a young Hussar officer and throughout his long, brilliant and varied appearance on the world stage was so frequently to be seen either participating in or directing military operations. 'His world,' wrote Sir Isaiah Berlin,

> is built upon the primacy of public over private relationships, upon the supreme value of action, of the battle between simple good and simple evil, between life and death; but, above all, battle. He has always fought. 'Whatever you may do,' he declared to the demoralised French ministers in the bleakest hour of 1940, 'we shall fight on for ever and ever and ever,' and under this sign his whole life has been lived.

Just as his life had been a pageant of achievement, so his funeral was a pageant of homage. As the Commanding Officer of his old regiment (originally 4th Hussars, by this time The Queen's Royal Irish Hussars – Churchill had been Colonel of both) I took part in the ceremony with my regimental comrades. We formed a Vigil Party for the Lying-in-State in Westminster Hall; we carried his Insignia and Standards in the Funeral Procession on 30 January; the Trumpet Major, Sergeant King, sounded Reveille in St Paul's Cathedral, and a Bearer Party took the Colonel of the Regiment on his last journey from Waterloo Station to Bladon and laid him to rest. Those of us who took part in that day will never forget it. We have not touched much in this book on the Army's ceremonial activities – it has been rather a picture of active service and battle – yet there is no other Army in the world, never has been, that could, under the splendid guidance and direction of the Household

Division, have produced the dignity, solemnity, drilled perfection and sheer emotion of the procession from Parliament Square to St Paul's, the Dead March from *Saul* played by innumerable bands, the soldiers with reversed arms lining the streets, and behind them Churchill's people, silent, grave, some weeping, all filled with pride and awe.* For those of us slow-marching in the procession who had been members of his regiment and had been presented to him both during the war and at later regimental occasions, there was a very special participatory elation. Churchill had joined the 4th Hussars in 1895, had soldiered with them in India, played in the winning regimental polo team, charged at Omdurman (although with another regiment), become their Colonel in the dark days of 1941 after serious losses in Greece, visited them no less than four times in war, attended their dinners and parades in peace, stayed on as Colonel after amalgamation with the 8th Hussars, and symbolized their twin mottos, *Pristinae Virtutis Memores* and *Mente et Manu* as no other man ever had or could. He had been, as one former Commanding Officer had put it, the greatest Hussar of them all. Back in our barracks in Germany a few days later, we held our own simple and brief Drumhead Memorial Service and during it I was able to remind the Regiment of the words with which Sir Isaiah Berlin had completed his infinitely rich miniature, *Mr Churchill in 1940:*

> A man larger than life, composed of bigger and simpler elements than ordinary men, a gigantic historical figure during his own lifetime, super-humanly bold, strong, and imaginative, one of the two greatest men of action his nation has produced, an orator of prodigious powers, the saviour of his country, a mythical hero who belongs to legend as much as to reality, the largest human being of our time.

After this great, unforgettable event, the Professionals returned to their profession, still, as we have seen, in many parts of the world, although the horizons were dwindling. Indeed, there was one cloud very close to hand. As the 1960s ended, there were some who had reason to recall the words of Patrick Pearse spoken at his court-martial for his part in the Easter Rising of 1916: 'You cannot conquer Ireland, you cannot extinguish the Irish passion for freedom. If our deed has not been sufficient to win freedom, then our children will win it with a better deed.' Whether the recent activities of the IRA, which in this particular phase of 'The Troubles' have now lasted for twenty years and show no

---

*One of the most remarkable things of the whole affair was that during the rehearsal on the preceding morning – it was done very early, about 4 am, in order to minimize the disruption to London's traffic – the streets were also lined with people, who wept just as copiously even though the principal actor was absent.

signs of coming to an end, would fall into this category may be questioned. But the fact is that as the British Army, as the Professionals, marched into the 1970s, they were to be confronted with one of the greatest tests of professional integrity, perseverance and skill that they had up to now encountered.

19

THE 1970s AND 1980s

What is the Army for?
Haldane, 1905

When Haldane asked this question upon becoming War Minister in 1905, he found that the answer was a very simple one. It was to provide two Army Corps to fight on the left flank of the French, and, as we have seen, when the moment came they did so with honour and distinction. Seventy years later the answer was less easy. Of course it is possible to generalize and say that in the 1970s, as so often before and since, the Army's task was to provide protection or support or security in those areas where it was both desirable and practicable to provide them. Or we may particularize and speak of many places and many occupations. Then we must speak first and foremost of Northern Ireland. Not many days have passed in the last two decades when we do not talk or read or hear of the Army's operations in Ulster. This patrol ambushed, that car-bomb defused, an allegation of brutality here, praise for a soldier's humanity and courage there – it is routine stuff. Yet in the last decade and now it largely affects the Army's business.

The two principal surviving Army Commands are the British Army of the Rhine and United Kingdom Land Forces. For both these commands Northern Ireland had and still has a profound influence on all those things which make up a soldier's life. This influence is felt by both the Rifleman, actually committed to the maintenance of law in Ulster, and by the General and his staff, who are not themselves there, but under whose command this rifleman normally is and who must see to it that the rifleman is properly equipped for operations. Weapons, readiness, well-being, the sinews of war – all these must be seen to so that he can carry out his task with confidence, conviction and success. The troops for Ulster have always largely come from the two commands, BAOR and UKLF, sometimes for a lengthy tour, sometimes a short one, and for the commanders concerned the seemingly endless Ulster commitment calls much of the tune. It conditions deployment; it conditions training (both training for Northern Ireland and training which is neglected because of it); it conditions movement and logistics; it conditions morale; it even conditions the soldier's place in society. Not all these conditions are to be deprecated. The prospect of being shot at or blown up by the IRA, like that of being hanged, concentrates the mind. Powers of command, of observation and alertness, marksmanship, cunning, anticipation, tactical skills, endurance, versatility and the ability to act quickly and properly in a tight corner – all these important military virtues are tested and enhanced.

But it would be wrong to suppose that having just completed a four-to-six month tour, in say, the Ardoyne, the soldier, whoever he may be, is looking forward to returning there in a year's time, when he will probably find peace or the rule of law and order not a jot nearer. He would rather be getting on with some other business, which has had to go by the board – completing an upgrading course to earn him more money and responsibility, refreshing or improving his particular skills as driver, signaller or fitter, enjoying a long-promised exercise in Kenya or the Oman, practising all-arms training in tank, infantry, artillery and engineer teams, or simply being with his family. That all these things could not and cannot be done is another way of saying that the Army always seems to be 'overstretched'. None of us in uniform during these last ten or twenty years can remember a time when the Army or the armed forces generally were not said to be suffering from overstretch. Yet whether caused by problems in Borneo or the Dhofar or Cyprus or Ulster, it is not a condition about which many regimental officers and soldiers would complain. On the whole such fare is what regiments thrive on. We might even say, in answering the question – What is the Army for? – that it is there to be overstretched while fulfilling its country's policies and protecting its country's interests, and not to sit idle in barracks unused. Many of the so-called emergencies overseas have had a stop; the Irish ulcer festers on. If we take a leap from the 1970s right up to the end of the 1980s, what do we find? In *The Times* of January, 1988, we read:

> The Army is to establish a new brigade headquarters to take over all security operations along the meandering 308-mile border with the Irish Republic. It comes in response to the belief that the Provisional IRA possesses substantial new supplies of sophisticated weaponry, including shoulder-launched surface-to-air guided missiles supplied from Libya.

The new formation, 3 Brigade ... will become operational in the summer only a few miles from the south Armagh border zone, and comprise units transferred from the two existing brigades in the province, 39 Brigade at Lisburn and 8 Brigade at Londonderry.

They will cede to the new unit the responsibilities for patrolling their respective stretches of the border and concentrate wholly on support of the Royal Ulster Constabulary elsewhere.

No increase is foreseen in current troop levels in Northern Ireland, which are now about 10,000 regular troops and 6,500 men and women of the Ulster Defence Regiment, both full-time and part-time volunteers.

These are large numbers for containing what must be thought of as a domestic matter. It is not in every newspaper that the Army's virtues are extolled, yet shortly after the murder of two British soldiers during IRA funeral processions in March, 1988, *The Sunday Times* had this to say:

The British Army has proved itself a superbly efficient and disciplined anti-terrorist force. Its professionalism is unmatched; what other army in the world would have resisted going on the rampage after last Saturday's harrowing murders of two of their own? Despite the ignorant efforts of much of the world's press to portray it as a colonial occupying force, the people of Britain should be proud of their army's peacekeeping role in Ulster, and Ireland should be grateful too.

As the security forces have mastered the techniques of urban guerrilla warfare, the IRA has been contained and even forced onto the defensive. Contrary to the impression often created by reports from the province, violence in Ulster is not spiralling out of control. In the 1970s the terrorists claimed on average more than 200 lives a year in Ulster, in the 1980s less than 80. We have come a long way from the peak of more that 450 deaths in 1972.

How do we explain the Army's excellence? Why has it acquitted itself with such dignity, patience, humanity, fairness, skill, moderation, discipline, humour and marked effect? That it has done so is something about which debate in the House of Commons, a chamber not always distinguished for accord, is unanimous. Despite all propaganda to the contrary, there is general agreement that the Army, by producing so effective a combination of military qualities, has kept the door open for manoeuvrings which might lead to political settlement. In saying this, it must be recognized that we are not speaking of military victory or even a draw. The circumstances prevailing in Ulster's urban jungle and bandit country would not allow such a result. There seem to be no means by which the hearts and minds of the Republicans can ever be won by Westminster; there has never been a clear, consistent, realizable political objective; the twenty years task of the Army has therefore been at best a Micawber-like holding operation; whatever the Anglo-Irish agreement may have yielded, it has not prevented Eire being a largely unassailable sanctuary and storehouse for terrorists; and if, as we have constantly seen elsewhere, a necessary condition for defeating insurgency against legal government is to win control of the population, then it is plain, always has been plain, that this condition is unattainable, and being so renders also unattainable defeat of the IRA.

Yet the soldiers have persevered. How have they done it? The answer lies in the quality of its people and its leadership. And this quality, so high and so consistent, owes almost everything to regimental and corps spirit and tradition. To the Commanding Officer, his little world is as dear and familiar to him as was that of Don Camillo. His commitment is absolute, his efforts untiring, his pride in the Regiment's achievements infinite. He knows that 90 per cent of the business of command is the people in it, and by knowing *them*, caring for them, encouraging them, training them to standards of perfection, and being a model of dedication and integrity, he has done all he can to bring about the reward of successful command – every task well done and the outfit itself in superb order. Indispensable to all this is the quality also of those commands, whether we are thinking of his subordinate officers, or of those whom Kipling immortalized with his 'man in khaki kit who could handle men a bit, With his bedding labelled Sergeant Whatsisname'; or of Thomas Atkins himself.

It is remarkable how far afield the gentlemen in khaki still position themselves. In Central America a battalion group continues to look after the security of Belize – with advantages, for the training there, quite apart from the change of scenery and task, can be first class. Some of the jungle in Belize was described by a Gurkha colonel (and there are few soldiers more experienced in jungle warfare) as the thickest and toughest bit of *ulu* he had yet encountered. On the other side of the world, in Hong Kong, we find more Gurkhas and other British soldiers, garrisoning what is still a Colony, and will be for some years yet. What is to happen to the Brigade of Gurkhas after 1997? It is to be hoped that even then we can still find a place for some battalions in the British Army, whether in Brunei or Cyprus or Belize, the Falkland Islands, BAOR or as part of our strategic reserve here at home, for they are among the finest, most loyal, bravest and most likeable soldiers ever to serve Britain.

Mention of the Falklands reminds us that we have a substantial force there (we will look at the 1982 war in the next chapter) and again for short periods it provides a not unwelcome variation from the rolling plains of Westphalia or the mean streets of Belfast. Between these extremes of west and east, we see a number of other stations. In Brunei the Sultan finds it prudent to position, and pay for, a battalion of Gurkhas. In Oman British soldiers still serve, some on loan, some temporarily contracted to the Sultan's Armed Forces, some practising reinforcement of the Gulf plans. In Cyprus we have both the garrison troops of our Sovereign Base Areas and our contribution to the United Nation peacekeepers. In Gibraltar a battalion mounts guard outside the Governor's Residence and makes sure that the apes are still on parade. There are innumerable and invaluable exercises in a host of foreign countries in pursuit of what is called adventurous training. Often training is combined with help for countries in need of it – the Royal Corps of Transport's air despatch experts dropping supplies from RAF Hercules aircraft to starving Nepalese or Sudanese or Ethiopians; the Royal Engineers building bridges or roads, power plants or schools and jetties in countries as widely apart as Malawi, Bangladesh, Kenya and Anguilla. The Army's activities are infinitely varied and it is always ready to go anywhere and do anything. The readiness, as Hamlet reminded us, is all.

Readiness is, of course, the watchword too of the British Army of the Rhine. Here, some fifty thousand strong, is what many have described as the best-trained and best-equipped army that we have ever had in peacetime. The claim survives examination. 1st British Corps with its armoured and artillery divisions, supported by RAF Harriers and Chinooks, is expert in mobile warfare, in meeting, slowing down and stopping any attack launched across the West German border. Every soldier likes to take pride in the excellence of and his mastery of the tools of the trade, and 1st British Corps is well served here. The infantry and guns are largely mounted in tracked armoured vehicles, latest among them being the renowned Warrior MICV (Mechanized Infantry Combat Vehicle), while the engineer material is imposing in its range and power. Chieftain and Challenger tanks provide the principal punch, the new Multi-Launch Rocket System reaches out further than ever before with its devastating salvoes, surveillance devices richly furnish vital information, helicopters give a new dimension to mobility and adaptability, the logistic teams are nimble and effective. The basic elements of combat – fire power and manoeuvre – are ever-present and are matched by the third essential, an excellent facility for command with reliable, secure signalling. Louis XIV once observed to Marshal Villeroi that he should pay particular attention to that part of the line which would bear the first shock of English Troops. Anyone thinking about taking on 1st British Corps in battle would do well to give it similar attention.

A hundred miles or so to the east of BAOR's most easterly garrison in West Germany is another British garrison – the Berlin Brigade. Together with French and American forces, it helps to keep West Berlin free and prosperous, an important pawn in a different sort of game. Lenin once argued that whoever controlled Berlin would rule Germany and whoever controlled Germany would rule Europe. In a sense it is still true, although this control and rule are now both multilateral and with the pie cut roughly in half. British soldiers like being stationed in Berlin where they enjoy excellent housing, plenty of sport (sailing, skiing in the Grunewald, polo, all the team games), superlative opportunities for going to concerts and the opera, including East Berlin, incentive to polish other languages. Above all it is *being there* and representing the finest Army in the NATO alliance which matters.

Whether we are thinking of the Rhine Army or Salisbury Plain or Hong Kong or the Springfield Road, in the mind's eye the British soldier is usually in combat kit with a gun in his hand, or with a tank beneath him, flying a helicopter, building a bridge under fire – in other words, a fighting man. Yet not only within the battalion or regiment, but throughout the Army as a whole, there is no end to the variety of activity and employment. When you think of a soldier in the Royal Army Ordnance Corps, you may picture, unless you are old-fashioned enough to think of Ordnance literally, a man issuing stores or running a depot or sitting at a desk. Look at the Honours and Awards list for Northern Ireland, however, and you will see that many of the George Medals and MBEs are collected by the RAOC for that two o'clock in the morning courage of defusing bombs. The butcher, the baker, the candlestick maker are all there still, the chaplain, the dentist, the pioneer, and more. In the dining-hall of any Army unit today, food is excellent. Quality, choice, presentation are, as they should be, outstanding. The Army Catering Corps, like the Coldstream Guards, is second to none. And the men who eat the food are themselves excellent – in their professionalism, their mastery of technology and their spirit. If you have had the good fortune, as I have, to visit a cavalry regiment one day, a workshop another, a hospital, an Apprentices' College, the School of Infantry, a computer classroom, an artillery battery, a helicopter squadron, a Royal Engineer Study Day, a Royal Military Police detachment, a recruit training depot, Royal Corps of Transport landing craft, a parachute platoon, a language training course, a pay office, a brigade headquarters – you begin to understand two things. First you see that there is almost no trade or calling or technique with which the Army is not concerned. Secondly you see that the commitment of those in charge, of those responsible for managing it all, is absolute. It is a combination hard to beat. What is more, this rule applies not just to the Regulars. The same is to be seen in the Territorial Army.

It is a rare experience to spend a weekend in a training area with a TA regiment. You arrive at perhaps mid-morning on Saturday. The month is February. Your helicopter is met by the Commanding Officer and the Regimental Sergeant-Major. Both are regular soldiers but wholly part of their TA regiment. You go to the dining hall where all ranks are having lunch. Many have motored through the previous night to be there on time. The atmosphere is one of cheerful comradeship mixed with an understanding of what service and duty are worth. There is a hubbub of discussion about the twenty-four hours to come, when adventurous, challenging, necessary exercises are to be done. For the next twelve hours you tour the regiment in the field. In small groups they are practising and perfecting their military skills – planning an airborne drop and an operational task, establishing communications with headquarters and passing messages, learning to live and survive in the open, displaying mastery of guns and explosives, reviving a near-dead man (simulated), crossing at night a fast-flowing and icy cold river with only their customary kits to aid them. You talk to one of the patrol. The sergeant in charge is a London taxi driver, his subordinates a mixture indeed – a doctor, a don, a cabinet maker, an underwriter. They set about their tasks quietly, determined, full of spirit and enthusiasm, committed, using their leisure to add something to their country's security and their own fulfilment. The pattern is repeated every weekend of the year in every county and many towns. Some units have a war role in BAOR, others are for Home Defence. They number in all some sixty to seventy thousand men. In Northern Ireland, more permanently on duty and in danger, are ten thousand of the Ulster Defence Regiment, whose casualty list lengthens with the years.

The TA is there, of course, to supplement the Regular Army in time of war or other emergencies. At present, in spite of the overstretch we have already looked at, the Army seems just able to carry out its peacetime jobs. With a total of some 140,000 officers and men (not including the Gurkhas or the Women's Royal Army Corps) it is able to man about fifty infantry battalions – the hard core and basis of it all – suitably supported by regiments and corps which provide reconnaissance, fire power, mobility – land and air – pioneering, administration, health, food, education, horses and dogs. The would-be soldier thus has a great variety of options. He may join the Royal Armoured Corps and be one of a Challenger tank crew or a Scorpion combat vehicle; he may join the Gunners, serve a pack howitzer or a nuclear-warheaded rocket; he may become a Sapper and be expert at building bridges and blowing them up. He may tinker with radio, sport a bearskin, mend every type of machine the Army has, operate computers, fly helicopters, cook, drive, be a policeman, or be a member of what Wellington was so anxious to have enough of at Waterloo, the British infantry. The choice is there; and the training is superlative.

Nowhere is it better than for the Army's leaders. Courses in tactics for young cavalry troop leaders, for platoon sergeants at the School of Infantry, for section leaders of the Parachute Regiment, for NCOs running a dining hall, for managers of a transport office – all of these are thorough, demanding and staffed by experts, who have mastered theory and practice. If there be a fault in the system, it is perhaps that too much time is spent in the classroom learning how to do it and too little at the be-all and end-all of the business, with the regiment, battalion, squadron or company. A young officer has to get the balance right, or he may find that in the twenty years between joining his regiment and commanding it, he is away for more than half. Yet never before has the young officer had such opportunities for academic distinction and military versatility. University degrees are well within his reach, he can switch from commanding a troop or platoon to becoming a pilot or parachutist or – if good enough – a member of the SAS; he may serve with the Brunei regiment or with the Sultan of Oman's armed forces, learning Malay or Arabic as he does so; he may go to the Royal Military College of Science or the Staff College or both. And all the time the sporting stage is there – horses, ski-ing, sailing, mountaineering, gliding, free-fall parachuting. It is all presented to him on a plate like an oyster, which he with sword may open.

We must not forget the Women's Services. They are part of the British Army. An officer or girl of the WRAC or QARANC, whether she is driving a car, supervising a Communication Centre, running a hospital ward, serving at table in a dining room or being a secretary in Whitehall, is elegant and articulate and possesses the knack of getting things done quickly and well. Recruiting is excellent, spirit is high and the contribution to the Army is enormous. If we talk of the monstrous regiment of women, we must bear in mind that the Army today is largely married, and the consequent need for houses, schools and shops is clear enough. Clear also is the point that if wives are not content that their husbands should be soldiers, sooner or later the husbands will feel the winter of discontent. Absence may make the heart grow fonder, but a husband's frequent and prolonged departure to Ulster or Belize, Cyprus or the Falkland Islands does not make a wife fonder of the Army. There are antidotes, of course – clubs, sporting amenities, trips and tours, special telephone centres for free calls, above all there is the comfort of belonging to a regimental family, but all these things do not prevent soldiers deciding to leave before their engagement is complete.

There was a time when, for reasons of both inclination and money, only the more senior officers and men were married, but now a man is sometimes married *before* he joins the Army. Certainly many young soldiers marry after joining. The adage, captains may marry, majors should, colonels must, would be laughed out of court today. We must not make too much of the Army's being married, for it does not interfere with the discharge of duty when duty calls, but it is something which Commanders at all levels must take account of. Nor is this all. There has been of late an exodus of many of the most promising young officers and men, often the very ones most likely to succeed and reach high rank – in time! Why? It is not just the lure of City money, not just a comparison of their way of life with that of their friends in business pursuits. It is a yearning for greater responsibility, for greater opportunity at a relatively early age, combined with the disillusion with the sameness, the dreary training pattern, the sheer unadventurousness of serving year in, year out, in BAOR. Both problems are correctable, but only if the Army Board displays imagination and determination in making fundamental changes in an officer's career pattern. He must gain experience in command, at every level, but could spend less time in undemanding administrative positions (which could go to promoted warrant officers or WRAC), and then, while not with his regiment, acquire some totally different and subsequently invaluable skill – in technology, in economic matters, in business management, in languages. There has always to be a challenge, a demand, a new source of inspiration, a permanent application of the spur. Moreover life has to be *fun*. Adventurous training all over the world is done and will continue. But the pattern of training has to be far more imaginative, realistic, varied and so testing (in a way that the SAS do it) that its successful execution becomes a worthwhile achievement in itself. Happily there are signs that *some* senior Army officers understand this danger of losing their most promising young people and mean to find a solution to it.*

The Army, like all servants of the establishment, has its critics. Its regimental system – envy of every other army in the world – is scoffed at by one group for its antiquity and overheads. Its bizarre variety of

---

* Among them is Major-General Michael Rose, many of whose ideas are reflected here after his discussions with me.

dress is scorned by another. Its training areas, say a third group, should be handed back to the public (incidentally the Army is the greatest conservationist for wild life of any landowner in the country). The Army's separateness from much of society – aggravated by its being in out of the way cantonments – is a target. The image of Colonel Blimp dies hard. Every peccadillo – a case of drugs, a misemployed soldier, a regimental sergeant-major of the old school, isolated instances of bully-ing – any whisper, any hint of such a fault in the Army is marked down for comment. Excellence, success, perseverance, high quality, loyalty, service, duty and commitment provoke little press enthusiasm. Look elsewhere and what do we find? The Germans long for our Army's discipline and traditions; the Americans yearn for a volunteer Army of such a calibre at so reasonable a cost; the Sultan of Brunei relies on his Gurkha battalion; the Sultan of Oman owes his throne to the British Army; the Argentinians did not greatly relish mixing it with the Para-chute Regiment, the SAS, the Royal Artillery and the Brigade of Guards; without the Army Ulster would disintegrate; were it to be withdrawn from Europe NATO would be in despair; were it to quit Cyprus the UN force would be unadministered; were it to leave Belize, Mexico and Guatemala would be snarling at each other again; Hong Kong's frontier security still relies on it for a few years yet. Arnold White was not so far wrong a hundred years ago in claiming that the average Englishmen, while not thinking greatly about it, believed that the British Army, although small,could do anything and go anywhere. The belief holds good today. The British Army is unique, omnipresent and effective. Trouble is still its business – not the creation of trouble, but its avoidance or suppression – not a bad *raison d'être*. Before we go to the South Atlantic to see how the Army sorted out a major piece of trouble, let us look at one more instance of how a handful of British soldiers helped to bring peace to an area which drew those with nostalgic longings for an up-to-date North-West Frontier to it – the Dhofar.

We have already seen the SAS dealing with Talib and the Djebel Akhdar in 1958. In the 1970s they were in the Dhofar again and remained there for years until the rebellion was finally defeated in 1976. It has all been admirable recounted by Major-General Tony Jeapes in his *Oper-ation Oman*. He was there commanding an SAS Squadron and later the Regiment itself, and explains that there were about two thousand guerrillas opposed by the Sultan of Oman's Armed Forces, about a brigade with air and naval support. The SAS part in it was to raise and train the Dhofari irregulars, the *firqats*, to fight for the Sultan. It was essentially a war about people, about winning support of the Djebel Dhofar tribesmen, with military action allowing civil development to complete the job. Tony Jeapes outlines in his book the strategy of 'Five Fronts' devised by the Commanding Officer of 22 SAS Regiment, Lieutenant-Colonel Johnny Watts, in other words five ways in which his men should support the campaign, not so much to eradicate the rebels, as to persuade them to change sides and join the Government forces. First it was essential, as in all such operations, to establish an intelligence cell; second, by means of an information team, to make known all that was being and would be done in civil development, with the benefits it would bring, while at the same time trying to neutralize the hostile broadcasts from Radio Aden; the next two lines of assistance concerned the all-important matter of health, both for the Dhofari people and their animals, and this meant providing a medical officer and a veterinary officer – all SAS men were, of course, themselves highly trained in medical skills; fifth and last came the actual raising of soldiers to fight for the Sultan, the so-called *firqats*. There was plenty of hard, adventurous stuff for the SAS men and their locally recruited tribesmen, of whom one SAS Officer observed that he was glad such a murderous looking lot were on his side. Some of the country was so inhospitable that it severely tested even the SAS, who well remembered the climb to secure an airstrip at Lympne, not far from the important djebel position at Jibjat:

It was a terrible march. The route itself lay across the negd, winding its way through the boulder-strewn wadis and across the flinty little plateaux. It was an area devoid of water and breeze. The night was hot and humid and before long, the combination of wrenching ankles and knee joints, the weight of their bergens and ammunition and the lack of water began to make itself felt even upon the SAS. The much less heavily equipped *firqats* began to throw away their rations to lighten their loads still further. The pace became slower and the final climb up the steep slope to Lympne seemed endless. At last no more than half the force stumbled on to the airstrip at 0435 hours and set about making it secure, but they were in no state to fight without a rest. Fortunately the *adoo* [enemy] were conspicuously absent and remained so for the rest of the day.

It was by such means that the Government demonstrated that their authority held good on the djebel as well as in the coastal towns. Once this was more widely done, the war could be taken to the enemy. They were hunted out of their wadi hiding places by combined SAS/*firqat* teams. It was still necessary, however, for the Government to win over the people as a whole by building water wells and dwellings and ensuring that the *firqats* living with their families and animals on the djebel had a market for their herds. Tony Jeapes has described how the cattle were driven down off the djebel to Taqa on the coast:

> Next day saw what must surely be unique in military history, a Texan-style cattle drive supported by jet fighter cover and 5.5-inch artillery. Amidst scenes like shots from a Boulting Brothers comedy mixed with a John Wayne Western, fire fights between pickets and *adoo* on the high ground, whoops of delight from the *firqat* and expressions of amused disbelief by the SAF and SAS, five hundred head of cattle were driven across the plateau and down the djebel to Taqa. Most of the animals were owned by *firqat* families, but many of them belonged to men serving in the *adoo*, and were 'confiscated' by the *firqat* during the drive.

This illustration of Government control made a deep impression on the people. Indeed during the year 1971 the situation had been transformed. At the beginning of the year the Government writ had run only at Salalah and in part of the plain; at the end all the coastal towns and the plain were included, there were firm bases on the djebel, 700 Dhofaris were under arms on the Government side, and the civil development programme for agriculture, medicine and education was making great strides. And it was the British Army in the form of the SAS Regiment that had devised and executed the strategy which had made it all possible. There was still much to be done, and more battles to be fought, notably one at Mirbat, when in July, 1972, some 250 *adoo* with artillery, machine guns and mortars attacked a small party of eight SAS, thirty armed tribesmen and a few *firqat* men. The gallantry of the defenders, commanded by the late Captain Kealy, together with some timely reinforcements and air strikes, saved the day, but it had been a serious business. The campaign went on. The Sultan's Armed Forces expanded, more *firqats* were raised, the SAS with their British Army Training Teams stayed on, the wadis were combed for *adoo*, many of whom changed sides, the Government development programme expanded. At the end of 1975 the Sultan declared that the war was over. It was not quite true, for fighting went on for some months more, but by the autumn of 1976 the SAS had withdrawn their last squadron from a campaign that had lasted for six years. The names of many senior British officers will always be associated with this success – Tony Jeapes, Johnny Watts, Peter de la Billière, John Graham, Tim Creasey, Ken Perkins, Jack Fletcher, John Akehurst. Akehurst had always insisted that the *firqats* were the key to the whole thing, they were the future of Dhofar, what the war was all about, and therefore must always be seen to be involved in the fighting. He was wholly justified in calling his book about it *We Won a War*.

It had been one of the very few wars – Malaya was another – in which the British Army had successfully defeated a Communist-inspired armed rebellion and it had dragged on for much of the 1970s. It had been one more illustration that trouble is the Army's business, albeit trouble of a relatively minor nature. As the 1980s got under way there was to be a kind of *fin de siècle* affair, an Imperial anachronism, a punitive expedition administering correction to 'lesser breeds without the law' in which the British Army, aided as always by the Royal Navy and Royal Air Force, was required to launch an invasion on distant shores and indulge in all-out full-scale war.

20

ORDERED SOUTH AGAIN

When you've shouted 'Rule Britannia,' when you've sung 'God save
the Queen,'
When you've finished killing [Argies]* with your mouth,
Will you kindly drop a shilling in my little tambourine
For a gentleman in khaki ordered South?

Kipling

The Falklands campaign had some things in common with the Russo-
Japanese war of 1904–5. It was fought at sea and on land. It was short
and it was victorious. Operations to re-take the Falkland Islands lasted
about ten weeks – from 2 April, 1982, when two carriers of the Royal
Navy, *Hermes* and *Invincible*, sailed from Portsmouth until 14 June when
General Menendez surrendered at Port Stanley. There were three main
parts to the operation – getting there, getting ashore and getting Port
Stanley. During the first part South Georgia was recaptured. The longest
part of the whole thing was getting there, from the beginning of April
when the Task Force sailed until 21 May when the main landings were
made at San Carlos; from the landings to victory took little more than
three weeks, although in this short time there were some very sharp
engagements. Much of what happened is such recent history and commanded such comprehensive reporting in books, newspapers and tele-
vision films that it hardly requires iteration in detail. Rather we should
perhaps see how the Army performed in battle conducted under such
remote and trying conditions, and we may begin with those British
troops who were first ashore both at South Georgia and the East and
West Falklands – the SAS.

The principal enemy to be conquered in South Georgia was not the

---

* In *The Absent-Minded Beggar* the word, of course, is 'Kruger'.

Argentinian forces, but the elements. Corporal Davey of 19 Troop, D Squadron, remembered that on 21 April, after several unsuccessful attempts, his troop was at last landed by helicopters on the Fortuna glacier. Almost immediately the weather deteriorated appallingly. 50mph winds with spindrift blocked the ammunition trays of the machine-guns. The trays were then frozen. Their plan had been to move east over the glacier to the coast and reconnoitre landing beaches at Leith, Stromness and Husvik, but the going was so difficult, hampered by deep snow and crevasses, heavily burdened by all the kit being carried, that in some five hours they succeeded in moving less than half a kilometre. The wind kept getting stronger, they were plagued by continuous whiteouts and obliged to seek shelter in a crevasse. Thereupon the so-called arctic tents showed their inadequacy with breaking poles and simply being torn away. They then spent what was described as an uncomfortable night wrapped in sleeping bags and preventing the tent from collapsing by sitting against its sides, but it was still necessary to go outside and dig the snow away every hour or they would have been buried. Next morning there was such a threat of frostbite and hypothermia that they had to signal HMS *Antrim* to be extracted by helicopter. How hazardous this was is illustrated by their losing two of the three helicopters sent to extract them. Fully laden, they crashed because whiteout caused the pilots to lose all their horizons. Happily the third helicopter eventually took them all back to the ship. Having failed to establish themselves ashore properly by air, the SAS then tried by sea and, together with some of the Royal Marines Special Boat Squadron men, did succeed in effecting landings at Stromness Bay and the northern whaling stations. These landings were then reinforced by more SAS and Royal Marines moved in by all available helicopters, and when these forces advanced against the Argentinian positions at Leith and King Edward Cove, all resistance quickly melted away and on 26 April the Argentinians surrendered.

Recapture of South Georgia was of greater symbolic than strategic importance, though it must have sent a chill down the backs of the Junta, who by this time would have realized that Britain meant business. There was still much to do before the main landings on East Falkland could take place, and again the SAS played their crucial part in establishing intelligence-gathering patrols ashore in order to provide the Task Force commanders with the necessary information both for planning the assault and giving Argentinian positions appropriate attention from naval guns and Harrier aircraft. They did not confine themselves, however, to this type of surveillance operation. In a daring raid, reminiscent of the original SAS activities led by David Stirling in the Western

Desert forty years earlier, the airstrip at Pebble Island, off the north-east side of West Falkland, was attacked and the eleven aircraft there destroyed, together with ammunition and explosives. It was another example of the SAS's ability to go more or less where they liked and do what they wanted.

Much of the credit for the successful landings at San Carlos on 21 May must go to Brigadier Julian Thompson, commander of 3rd Commando Brigade, who was not only jointly responsible for planning the operation, but was in charge of the land battle during its initial, decisive stages. He has given his own clear and modest account of it all in an excellent book.* Of course, the Royal Navy's and Royal Air Force's part in it was indispensable and was brilliantly executed, and Julian Thompson was fortunate in having under his command such highly trained and experienced units as 40 and 45 Commando, Royal Marines, and 2nd and 3rd Battalions of the Parachute Regiment. The assaulting troops were 40 Commando and 2nd Parachute Battalion who were to land astride San Carlos settlement, and were to be followed by 45 Commando and 3rd Parachute Battalion. Fortunately the landings were not opposed, and during the morning all battalions secured their objectives – 40 Commando occupied San Carlos, 2 Para secured Sussex Mountains in order to protect the beach-head, 45 Commando were at Ajax Bay, and 3 Para went to Port San Carlos. Then the whole business of getting ashore supporting weapons, including the vital Rapier air defence missiles, stores to build Harrier and helicopter landing zones, light tanks, artillery, ammunition, supplies, headquarters and the whole paraphernalia of war on land, got under way. The main Argentinian resistance during the first few days came not from their Army on the islands, but from their gallant Air Force pilots operating from the mainland. After four days about thirty Argentinian aircraft had been shot down, but they had succeeded in hitting ten British ships. One of the losses during this first phase was *Atlantic Conveyor*, which contained the vital Chinook helicopters, together with six Wessex, all of which were to be used for a rapid advance on Port Stanley. Without them Julian Thompson was obliged to revise his plans, and having received orders from Northwood (Headquarters of Commander-in-Chief, Fleet, and the Joint Operations HQ for the whole operation) to get on with it, he made it clear to his subordinate commanders that, if necessary, they would walk to Port Stanley. Many of them did, so that what Thompson called the LPG, the leather personnel carrier, or plain boot, was to have

---

* *No Picnic*, Leo Cooper.

a major role in it all, and was to give birth to a new word in our military vocabulary – *yomping*.

It was clear, however, that getting to Port Stanley by boot would take some time, and the political and military chiefs in London wanted some successes, beyond merely consolidating the beach-head and beginning the long march east, to silence criticism and justify the decision to embark on what some regarded as a risky and unimportant side-show. It was therefore determined to attack and take Goose Green, where there was an airstrip and a settlement normally housing some eighty islanders. It was quite irrelevant to the principal objectives of capturing Port Stanley and dealing with the main part of the occupying enemy forces. Nevertheless something had to be done, and Goose Green was within reach. Besides, no one had any better ideas. Hardly proper grounds for undertaking what turned out to be a difficult operation, but as Major Keeble, second-in-command of 2 Para [who took over command when Lieutenant-Colonel H. Jones was killed – he was posthumously awarded the Victoria Cross for his gallant and selfless leadership] admitted months after the war was over; 'It would be a thermometer – you could test the water. I think that is probably why we went.'

2 Para had a formidable fighting reputation – from the epic struggle at Arnhem to the Rhine crossing and dash to Schleswig Holstein, their counter-insurgency operations in the Middle East, Suez, dealing with Indonesian guerrillas in Borneo and with the 'troubles' in Northern Ireland. Moreover they had at the time a Commanding Officer determined to maintain and enhance this reputation. There was no doubt about their doing so in the battle for Goose Green. It was a difficult task – to advance some three miles over open, bare country with no cover other than that afforded by folds in the ground. Two features, Boca Hill and Darwin Hill, occupied by the enemy in well-prepared entrenchments and machine-gun emplacements, barred the way. The parachutists had artillery support and their own Milan missiles, but when they asked for additional assistance of Scorpion tanks from The Blues and Royals, the answer given was that these vehicles were required for other operations. This refusal to provide armoured support was a bad mistake, as their close cooperation with the advancing troops could have been decisive in quelling Argentinian opposition far more quickly. In the event 2 Para's attack bogged down before either Boca Hill or Darwin Hill had been taken, and the Commanding Officer, Lieutenant-Colonel H. Jones, in a brave attempt to silence a suddenly discovered and unsuspected machine-gun post, had been killed. Major Keeble then had the unenviable job of taking over command of a battle that seemed

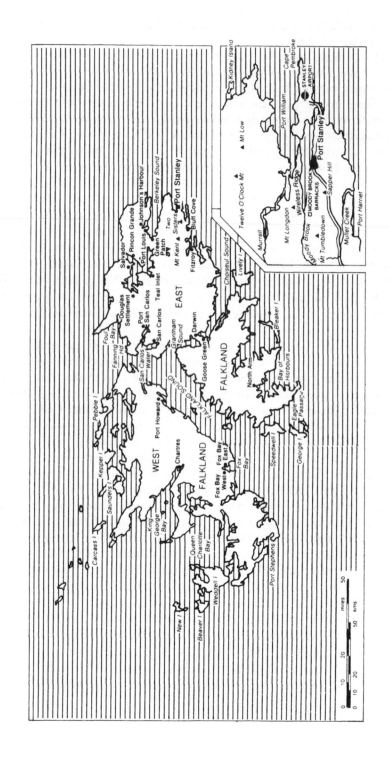

in danger of going wrong. He was more than up to the job. 'We had to keep going,' he recorded later. 'There was artillery coming down, we had a battle to fight. You cannot suddenly burst into tears or anything. You have got to get on. There were people's lives depending on what I actually did at that point – *me*.' Seeing that the key to the battle was Boca Hill, he brought heavy artillery and Milan fire on to the enemy positions, while moving 'D' Company forward to outflank it. The Argentinians gave up and soon afterwards Darwin Hill was in 2 Para's hands as well. They still had to capture the School House and the airstrip, but by a combination of artillery fire, air strikes from Harriers and dogged infantry action, Keeble and his men won a remarkable victory. When the Argentinians surrendered, he was astonished to find that his 450 parachutists had overcome some 1,600 of the enemy – a far greater number than British intelligence had estimated. But in a battle like this it was not numbers that mattered. It was spirit and will power. Keeble summed it all up admirably: 'We had been given all this garbage about their equipment and their food, and dysentery being rife. All that was really irrelevant. We knew when we got to the Falklands that we would have the same problems, trench foot, shortage of this and that. The question which decides it all is whether they want to fight. There was not a man in 2 Para who did not want to do that operation. *Their* weakness even before we had attacked is that they did not really want to fight.' Keeble was echoing Winston Churchill here, and how proud that great warrior would have been of 2 Para's magnificent performance.

There were still plenty of dramatic, tragic and triumphant incidents in the Falklands war – the rapid capture of Fitzroy by helicopter-borne troops, the terrible casualties suffered by the Welsh Guards and others aboard *Sir Galahad*, and the relentless advance on and capture of Port Stanley, which involved set-piece attacks by night on prepared defensive positions, calling for the very highest standards of training, courage and leadership. All those involved in these attacks – the Royal Marine Commandos, the Parachute Regiment, the Scots Guards – acquitted themselves with faultless upholding of their matchless tradition. One of the Scots Guards company commanders, Major Kiszely, remembered what it was like during the attack on Tumbledown Mountain:

We did fix bayonets because I believe bayonets kill people and are useful. It certainly saved my life. As we were charging up, I looked round and saw coming out of a hole in the ground – not a trench, but a hole – this figure with a weapon, almost from behind. I swung round and pulled the trigger. I heard the click. What you're meant to do is to count your rounds – twenty rounds in a magazine and you count from one to twenty. Of course, it doesn't work like that. 'Click'. So there was only one thing to do and without a moment's hesitation you do it. I struck him in the chest and he fell back into the hole. At the time it did not shock me. I was too busy. Immediately afterwards I didn't bother to wonder whether he was dead or anything else and I ran on. Looking back on it now, it is not something I am proud of at all. I knew he was going to kill me but I derive no pleasure from sticking a bayonet into another person.

As these battles to capture the high ground overlooking Port Stanley were in progress, the SAS were again active in trying to arrange for the Argentinians to surrender without resorting to the necessity for a full-scale assault on the capital itself which might have involved heavy casualties, not only to the military people on both sides, but to the Falkland Islanders themselves. As usual who dared, won. On 6 June they had succeeded in establishing contact with the Argentinians at Port Stanley and during the following week, a psyops campaign was mounted, designed to convince the enemy that further bloodshed was pointless, that their military position was hopeless, and that as they had put up a good fight in the circumstances, the best thing would be to lay down their arms now rather than go down in history as the butchers of Port Stanley. It worked, and on 14 June the SAS Commanding Officer, accompanied by the Spanish-speaking Royal Marine Captain Bell, con-ferred with General Menendez, who eventually agreed to the conditions of surrender. It then required only formal signature by Major-General Jeremy Moore, the overall land force commander, and the Falklands war was over. The British Army, with the whole-hearted and indispensable support it always enjoyed from the Royal Navy and Royal Air Force, had shown that improvisation, adaptability, determination and sheer refusal to be duped or dismayed could triumph over a greatly numerically superior enemy eight thousand miles from England's shores. It was almost a return to what had happened so frequently and comparably far away in the 1890s when this story began. Ordered south again, the gentlemen in khaki had conquered again. Max Hastings, who was there throughout and who writes better about war than most correspondents, gives us a feel for what the last day of this particular war was like for him:

> I awoke from a chilly doze on Monday morning to find a thin crust of frozen snow covering my sleeping-bag and equipment in the dawn. Around me in the ruined sheep pen in which we lay, a cluster of snow-covered ponchos and rucksacks marked the limits of battalion headquarters. The inexhaustible

voice of Major Chris Keeble, second in command 2 Para,* was holding forth into a radio handset as decisively as it had been two hours earlier when I lost consciousness. All firing in front of us, where the battalion's rifle companies had stormed a succession of enemy positions in the darkness, was ended. Desultory Argentinian shells were falling on untenanted ground some 600 yards to the right. We could hear heavy firing of all calibres further south, where the Guards and Gurkhas were still fighting for their objectives.

Hastings then went forward, guided by a paratrooper who talked to him about John Greenhalgh, a Gazelle helicopter pilot, who seemed able to fly anywhere at night without any special vision aids and who endlessly brought ammunition forward and took the wounded back. There were former enemy positions, now abandoned with innumerable weapons left lying about, plenty of ammunition and food. Then they saw the Scorpion and Scimitar tanks of The Blues and Royals which had given such excellent fire support to the battalion during its attack. Hastings talked to an artilleryman, a Forward Observation Officer, who seemed to have less idea as to what was going on than Hastings himself. Suddenly there was news and very welcome news. The enemy was running away. Everyone was then in haste to get further forward and Hastings got a lift on one of the Household Cavalry Scimitars and joined more of 2 Para's soldiers:

> They were looking upon the wreckage of a cluster of large buildings at the head of the estuary, perhaps three hundred yards beneath us. It was the former Royal Marine base at Moody Brook. Two or three miles down a concrete road east of it, white and innocent in the sudden winter sunshine stood the little houses and churches of Port Stanley ... the climax of all our ambitions, apparently as distant as the far side of the moon at breakfast, lay open for the taking.

On they went, eager to be first into Port Stanley. Only an order from higher headquarters halted them. Max Hastings, however, did not halt. He walked on into the capital, chatted to some Argentinian soldiers, and at length made his way into 'that well-known Stanley hostelry *The Upland Goose*', approaching it along a road filled with lines of cowed Argentinian soldiers. When he went in, the host told him that he knew the British would come. They had just been waiting for the moment. 'It was,' said Hastings, 'like liberating an English suburban golf club.' That afternoon the surrender document was signed.

It had been a remarkable campaign and there were plenty of lessons to be taken note of for the future; the absolute need for some sort of

* David Chaundler, parachuted in, had taken over command.

amphibious capability if such things were to be done again; the over-riding importance of good, accurate, up-to-date intelligence; the use of the right troops – hard, versatile, determined (this is where units like the Royal Marines, the Parachute Battalions, the Gurkhas, who also do all sorts of other jobs, were so valuable); the indispensability of Royal Navy carriers with the Harriers and helicopters (just as Falstaff was not only witty himself, but the cause of wit in other men, so the helicopter lends even greater power to other weapons by its giving them infinite momentum, supply and mobility*; having a strategic reserve at a peak of readiness; and, of course, having the will to take on great odds. Will all these lessons be taken note of as we move into the 1990s?

* Fire power from the Royal Artillery was a crucial factor in persuading the Argentinians to surrender.

21

KEEPING HONOUR BRIGHT

War, in Shakespeare, is usually a positive spiritual value, like love.
There is a reference to the soldiership of the protagonist in all the
plays ... Soldiership is almost the condition of nobility, and so the
Shakespearian hero is usually a soldier ... [he] becomes automatically
a symbol of faith in human values of love, of war, of romance in a
wide and sweeping sense. He is, as it were, conscious of all he stands
for: from the first to the last he loves his own romantic history.

G Wilson Knight

If we soldiers did not love our own romantic history, we would hardly
write about it. War as highly coloured romantic adventure may have
gone out of fashion, yet Shakespeare's plays have got plenty of good
advice for the soldier. One of the best pieces of advice is given to us by
Ulysses in *Troilus and Cressida*. He points out that the wallet at Time's
back into which go alms for oblivion is simply a vast receptacle for
ingratitude, of benefits forgot if you like, and that all the past good deeds
are quickly devoured and put out of mind. Only perseverance keeps
honour bright. If there is a single feature in the British Army's conduct
during these last hundred years, which might be lifted from all the
others, then surely it is perseverance. It was perseverance – both that
of Kitchener and the ordinary soldier – that in the end persuaded the
Boers to sue for peace in South Africa; the perseverance of the infantry
during the Great War in fruitlessly attacking well-nigh impregnable
positions through mud and barbed wire in the face of deadly machine-
gun and shell fire puzzles today's historians, but inspires infinite admiration; Churchill's perseverance and the response he wrung from the
nation against seemingly impossible odds will always be remembered as
a finest hour; the Army's campaigns in Malaya, in Korea, in southern
Arabia, in what looks like being another thirty years war in Northern

Ireland – all have been characterized by courage, skill and perseverance. They have kept the British Army's honour bright.

Why has it been able to persevere so successfully? Those readers who have followed the fortunes of various regiments in this account of what the British Army has done during the last century will not pause in giving their answer. It is a combination of qualities and conditions – tradition to be maintained, fine leaders who compelled a taste for duty, service, loyalty, honour, the sheer calibre of Thomas Atkins, a commitment to do well the task in hand, much of it all springing from the priceless regimental system which the Army has created and preserved. Coriolanus summed it all up in a few lines:

> If any think brave death outweighs bad life,
> And that his country's dearer than himself,
> Let him alone – or so many so minded –
> Wave thus to express his disposition,
> And follow Martius.

We have seen in all the campaigns recorded here how very many were so minded. Is there something in it to be learned by future generations, as I suggested and hoped in my Foreword? We often hear that a soldier, or for that matter everyone, should study history. Vindication for this view varies. On the one hand, we find in a letter to Sir Frederick Wallace from his father this recommendation: 'In all professional study it is essential for a soldier to remember that the object is not to acquire information about past operations, but to improve his judgement as to what ought to be done under conditions of actual war.' Walter Raleigh, while agreeing in principle, puts it more succinctly: 'The end and scope of all history is to teach by examples of time past such wisdom as may guide our desires and actions.' Veronica Wedgwood leaves us in no doubt as to her philosophy: 'Facts alone, even if they are proven beyond doubt, do not amount to history. It is the examination of the personalities involved and the interpretation of their characters that make events intelligible.' That brilliant historian, Michael Howard, tends to give us the events, 'to show what really happened', rather than concentrating on interpreting character. Shakespeare dramatizes character without worrying too much about the accuracy of events. We may perhaps allow Henry James the last word on this point with his indisputable 'What is character but the determination of incident? What is incident but the illustration of character?' How totally Shakespeare's characters determine incident – the Macbeths at Inverness, Brutus at Sardis, Harry the King at Agincourt; how relentlessly the plays' incidents illustrate character – Desdemona's handkerchief and Othello's jealousy, Falstaff's attempt to exploit the death of Hotspur, Antony's putting love before honour when Cleopatra flees during the sea-fight. We will continue to read and see Shakespeare's plays for the people in them and the things they say, for their dramatic characterization and beautiful verse, and those soldiers aspiring to the rank of general officer will do well to take note of Macbeth's rhetorical question:

> Who can be wise, amaz'd, temperate, and furious,
> Loyal, and neutral, in a moment?

for with these words Macbeth, himself a general, defines all too well the multitudinous moods required of a military commander in the field. It is, of course, not only Shakespeare's soldiers, with their thrilling language, and what Professor Wilson Knight called 'the quality of soldiership in all its glamour of romantic adventure' – it is not only Shakespeare's military heroes that entertain us so fully. If we turn to the present, our bookshelves are full of Evelyn Waugh and Anthony Powell, of George Macdonald Fraser and Bernard Cornwell. How we treasure Conan Doyle's Brigadier Gérard or C.S. Forester's Peninsula War stories, all this to say nothing of the biographies of our great soldiers and the histories of our endless campaigns. Yet we turn to novelists with particular affection. No novelist honoured the soldier more or captured him in prose and verse more completely than Rudyard Kipling, and in his introduction to *The Complete Barrack-Room Ballads*, Charles Carrington does much to explain how he did it. 'Kipling,' he writes, 'enables us to share the experience of Tommy Atkins, the traditional British solider,' adding that 'all the evidence he allows is what the soldier said.' Much of what Kipling heard came from the old soldiers, who served on the North-West Frontier of India and told their tales of active service there – it was a kind of training ground for battle – 'while the young reporter applied an attentive eye and ear'. Then with a matchless pen, Carrington tells us:

> He wrote not only of the vice-regal court and its gossip, but of engineers and district officers, law courts and opium dens, cholera epidemics and race riots, illicit love affairs across caste rules, drop-outs from British society. With loving sympathy he visualized the Indian scene, writing delightfully of Indian children; and, rather late in the day, he came to the British 'Tommies', a new low caste in caste-ridden India, recruited from the lowest of unskilled labourers, scarcely to be ranked as *sahibs*. What sort of men were they, then, this fellowship of professional fighters, who rejected the proprieties and inhibitions of Victorian society, who appeared sometimes in the police court news as drunken disorderly reprobates, and sometimes as heroes of romance,

the 'Thin Red Line' of Balaclava, the storming column of Delhi, the defenders of Rorke's Drift. Search English literature and you will find no adequate account of the British soldier, what he thought of his officers, and what he talked about the night before the battle, between Shakespeare's *Henry V* and Kipling's *Barrack-Room Ballads*. The British tradition was not favourable to soldiers; ever since Cromwell's day, hostility to a standing army had been an underlying factor in British politics. The sailor, the 'jolly Jack Tar', was the national hero, not the soldier.

It was left to later writers to make a hero of the soldier once again, but in Kipling's day there was plenty of heroic stuff about the soldier. As Charles Carrington reminds us, in a leader of *The Times*, dated 25 March, 1890, Humphry Ward praised Kipling as 'the discoverer of "Tommy Atkins" as a hero of realistic romance'. It did not matter how small the British Army was at this time, it 'was strictly professional and class-conscious; its officers were exclusively "gentlemen", giving their loyalty directly to the crown; the rank and file were drawn from the unskilled labourers, and recruiting was good when employment was bad. All armies live by *esprit de corps,* the comradeship of men who are willing to live and die together. Perhaps no army since the Roman legions has had so strong a sense of regimental unity as the old British regular army, or so strong a sense of loyalty.' It is, however, not just the old British regular army which enjoyed these priceless assets of regimental unity and loyalty. They are there today as strong as ever and will be tomorrow.

Kipling's *Ballads* give us unforgettable pictures of the gentlemen in khaki – infantry, gunners, sappers, the cavalry, the mounted infantry. An infantry battalion is on the move:

> We're marchin' on relief over Injia's coral strand,
> Eight 'undred fightin' Englishmen, the Colonel, and the Band;
> Ho! get away you bullock-man, you've 'eard the bugle blowed,
> There's a regiment a-comin' down the Grand Trunk Road;
> > With its best foot first
> > And the road a-sliding past,
> > An' every bloomin' campin'-ground exactly like the last...

There is O'Kelly, the cavalry soldier, who has heard 'the Revelly' in every part of the globe from Hong Kong to Lucknow, from Leeds to Lahore, who is old and nervous now, cast from the Service, with an inadequate pension and little prospect of employment, but he remembers past glories:

> Oh, it drives me half crazy to think of the days I
> Went slap for the Ghazi, my sword at my side,
> When we rode Hell-for-leather
> Both squadrons together,
> That didn't care whether we lived or we died.

Now, this late Troop-Sergeant-Major is glad if he can get the job of a messenger delivering a letter. 'Think what 'e's been, Think what 'e's seen, Think of his pension an' – Gawd Save the Queen!' The Sapper is in no doubt about his superiority over all other regiments and corps – the Infantry of the Line is simply a man with a gun in his hand; cavalry is only what horses can stand; artillery moves by leave of the ground; but we, the sappers, do something all round. In short Her Majesty's Royal Engineers are like no one else:

> I have stated it plain, an' my argument's thus...
> There's only one Corps, which is perfect – that's us.

The Royal Artillery, with their proud motto, Ubique, would not agree:

> Ubique means that warnin' grunt the perished linesman knows,
> When o'er 'is strung an' sufferin' front the shrapnel sprays 'is foes;
> An' as their firin' dies away the 'usky whisper runs
> From lips that 'aven't drunk all day: 'The Guns, Thank Gawd, the Guns!'

We have met the mounted infantry already and seen that in the Boer War, with their peerless coalition of fire power and mobility, they provided the answer to Kitchener's problems. Here they are again:

> I wish my mother could see me now, with a fence-post under my arm,
> And a knife and a spoon in my putties that I found on a Boer farm,
> Atop of a sore-backed Argentine, with a thirst that you couldn't buy.
> I used to be in the Yorkshires once
>   But now I am M.I.
> We're trekkin' our twenty miles a day an' bein' loved by the Dutch,
> But we don't hold on by the mane no more, nor lose our stirrups – much;
> An' we scout with a senior man in charge where the 'oly white flags fly.
> We used to think they were friendly once
>   But now we are M.I.
> I wish my mother could see me now, a-gatherin' news on my own,
> When I ride like a General up to the scrub and ride back like Tod Sloan,
> Remarkable close to my 'orse's neck to let the shots go by.
> We used to fancy it risky once
>   But now we are M.I.
> I wish myself could talk to myself as I left 'im a year ago;

I could tell 'im a lot that would save 'im a lot on the things that 'e ought to
  know!
When I think o' that ignorant barrack-bird, it almost makes me cry.
I used to belong in an Army once
    But now I am M.I.

This ballad characterizes absolutely the Tommy's acceptance of the
unexpected, his total adaptability to changing circumstances, his pride
and satisfaction in the accomplishment of another skill, his cheeky
defiance of risk, the enemy and his own military hierarchy. There was
nothing wrong with the Victorian soldier of the 1890s. Nor is there
anything wrong with the Elizabethan soldier of today. He may be better
educated, better paid, better equipped, but his spirit, always reinforced
by pride in regiment or corps, is not very different. Today's soldier,
however, suffers one great disadvantage compared with the Tommy of
a hundred years ago. His field of operations is so limited. How he must
envy the opportunity, the adventure, the challenge, the mystery and
romance, the sheer *range* of soldiering that was spread before his Victorian predecessor. There is no 'Burma girl a-setting' thinking of him
by the old Moulmein Pagoda. There is no 'Troopin', troopin', troopin'
to the sea for our Army in the East'. Afghanistan's plains may have been
littered with Soviet soldiers, lying out wounded and waiting for the
women to cut up what remained, but for the British soldier, the North-
West Frontier and the Great Game are gone for ever. The counter-
insurgency wars are over, except for one too close to home. There are
no colonial garrisons to man, no little wars to fight, no expeditions to
mount. Even though there is peace to be kept in many a former part of
Empire, whether East of Suez, the Caribbean, Africa or the Middle
East, it is no longer for the gentlemen in khaki to do it. Belize, Hong
Kong, Cyprus – that is the sum of it. What is the antidote to this dearth
of professional purpose? I will reply in one word – *training*! But not the
way we train now. The British Army has never trained seriously. We
play at it. Even in war, I remember well, we hardly did any training at
all, although motive was not lacking. When my regiment, 4th Hussars,
moved from the Middle East to Italy, you might have supposed that we
would have undergone an intensive period of getting used to totally new
conditions of battle – roads, tracks, villages, towns, mountains, rivers,
vine-yards and farms – and urgently have sought advice from other
regiments which had already been in action there. Not a bit of it! In
the few months between arriving and going into action, our principal
concerns were looking at all the beautiful things, going to the opera and
swimming. What could our colonels and generals have been thinking

of? 'Markin' time to earn a K.C.B.?' Now that there is no war, however, perhaps the Army could turn its attention to training properly. I am not talking here of what goes on in the British Army of the Rhine, where some degree of mastery over weapons [despite absurd rationing of live ammunition and shortage of simulators] does go on. I am talking of training for *war* – building up to and testing that pitch of mental and physical hardness which is capable of surmounting infinite fatigue, stress and endless demand on imagination, clarity, accuracy and character. Only the SAS do it properly. Let them take a lead in making others to it properly too. There is no need for tanks, guns or helicopters to be involved. Mountains, boots, bad weather and *ideas* are all that you need. Happily, some of the training which regiments undergo before serving in Northern Ireland is on the right lines. There is room for extending this practice more widely.

We have looked here upon this picture and on this. What have we seen? In the 1890s we have seen what was essentially an Imperial Army, recruited, trained, deployed and used to keep the British Empire intact, fighting many little wars, mainly against ill-armed natives, invariably winning, or at least not losing them, a small, professional army of volunteers, taking infinite pride in their regiments' traditions and battle honours, and in action living up to them time after time. As we move into the 1990s we still see a small, all-volunteer army of professionals, organized in the same regiments and corps, although many of these regiments amalgamated, and with the change of name, still cherishing the same proud traditions and still when action calls maintaining and enhancing their record of achievement and honour. But gone is the Imperial connection. Some minor peace-keeping in Cyprus and Belize; a garrison in the Falkland Islands to keep the Argentinians from making fools of themselves again; some frontier watching in Hong Kong; a Gurkha battalion to secure the Sultan of Brunei; some assistance to Arab rulers – these relics of our Imperial past trickle on. But the Army itself is now a European Army, its cream deployed in Germany, declared to the NATO alliance, or here in this country ready to reinforce NATO, on the flanks or in the centre, with only the distraction of Ulster to remind our soldiers of the unchanging condition of their lives – trouble is their business. Between 1890 and 1990 the British Army has been more or less continuously in action. During this Hundred Years' War, the Army may have lost a few battles. It rarely lost a campaign. It never lost a major conflict. And during that time there were two wars of such magnitude, such consequence and such horror that we need not wonder at the record left of them by such literary giants as Siegfried Sassoon and Robert Graves, Evelyn Waugh and Anthony Powell. Perhaps the nation's affection for and confidence in the Army today is reflected by the popularity of fictional portraits of soldiers published in recent years, whether we are thinking of that howling cad, Flashman,* who, despite all his funk and poodle-faking, won more campaign medals than most of his contemporaries, to say nothing of the Victoria Cross. Richard Sharpe,† of course, is a real hero, and may he and Sergeant Harper go on marching. Stories about soldiering seem to have an almost limitless capacity to grip the military imagination of every age, and yet remain unique and intact in their own particular age.

The British Army has almost always been fighting some enemy somewhere. What has it been fighting for? India, the Empire, trade, expansionism, survival, gain, against unspeakable evil and tyranny, for mercenary purposes. There is something more than that. Often it fought for the Regiment, for comrades, for The Queen, for a leader who would not take no for an answer, for honour. There are still those of us who believe that in the end what the British Army will be remembered for and reward those of us who have served in it and pull others to it in the future is an acknowledgement that the winning of honour, the performance of duty and the fulfilment of service are in themselves rewards more lasting than material matters. The publican in Winifred Holtby's *South Riding* says at one point: 'If I had *six* sons, I'd put them all in the Army. The King's Uniform! You can't beat it.' Those of us who have worn The King's uniform and The Queen's would agree. You can't beat it. It is the surest way of keeping honour bright.

---

*Not forgetting that other great creation of George MacDonald Fraser, Private McAuslan, who despite being the World's Dirtiest Soldier and more or less permanently a janker-wallah still understands what it is to be part of a fine Regiment.

†In Bernard Cornwell's splendid series, Richard Sharpe, a Rifleman [95th] has to contend not only with the French Army, but with some of the less enlightened officers of his own Army too.

22

A TIME OF CHANGE

> In a progressive country change is constant; and the great question is not whether you should resist change which is inevitable, but whether that change should be carried out in deference to the manners, the customs, the laws, and the traditions of a people, or whether it should be carried out in deference to abstract principles, and arbitrary and general doctrines.
>
> *Disraeli* 1868

Disraeli, of course, was in no doubt that the former recipe was the proper one for managing the country, and we similarly should be in no doubt that in effecting inevitable change in the British Army's size, structure and capability, we should do it in deference to the manners, customs, laws and traditions of the Army itself. We have seen in the foregoing chapters that the Army's conduct in waging campaigns of infinite variety was distinguished by courage, skill and perseverance. Why was it able to persevere so successfully and in doing so keep bright the British Army's honour?

The answer is not a simple one. In the first place it was the mere condition of being so continuously in action that had given officers and men alike confidence, experience and adaptability, had refined strategic know-how, tactical skills, leadership, administration, and the business of command. It had also developed weapons and equipment appropriate to the tasks in hand. But there was more to it than the obvious, tangible need for good leaders, sound training, proper tools of war. There was a tradition to live up to, a determination not to let your comrades down, a pride in past achievement, loyalty to and trust in your 'mates', all reinforced by the innate quality of the British soldier, the dedication and professionalism of the officers and a kind of inborn conviction that the British Army could go anywhere and do anything. Much of this invincible combination sprang from the priceless regimental system which the Army had created and – some ill-advised meddling of recent times notwithstanding, meddling which contradicted Disraeli's dictum – more or less preserved.

Much has happened in recent years. The new millenium has brought with it a significant change of purpose for the British Army, changes too of size, deployment, organization, equipment, role, uniforms, conditions of service, enemies it fought, countries it fought in, results it achieved. Yet there is one thing which we trust has *not* changed - its reputation. How shall we put this trust to the test?

We may do so by examining what the Army has been up to during these last two decades and whether it has maintained its record of perseverance and success in the light of different challenges and different objectives. During the century examined by *Gentlemen in Khaki* the Army did its stuff almost exclusively in pursuit of British interests right up to the time of re-taking the Falkland Islands in 1982. This operation was entirely a national one, executed to restore legitimate sovereignty to British territory after its illegal seizure by a foreign power, and it was done without allies, although France and the United States were not unfriendly in their supply or non-supply of warlike material to one side or the other. Indeed it might be said that the Falklands war was the *last* purely national one waged by this country. It could hardly be foreseen that although the British Army was no stranger to peace-keeping activities with allies under the auspices of the United Nations, the military ventures still to come would *all* be undertaken either in support of United Nations initiatives or as a partner with the United States. We may therefore ask what sort of tasks awaited the British Army in the new millenium and what sort of Army would we need to carry them out?

To pontificate about the past is one thing. To do so about the future, another. The first is easy, the second less so. Yet in writing an article for *Blackwood's Magazine* in June 1979 – ten years before *Gentlemen in Khaki* was published – I ventured to predict what sort of Army we would have in the year 2000 and what it would be up to. Doing so meant, of course, predicting also the broad political and strategic conditions of the years ahead. For my background, therefore, I suggested that between 1979 and the beginning of the 21st century the Soviet Union would disintegrate; the Warsaw Pact be dissolved; American ties with Europe be loosened; the Northern Ireland emergency would end; Europe would get more involved in African and Middle Eastern affairs;

terrorism in Great Britain would continue; there would be a European Defence Force; and that our defence budget, unless increased in real terms, would be unable to sustain the current level of armed forces and their equipment. Easy enough to have predicted, no doubt, and not wide of the mark, although I was quite wrong about Hong Kong.

Following on from these likely circumstances, I forecast that the sort of Army we should have in the early 2000s would still be built round horse, foot, guns and sappers; the regimental system would be preserved as it is the best system of raising, grouping, training and commanding men in battle that any Army has yet devised; there would be fewer fighting regiments, perhaps only seventy or so – fifteen armoured, fifteen artillery, forty infantry, some sappers and Army Air Corps units; supporting corps would be scaled down accordingly; the Army's strength might be little more than 100,000 and it would be deployed in Germany, in the UK, in lingering garrisons like Cyprus and Gibraltar, and wherever else it was required to protect British interests [in 1979 the Falklands war was not far off] or fulfil international undertakings; above all the Army would receive recognition of the nation's debt to it – alas the Blair/Brown government has in this respect failed the nation and let down the Army – and, so I conjectured, would be well-found, well-trained, well-equipped, well-paid, well-accommodated; well-led and well aware that trouble was their business and that this business would be conscientiously discharged. I suggested that trouble would beckon the Army once more in the Middle East, would invite us to mount rescue operations in Africa, would be required to combat terrorism and might even seduce us into playing The Great Game once more. Well, there was plenty of trouble to come – in Iraq, in the Balkans, Sierra Leone, Afghanistan. Would the Army maintain, even enhance its reputation for dogged perseverance and eventual triumph in tackling these new, unexpected commitments? Before we answer the question we must see how the Army Board reacted to the changing strategic circumstances which I have outlined.

If there is one thing that politicians of all parties have in common – apart from regularly increasing their own emoluments – it is that of an unending eagerness to reduce the armed forces. Any condition will do. In this case it was the supposed advantage that would occur from the break-up of the Soviet Union and collapse of the Warsaw Pact. There would, it appeared, be a Peace Dividend. What these men of government failed to realise or acknowledge was that relaxation of the iron grip which had been imposed on liberal aspirants for change would allow, indeed encourage, trouble to bubble up all over the place.

Even the Army Board, in considering the Army's future structure, allowed hope to triumph over experience. In doing so they were guilty of two major errors. The first was to reduce the number of armoured regiments and infantry battalions by too much, respectively to eleven and thirty-six. How they must long now for my demand for fifteen armoured and forty infantry, faced as they are with both Iraq and Afghanistan. The second error was to meddle with the infantry's unique, precious regimental system. It may be doubted whether the Army Board pundits during their consideration of the Infantry's reorganisation consulted Bernard Fergusson's excellent *The Trumpet in the Hall*. He reminds us of Wavell's saying to him: 'Never forget: the Regiment is the foundation of everything'. This was in 1935 at a time when, as Fergusson put it 'the first assaults were being made upon the regimental system'. Although circumstances were very different then 'the idea was to link the various Regiments of the Line in bunches of five or six', a device which the War Office called the 'Group System'. The plan was put to all Regiments and was rejected outright by all but two, neither of which had a reputation for contented competence. It may also be doubted whether the works of Arthur Bryant were examined. Had they been, this passage, referring to Wellington's reliance on the Army's great strength – its regiments – might have given them pause:

> Pride in the continuing regiment – the personal individual loyalty which each private felt towards his corps gave to the British soldier a moral strength which the student and administrator ought never to underestimate. It enabled him to stand firm and fight forward when men without it, however brave, would have failed. To let down the regiment, to be unworthy of the men of old who had marched under the same colours, to be untrue to the comrades who had shared the same loyalties, hardships and perils were things that the least-tutored, humblest soldier would not do.

Fergusson also drew our attention to the memoirs of Lord Wolseley, a former Army C.-in-C. who wrote: 'Keep your hands off the Regiments, you iconoclastic civilians who meddle and muddle in Army matters: you are not soldiers, and you do not understand them'. And what mattered was that the proposed 1935 Group System was so emphatically dismissed by regiments.

History repeats itself, it seems, and the 2004 Army Restructuring simply put into effect another sort of Group System. The sheer absurdity of it perhaps best illustrated by the measure which first merged The Devonshire and Dorsetshire Regiment with The Royal Gloucestershire Regiment – both renowned for their magnificent record and traditions – and then turned themselves into light infantry as part of The Rifles, this latter distinction surely being the preserve of the The 60th, The 95th and The 43rd/52nd. What were the reasons given for all this meddling? Greater stability, ease of individual movement between battalions, more flexibility, less re-roling. Stability would be better served by having more battalions and more circumspection in undertaking far-flung campaigns; movement between battalions has long been practised; flexibility springs from adaptability, not from organized conformity; re-roling is almost second nature to those who have served in the Army since the war and undertaken an infinite variety of operational duties.

The trouble sprang from the Army Board's pursuit of a chimera. They conceived that by abandoning the so-called Arms Plot [the planned re-roling and redeployment of infantry and armoured regiments] more of these fighting units would be available for operations, as fewer – so they argued - would be tied up with their change of role. The Treasury were, of course, quick to seize on what they classified as 'spare' regiments and battalions, and the Army Board were hard put to justify even the 36 battalions, the eventually agreed number. So the group system emerged. More to the point would have been how to avoid the severe overstretch caused by waging unnecessary and unwinnable campaigns in Iraq and Afghanistan with inadequate resources and inappropriate weapons. Had the Army Board seen fit to insist on the retention of 40 infantry battalions and 15 armoured regiments, and insisted also on correcting some of the failings which have led to soldiers' discontent – by ensuring proper pay, adequate and relevant equipment and weapons, excellent accommodation for single soldiers and married ones – this overstretch could have been prevented and the premature resignations of experienced, valued officers and men, tired of such neglect – could have been staunched.

Yet these things were not done and the resultant hotchpotch which took away some of the noblest names of British infantry regiments can but put us in mind of Othello's despairing cry that he had thrown a pearl away richer than all his tribe. Let this be the epitaph of that particular Army Board. But now we must see how gallantly and how well, despite this untimely meddling, those regiments deployed to new theatres of war conducted themselves when required to liberate

Kuwait, bring peace of a sort to the Balkans, save Sierra Leone from chaos, and however misguided in concept, interfere once more in the affairs of Iraq and play a new sort of Great Game in Afghanistan.

We will take a look at these campaigns shortly, but first we will do well to observe that a great change was beginning to take place in the conduct of British foreign policy and hence in the Army's employment. As noted earlier the Falklands affair had been an action in support of essentially British interests, although it may also have sent a useful message to military dictators other than Galtieri not to get too big for their boots.

But when it comes to our interference in Iraq and other places, whether the Balkans or Afghanistan, we come face to face with the question which was posed by Haldane in 1906: 'What is the Army for?' Apart from protecting our Imperial concerns, he was soon to discover that it was to come to France's aid should Kaiser Wilhelm II ignore Bismarck's advice and see himself as an all-conquering War Lord. If we pose the question again now – or from the time Blair assumed the mantle of office – we may return a different answer. We may say that no longer was the Army's task simply to contribute to the defence of the realm and fulfil certain treaty obligations, but in addition to assume a kind of moral strategy, which would include supporting the US by preventing genocide in ethnic cleansing, bring 'democracy' to some countries to whom such a political concept was not merely foreign, but undesirable, and also supporting the United States, whose President seemed bent on regime changes and was determined to counter the threat of al-Qaeda which had made clear how real this threat was by the so-called 9/11 act of murder most foul.

We all know now how bogus was Blair's justification for joining the United States in the attack on Iraq which began in 2003. There were no WMDs and neither Bush nor Blair was prepared to exercise restraint and obtain UN approval for their descent on Iraq. Yet what was lacking from the very outset of this campaign was what is fundamental to the successful pursuit of overseas military adventures – an absolutely clear aim of military operations and an equally clear plan of action once the military side of the business is completed. This fatal lack of clarity landed the British Army in a quagmire of uncertainty, loss of life and ineffectual activity.*

This strategic bungling of what might be called the second Gulf War is admirably illustrated by comparing it with the First Gulf War,

* The war-mongers should have recalled General Templer's shrewd question during the Suez fiasco: 'We can take Cairo if you like. But what do you want us to do then?'

the wholly justifiable and successful ejection of Iraq's armed forces from Kuwait after Saddam Hussein's invasion of that country in 1991, and we will now examine this earlier campaign before contrasting it with the latter one. It was on 2 August 1990 that the strong man of Iraq made another of his customarily faulty calculations and despatched his armed forces to overwhelm Kuwait. Not only did the Iraqi army rapidly occupy that country. They threatened Saudi Arabia. In short there was a first class crisis in the Arabian Gulf, and for once the United Nations acted swiftly and decisively. On the very day of the invasion Resolution 660 condemned Iraq's action and demanded their withdrawal. Further Resolutions put an embargo on trade with Iraq, imposed a naval blockade, restricted air flights, authorized the detention of Iraqi shipping, and most important of all approved the means necessary to drive Iraqi forces from Kuwait if they had not already quitted the country by mid-January 1991. Now was the moment for Margaret Thatcher to demonstrate once more that she really was an Iron Lady and she seized the chance with both hands.

Her bullying of George Bush père persuaded him not to 'wobble' and a powerful Coalition force assembled both in Saudi Arabia and at sea. In his excellent autobiography that exceptionally able and intrepid soldier, Peter de la Billière, explains that as the build-up of US, British and other countries' armies and air power gathered pace from September 1990 onwards, so 'our posture changed from one of defence to that of offence: from seeking to contain the Iraqis, we swung round to the aim of driving them from Kuwait, first by threats and finally by force'.

Force it had to be for Saddam Hussein showed no inclination to withdraw. Intelligence sources revealed that the Iraqi army had deployed in Kuwait and on the frontier with Saudi Arabia some half million men in strong defensive positions supported by artillery and armour. It was also believed that the Iraqis possessed chemical and biological weapons and were prepared to use them. Allied strategy had the virtue of being both simple and sound. It was to build up their own armies to an adequate strength, then launch air attacks on Iraqi positions to halve their capability, and only then advance with ground troops to overwhelm and destroy the enemy. Simplicity and soundness, coupled with great numerical superiority, were quick to pay dividends. The air war began on 17 January 1991 and was strikingly effective. During the next five weeks the Iraqi air force ceased to exist, their command and control neutralized, their navy shattered. At the same time the Iraqi army deployed in defensive positions was subjected to such prolonged harassing that when the Allied ground assault was launched on 24 February, it was all over bar the shouting in four days.

How did the British division get on? Peter de la Billière, commander British Forces, Middle East, gives high praise to his subordinate commanders, in particular the divisional commander, Rupert Smith, a man after his own heart, calm, unorthodox, of independent spirit and wholly to be trusted to carry out orders without further direction. He was just the man for what was to come. Equally reliable, thrusting and imaginative was the 7th Armoured Brigade commander, Patrick Cordingley, who set about preparing his brigade for desert fighting, something of a change from the tasks envisaged in the British Army of the Rhine for which armoured and infantry soldiers had so long trained. Patrick Cordingley was comparably fortunate in that one of the regiments in his brigade was my own – The Queen's Royal Irish Hussars, commanded by Arthur Denaro.

The overall commander, General Schwarzkopf, US Army, had to bear in mind, of course, what the Iraqis might do while the Coalition forces were building up to the required strength. Fortunately Saddam Hussein had little understanding either of what he was up against or what sort of strategy would be most effective in dealing with it. He did little except reinforce his static defences. Meanwhile Schwarzkopf decided rather than make his main thrust a frontal attack into Kuwait from the south, he could most effectively use his powerful armoured forces in a bold, wide left hook which would sweep in from the western Iraqi desert and so take the more competent Republican Guard troops in the flank. What is more Peter de la Billière persuaded Schwarzkopf that the British armoured regiments, equipped with formidable Challenger tanks, were ideally suited for operating in the open western desert.

John Keegan, whose fame as our most distinguished military historian has never been greater, pointed out in his book about the Iraq war that Saddam Hussein's gross misappreciation of what the Coalition forces were capable of led him into a fatally vulnerable deployment of his army. He concentrated it between the head of the Gulf and the Wadi-al-Batin, with its foremost positions manned by some thirty divisions of the regular army, and in depth behind half a dozen divisions of the far steadier Republican Guard, ready either to support the defences or mount counter-attacks. Thus the Iraqi dispositions were such that they invited an outflanking attack by the Coalition. This invitation was not declined, and Allied strategy was essentially to pin the enemy forces in their defensive positions while executing a bold and wide sweep from the western desert, so taking Republic Guard divisions from the flank, then encircling and rolling up the entire Iraqi defences – in short a classic manoeuvre. The plan worked perfectly declared John Keegan.

Day 1 saw United States and Arab forces attacking Iraqi positions and knocking out their tanks, while the outflanking armoured units moved further north and east in the desert. On Day 2 these armoured formations began to threaten Iraqi reserve positions, while the third day saw further advances by the frontally attacking US and Arab forces and a deeper penetration by the left-flanking armour against the Iraqi rear. Finally on the fourth day, while the US and Arab armies completed their liberation of Kuwait, the outflanking desert columns reached the Euphrates thus trapping the rest of the Iraqi's army.

These grand manoeuvrings are airily described, but for those on the ground there was the prospect of battle, of shooting at some unknown adversary and being shot at. That real war was on the menu was made plain by Peter de la Billière, who on 13 January 1991, four days before the air war began, spoke to all Commanding Officers and warned them that real live fighting was now inevitable. Up to this time there had been some expectation that the United States-Iraqi talks in Geneva might lead to a negotiated settlement, but this had proved illusory. The chips were down, and those who now knew that there was some fighting to be done underwent a kind of mental readjustment. On the whole this removal of uncertainty had brought with it a sort of relief, and the trooper in his Challenger, the private soldier in his Warrior were conscious of a sense of excitement and anticipation of the trial to come. Besides there was much to do in preparation for the day of battle, including the tedious business of climbing into and out of NBC kit, in case the threat of enemy chemical weapons should turn out to be a real one.

For the ordinary soldier the eloquence, determination, confidence and assurance of his officers may be a comfort. For a Commanding Officer the knowledge that he is shortly to take his Regiment into action against a foe known to be well-equipped and possessing weapons of a particularly nasty sort concentrates his mind. It is, however, a relief that he, more than most, has much to do, and has little time for introspection. There is also the heartening reflection that you are part of a great team, supported by tried and trusted subordinates, commanded by sound, confident, competent generals. Furthermore, letters from home are precious and advice from former

Colonels of the Regiment – 'get plenty of sleep and don't worry' – is welcome.

There was much to be done before the day of action arrived. Regiments were required to move to new concentration areas, and despite the supposedly limitless space provided by the desert, as 7th Armoured Division redeployed, together with formations from other Coalition nations, there seemed to be an endless dispute between rival columns for the right to get forward, resulting in the overtaking of slower vehicles by impatient thrusters and so exposing themselves to further hazards from empty trucks hurtling in the opposite direction. This particular move took six hours, double the estimated time, but what a relief it was to find the advance party well established in the new position. Yet there is still no immediate prospect of battle, as the Divisional Commander, Rupert Smith warns his subordinates that the air war must continue for two more weeks before ground troops will be committed to action,

There is, however, still plenty of talking to be done. Rupert Smith and Patrick Cordingley regularly visit their regiments to brief the soldiers on the latest situation and succeed in conveying their own confidence to all ranks. It is clear that the air strikes are proving most effective. Other visitors inevitably include the press, and the troops are fortunate in engaging the sympathy and support of such veterans as Martin Bell and Kate Adie.

'Three-quarters of a soldier's life,' observed Rosenstock-Huessey, 'is spent in aimlessly waiting about'. The officers and men of my Regiment, The Irish Hussars, might be forgiven for agreeing that there was a good deal of waiting about to be endured during the first Gulf War, but they would emphatically disagree that it was aimless. The cold, wet weather did not interfere with sand model exercises designed to simulate the forthcoming advance, and time spent in perfecting the preparation of weapons and equipment was never wasted. During one of his visits to the Regiment, Patrick Cordingley reads Kipling's ever popular poem *If*. Arthur Denaro recalled that it was both moving and inspiring. He also remembered sitting on his thunder-box one morning, reading articles about stalking and grouse shooting, while reflecting that there would shortly be a different type of shooting to be indulged in. Would the Regiment get through it all successfully?

On 5th February 1991 7th Armoured Division was once more on the move, this time from concentration to staging area, some 50 kms with thousands of vehicles, some wheeled, some tracked, crossing and recrossing each other. This move was designed to get 7th Armoured Brigade into a counter-penetration position, some 50 kms forward by first light next morning, a formidable undertaking. Yet it was done, and next day the whole brigade, Irish Hussars centre, Staffordshire Regiment left, Royal Scots Dragoon Guards right, was deployed in its planned position. The achievement of this tricky redeployment gave everyone involved great confidence both in their equipment and in themselves, a great morale booster for what was still to come.

The real thing was still nearly three weeks away, but when it came all the mounting confidence was more than justified. By midday on 24th February The Irish Hussars had gone through the minefield breach and reached their Forming-Up-Place, passing surrendered Iraqi prisoners of war, and were poised and ready to lead the brigade, indeed the whole British division into Iraq. Off they went, D Squadron in the van, A Squadron left, B Squadron right. As the Regiment advanced they found themselves facing an enemy position, but they pushed on to a planned phase line in rain and darkness, with The Royal Scots Dragoon Guards on the right making contact with the enemy and knocking out six Iraqi tanks and taking prisoners.

After an artillery barrage on suspected enemy positions, The Irish Hussars pushed on again with lots of Iraqi soldiers wielding white flags in surrender, until Cordingley ordered a halt at the next phase line. Next morning D Squadron reports enemy vehicles approaching, moves forward to fire positions to engage them, knocks out half a dozen or so, while others sheer off to the north. At six o'clock the Regiment pushed forward to another report line and engages Iraqi T55 tanks, scoring more kills and taking more prisoners. After further action accompanied by violent sand storms – 'strong enough to blow your steel helmet off' – The Irish Hussars consolidate their position on the next objective. The next two days are sufficient to wrap up the whole thing. A new plan is made to seize ground behind the Iraqi defences and cut the enemy off from withdrawal. It works and the Irish Hussars reach their objective by 8 o'clock on the morning of 28th February. General Rupert Smith arrives and congratulates Arthur Denaro. The Regiment moves to a final leaguer and a cease fire is declared and holds. Denaro notes in his diary: 'I really believe the war is over which is tremendous. A hundred hour war. And we have done it. The Regiment has done it so well, really magnificent. Every man playing such an important part; such good lads. Let us go home now, safe and sound'.

Such were some of the jottings of a regimental commander. How did it all appear to the overall British commander, who saw his whole career – a star-studded one, personifying gallantry, imagination and perseverance – as equipping him to take command of all British forces in the Middle East at this particular time, for this particular purpose? I refer, of course, to Peter de la Billière. He had always seen the British division's role as one to protect the US VII Corps' right flank as it executed its bold left hook against the Iraqi Republican Guard. After gaps in the enemy's minefield had been cleared, Rupert Smith's division, led by 7th Armoured Brigade had advanced on the afternoon of 25th February. By pushing forward, first with this brigade, next with 4th Brigade, and supported by artillery. including multiple rocket launchers, the division made its way to a series of objectives to surround enemy concentrations and knock out their tanks and guns. While the British troops were equipped to cope with gas attacks, there were none. The British also possessed two crucially valuable pieces of technology – a system of telling vehicle commanders exactly where they were, together with special gun-sights which enabled tanks to fire their main armament with deadly accuracy at night. The surprise achieved by this wide outflanking attack by the British and American divisions was vividly demonstrated by the revelation that many of the Iraqi tanks were dug in facing south and unable to manoeuvre to face an assault from the west.

We have seen from Arthur Denaro's account of things that at dawn on 28th February, 7th Armoured Brigade got the whips out and made its final advance across the desert at 40 Kilometres per hour, reaching their final objective astride the Kuwait-Basra road, while thousands of Iraqis were either surrendering or fleeing north-eastwards. At 8 o'clock that morning the order came to suspend offensive operations. 'By then', wrote de la Billière, 'after three days and nights with practically no sleep, officers and men were grey-faced with exhaustion, and Rupert Smith, realizing how much people's faculties had been eroded, took to issuing all orders in written form. His division had advanced three hundred kilometres, destroyed most of three Iraqi armoured divisions, and taken more than seven thousand prisoners'. At a press conference that evening, de la Billière urged the British people to ring their church bells 'because the British service men and women in the Gulf have won a great victory'. It is pleasing to record that they did.

In the closing part of his autobiography, Peter de la Billière poses the question which has puzzled many an observer and commentator. Should the Coalition forces have followed up their victory by going on to Baghdad, with a view presumably to removing Saddam Hussein and establishing some other form of of government. There could be no other reason for doing so. For many reasons de la Billière rejects the idea and believes it was right to stop the war when they did. Saddam Hussein would certainly not have waited about to be captured. Whether he would have disappeared somewhere within Iraq or sought refuge in some other Arab country hardly matters. But what would the Coalition forces have done in Baghdad, with no government to deal with, the country itself in ruins, and no plans whatever to assume control, to say nothing of resources? Besides, such a move would not have been supported by other Arab countries. Nor indeed was there any United Nations backing for it. The Coalition's task had been to liberate Kuwait and that they had done. So far we may go along with de la Billière's views, but when he suggests that we should have insisted on Saddam Hussein's surrendering himself with a view to signing a peace treaty which would authorize the UN to conduct inspections of Iraq's military capabilities, and further proposes that the Coalition Forces should occupy southern Iraq until Saddam complied, I part company with him. With his astonishing ability to paint defeat as victory and with his seemingly unassailable position as not just Iraq's leader but also as a kind of Pan-Arab champion, Saddam would have sat tight, built up his forces again, harassed the UN forces in the south, and by his defiance won more golden opinions from those not wholly disposed to support American policy. There would also have been the vexed question of oil. But leaving all that aside , there had never been any intention of invading Iraq with a view to its occupation and administration. Therefore no plan of any sort existed to do so. And we have only to think of the appalling and bloody chaos which followed the more recent Iraq war to conclude that the decision not to follow up the successful ejection of Iraqi forces from Kuwait by going on to Baghdad was the right one. But this does not excuse the failure to plan for the aftermath of a successful campaign.

One of the final points made by Peter de la Billière in his autobiography is that if our politicians decide to commit our armed forces to war, they must 'have the courage to listen primarily to the advice of their military commanders' and 'must commit all available resources and finance . . . to ensure that their military forces have everything they need to win as quickly as possible'. Alas, there are some instances in conflicts still to be described where political courage and commitment have been wanting.

The relatively small affair in Sierra Leone in the year 2000, however, was not of them. Just how small it was, involving a thousand or so British soldiers, is emphasized by recalling that the Iraq war had demanded the presence of some 45,000 service men and women, the most numerous deployment of British forces beyond Europe since the Second World War. The complexities of the struggle for power in Sierra Leone need not concern us here. What is important is that the intervention of British forces there was crucial to the re-establishment of legitimate government. However much we may deplore some other military adventures of Mr Blair, we may perhaps concede that action in Sierra Leone was both politically sound and militarily effective. That it was the latter was, of course, because of the boldness, skill and sheer effectiveness of the British Army and the Royal Marines. That it was the former was after all in keeping with Mr Blair's pledge to protect and help those African leaders who would suppress corruption, promote their economies and encourage democracy.

In May 2000 the United Nations Mission in Sierra Leone claimed that they had disarmed some 24,000 of the so-called Revolutionary United Front, whose leader was Foday Sankoh. But the RUF, taking advantage of Nigeria's withdrawal of UN committed troops, while claiming to cooperate with Zambian and other UN forces, began to mount sustained attacks on these forces. It was then that the arrival of British troops prevented a coup by Sankoh to take over Sierra Leone's government. The 1st Battalion, Parachute Regiment and 42 Commando, Royal Marines, deployed in Freetown and secured the airport at Lungi. They then conducted evacuation of non-Sierra Leoneans, particularly those from Western Countries, and then the Parachute battalion positioned itself to secure the important areas – airport, sea port and Freetown itself. In his admirable account of the whole affair, Lansana Gberie shows how a small but resolute group of British soldiers could have a profound influence on the turn of events:

> The British deployed the Parachute Regiment's Pathfinder Platoon near Lungi under the command of Sergeant Stephen Heaney. That week RUF troops, trying to capture the airport, attacked the platoon at night but were repulsed; over twenty of the rebel force, which outnumbered the British five to one, were killed, with the British sustaining no casualties. The operation helped to convince the RUF, if this was needed, that it was up against a very powerful enemy indeed. Sankoh's arrest less than two

weeks after this incident completed the demoralisation of the RUF. The UN mission had been saved from imminent collapse.

Nor was this all, There was shortly to be another demonstration of what could be achieved by small numbers of British soldiers who were trained to combine careful planning with dash, skill and action which surprised and dismayed their enemies. Among the numerous guerrilla groups seeking to overthrow the government of President Kabbah was one with a notably evil reputation. They called themselves the West Side Boys and were the remnants of the so-called People's Army led by Major Koroma. This group succeeded in capturing eight British soldiers, whom they then held hostage, demanding new elections and the resignation of Kabbah. During negotiations to resolve the crisis, this group was short-sighted enough to insist on being supplied by the British with food and radio equipment, which in turn led to their revealing where their hideout in the bush was, and where the hostages were being held. With the indispensable aid of the SAS – almost always crucially involved in the resolution of such difficulties – a raid on their positions was launched by British parachute troops which was an instant success. Twenty six of the rebels were killed, their leader, a Major Kallay, was taken and the eight hostages freed.

This was in September 2000 by which time there were about one thousand British troops in Sierra Leone, and one of their tasks was to retrain the local army. It was done most effectively and by early in the following year, between four and five thousand of Sierra Leone's army had completed their training. Meanwhile there had been a further ceasefire agreement between the UN and the RUF, which together with an impressive military display of strength by the Royal Marines convinced the RUF that it was time to honour their pledge to disarm, a process which was largely completed by January 2002. Four months later a general and presidential election was held. Kabbah obtained 70 per cent of the vote, and as Lansana Gberie puts it: 'Sierra Leone was once again declared at peace'. Mr Blair could bask in the reflection that Britain was rewarded with the largest share of praise for bringing peace to Sierra Leone. In speculating on this point Gberie observes that the answer lies in the timing of British intervention, the resources made available and the sheer experience and reputation of British troops. 'No one failed to notice', he writes, 'that it was the robust presence of the British troops that prevented the total collapse of the UN mission and a relapse into violence'.

We come now to the events of 11 September 2001 which changed everything. These events, writes John Keegan, or '9/11 as the day soon became universally known – caused shock throughout the world. In the United States, it provoked a revolution, changing national sentiment and redirecting national policy'. Up to this time the United States had taken the lead in cementing a Western alliance which had successfully maintained peace in Europe, such distractions as Kosovo notwithstanding. Now, seeing enemies everywhere, the United States concentrated more firmly on its own security, with the added watchword that those who were not on side would be regarded as positively hostile. The result of this totally revised strategic posture was war – war in Afghanistan and war in Iraq, At this time Great Britain, whose Prime Minister was, as Libby Purves most felicitously put it, 'naïve, vain and unreflecting' took the fateful step of allying itself closely to United States policy and became heavily committed to both these wars.

At this point it is meet to remind ourselves of the two great rules of strategy, each of which is dependent on the other. The first is correctly to select your primary object. This is the master rule. The second rule is so to concentrate and deploy your forces that you achieve the object. There is perhaps a third rule, which obvious though it is, is sometimes ignored or distorted or manipulated to conform to the conclusion which its manipulators desire. This third rule is that your strategic intelligence must be indisputably accurate, based on concrete fact, so that sound conclusions may be drawn from it. There must be no devious speculation, no over emphasis or under emphasis to guide the decision makers this way or that. The manner in which these assuredly well-founded principles of war could be honoured both in the breach and the observance could hardly be better illustrated than by comparing our two recent adventures in Iraq – the first Gulf War and the current debacle.

As we have seen the first of these two wars was a straightforward affair. Saddam Hussein had invaded Kuwait and threatened Saudi Arabia. The strategic object was therefore clear – to prevent further Iraqi aggression and to liberate Kuwait. All that was needed to achieve this object was to deploy and then employ sufficient military force. What is more the intelligence was accurate and appropriately acted upon. What was not done was to consider action which might be both possible and proper *after* the achievement of the main object. But all in all the strategy was correctly selected and effectively pursued. How utterly different is the story when we come to consider the second Iraqi adventure.

If we now pose the question as to whether the critical rules of strategy were properly considered or observed for the invasion of Iraq in 2003, we are likely to get a dusty answer. What was the primary object in this case? It depends whom you ask. George W Bush would presumably say that it was a response to the terrorist attack on the Twin Towers of 11 September 2001 and part of the United States' determination to deal with al-Qaeda; Alan Greenspan, on the other hand, would say it was all about oil; the dossier-bearing Mr Blair would waffle about weapons of mass destruction – later shown to be illusory – and the establishment of a democratic regime in Iraq, despite the oxymoronic sin of placing the words, Arab and democracy, side by side. Others might argue that Saddam Hussein's regime had to be changed as it constituted a general threat to Middle Eastern stability. Ironically the very reverse seem to have resulted.

But we have perhaps said enough to establish that the object of the whole operation was far from clear. Equally uncertain was what was to be done when Saddam Hussein had been removed, and this uncertainty or unwillingness to face the issue was to lead to appalling errors of management when the initial conflict was over. As if these circumstances were insufficient to bring about a situation which seemed to defy control or order or a peaceful progress to cooperation between the various sources of power, the Coalition was doomed from the start by the ignorance, arrogance and malign influence of the US Secretary of Defence. It is no surprise to discover when we come to the second great strategic rule – to concentrate and deploy your forces in such a way as to achieve the primary object – that here too there is a lack of clarity, purpose or certainty simply because the object itself was so confused. Since our purpose here, however, is to describe how the British forces conducted themselves, we may leave aside the political blundering and strategic misapprehension of Mr Blair [no one now believes that his support for the Iraq affair was other than his slavish eagerness to cosy up to George W Bush] and take a look at the difficult tasks our soldiers had and how well they carried them out. We will take a look at Afghanistan later.

The British contribution to the invasion of Iraq in 2003 was substantial. Apart from naval and air forces, an entire division was deployed, made up of 7th Armoured Brigade, veterans of the earlier Iraq war, and two specialised brigades, 16 Air Assault and 3 Commando. The Assault Brigade had two parachute battalions, 1st and 3rd, and 1st Battalion, The Royal Irish Regiment, whose Commanding Officer, Lieutenant-Colonel Tim Collins showed that the days of pre-battle rhetoric, so effectively employed by Henry V at Agincourt, were not over. He found words which did not merely steel his soldiers' hearts, but confirmed Napoleon's point that one of the qualities inherent to a successful commander was eloquence such as appeals to soldiers. Indeed Collins' words rang triumphantly round the world*, and the fine performance of his battalion confirmed their inspiring effect. The British division was required to make for the Shatt el-Arab and Basra. The divisional commander, Major-General Brims, was determined to avoid a serious fight for Iraq's second largest city. He therefore invested it, and from 23 to 31 March, deployed his intelligence gathering agents, including both SAS and SBS teams, plus other infantry patrols, to discover whether it would be possible to occupy Basra without too much bloodshed.

Some blood was shed however. On the night of 26/27 March, some fifteen Iraq T-55 tanks were unwise enough to make a sortie towards the British lines, only to be encountered at first light by a squadron of The Royal Scots Dragoon Guards, equipped with the vastly superior Challengers, which swiftly knocked out their opponents with no loss to themselves. By the end of the month General Brims felt that he had a sufficiently clear picture of what was going on in Basra to behave more aggressively by sending small parties of observers and snipers to attack Ba'ath leaders and enemy soldiers. Meanwhile many of Basra's inhabitants, who were primarily Shi'a Muslims, and intolerant of Saddam Hussein's Sunni Muslims of the Ba'athist party, were leaving the city. Next, further ventures into Basra were made to destroy Ba'athist positions. For this task the speedy, well-armed Warriors, with which the British infantry were equipped, proved invaluable. Finally General Brims sent in his troops to assault and capture the city. He was rewarded by instant success. It is pleasing to record John Keegan's comment that British commanders had great confidence that their soldiers would fight with spirit and effect. 'The regimental system ensures this'.

Brims organized his forces into battle groups, each composed of infantry companies in their Warriors and armoured squadrons with Challenger tanks. There was some resistance from the so-called fedayeen, groups of terrorists from countries other than Iraq, including Moroccans, Syrians and Algerians, but such resistance was no match for the British infantry's skill and fire power. By the end of 6 April, General Brim's forces were masters of Basra, and next day the

* Collins had himself, I believe, been influenced by another's eloquence as to a soldier's duty and conduct in the field.

battalions of 16 Air Assault Brigade, two from the Parachute Regiment plus Colonel Collins' Royal Irish Regiment occupied the city. On the day after that the British troops, anxious to demonstrate their commitment to restore everyday order, discarded their body armour and steel helmets for the more reassuring regimental headgear, and climbing out of their armoured vehicles, strolled among the inhabitants, with instructions, as John Keegan puts it, 'to smile, chat and restore the appearance of normality' and start once more that well known process, begun some fifty years earlier and continued all over the world, of winning the battle of hearts and minds. This was not to prove as easy as had been hoped, but nevertheless, as John Keegan has told us, the British had every reason to be satisfied with what their soldiers had achieved:

> The British campaign had been an undoubted success. They had secured all their objectives – the Fao peninsula, the Shatt el-Arab, the oil terminals, Iraq's second city – quickly and at minimal cost. British loss of life was slight. They had also conducted their war in a fashion that appeared to leave them, as the representatives of the coalition, on good terms with the southern population of defeated Iraq. The inhabitants of Basra made it clear, to the British soldiers who took possession of their city, that they were glad to be rid both of the representatives of Saddam's regime and of the foreign fighters who supported it. If a new Iraq were to be created from the ruins of the old, Basra seemed the most promising point at which to start.

Winning the peace, however, is frequently a much more difficult affair than applying military force to bring peace about. It was not long before the influence of al-Qaeda, the emergence of militia groups, the interference of Iran combined to make life unpleasant for the British regiments in the south of Iraq. Small arms fire, rockets and road-side bombs were the principal threats, as the experience of The Queen's Royal Hussars record. In April 2006 the Regiment's battle group took over from The Royal Scots Dragoon Guards at Abu Naji camp with C Squadron and two companies of infantry. Within three weeks they had their first contact with an enemy ambush near the River Tigris and killed seven or eight terrorists. Life in the camp could be most disagreeable and during the four months that they were there, they had been subjected to nearly three hundred rocket and mortar attacks. There was also the intemperate weather. It was quite common for temperatures of over 60 degrees Celsius *in the shade* to be reached, while conditions in the infantry's Warriors and the Regiment's

Challenger tanks were a daily burden. Outside the camp on patrol there was a constant threat of road-side bombs and ambushes with automatic weapons. In particular the lines of communication were vulnerable and obvious targets for the insurgents. Yet the battle group always reacted robustly to these constant attacks, earning itself a high reputation and resulting in the award of a number of Military Crosses, Mentions in Despatches and Conspicuous Gallantry Crosses.

In August The Queen's Royal Hussars battle group quitted Abu Naji and deployed in the desert. It was a great relief to be free of the enemy mortar and rocket attacks and of the constraints imposed by a fixed base. The Regiment released its infantry companies to reinforce Basra itself, but assumed command of a Queen's Dragoon Guards squadron, and together, using Landrovers rather than tanks, they patrolled among the Iraqis who needed their help, rapidly earning their trust and respect, and as a result sustained only two attacks, which did no more than inflict minor casualties. It was possible for the Commanding Officer to record that the Regiment 'went to Iraq and did their duty with skill, panache and a surfeit of bravery' of which they could be profoundly proud. There were, however, still some casualties to be reckoned with even after withdrawal from Iraq for – again the Commanding Officer – 'prolonged exposure to such a high level of heat, threat, fear, death and destruction does deep-rooted damage to the best trained soldier and we continue to look after everyone with this in mind.'

Now at the time of writing there has been a further change in the deployment and mission of the British troops in southern Iraq. Withdrawal altogether from the vulnerable bases in Basra itself, with a readiness to come to the assistance of Iraqi security forces, now responsible for control of Basra, should this be necessary. Concentrated at the air base outside the city, with the intention of reduction first to some five thousand, later to half that figure, we may perhaps conclude that for the British soldiers, the Iraqi adventure is approaching its end. Not so in Afghanistan, where a very different sort of war is being waged. But before we take a look, let us peer briefly at what happened in Kosovo

We have taken note of the three positive maxims of strategy by which those intent on waging war would do well to be guided – get your intelligence right; select correctly your prime object [this is the master rule]; deploy and employ force necessary to achieve this object. We may also acknowledge that there are three negative maxims which it would be prudent to observe: don't march on Moscow; don't get involved in the Balkans; don't invade Afghanistan. The British Army has succeeded in avoiding an expedition to seize Moscow, but has not evaded involvement in Afghanistan or the Balkans, as many books by those in charge, including those by Michael Rose and Mike Jackson, have testified.

We will come to the former theatre of war later, but it will be as well to record that the Kosovo business brought credit on British political and military men. Indeed it may be said, even now at the time of writing that the business may be far from finished as Kosovo declares independence from Serbia, and our spearhead battalion, in this case The Welsh Guards, is warned to be ready for deployment there. Kosovo was a humanitarian operation, embraced by both United Nations and NATO. Not to have intervened might have resulted in the most appalling ethnic conflict to have ravaged that troubled land of Serbs, Albanians and Kosovars, a blood bath to have rivalled the Bulgarian atrocities which so troubled William Gladstone in 1876.

British troops conducted themselves admirably and their presence enabled General Jackson to defy orders from SACEUR, the US General Wesley Clark, to seize from the Russians Slatina airport, near the capital, Pristina, and make his celebrated comment that he was not going to start the Third World War for Clark. Not that it would have done, of course, but there are fleeting moments in a soldier's life when he is presented with the opportunity of saying something for posterity and this was one of them. Intervention in Kosovo also had the beneficial effect of bringing about the downfall of that sinister figure, Slobodan Milosevic. A report from an armoured squadron commander, whose task in 2002 was to help maintain in Kosovo 'a safe and secure environment in order to establish conditions for a peaceful and democratic society' talks of so-called surge operations, which called for deploying widely for weeks at a time, living under canvas, recovering vehicles which had become bogged and half-drowned, and doing all they could do ensure that the environment did remain safe and secure.

The report goes on to explain that much of their time was taken up with searching houses and vehicles for weapons and to curb smuggling. Some of these operations were undertaken with other national contingents, such as the Norwegians. A joint combing of the Drinica Valley succeeded in revealing former defensive positions of the Serbian Army and was further rewarded by finding weapons. Later one troop of the Squadron joined a Finnish battalion and deployed with them to Mitrovica in northern Kosovo to conduct further searches and public order training. Despite language difficulties one perseverant trooper was able to perfect his ability to calm and control frustrated, impatient Kosovan drivers by sheer force of personality.

The Squadron was also engaged in cooperating with Czechs and Slovaks for search operations in the boundary area between Kosovo and Serbia. Two troops were required to make further searches of trucks and heavy goods vehicles in Pristina itself, where some of the troopers found the change from the natural scenic beauty of the countryside enhanced by the presence 'of highly decorative females in summer attire'. Next came what was described as the highlight of the tour – deployment to the Macedonian Border in the United States' sector. Here they were to support a US battalion, known as The Vanguards, and were allocated an area of operations, where they established observation posts, patrolled against cross-border smuggling and gun running, conducted area searches which resulted in the detention of known extremists. All in all it had been a challenging and rewarding tour. At the time of writing we still have a commitment in Kosovo and the British Army will continue to provide a surveillance capability there. But, of course, this commitment pales in extent and consequence when compared with what is going on in Afghanistan.

Our military adventures in that wild, intriguing country have not always been crowned with notable success and our minds must inevitably go back to the campaign which provided a truly stupendous example of how not to conduct military operations against the tribesmen of Afghanistan.

The retreat from Kabul in January 1842, humiliating finale to the First Afghan War, fulfilled exactly the prediction made by General John Keane, who in 1839 had commanded the expedition which took Kabul and restored the despised, yet legitimate ruler, Shah Shuja, to the throne. There would before long, said Keane, be a 'signal catastrophe'. Just how signal it was may be judged by the measure of the British Army's defeat. On 6 January 1842 some 4,500 soldiers, with 600 of the 44th Foot (Essex Regiment) and a troop of Horse Artillery – the rest were East India Company troops, including 1,000 cavalry – set off from Kabul accompanied by some 12,000 camp-followers and families.

This heterogeneous column of redcoats, sepoys, camp followers and animals – apart from the horses, there were thousands of camels, mules and bullocks – faced a march of about a hundred miles to Jalalabad over mountain passes as high as 5,000 feet, in icy winter weather, with snow everywhere, inadequately clad, hungry, with no assured supplies and no protection from the hazardous passages through a series of defiles made for ambush. Had most of them reached Jalalabad in any sort of order, without interference by, even with the aid of, the Afghans, it would have been an astonishing achievement, indeed a near miracle. But given that they would be subjected to constant attack, ambush, harassment and treachery – and this is what happened from the moment they left Kabul – it was hardly surprising that the whole unfortunate multitude (except for one man who did reach Jalalabad) was either killed, dispersed, starved, captured or horribly wounded and left to die. Yet despite the almost total collapse of discipline, there were individual acts of heroism and sacrifice which even today must excite our wonder.

No such admiration may be levelled at the British commander, Major-General William Elphinstone, who is colourfully described by that dastardly, yet somehow *simpatico* warrior. Flashman (in George MacDonald Fraser's book): 'I will state unhesitatingly, that for pure, vacillating stupidity, for superb incompetence to command, for ignorance combined with bad judgement – in short, for the true talent for catastrophe – Elphy Bey stood alone . . . Elphy outshines them all as the greatest military idiot of our own or any other day'. We must be thankful that there is no room for such military idiots in the British Army of today, yet it would be interesting to learn whether any of our political or military leaders studied the progress of former campaigns in Afghanistan before embarking on the current one.

However much we may question the strategic purposes of our more recent operations in Afghanistan, at least the commanders on the ground are competent enough. It is when we come back to our master rule of strategy that doubts begin to emerge. What is the primary object of our being there? To defeat the Taleban? To bring democracy to a country that has always been run by one war lord or another? To root out al-Qaeda once and for all? To suppress the opium trade? To squash other sources of Islamic terrorism? We need only to pose such questions as these to see how absurdly unattainable they are. Despite shortages of weapons and equipment indispensable to the proper handling of operations – shortages for which ministers and officials in Whitehall are wholly responsible – our soldiers have shown great fortitude, skill, courage and perseverance in taking on the Taleban on their own ground. In most cases these operations have been successful. The trouble is that these successes have contributed little to realizing the supposedly real purposes of these soldiers being there at all –

peace, harmony, the restoration of essential services for an agreeable life, an end to the extremes of Islamic fanaticism, stable government, loyal, reliable security forces. At the beginning of his admiral book, *Battlefield Afghanistan*, Mike Ryan writes: 'Afghanistan has been the graveyard for many, and provided salvation for few – yet they still kept coming. Why? Because this beautiful yet troubled landlocked country is of immense strategic importance'. From the West's point of view, it may be assumed, what is important is that Afghanistan should not be hostile, or harbour elements which have declared their hostility, to Western interests. How is this to be achieved? Before we answer that question, we will do well to take a look at the British Army's recent record in that 'troubled landlocked country'.

As a result of 9/11 it was clearly necessary for the United States to take some action. Convinced, as the USA was, that al-Qaeda under the leadership of Osama bin Laden, had planned and executed the attacks on New York's World Trade Centre, and that Afghanistan, ruled as it was by the Taleban, was providing refuge and support for al-Qaeda terrorists, the USA with British support conducted a military campaign to remove the Taleban from power. In this they were successful and the Taleban regime fell in late 2001. There then began an international effort embracing an unlikely variety of organizations – NATO, the UN, the G8, the EU and the World Bank – to bring stability to Afghanistan and to embark on a programme of reconstruction. For this programme to succeed, it was clearly essential that the country should enjoy security, and it was with this strategic interest in mind that forces of the United Kingdom were committed to Afghanistan.

It was early in 2006 that the British contribution to the International Security Assistance Force was defined. Royal Engineers and a Royal Marine Company from 42 Commando would deploy to Helmand province together with a force of 3,300, composed of 16 Air Assault Brigade plus the 3rd Battalion, Parachute Regiment; Task Force HQ would be at Lashkar Gar, and helicopter support would be provided by 8 Apaches, 4 Lynx and six Chinooks. Alas, the whole thing has gone wrong. In an article for *The Sunday Times*, 3 February 2008, Simon Jenkins pointed out that there was a crisis created by London and Washington, who 'have no strategy for the continuing occupation of Afghanistan'. Instead there is dissension. The USA accuse Britain of not fighting the insurgents vigorously enough; the British are angered by the American destruction of Helmand's poppy crop, the only source of income for the inhabitants – hardly the best recipe for winning hearts and minds. In short Jenkins concludes what many observers have long maintained that 'Afghanistan is a nasty war we can never win'. He might have added that fighting a war on two fronts is not a strategic course to be recommended. The IFS of history are notably capricious, but put the case that from 2001 onwards, we had concentrated solely on Afghanistan, leaving Iraq alone for for the time being, and in alliance with the United States and other NATO countries, seen to it that President Karzai would enjoy a period of security, reconstruction and re-emergence of the Afghan military and police forces, whilst supporting a judicious policy of granting some political and administrative power to the tribal leaders, while at the same time giving the Taleban no respite, put the case that this had been our strategy, is it not possible that by now the position of Afghanistan would be far more favourable than it actually is. But back to reality!

If ever a conflict qualified to be one of what Kipling called the savage wars of peace, then the British Army's fight against the Taleban is a first class candidate. It was a far cry from Dr John Reid's announcement in January 2006 that this country would send several thousand British troops to Helmand in southern Afghanistan for three years to help with the country's reconstruction and from whence they 'would be happy to leave without firing a shot!' Alas, it turned out to be rather different. As Mike Ryan records: 'Life for any British soldier involved in direct combat operations was extremely difficult as they were experiencing the most intense and sustained attacks on any British force since the Korean War. They had not just stirred up a hornets' nest – they were in it. The controversial decision to set up so-called platoon houses in certain Taleban-held areas of Helmand was made at the request of the provincial governor, who wanted an aggressive stance to be taken. And nobody in the British Army does aggression better than the Paras'.

These platoon houses were like thorns in the Taleban's flesh. Set up in positions commanding a town or village, they had the effect of dissipating the Taleban's domination of the local people, who were thus able to switch their loyalties, simply because the Taleban were now more concerned with attacking the platoon houses. In short a wholly different state of affairs had been created. Yet, as the Paras themselves conceded they were themselves inviting attack, had become what they called 'bullet magnets'. Many were the stories of such attacks. For our purposes here, one highlighted by Mike Ryan will serve. It was at Sangin, occupied by the Parachute Regiment in mid-2006, together with Royal Marines. It became known as the Red House, by virtue of the red berets worn by the Paras, and more chillingly because of British soldiers' blood spilt there:

> In July 2006 it was cut off and surrounded by the Taleban, leading to a vicious and sustained series of firefights that lasted for almost five weeks. During this period there were only three days in which the Taleban failed to mount an attack.
>
> Despite being a bloody month for both 3 Para and the Taleban, neither side broke. When news of the battle first reached the UK, there was outrage amongst the British public. Why had the Paras seemingly been abandoned?

Thus Mike Ryan, who goes on to explain that during this vicious contest the supply of food and ammunition for the British was faulty, and they were obliged to forage for provisions in the local villages and make do with ammunition for their .50 calibre machine guns which would fire only single shots and not automatic. Ryan also expressed his profound admiration for the soldiers and Royal Marines who endured these daily onslaughts for weeks on end, until eventually relieved by American and Canadian troops. We may most emphatically endorse this praise and agree too that the 'British forces are superb at engaging the Taleban and removing them from the various places that they hide out in. But all this effort is wasted if they cannot hold this ground. All the Taleban have to do is to wait for them to go'.

One of the conclusions reached by Mike Ryan is that British soldiers are facing what he calls 'a combat burnout' in that repeated tours of operational duty with insufficient time at home are causing the breakdown of marriages and families. So what is to be done? His answer is that we must either increase the size of the Army – and here I may perhaps reiterate my own estimate of the need for 40 infantry battalions, not 36, and 15 armoured regiments, not 11 – to do away with overstretch, or so adjust HMG's foreign policy that we do not allow ourselves to become overcommitted. It is a view emphatically endorsed by both today's field commanders and by three former Chiefs of Defence Staff. Both of these sources have repeatedly warned the government about the dangers of military overstretch, which results in experienced officers, NCOs and men electing to leave the service prematurely. They also have made it clear that 'inadequate supplies, underfunded operations, poor housing and medical support, derisory compensation for injury' – all have had their negative effect on the morale and well-being of the armed services. There is but one remedy. The government must spend more money on the armed forces. Lord Guthrie, who heads the UK National Defence Association, has made it clear that with wars in Iraq and Afghanistan 'we are quite honestly struggling and I don't know how much longer the services can go on like this'. The Association calls for current defence spending of some two per cent of gross national product to be increased to three per cent. Will ministers listen and act? We may recall that when Ludendorff declared that the British soldiers would fight like lions in the Great War, Hoffman reminded him that they were led by donkeys. Our soldiers are fighting like lions in Afghanistan now and are commanded by highly competent generals. But they were put there by a parcel of political donkeys.

The political donkeys have failed in the one respect for which they are specifically responsible and in theory possess the training and experience – the making of policy and provision of the means to put policy into practice. If we leave aside for the moment Mr Blair's gross mishandling of foreign policy, and turn instead to the more recent version of what can only be called 'interventionism', we observe that the new, young, inexperienced foreign secretary has come up with the idea of regimes which have some claim to be classified as democratic being offered by this country some guarantee of security if threatened by insurgency. Long before Mr Miliband made this declaration, the British Army's action in Sierra Leone had illustrated how this theory could work in practice. But when we contemplate the situation in Iraq and Afghanistan, can we say that intervention has promoted security? The notion is fanciful.

What is not fanciful is the utter failure of ministers and defence chiefs to follow a declaration of policy – in this case that of coming to the rescue of deserving regimes by assistance with their security – by providing our armed forces with the equipment and support indispensable for the prosecution of the agreed policy. As many commentators have emphasized: what is the relevance of Trident, of European fighter aircraft, of submarines, when what is actually and urgently needed are full strength infantry battalions, equipped with bomb-proof armoured vehicles, body armour, night vision and shooting devices, long range automatic machine guns, helicopters galore, first class and instantly available medical support? If we have learned anything at all from the campaigns which the British Army has waged since 1990, surely there it is.

I said at the outset that we would take a look at the Army's performance during the last two decades. In doing so it will be as well to acknowledge that there have been some disturbing reports that

British soldiers have ill-treated, even killed, Iraqis, who may or not have been insurgents. But such reports are rare and will no doubt be thoroughly investigated and dealt with. If we look at the whole picture, however, we see the British soldier boldly storming to victory in the first Gulf War, preventing ethnic cleansing in Kosovo, wrestling gallantly with ever more difficult conditions during the second Iraq invasion, restoring stability in Sierra Leone with minimal forces, and replaying the Great Game in Afghanistan with dogged defiance against ever growing difficulties. Operation *Eagle's Summit* to deliver turbine to Kajaki in August/September 2008 showed the British Army at its bold and brilliant best. *Shabash!*

Earlier I posed the question – has the British Army's reputation for skill, courage and perseverance, so strikingly illustrated by its performance between the years 1890 and 1990 pictured in *Gentlemen in Khaki* and reiterated here – has this reputation been preserved? Who can doubt it? Just as campaigns in the Sudan, in South Africa, Flanders, Gallipoli, whilst not always strategically wise or morally justified, had confirmed the British soldiers' versatility and doggedness, so this tradition for hanging on, no matter what the odds, was renewed during the Second World War. We need to think of only El Alamein, Cassino, Kohima, Normandy, Arnhem. It was further demonstrated by a whole series of counter insurgency campaigns in the Far East, the Middle East, even at home which our soldiers conducted from 1948 until overtaken by a different sort of challenge in the South Pacific and Mesopotamia.

It is when we come face to face with the *purpose* of all these wars that our current involvement in Iraq and Afghanistan may present us with a puzzle. No one would deny that the two World Wars had to be fought; few would hesitate to agree that those campaigns which gave independence to Malaya, survival to Malaysia, freedom from bullying to Oman, a brighter future to Northern Ireland and so on were necessary and proper. In each case the purpose was both clear and justifiable. So positive a view can hardly be taken in the case of Iraq or Afghanistan. Let us look at Afghanistan first. It is the simpler of the two.

If we could say that the overall purpose of war in Afghanistan were to effect a regime change by turning out the Taleban and inserting instead some kind of provincial government with President Karzai as the nominal head of a central authority, and at the same time search for and find Osama bin Laden in order to suppress the terrorist campaign initiated by him and al-Qaeda, then we might concede that there has indeed been a change of regime, however confused and nugatory it may be. But as for bin Laden and al-Qaeda - a blank. When we contemplate Karzai's position and his all too ready condemnation of the British action in his country – 'bungling military operations in Helmand and setting back prospects for the area by 18 months', – we may perhaps question whether this particular regime change has been for the good. The two great requirements of security and reconstruction seem to be as elusive as ever. We may also recall by glancing back that previous attempts to impose a change of regime on the Afghan people were not crowned with success.

In 1839 the British had turned out the then ruler of Afghanistan, Dost Mahommed, who in fact was pro-British, and had installed instead the flabby, vicious, despised Shah Shuja, whom no one wanted even though he might have been the rightful ruler. The result of it all was the disastrous retreat from Kabul which we have already touched on, and the reinstatement of Dost Mahommed who proved to be a good friend to the British. It all went to confirm what the one real expert on Afghanistan's affairs of that time, Sir Alexander Burnes, had always maintained: 'We shall never settle Afghanistan at the point of a bayonet'. Yet this is exactly what we are now once more trying to do. And once again there is installed a President who wields no power beyond the confines of Kabul. Whether British troops in Helmand total 7,000 or even more when we wind down in Iraq, there will be no solution to that troubled region until someone both acceptable to the people there and feared by the Taleban is restored to power, and according to Anthony Lloyd that man is Sher Mohammed Akhunzada, warlord and former Helmand governor. There is another aspect to all this - the appalling and spiralling cost to the British economy of our commitment to Afghanistan which some prophets of doom consider must persist for at least a decade. It is to be hoped that if this is so, those British troops invited to serve there will be properly equipped to deal with the indiscriminate road bombs and powerful guns employed by the Taleban. If a way forward for Afghanistan, however difficult to execute, is at least identifiable, can the same be said of Iraq?

We must distinguish here between what the British can do and what the Iraqis can do for themselves. The United States' surge operations have brought some relief to the central Baghdad area and encouraged Shia and Sunni alike to reject insurgent activity; in the north the Kurds maintain some stability, despite Turkish Army incursions to discourage their own Kurdish separatists; in the south the 2,500 British troops, formerly fighting against Basra insurgents, have now withdrawn to the Air Station so-called, and virtually sit there without a purpose. They might as well be withdrawn for all the good they are doing. But with such withdrawal must go an admission that the great aim of effecting democracy and reconstruction has not been achieved.* No WMDs were found. Al-Qaeda is still in business. British soldiers have little to do but watch their own backs. Blair's great mission has failed. We would have done better not to have invaded Iraq in the first place. There is certainly no point in keeping British soldiers there now. And again the cost is crippling. It may be argued, of course, that their presence at the airfield does protect this vital facility, provides some supply route security and they can be called upon – as indeed they have been – to return to Basra in support of Iraqi forces.

Opinion as to what should now be done about Afghanistan is divided. Some journalists, like Simon Jenkins and Matthew Parris are clearly for getting out. Indeed Jenkins reaches an extravagantly high tide of purple prose when he recommends an end to fighting the Pashtun and a return to tribal autonomy. 'Fate has handed it [Pashtunistan] a starring role in Britain's nastiest war in decades . . . To have set one of the world's most ancient and ferocious people on the warpath against both Kabul and Islamabad takes some doing. But western displomacy has done it. Now we must begin the agonising process of escaping that appalling mistake'. Matthew Parris is inclined to agree, and talks of keeping thousands of troops in a barbarous place, in the openended support of a puppet government 'led by a man who wears elegantly tailored clothes and speaks nice English but whose writ hardly runs'. What is to be done? To stick around in Helmand, with mounting casualties, tolerating a poppy-elimination policy we don't support, with occasional nominal successes in re-taking a village here or there, hoping like Mr Micawber for something to turn up? One correspondent of *The Times* recommends a kind of Marshall Plan for Afghanistan – economic, industrial and social regeneration. Easily said, but who is to ensure that al-Qaeda and the Taleban do not disrupt it all? Would this mean switching our resources elsewhere for the war on terror? The truth is that the Afghans will never tolerate foreigners attempting to run their country for them. A return to tribal authority, supported by some centrally controlled distribution of resources, overseen by the UN would provide the stability and security required for the so badly needed reconstruction of Afghanistan. While the British Army is ready to counter terrorism

---

* Elections early in 2009 were, however, encouraging.

and restore security and stability to far off countries in need of such support, it must be against a background of acting from a firm base of authority and control. But let there be an end to pointless losses of gallant, perseverant soldiers.

If it may be said that despite all the courage and determination displayed by British regiments in Helmand, the campaign there will end in frustration and failure, how much more so can the same be said of the Iraq adventure. In his book *Blair's Wars*, John Kampfner points out that the then Prime Minster's reputation had been badly damaged by his interference in Iraq. Even after the initial military progress, by the spring of 2004 Iraq was descending into anarchy. That there have been more encouraging developments since then, that Iraqi security forces have exerted control in Basra, with British soldiers positioned nearby to come to their support if need be, is something. But how long HMG intends to keep them there is another. Indeed the very purpose of their continued deployment is itself in question, for when the joint Iraqi/US operation to pacify Basra was launched in March 2008. British forces, willing and eager to assist, were prevented from doing so by the veto of their own Defence Minister to the dismay of the British troops. Insurgency of one sort or another will persist, encouraged and supported no doubt by Syria and Iran. All in all if we look at the various wars which Blair chose to participate in, only that in Sierra Leone can be counted an unqualified success. Iraq and Afghanistan drag dangerously on; Kosovo seems set to disrupt the Balkans once more, and British regiments are stretched to the limit and beyond to fulfil commitments imposed upon them by a set of politicians, green in judgement and incompetent in deed. If ever a Minister of Defence of Denis Healey's character, grasp of both strategic matters and technological detail, dominant in Cabinet and blessed with human understanding, were needed, it is now. Yet look at the calibre of those minister now responsible for defence matters – and despair! Having done so, we must then tell them what to do.

For the British Army a period of fewer operational commitments is imperative if the current overstretch and discontent are to be cured. Moreover HMG must recognize that if this country is to pursue a foreign policy which requires the deployment and application of force, more money must be forthcoming. Yet at this very time of writing there is governmental talk of *cutting* the Defence Budget by £1 billion. Such wanton stupidity must cease. If the Army, as required in my Blackwood's article of June 1979, is to be well-found, well-trained, well-equipped, well-paid, well-accommodated, well-led and well aware that trouble will continue to be its business, then the money must be found. The nation's everlasting debt to the Army must be acknowledged and paid. If not, the native hue of resolution will be sicklied o'er with the pale cast of thought; and enterprises of great pitch and moment will find their currents turning awry and losing the name of action. And no more interference with the regimental system. It is the heart and soul of the British Army. For many of us it is the *raison d'etre* of having been a soldier, an honour long cherished. In contemplating the future we should bear in mind how well the British Army has served the nation. Now it is time for the nation to respond by serving the Army well. Give me a sufficiency of infantry battalions and armoured regiments – as indicated earlier – backed by a proper level of supporting arms; give me the mobility of enough helicopters; give me naval and air support; give me bomb-proof carriers and guns which work; give me above all a defence budget which provides what I want, as outlined above, and I will guarantee that the British Army will play an honourable and successful part in any future NATO controlled campaigns of interventionism. But if this means a policy of more Iraqs and Afghanistans then it is a policy which will be more honoured in the breach than the observance.

BIBLIOGRAPHY

Anglesey, Marquess of, *A History of the British Cavalry*, Leo Cooper

Articles in *The Times*, *The Sunday Times*

Barker, A.J., *Dunkirk: The Great Escape*, Dent

Baynes, John, *Morale*, Cassell

Berlin, Sir Isaiah, *Mr Churchill in 1940*, John Murray

Brett-Smith, Richard, *Berlin '45; the grey city*, Macmillan

Churchill, Winston S., *The Second World War*, Cassell

Crisp, Robert, *Brazen Chariots*, F. Muller

Crossbelts: Regimental Journal of The Queen's Royal Hussars

de la Billière, General Sir Peter, *Looking for Trouble*, Harper Collins 1994

Ensor, Sir Robert, *History of England 1870-1914*, Oxford U.P.

Fergusson, Bernard, *The Trumpet in the Hall*, Collins

Fitzherbert, Margaret, *The Man Who Was Greenmantle*, John Murray

Fortescue, Sir John, *A History of the British Army*, Macmillan

Gberie, Lansana, *A Dirty War in West Africa*, Hurst & Company, 2005

Gilbert, Martin, *Winston S. Churchill*, Heinemann

Hackett, Gen. Sir John, *The Profession of Arms*, Sidgwick & Jackson
                        I Was a Stranger, Chatto & Windus

Hastings, Max, *The Oxford Book of Military Anecdotes*, Oxford U.P.

Jeapes, Tony, *SAS Operation Oman*, Kimber

Judah, Tim, Kosovo, *War and Revenge*, Yale Nota Bene, 2002

Kampfner, John, *Blair's Wars*, The Free Press, 2004

Keegan, Sir John, *The Iraq War*, Pimlico, 2005

Kipling, Rudyard, *The Complete Barrack Room Ballads*, Ed. Charles
    Carrington, Methuen

Kitson, Gen. Sir Frank, *Bunch of Five*, Faber

Legion, The Royal British Legion Magazine, Winter 2007, Spring 2008

Longford, Elizabeth, Wellington, *The Years of the Sword*, Weidenfeld
    & Nicolson

Macaulay, *History of England*, Dent
Mackenzie, Jean, *The Children of the Souls*, Chatto & Windus
McGuffie, T. H. (Ed), *Rank and File*, Hutchinson
Mason, Philip, *A Matter of Honour*, Cape
                    The Men Who Ruled India, Cape
Morris, James/Jan, *Pax Britannica Trilogy*, Faber
Majdalany, Fred, *Cassino: Portrait of a Battle*, Longmans
                    The Monastery, John Lane, The Bodley Head
Moorehead, Alan, *The End in Africa*, Hamish Hamilton
Lindsay, Sir Martin, *So Few Got Through*, Cassell
Orgill, Douglas, *The Gothic Line*, Heinemann
Pocock, Tom, *East and West of Suez*, The Bodley Head
Priestley, J. B., *The Edwardians*, Heinemann
Ryan, Cornelius, *A Bridge Too Far*, Hamish Hamilton
Ryan, Mike, *Battlefield Afghanistan*, Spellmount, 2007
Samwell, H. P., *An Infantry Officer with the 8th Army*, W. Blackwood &
    Sons
Slim, Viscount, *Defeat into Victory*, Cassell
Taylor, A.J.P., *English History, 1914-1945*, Oxford U.P.
Tuchman, Barbara, *August 1914*, Reprint Society, London
Walder, David, *The Chanak Affair*, Hutchinson

INDEX